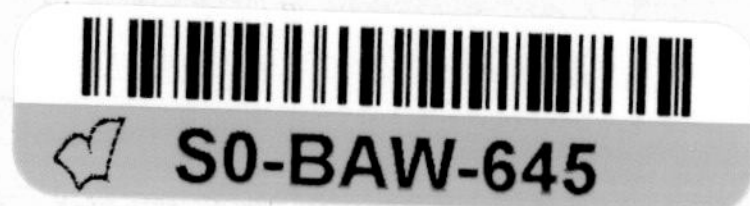

THE "SYROHEXAPLARIC" PSALTER

SOCIETY OF BIBLICAL LITERATURE
SEPTUAGINT AND COGNATE STUDIES SERIES

Edited by
Claude E. Cox

Number 27

THE "SYROHEXAPLARIC" PSALTER

Robert J.V. Hiebert

THE "SYROHEXAPLARIC" PSALTER

Robert J.V. Hiebert

Scholars Press
Atlanta, Georgia

THE "SYROHEXAPLARIC" PSALTER

Robert J.V. Hiebert

Library of Congress Cataloging-in-Publication Data

Hiebert, Robert J.V. (Robert James Victor)
The Syrohexaplaric psalter / Robert J.V. Hiebert.
p. cm. -- (Septuagint and cognate studies series ; no. 27)
Revision of the author's thesis (Ph.D.) -- University of Toronto, 1986.
Includes Syriac text of the Psalms in the Syrohexapla version.
Includes bibliographical references.
ISBN 1-55540-431-6. -- ISBN 1-55540-432-4 (pbk.)
1. Bible. O.T. Psalms--Criticism, Textual. 2. Bible. O.T. Psalms. Syriac--Versions--Syrohexapla. I. Bible. O.T. Psalms. Syriac. Syrohexapla. 1990. II. Title. III. Series.
BS1430.2.H54 1990
223'.2043--dc20 89-29647
CIP

Printed in the United States of America
on acid-free paper

To my wife, Karen,
for her constant support
and loving encouragement

TABLE OF CONTENTS

PREFACE

This study of the so-called Syrohexaplaric Psalter is a slightly revised version of a Ph. D. thesis submitted at the University of Toronto in 1986. It is in part an outgrowth of my work as a Research Assistant for The Byzantine Psalter Project which was established for the purpose of delineating textual groups within the large Byzantine (*L*) family of Greek Psalms Mss. This is the textual family with which Alfred Rahlfs, in his edition of the LXX Psalter (*Psalmi cum Odis*), associates the version which is the focus of the present investigation.

The materials gathered for this study include eight unpublished Syriac Mss of the Psalms. I am indebted to the following institutions for providing me with microfilm copies of these Mss: the British Museum, the Cambridge University Library, the Bibliothèque Nationale, the Vatican Library, and the Peshitta Institute of Leiden. I am also grateful to the staff of the University of Toronto's Interlibrary Loan Service who assisted me in procuring these and other much-needed materials.

During the period of my doctoral studies, I was privileged to receive five academic awards: three Ontario Graduate Scholarships (1979-82) and two Social Sciences and Humanities Research Council of Canada Fellowships (1982-84). I am thankful to both the Ontario and Canadian governments for these awards.

The fourth chapter of this study involves a comparison of my Syriac edition with the various groups of the Greek *L* family. The delineation of these groups proved to be a long and arduous task whose completion was facilitated by computer analysis. In this connection, I would like to thank Mr. Mark Dornfeld, a Ph. D. student at the University of Toronto's Department of Near Eastern Studies, for the long hours he spent setting up the computer program.

To Professor John Wevers of the Department of Near Eastern Studies, University of Toronto, I express my appreciation for his helpful advice relating both to the preparation of the edition and to other textual matters.

The greatest debt of gratitude, however, I owe to Professor Albert Pietersma, my thesis supervisor. His patience and encouragement coupled with a persistent demand for thoroughness and clarity were of immense benefit to me in the production of this study. Nevertheless, the responsibility for any errors or other shortcomings which may yet remain rests solely with me.

SIGLA AND ABBREVIATIONS

*	the original reading of a Ms
c	a later correction or one of uncertain origin (e. g. an erasure)
c pr m, c pr m	a correction by the first hand
s	the suppletor of a Ms
txt, txt	the textual reading of a Ms
mg, mg	the marginal reading of a Ms
mg†	a SyrPs reading situated in the margins of *fg* when the Peshitta has a shorter text
mg	used when the transliterated equivalent of διάψαλμα appears in the margins of *fg* rather than within the lines of their interlinear text
+, add.	addition
>, om.	omission
|	change of line, column, or page
‖	a break between readings of a verse in the apparatus
∩, prbl.	parablepsis
※, ast.	asterisk
÷, ÷, ob.	obelus
⸓, ⸔, ⸕, :, metob.	metobelus
ܵ	Syriac letter uncertain
ν̣	Greek letter uncertain
κ̂ς̂	Greek scribal abbreviation, e. g. κυριος
πλειο/ωσιν	some Greek Mss attest the letter to the left of / while others attest the letter to the right of

it (when / appears within a word)

(ν) the Greek letter is lacking in some Mss, e. g. εστι(ν)

[ ] a lacuna in a Ms

< > an omission in a Ms which is restored by this writer

⟦ ⟧ an abbreviation in a Ms which is restored by this writer

« » hexaplaric material, not recorded by Field, which has been retroverted into Greek by this writer

{ } brackets surrounding H-P Mss not cited by Rahlfs in *Psalmi cum Odis*

≈ equivalent

MT Masoretic Text

LXX Septuagint

Pesh Peshitta

SyrPss any or all Mss collated for this study's Psalter edition

SyrPs the Psalter revision ascribed to Paul of Tella in this edition

SyrPs^{a} the Psalter revision ascribed to Thomas of Harkel in this edition

SyrPs^{b} the Psalter tradition which displays features of both SyrPs and SyrPs^{a}

a Milan, Ambr. Libr., C. 313. Inf.; eighth or ninth century *b* Br. Mus., Add. 14,434, folios 1-79; eighth century

c Br. Mus., Add. 14,434, folios 80-128; eighth century

d Br. Mus., Add. 17,257, folios 84-94; thirteenth century

e Cambridge, Univ. Libr., Orient. 929; specifically the Syriac column of this polyglot Ms; fourteenth century

e^g the Greek column of the Cambridge polyglot Ms

e^h the Hebrew column of the Cambridge polyglot Ms

f Baghdad, Libr. of the Chald. Patr., 211; twelfth century

g Vat. Libr., Borg. sir. 113, f. 1-135; nineteenth century

h/h_1 Baghdad, Libr. of the Chald. Patr., 1112; twelfth/fifteenth centuries

j Paris, Nat. Libr., Syr. 9; thirteenth century

k Moscow, Publičnaja Biblioteka S.S.S.R. im. V. I. Lenina, Gr. 432; eighth century

α′ Aquila

σ′ Symmachus

θ′ Theodotion

ε′ Quinta

ϛ′ Sexta

εβρ′ ὁ Ἑβραῖος

absc. abscissus

abscond. absconditus

bis scr. bis scripsit (-serunt)

c. cum

fin. finis

^{frt}, frt fortasse

hab. habet (-ent)

homarch. homoioarchton

homtel. homoioteleuton

hpgr. haplographice

$^{\text{inc.}}$, inc. incertum

init. initium

inscr. inscriptio

$^{\text{int.}}$, int. interlinearis

Ms(s), ms.(mss.) manuscriptum (-ta)

pr. praemittit (-tunt)

pr m prima manu

ras. rasura

rel. reliqui

s. sine

sey. s^{e}yāmē

sil e silentio H-P (cf. Rahlfs, *Psalmi cum Odis*, pp. 7, 63)

sub lin. sub linea

sup. lin. supra lineam

sup. ras. supra rasuram

tr. transposuit (-suerunt)

u., uu. uersus

uar. uariatio (-ones)

uid., uid. ut uidetur

BDB F. Brown, S. R. Driver, and C. A. Briggs, eds., *A Hebrew and English Lexicon of the Old Testament* (Oxford: Clarendon Press, 1907 [Repr. 1974]).

BHS K. Elliger, W. Rudolph, et al., eds., *Biblia Hebraica Stuttgartensia* (Stuttgart: Deutsche Bibelstiftung, 1967/77).

CSCO Corpus scriptorum christianorum orientalium

Field F. Field, *Origenis Hexaplorum quae supersunt*, 2 vols. (Oxford: Clarendon Press, 1875).

H-P R. Holmes and J. Parsons, eds., *Vetus Testamentum Graecum cum variis lectionibus*, vol. 3 (Oxford: Clarendon Press, 1823).

H-R E. Hatch and H. A. Redpath, *A Concordance to the Septuagint and the Other Greek Versions of the Old Testament*, 2 vols. including Supplement (Graz: Akademische Druck- u. Verlagsanstalt, 1975).

Rahlfs (in the apparatus) A. Rahlfs, ed., *Septuaginta*, vol. 10: *Psalmi cum Odis* (Göttingen: Vandenhoeck & Ruprecht, 1931).

Reider J. Reider, *An Index to Aquila*, completed and revised by N. Turner, Supplements to Vetus Testamentum 12 (Leiden: E. J. Brill, 1966).

S.-St. A. Rahlfs, *Septuaginta-Studien* 1-3 (Göttingen: Vandenhoeck & Ruprecht, 1965).

THGD J. W. Wevers, *Text History of the Greek Deuteronomy*, Mitteilungen des Septuaginta-Unternehmens 13

(Göttingen: Vandenhoeck & Ruprecht, 1978).

THGG J. W. Wevers, *Text History of the Greek Genesis*, Mitteilungen des Septuaginta-Unternehmens 11 (Göttingen: Vandenhoeck & Ruprecht, 1974).

VT *Vetus Testamentum*

ZAW *Zeitschrift für die alttestamentliche Wissenschaft*

Note: For a description of the witnesses to the LXX of Psalms, and their designations, see Rahlfs' *Psalmi cum Odis*.

INTRODUCTION

The present study has as its object the Syriac Psalter commonly attributed to Paul, bishop of Tella in Mesopotamia. This version of the Psalms is distinct from the Peshitta Psalter, a Syriac translation of the Hebrew Psalms,[1] in that it closely follows the Greek. The Psalms text found in Ms Milan, Ambr. Libr., C. 313. Inf. is usually regarded as Paul's Psalter *par excellence*.[2] Alfred Rahlfs, in his edition of the LXX Psalms, describes this text as "die syrische Übersetzung aus dem Griechischen, von Paul von Tella 616/7 n. Chr. verfasst."[3] Apart from another very fragmentary Ms, this complete text is the only published exemplar of the Syriac Psalms associated with Paul.[4] Antonio Ceriani, in the notes accompanying his edition (*Codex Syro-Hexaplaris Ambrosianus*), records some selected variant readings from four other Psalter texts.[5] Yet since the publication of this edition, three additional Psalms Mss with continuous texts, and several others with non-continuous or glossed texts, have come to light. An urgent *desideratum*, therefore, is a new edition which incorporates all additional evidence.[6]

The Psalter edition offered in this study is a diplomatic, not a critical, edition. The text of Ceriani's Ambrosian Psalter is reproduced, and an apparatus of variant readings from nine other collated Mss is supplied. As a perusal of that text and the numerous variants in the apparatus will show, one cannot speak of *the* Syriac Psalter. There are, in fact, three discernible text traditions represented (see chapter five). In this study, the majority text is designated SyrPs, and the two minority traditions are termed SyrPs^{a} and SyrPs^{b}, respectively.[7] SyrPss is an all-embracing designation which can refer to any or all Mss collated for this edition without regard to these component groups.

Paul of Tella's version of the Old Testament, the Syrohexapla, is a translation of the fifth column of the Hexapla, the monumental work attributed to the third century Christian scholar, Origen.

Origen assigned to the fifth column his version of the current Greek text, which he brought into closer conformity with the Hebrew. He marked with an obelus (÷) those words or phrases in the Greek which had no equivalent in his Hebrew text. When the Greek text was shorter than the Hebrew, he remedied the deficiency from one of the three second century A. D. translators—Aquila, Symmachus, or Theodotion[8]—and marked the addition with an asterisk (※). A number of SyrPss Mss contain these Aristarchian signs. Rahlfs lists the relevant passages for the Psalter of *Codex Syro-Hexaplaris Ambrosianus* (*a*), the foremost member of SyrPs, and for two of its companions in that group, Mss *b* and *c*.[9] Nevertheless he maintains that this text tradition is not typically hexaplaric in the sense of being a consistent and reliable witness to Origen's fifth column. However, in view of the fact that he does not undertake a thoroughgoing comparison of the hexaplaric Psalter with SyrPss, it is evident that his conclusion must be subjected to critical review. A major portion of the current study is devoted to this task.

The Syriac Psalter text which Rahlfs uses for his LXX Psalms edition is that of *Codex Syro-Hexaplaris Ambrosianus*.[10] After concluding that it is essentially non-hexaplaric, Rahlfs determines that it is to be grouped with his (Byzantine) *L* family of texts.[11] This family embraces the great mass of Greek Psalter Mss (nearly 1000 in all),[12] which Rahlfs fails to break down properly into textual groups. Indeed, Rahlfs employs only about 100 of these *L* Mss, all of which were previously collated for the Holmes and Parsons LXX edition (hereafter H-P), but which were not recollated by Rahlfs.[13] Another facet of the present investigation is the delineation of textual groups within the *L* family, and an examination of the relationships between those groups and SyrPs, SyrPs^{a}, and SyrPs^{b}.[14]

The textual diversity of the Syriac Ms evidence makes it clear that the work of more than one translator or recensionist is represented. The fact that none of the three Syriac text traditions is essentially hexaplaric raises the question as to whether Paul of Tella had anything to do with them. It is evident, therefore, that the problem of the origins of SyrPs, SyrPs^{a}, and SyrPs^{b} must be addressed. This very important part of the present investigation is based on a careful consideration of literary references and detailed textual analysis.

A number of the Mss of this Syriac Psalter edition contain an extensive marginal apparatus of primarily hexaplaric readings from Aquila, Symmachus, Theodotion, Quinta, and Sexta.[15] The Psalter of *Codex Syro-Hexaplaris Ambrosianus* is the best witness to this apparatus. Frederick Field has, apart from a few slips, carefully recorded the hexaplaric readings of this Ms in *Origenis Hexaplorum quae supersunt*,[16] also including variants from fragmentary Mss *b* and *c*. Besides the hexaplaric marginal readings attested by these three Mss, there is a relatively small number of additional ones found in other SyrPss Mss. Since the focus of this study is the text of SyrPss, no comprehensive analysis of this marginal apparatus is undertaken. However, a concluding appendix contains corrections of, and supplements to, Field's evidence.

The plan of this study is as follows. Chapter one contains descriptions of the Mss collated for this Psalter edition. The edition itself is found in chapter two. Chapter three is concerned with the investigation of hexaplaric influence on SyrPss. Chapter four examines the relationship between SyrPs, SyrPs^{a}, and SyrPs^{b}, on the one hand, and *L*, on the other. In chapter five, the problem of the origins of these three text traditions is analyzed. The appendix contains hexaplaric material from Ms margins which is not found in Field.

I

DESCRIPTIONS OF THE SYRIAC MANUSCRIPTS

A total of ten Mss were collated for the edition of the Psalter produced for this study. They range in date from the eighth to the nineteenth century. Apart from two texts (*a* and *k*), which were available to the present writer in published facsimiles, these Mss were collated from microfilm copies (see Preface).

A. Milan, Ambr. Libr., C. 313. Inf. (= *a*, Ceriani's A).[1]

Vellum, 193 folios, 2 columns per page, approximately 55 lines per column. This Ms originated in the Syrian monastery of the Nitrian Desert in Egypt, Dair as-Suryan.[2] It is written in an elegant Estrangelā hand of the late eighth or early ninth century and was published by Antonio Ceriani in his facsimile edition of 1874.[3] In addition to all 151 Psalms (folios 6b-38b),[4] this Ms contains the Syrohexapla of Job, Proverbs, Ecclesiastes, Song of Songs, Wisdom of Solomon, Sirach, the Twelve Minor Prophets, Jeremiah, Baruch, Lamentations, the Epistle of Jeremiah, Daniel, Susanna, Bel and the Dragon, Ezekiel, and Isaiah. It is apparently of the same age and make-up as the now lost Ms which was in the possession of Andreas Masius (1514-1573). He frequently quoted from this Ms in his *Syrorum Peculium*,[5] and in his posthumously published studies on Deuteronomy 17-34[6] and the book of Joshua.[7] Tragically, the Ms itself was never published. It apparently contained, in whole or in part, at least the following books: Deuteronomy, Joshua, Judges, I-IV Kingdoms, Paralipomena I-II, Esdras, Esther, Judith, and Tobit.[8] Probably *a* and Masius' Ms were the component volumes of a once complete Ms of the Syrohexapla.[9]

Folios 1a-6a of *a* contain part of an introduction to the Psalter[10] featuring extracts from Hippolytus, bishop of Rome, Basil, bishop of Caesarea of Cappadocia, Eusebius, Athanasius, bishop of Alexandria (from his *Letter to Marcellinus*), Origen, and Epiphanius, bishop of Cyprus. Also included is an explanation of Hebrew names and terms in the Psalter. At various intervals in the margins of the Psalter text itself, there are excerpts from the writings of Athanasius, Hesychius, presbyter of Jerusalem, and Cyril of Alexandria. Other marginal material includes some explanatory scholia, a number of Greek words written in Greek characters, the occasional transliterated Hebrew reading, and, most importantly, many hundreds of hexaplaric readings from Aquila, Symmachus, Theodotion, Quinta, and Sexta. The hexaplaric notes of *a* have been recorded in Field.[11] The Psalter text of *a*, the foremost member of the SyrPs group, is reproduced in this edition.

B. Br. Mus., Add. 14,434, folios 1-79 (= *b*, Ceriani's B).[12]

Vellum, 79 folios, 1 column per page, 22-27 lines per column. This, like *a*, is a Nitrian Ms from the Syrian monastery, written in an Estrangelā hand of the first half of the eighth century. It contains: 1:5 ܐܦ ܠܐ (*pro* ܐܦܠܐ)-4:9(8) ܘܐܝܬܒܢܝ; 6:2(1)-7:8(7); 8:7(6)-9:12(11) ܨܒܘܬܗܘܢ; 15:4 ܐܦܠܐ-17:39(38); 25:4 ܘܥܡ-36:12; 39:7(6) ܢܩܒܬ-40:3(2) ܩܐܝܡ; 41:1(inscr.)-41:12(11) ܒܝ (*pro* ܒܟܝ); 51:1(inscr.)-63:6(5) ܦܬܢܐ; 64:10(9) ܬܫܒܚܬܐ-71:5; 71:19 ܥܒܕܬ-74:4(3); 75:10(9) ܕܐܠܗܗ ܕܝܥܩܘܒ (*pro* ܕܝܥܩܘܒ)-76:14(13); 77:8 ܕܪ ܕܪ 2°-77:25; 77:43 ܘܐܬܕܡܪܘܬܗ-78:8 ܕܐܬܬܥܝܬ; 84:13(12) ܘܐܠܗܐ-94:7 ܕܝܠܗ; 100:6-102:2 ܒܡܕܢܚܐ; 103:31 ܥ[ܒܕܘ]ܗܝ-105:9 ܘܥܡ; 118:96-118:114; 141:5(4) ܢ[ܦ]ܫ-143:9 ܠܟ 1°; 144:21 ܥܠܡ-146:6 ܡܪܢܐ; 149:4-151:2 ܘܐܘܪܓܢܐ.

Ms *b* has fragments of the same introduction as in *a*, with only imperfectly preserved extracts from Hippolytus, Basil, Eusebius, Athanasius, and Origen, as well as the explanation of Hebrew names and terms. Like *a*, it has in its margin excerpts from the writings of Athanasius, Hesychius, and Cyril, and the important apparatus of hexaplaric readings, along with the other marginal material. However, unlike *a*, it includes a Latin rendering of 40:2(1)-3(2) ܩܐܝܡ on folio 29b:

> Beatus qui intelligit sup egenum et pauperem. in die mala liberabt (*sic*) eum dñs. dñs conserut (*sic*) eum et uiuificet eum· et beatū faciat eum in terra.

This Latin text seems to be of a considerably later date than the original Syriac text of the Ms, though it was probably penned before the twelfth century. This constitutes one of the very rare instances of a Latin note in a Nitrian Ms.[13] Textually, Ms *b* is a member of SyrPs.

C. Br. Mus., Add. 14,434, folios 80–128 (= *c*, Ceriani's C).[14]

Vellum, 49 folios, 1 column per page, 23–29 lines per column. This Ms from the Syrian monastery in the Nitrian desert is written in Estrangelā script of the eighth century. It contains: 9:34(33) ܐܡܪ-20:6(5); 21:29(28)–32:17; 33:23(22) ܬܫܪܘܢ-58:16(15) ܠܡܐܟܠ; 60:5(4) ܐܚܙܝܬ-72:3 ܫܝܢܐ. This text, too, is prefixed with fragments of the introduction found in *a* and *b*, with extracts from Basil and Eusebius preserved. It also has the same marginal material, including comments from Athanasius, Hesychius, and Cyril, as well as the apparatus of hexaplaric readings. The Syrohexapla of Ode 8 (= Dan. 3:52–88) and a Psalter *subscriptio* are appended to the Psalms in folios 127a–128b. Certain readings in the text of the Ode are marked as Theodotionic.[15] Also featured in the Ode are marginal readings, most of them attributed to Theodotion.

Ms *c* was written by a scribe from the city of Amid (modern Diyarbakir).[16] Textually, it is a member of SyrPs.

D. Br. Mus., Add. 17,257, folios 84–94 (= *d*, Ceriani's E).[17]

Paper, 11 folios, 1 column per page, 10–11 lines per column. This Ms from the Syrian monastery in the Nitrian desert is written in Sertā script, in a hand of the thirteenth century. It contains: 59:4(2) ܐܪ̈ܥܬܐ-62:8(7) ܒܡܫܬܐ (*pro* ܘܒܡܫܬܐ); 101:2(1) ܘܡܫܒܚ-102:17 [ܒܬܫ̈ܡܫܬܐ. It has no marginal material at all, and thus no hexaplaric apparatus. The Ms also lacks Psalm titles[18] and does not represent διάψαλμα. It is included with the SyrPs textual group.

E. Baghdad, Libr. of the Chald. Patr., 211 (= *f*, also known as Mosul Cod. 4).[19]

Paper, 161 folios, 1 column per page, 16-21 lines per column. The colophon of this Ms states that it was written in the city of Maragāh in the district of Adorbaiğan by a scribe from the district of "the blessed city," Edessa, in 1438 A. Gr. (= 1126 A. D.).[20] The Ms contains in folios 8b-152a: 1:1-16:15; 17:14(13) ܡܢ-74:11(10); 77:1(inscr.)-80:13(12) ܚܠܦܝܢ; 82:1(inscr.)-151:7. It has the Peshitta text[21] in bold Estrangelā script and the SyrPs text written in interlinear fashion in small Nestorian script (with some Sertā character forms). The interlinear text is not continuous, but appears where SyrPs and the Peshitta differ.[22] Psalm titles are found on the Peshitta line in the Peshitta hand, though they are penned with different (lighter) ink than is used for both the Peshitta and SyrPs texts. The titles are those attested by most other Mss, though at times with variations, and are collated for our edition. Obviously, one cannot make definite statements about the interlinear text where it is not explicitly quoted.[23] Thus, *e silentio* conclusions regarding *f* cannot be drawn in the Psalter edition prepared for this study. Yet, whenever *f* attests part of a given reading which is being investigated, that reading is designated f^{pars}. Psalm 151, not part of the Peshitta canon, is written in the Estrangelā script used throughout this Ms for the Peshitta text, with obviously no interlinear material.

The *f* Psalter also features a commentary, with exegetical remarks in small Sertā script following each Psalm.[24] This commentary consists of extracts attributed to Church Fathers such as Athanasius, Cyril of Alexandria, Daniel of Ṣalaḥ, Didymus, Eusebius, Hesychius of Jerusalem, Ignatius, Origen, and ܬܐܘܠܘܓܘܣ (i. e. the Theologian, an epithet used especially of Gregory Nazianzen).[25] In addition, there is much marginal material. Besides scholia, and Greek and transliterated Hebrew readings, one finds the apparatus of hexaplaric readings which is featured as well in *a*, *b*, and *c*.

Prefixed to the text are significant portions of the introduction which the Mss just mentioned also preserve in varying degrees of completeness. Extracts from Hippolytus, Basil, Eusebius, Athanasius, Origen, and Epiphanius are represented in *f*.

Following the Psalter text of *f* are the Odes. Folios 152a-156b contain the Peshitta of Odes 1 (= Ex. 15:1-21)[26] and 2 (= Deut. 32:1-43) with interlinear (non-continuous) Syrohexapla, commentary, marginal hexaplaric notes, and scholia, etc. Between Odes 1 and 2 is the Peshitta text of Is. 42:10-13. In folios 160a-161b (after the colophon) is added, in Sertā script, the Peshitta of Odes 3 (= I Kingd. 2:1-10), 4 (= Hab. 3:2-19), 5 (= Is. 26:9-19), 6 (= Jon. 2:3-10), 8 (= Dan. 3:52-90), and 9 (= Lk. 1:46-55). The Ms concludes with some additional material including the Lord's Prayer, the Beatitudes, the Creed of "the 318 Holy Fathers" (i. e. the creed associated with the First Council of Nicaea in 325 A. D.),[27] and a hymn. The *f* Psalter is part of the SyrPs textual group.

F. Vat. Libr., Borg. sir. 113, f. 1-135 (= *g*).[28]

Paper, 135 folios, 1 column per page, approximately seventeen lines per column. This Ms is a copy of *f*, written in Barṭellī in 1868. Both the Peshitta[29] and the interlinear lines of *g* are in Sertā script. In addition to the fact that textual differences between these two Mss are few, other indicators point to *g* being a copy of *f*. These include the fact that *g* exhibits the same physical layout of Peshitta plus interlinear text as is found in *f*, and the fact that illegible letters or words in *f* are often represented by dots in *g*. However, at times it is clear that the *g* scribe was able to make out more of the *f* text than is decipherable in this writer's microfilm copy of it.[30]

Apart from its usefulness in deciphering the text of *f*, *g* is also important because it was made when the leaf with 80:13(12) ܟܠܗܘܢ-81:8 was still extant in *f*, its exemplar. Ms *g* does not, however, have the commentary which follows each Psalm in *f*. Marginal materials, including the hexaplaric apparatus, are, however, reproduced. Ms *g* (which is, of course, included with the SyrPs group) is not cited in the apparatus of this edition, except when it diverges from *f* with a textually significant reading or when *f* is defective.

G. Cambridge, Univ. Libr., Orient. 929 (= *e*).[31]

Paper, 187 folios, 2 columns per page, approximately 30 lines per column. This is a fourteenth century polyglot Ms of uncertain origin[32] with the Psalms and Odes in four languages arranged in two columns per page. Each left hand page has Arabic on the left side and Syriac (in a hand which combines Estrangelā, Nestorian, and Sertā character forms) on the right (*e*), while each right hand page has Greek on the left side (*e*^{g}) and Hebrew on the right (*e*^{h}). From all indications, the same scribe is responsible for all four columns.[33] The only clue as to his identity comes from an occasional marginal note in which he makes reference to "us Syrians" (ܕܝܠܢ ܣܘܪܝܝܐ).[34] The Syriac Psalms are contained in folios 1a-184a: 16:5 ܐܚܒܠܐ-17:34(33); 19:6(5) ܒܟܠܗܘܢ-51:4(2) ܐܬܢܥܒ; 52:4(3) ܐܨܒܐ-145:5 ܚܠܐ; 146:7 ܪܟܢ-148:13 ܢܦܫܗ; 150:2 ܕܪܒܘܬܗ-151:7 ܒܝ. With the focus on the Syriac and Greek columns, here is the arrangement of the last several folios of the Ms in this writer's microfilm copy:

184b-185a: missing;

185b: 151:7 σπασάμενος-fin., plus Ode 1:1-8 ἐπάγη 1° (-γει *e*^{g}) = Ex. 15:1-8;

186a: Ode 2:8 ܕܐܕܡ (≈ Ἀδάμ)-15 ܘܐܟܠ (= καὶ ἔφαγεν) = Deut. 32:8-15;

186b-187a: missing;

187b: Ode 2:15 Ἰακώβ-23 = Deut. 32:15-23.

Very little hexaplaric material is found in *e*.

Although there are other polyglot Mss of the fourteenth century,[35] *e* is apparently unique among Christian Mss of this period in that it contains a Hebrew column. The Hebrew text, complete with vocalization and accent signs, is Masoretic.[36] Hebrew influence is exhibited to a remarkable degree in the Syriac column of *e*, as indicated by the following phenomena:

1/ the frequent interlinear glossing of words in the Syriac column so as to give more exact readings, even transliterations, of the Hebrew;[37]

2/ the not uncommon use of the obelus to mark words in the Syriac column which are absent in the Hebrew;

3/ the prefacing of verses in the Syriac column with the appropriate Hebrew letters to indicate the acrostic nature of a Psalm in Hebrew;[38]

4/ the references to the Hebrew in a number of philological and exegetical annotations in the margins of the Syriac column.[39]

As far as the textual character of the Greek column (*eG*) is concerned, it aligns itself with *L*, the large Byzantine family of Psalter texts. Based on Ms collations done for The Byzantine Psalter Project, *eG* and 1819 comprise the *L*[16] group within that family. The Syriac text of *e* is a member of SyrPs.

H. Baghdad, Libr. of the Chald. Patr., 1112 (= *h* and *h1*, also known as Diarbakir Cod. 2).[40]

Vellum, 140 folios,[41] 1 column per page, 22-23 lines per column. Folios 1a-127b of this Ms are written in Nestorian script of the twelfth century (= *h*), but folios 128a ff. (beginning with Ps. 146:8 ܠܐܙܕܐ) in Sertā script of about the fifteenth century (= *h1*). The following portions of the Psalter are extant: 1:5 ܢܬܗܡܐ-12:3(2) ܠܐܡܚܠ 2°; 14:1 ܘܡܢܘܒܐ-39:13(12) ܕܝܠܟ 1°; 40:12(11) ܡܢܗܘܢ-149:7.[42] Folios 130a-140a contain, in the following sequence, Odes 1 (= Ex. 15:1-19), 2 (= Deut. 32:1-43), 5 (= Is. 26:9-19), 3 (= I Kingd. 2:1-10), 4 (= Hab. 3:1-19), 6 (= Jon. 2:3-10), 7 (= Dan. 3:26-45), and 8 (= Dan. 3:52-88).

The Psalter portion of *h*/*h1* actually embraces not one, but three, text traditions: 1:5 ܢܬܗܡܐ-27:6 (where extant) = SyrPs[a]; 27:7-146:8 ܕܡܦܩܬ (where extant) = SyrPs[b]; 146:8 ܠܐܙܕܐ-149:7 = SyrPs. There is only one hexaplaric reading in the margin—that being the Aquilanic reading in 146:8 which falls within the SyrPs section (cf. Field).

I. Paris, Nat. Libr., Syr. 9 (= *j*, Ceriani's D).[43]

Paper, 374 folios, 2 columns per page, approximately 25 lines per column. This Ms is written in Sertā script of the thirteenth century. Folios 165b-228a contain Psalms 1-151 in a text like that of *h*[44], but unlike that of h_1. Thus, in *j*, 1:1-27:6 = SyrPs^a; 27:7-151:7 = SyrPs^b. Elsewhere, this Ms contains a shortened Peshitta text[45] of other Biblical books. The order of books in folios 1b-354b is: the Pentateuch, Joshua, Judges, I-IV Kingdoms, Job, Psalms, Proverbs, Wisdom of Solomon, Ecclesiastes, Song of Songs, Sirach, Isaiah, the Twelve Minor Prophets, Jeremiah, Lamentations, Ezekiel, Daniel, and Bel and the Dragon. Folios 355-374 contain exegetical fragments on parts of the Old Testament: Genesis, Kingdoms, Job, Joshua, and Ezekiel.

The margins of *j* feature comments, some attributable to the original scribe, others to a later one. The comments of the first hand are derived, for the most part, from the works of Jacob of Sarug and Jacob of Edessa. Others come from Severus of Antioch, St. Nilus, St. Maximus, Mār Isaac, St. Ephraem, Epiphanius, Dionysius bar Ṣalibi, Philoxenus, and Hippolytus. The comments of the second hand are mostly anonymous. In the Psalter, there are marginal comments attributed to Severus of Antioch in the first hand, and anonymous comments in the later hand. However, very few marginal hexaplaric readings are to be found.

It is not uncommon to find that *j* has been erased and that a first hand correction has been written over the erasure. At times it is possible to discern that the erased material is a Peshitta reading. Original readings in *j* (and other Mss) which can still be deciphered are recorded in this edition. Otherwise, material written over erasures is designated sup. ras.

J. Moscow, Publičnaja Biblioteka S.S.S.R. im. V. I. Lenina, Gr. 432 (= *k*, also known as Norov 74).[46]

Vellum, 4 folios, 3 columns per page, approximately 35 lines per column. This is an eighth century triglot Psalter Ms with Greek,[47] Syriac (in a hand which combines Estrangelā and Nestorian character forms), and Arabic columns on each page. It was carelessly published by N. Pigulewskaya in the facsimile edition of 1954.[48] It contains: 70:7-16 ܬܫܒܘܚܬܟ (*pro* ܬܫܒܘܚܬܗ); 73:4 ܕܠܝܬ [ܗܫܬܐ] (*pro* ܕܠܝܬ)-14 ܒܨܦܪܐ; 77:28-38 ܚܡܬܗ; 79:9(8) ܐܠܗܢ-18(17) ܘܐܠܗܢ. There are no marginal hexaplaric notes.

The Syriac text of *k* is aligned with that of *h* and *j* in this part of the Psalter, i. e. SyrPs^{b}. The Greek text follows that of Rahlfs' *L* family, with which the A group (A 1219 55) often agrees.[49] Unfortunately, the Greek text of *k* (1102) is not extant in any of the four blocks of text selected for The Byzantine Psalter Project. It cannot, therefore, at this stage be associated with any of the groups which comprise the *L* family.

II

THE TEXT OF SYRPSS

As stated in the introduction, the edition of the SyrPss Psalter produced for this study is a diplomatic edition. The lemma is a modified form of Ms *a* (reproduced from *Codex Syro-Hexaplaris Ambrosianus*), in which obvious mistakes have been corrected and lacunae have been filled. These deficiencies in *a* are recorded in the first apparatus. Variants to the lemma from our SyrPss Mss are contained in the second apparatus. However, there are four categories of variants which are not included in the second apparatus:

1/ insignificant scribal errors which result in nonsense readings;

2/ obeli in *e* which are not attested by the other Mss (see the description of *e* in chapter one);

3/ instances in which only *h*, *j*, and/or *k* attest a substantive with the independent possessive pronoun (i. e. the ܕܝܠ form) whereas the other witnesses have the pronominal suffix attached directly to the substantive;

4/ cases of avoidance by *h*, *j*, and/or *k* of the proleptic suffix before ܕ in genitival constructions when the other Mss have it.

The preference for the ܕܝܠ form and the avoidance of the proleptic suffix before ܕ in genitival constructions are characteristic of *hjk*, whereas the directly attached pronominal suffix and the proleptic suffix before ܕ are typical of the other Mss. The recording of *hjk* variants in such instances would needlessly clutter the apparatus. This can be prevented, however, by listing exceptions to the rule for these three Mss. Consequently, it may be presumed that, in all other relevant instances, Mss *hjk* have the ܕܝܠ form and lack the proleptic suffix.

Below is a list of cases not recorded in the second apparatus in which *h* and/or *j* attest to a substantive with the directly attached pronominal suffix rather than the ܕܝܠ form (*k* always has the latter). Excluded from this list are noun-root prepositions (like ܩܕܡܝܟ, ܠܘܬܗ, and ܚܕ̈ܪܝ) with attached suffixes. Mss *hj* normally follow the lemma in such instances. However, when they do not, the reading is recorded in the apparatus. Verse numbering in this and subsequent lists, as well as in the text and apparatuses, is that of Ceriani's edition of *a*, *Codex Syro-Hexaplaris Ambrosianus*, except for Pss. 113, 115, and 147 (where Psalm division in the LXX and the MT differs) in which the Greek number appears first and Ceriani's follows in parentheses. In the present list, when *h* and/or *j* do/does not agree with the lemma, the lemma is written before the square bracket. The only Ms support for the lemma which is mentioned in such instances is that of *h* or *j* when these two Mss diverge and one or the other attests the textual reading. No special mention is made of abbreviations when their *plēnē* form is not in doubt:

5:7 ܕܪ̈ܚܡܝ *hj*
9:21 ܢܡܘܣܝ *hj*
33:7 ܕܪ̈ܢܟܘܗܝ *hj*
33:13 ܠܚܝ̈ܝ *hj*
34:16 ܢܫ̈ܝܗܘܢ *hj*
34:17 ܡܚܘܪܐ ܡܒܝܫܬܗܘܢ *hj*
36:39 ܘܡܥܕܪܢܗܘܢ *hj*
37:7 ܕܠܒܝ *hj*
37:22 ܡܢܘܪܝ *hj*
38:9 ܦܘܡܝ *hj*
39:15 ܡܥܠܠܗܘܢ *j*
43:10 ܘܚܝ̈ܠܢ *hj*
43:18 ܥܩ̈ܒܝ *hj*
43:24 ܠܡܢܥܘܬ *hj*

44:10 ܒܢܬܟ *h*] ܒܢܬܐ *j* (sicut *e*)
45:6 ܡܢܗ *hj*
48:6 ܚܝܠܗܘܢ *hj*
48:10 ܒܩܒܪܗܘܢ *hj*
48:11 ܘܩܢܝ̈ܢܗܘܢ ܒܬ̈ܝܗܘܢ *hj*
48:11 ܫܡ̈ܗܝܗܘܢ *hj*
48:13 ܒܦܘܡܗܘܢ *hj*
48:14 ܘܒܕܪ̈ܗܘܢ *hj*
48:14 ܠܥܘܫܢܗܘܢ *hj*
49:1 ܠܡܥܪ̈ܒܘܗܝ *hj*
54:4 ܠܒܝ *hj*
54:15 ܒܐܘ̈ܪܚܬܗܘܢ *hj*
56:7 ܠܒܝ 1° et 2° *hj*
58:inscr. ܠܒܝܬܗ *hj*

58:7 ܒܦܘܡܗܘܢ *hj*
65:7 ܒܚܝ̈ܠܗܝ *hj*
69:1 ܒܡܘܕ̈ܝܢ *hj*
70:16 ܙܕܝܩܘܬܐ ܕܝܠܟ]*h* ܙܕܝܩܘܬܟ *j*
76:2 ܡܠܬܗ *hj*
76:6 ܠܒܗ *hj*
77:3 ܘܐܦܐ ܕܝܠܝ]*j* ܘܐܦܝ *h*
84:9 ܕܕ̈ܝܠܗܝ *hj*
87:5 ܐܢܫ]*j* ܐܡܗ *h*
87:9 ܥܝܢܝ *hj*
87:15 ܢܦܫܝ *hj*
103:22 ܘܒܡܥܪ̈ܝܗܘܢ *hj*
107:1 ܠܒܝ 1° et 2° *hj*
113:21(115:13) ܠܕ̈ܚܠܘܗܝ *hj*
118:10 ܠܒܝ *hj*
118:11 ܒܠܒܝ *hj*
118:80 ܠܒܝ *hj*
118:82 ܥ̈ܝܢܝ *hj*
118:152 ܣܗܕ̈ܘܬܟ *hj*
128:2 ܐܝܕܝ *hj*
128:7 ܐܝܕܗ *hj*
131:15 ܠܚ̈ܝܕܗ *hj*
133:2 ܐܦܐ ܕܐܗܪܘܢ]*j* ܐܦܘܗܝ *h*
142:inscr. ܒܗ *hj*
151:7 ܪܝܫܗ *j*

In addition to the preceding readings, there are a number of instances in which it seems that *j* originally had the directly attached pronominal suffix but that it was corrected by the first hand to the ܕܝܠ form:

30:24 ܠܚܣܝܕܐ ܕܝܠܗ]*j**(uid.) ܠܚܣܝ̈ܕܘܗܝ *hj*c pr m

104:37 ܫܒ̈ܛܐ ܕܝܠܗ]*j**(uid.) ܫܒ̈ܛܘܗܝ *hj*c pr m

105:27 ܐܬܘ̈ܬܐ ܕܝܠܗ]*j**(uid.) ܐܬܘ̈ܬܗ *hj*c pr m

109:5 ܕܪܘܓܙܐ ܕܝܠܗ]*j**(uid.) ܕܪܘܓܙܗ *hj*c pr m

110:1 ܠܒܐ ܕܝܠܝ]*j**(uid.) ܠܒܝ *hj*c pr m

142:11 ܥܒܕܐ ܕܝܠܟ]*j**(uid.) ܥܒܕܟ *hj*c pr m

145:10 ܐܠܗܐ ܕܝܠܟܝ]*j**(uid.) ܐܠܗܟܝ *hj*c pr m

146:5 ܣܘܟܠܐ ܕܝܠܗ]*j**(uid.) ܣܘܟܠܗ *hj*c pr m

148:14 ܠܚܣܝ̈ܕܐ ܕܝܠܗ]*j**(uid.) ܠܚܣܝ̈ܕܘܗܝ *j*c pr m

What follows next is a list of cases not recorded in the second apparatus in which *h*, *j*, and/or *k* attest the proleptic suffix before ܕ in a genitival construction:

18:1 ܫܘܒܚܗ *hj*
28:3 ܩܠܗ *hj*
28:4 ܩܠܗ 1° et 2° *hj*
28:5 ܩܠܗ *hj*
28:7 ܩܠܗ *hj*
28:8 ܩܠܗ *hj*
28:9 ܩܠܗ *hj*
32:5 ܪ̈ܚܡܘܗܝ *hj*
33:19 ܐܘ̈ܠܨܢܘܗܝ *hj*
33:21 ܓܪ̈ܡܘܗܝ *hj*
35:11 ܘܐܝܕܗ *hj*
36:23 ܗ̈ܠܟܬܗ *hj*
39:4 ܫܡܗ *hj*
45:4 ܓ̈ܠܠܘܗܝ *hj*
45:8 ܚܝ̈ܠܘܗܝ *hj*
47:9 ܒܡܕܝܢܬܗ *hj*
47:10 ܒܗܝܟܠܗ *hj*
49:1 ܡܥܪ̈ܒܘܗܝ *hj*
51:inscr. ܠܒܝܬܗ *hj*
52:5 ܓܪ̈ܡܘܗܝ *hj*
71:20 ܒܪܗ *hj*
72:28 ܒܡܬܪܥܝܬܗ *hj*
77:31 ܘܪܘ̈ܓܬܗ *k*] ܘܪܘ̈ܓܬܐ *hj*
79:15 ܒܪܗ *hjk*
79:17 ܒܪܗ *hjk*
86:inscr. ܠܒ̈ܢܘܗܝ *hj*
90:1 ܒܡܛܪܘܬܗ *j*] ܒܡܛܪܘܬܐ *h*
100:8 ܡܕܝܢܬܗ *hj*
113:19(115:11) ܕ̈ܚܠܘܗܝ *hj*
118:62 ܒܕܝܢ̈ܝܗ *hj*
143:3 ܒܪܗ *hj*

A few points about this edition remain to be explained. Some of these have already been mentioned at various junctures in the introduction and chapter one, but they are reiterated here for the sake of convenience. First, Mss of the SyrPs and SyrPs[a]/SyrPs[b] traditions are grouped separately in order to reflect the distinctiveness of those traditions. Second, *g*, the copy of *f*, is not cited except when, on rare occasions, it differs from *f*, or when *f* is defective. Third, *e silentio* conclusions cannot be drawn regarding readings in *fg* due to the fact that their interlinear SyrPs text is non-continuous—consisting, in effect, of a series of glosses on the Peshitta text. Thus, in the list of extant witnesses on each page of the edition, *f* and *g* are enclosed in parentheses as a reminder to the reader of the incompleteness of their evidence. Absolute certainty with regard to the testimony of these two witnesses could, of course, only be achieved through the recording of their affiliation (when they do supply textual evidence) with either the lemma or the variant for each entry in the apparatus.

Fourth, Mss other than *fg* which are only partly extant on a given page of the edition are likewise placed in parentheses. The reader may consult the appropriate Ms description in chapter one for a record of what remains of each such text. Exceptions to the parenthesizing of deficient Mss in the edition occur when lacunae are limited to isolated words or phrases. In such cases, the deficiencies of the incomplete Mss are specified where relevant in the apparatus. Fifth, on those occasions when Ms support for the lemma reading is explicitly cited in the apparatus (e. g. when *f* and *g* do not agree, see Ps. 54:4), not necessarily all attesting Mss are mentioned. As always, the list of extant witnesses on the relevant page of the edition should be consulted in order to determine the full extent of Ms support for the lemma reading. Sixth, in addition to its being positioned above the second apparatus, the first apparatus is distinguished from the latter by the inclusion of the Psalm number with that of the verse in each reference.

We now present the text of SyrPss, which is the focus of the present study.

I

1 [illegible]
[illegible]
[illegible]
[illegible]
2 [illegible]
[illegible]
3 [illegible]
[illegible]
[illegible]
[illegible]
[illegible]
4 [illegible]
[illegible]

I
[illegible]
5 [illegible]
[illegible]
6 [illegible]
[illegible]

II
1 [illegible]
[illegible]
2 [illegible]
[illegible]
[illegible]
3 [illegible]
[illegible]

a(bfg) (h)j

INSCRIPTIO

a [illegible]

f [illegible]

g [illegible] [2° [illegible] *g*c [illegible] | *g** [illegible]

j [illegible]

I

1. [illegible] *j* | [illegible] *j* | [illegible] > *j*
2. [illegible] > *j*
3. [illegible] c. sey. *f* | [illegible] c. sey. *a**(sed punctum prius inductum est pr m) *j* | [illegible] *j* | [illegible] *g* [illegible] *f j*
4. [illegible] 1° et 2°] + [illegible] *j* | [illegible] > *j* | [illegible] *j*
5. [illegible] *j* | [illegible] *b* | [illegible] *hj*; [illegible] fuid. *g*
6. [illegible] *hj* | [illegible] c. sey. *b hj* | [illegible] *hj*

II

1. [illegible] *hj* | [illegible] *hj*
2. [illegible] *bf hj* | [illegible] *hj* | [illegible] *hj* | [illegible] + [illegible] *hj*
3. [illegible] *hj*([illegible] pro [illegible]) | [illegible] *h* | [illegible] *hj*

II

[illegible] 4
[illegible] 5
[illegible] 6
[illegible] 7
[illegible] 8
[illegible] 9
[illegible] 10
[illegible] 11
[illegible] 12

II

[illegible]

III [illegible]

1 [illegible]

2 [illegible]

3 [illegible]

4 [illegible]

5 [illegible]

6 [illegible]

7 [illegible]

8 [illegible]

ab(fg) hj

4. [illegible] s. sey. *j* | [illegible] *hj*
5. [illegible] *j**(uid.) (= Pesh), sed c pr m
6. [illegible] *h*, [illegible] *j*
7. [illegible] *f* | [illegible] *j*
8. [illegible] *hj* | [illegible] *hj* | [illegible] c. sey. *f*; [illegible] *j* | [illegible] *hj*
9. [illegible] *hj* | [illegible] *hj*
11. [illegible] > *hj*
12. [illegible] *hj* | [illegible] *h*; [illegible] *j* | [illegible] *hj*

III

Inscr. [illegible] *a*mg*b*mg*f*mg(uid.)*g*mg (*f*mg*g*mg adsignant lectionem σ', sed cf. Field) | [illegible] *hj* | [illegible] *f* (*g* hab. [illegible]) | [illegible] *f j*, [illegible] *h*
1. [illegible] *hj* | [illegible] *hj*
2. [illegible] *hj* | + [illegible] *hj*
3. [illegible] *h*
4. [illegible] *hj* | [illegible] *b hj*
5. [illegible] *hj*
6. [illegible] *j* | [illegible] *hj*
7. [illegible] *hj* | [illegible] *f* | [illegible] *hj*
8. [illegible] > *hj*

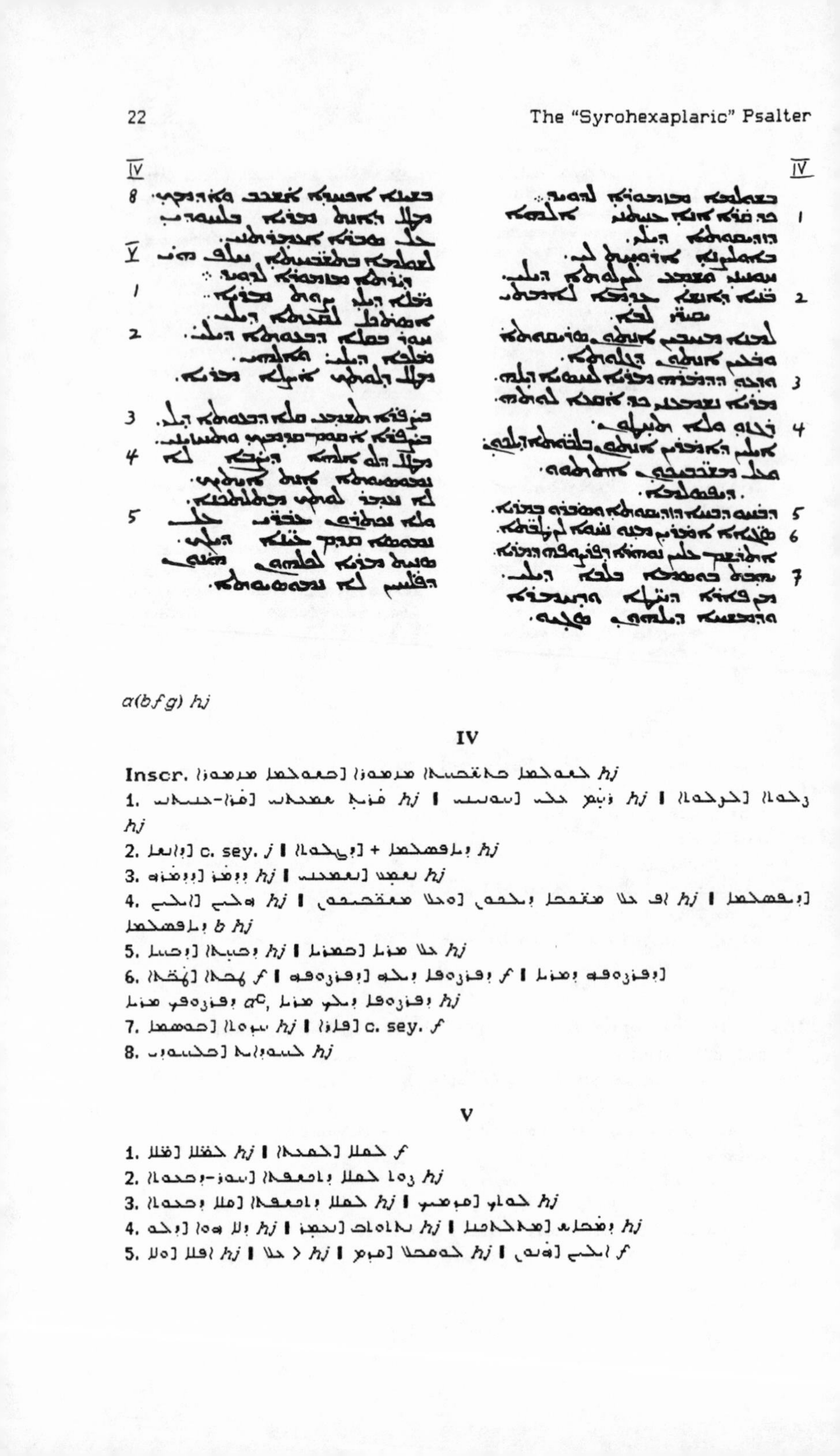

IV

[illegible]
1 [illegible]
2 [illegible]
3 [illegible]
4 [illegible]
5 [illegible]
6 [illegible]
7 [illegible]
8 [illegible]

V

[illegible]
1 [illegible]
2 [illegible]
3 [illegible]
4 [illegible]
5 [illegible]

a(bfg) hj

IV

Inscr. [illegible] *hj*

1. [illegible] *hj* | [illegible] *hj* | [illegible] *hj*

2. [illegible] c. sey. *j* | [illegible] + [illegible] *hj*

3. [illegible] *hj* | [illegible] *hj*

4. [illegible] *hj* | [illegible] *hj* | [illegible] *b hj*

5. [illegible] *hj* | [illegible] *hj*

6. [illegible] *f* | [illegible] *f* | [illegible] a^c, [illegible] *hj*

7. [illegible] *hj* | [illegible] c. sey. *f*

8. [illegible] *hj*

V

1. [illegible] *hj* | [illegible] *f*

2. [illegible] *hj*

3. [illegible] *hj* | [illegible] *hj*

4. [illegible] *hj* | [illegible] *hj* | [illegible] *hj*

5. [illegible] *hj* | [illegible] < *hj* | [illegible] *hj* | [illegible] *f*

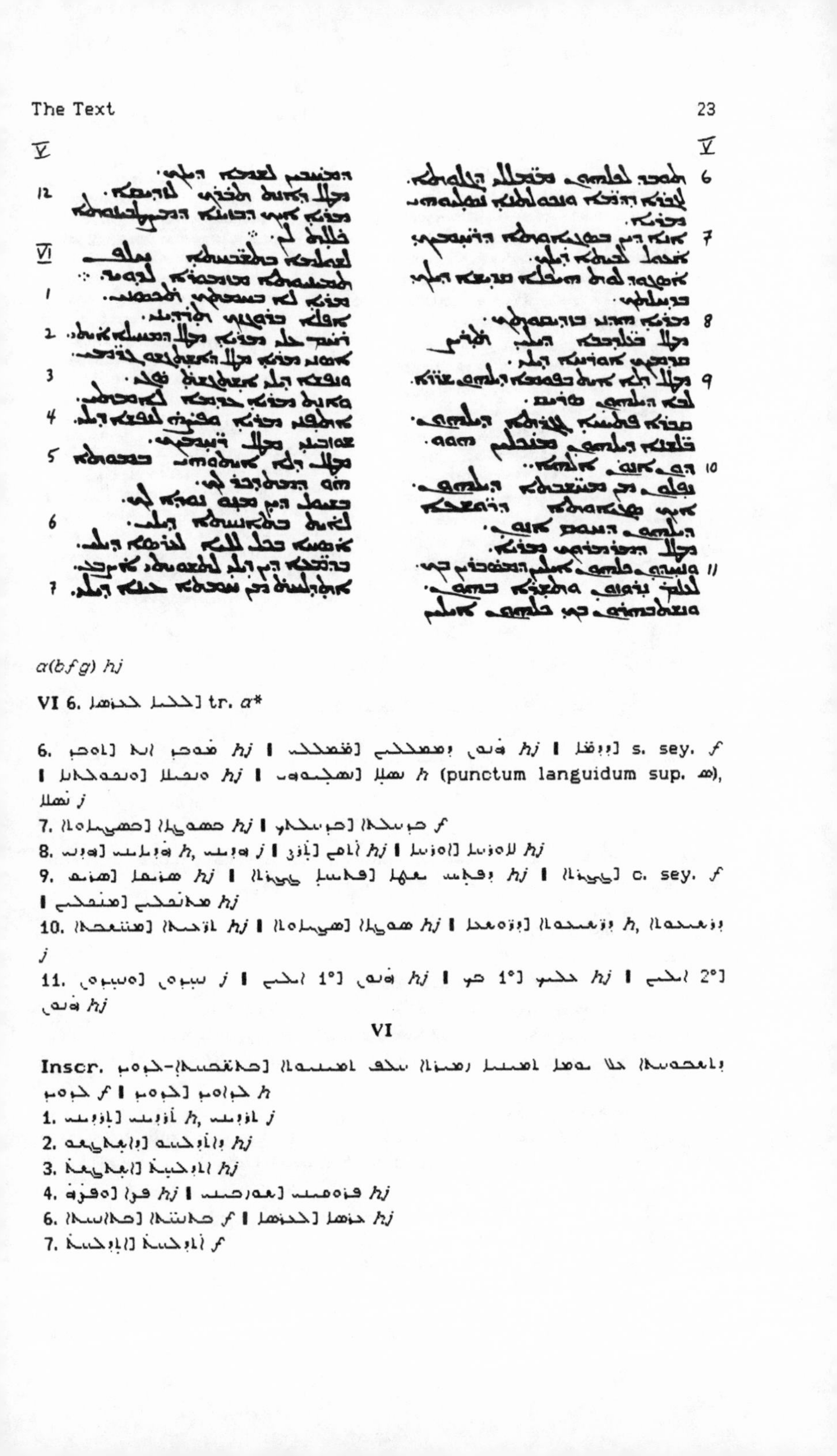

V

6 [illegible]

7 [illegible]

8 [illegible]

9 [illegible]

10 [illegible]

11 [illegible]

12 [illegible]

VI

1 [illegible]

2 [illegible]

3 [illegible]

4 [illegible]

5 [illegible]

6 [illegible]

7 [illegible]

a(bfg) hj

VI 6. [illegible]] tr. *a**

6. [illegible]] [illegible] *hj* | [illegible]] [illegible] *hj* | [illegible]] s. sey. *f* | [illegible]] [illegible] *hj* | [illegible]] [illegible] *h* (punctum languidum sup. [illegible]), [illegible] *j*

7. [illegible]] [illegible] *hj* | [illegible]] [illegible] *f*

8. [illegible]] [illegible] *h*, [illegible] *j* | [illegible]] [illegible] *hj* | [illegible]] [illegible] *hj*

9. [illegible]] [illegible] *hj* | [illegible]] [illegible] *hj* | [illegible]] c. sey. *f* | [illegible]] [illegible] *hj*

10. [illegible]] [illegible] *hj* | [illegible]] [illegible] *hj* | [illegible]] [illegible] *h*, [illegible] *j*

11. [illegible]] [illegible] *j* | [illegible] 1°] [illegible] *hj* | [illegible] 1°] [illegible] *hj* | [illegible] 2°] [illegible] *hj*

VI

Insor. [illegible]] [illegible] *h* | [illegible]] [illegible] *f* | [illegible]

1. [illegible]] [illegible] *h*, [illegible] *j*

2. [illegible]] [illegible] *hj*

3. [illegible]] [illegible] *hj*

4. [illegible]] [illegible] *hj* | [illegible]] [illegible] *hj*

6. [illegible]] [illegible] *hj* | [illegible]] [illegible] *f*

7. [illegible]] [illegible] *f*

VI

[illegible]
8 [illegible]
[illegible]
[illegible]
9 [illegible]
[illegible]
10 [illegible]
[illegible]
[illegible]
VII [illegible]
[illegible]
[illegible]
1 [illegible]
[illegible]
2 [illegible]
[illegible]
3 [illegible]
[illegible]
4 [illegible]
[illegible]
5 [illegible]
[illegible]

VII

[illegible]
[illegible]
6 [illegible]
[illegible]
[illegible]
[illegible]
7 [illegible]
[illegible]
8 [illegible]
[illegible]
[illegible]
9 [illegible]
[illegible]
[illegible]
10 [illegible]
[illegible]
11 [illegible]
[illegible]
[illegible]

a(bfg) hj

8. [illegible]] [illegible] *hj* | [illegible]] [illegible] *hj* | [illegible]] [illegible] *hj*; [illegible] *f*
9. [illegible]] [illegible] *hj*
10. [illegible]] [illegible] *h* | [illegible]] [illegible] *b* | [illegible]] [illegible] *hj*

VII

Inscr. [illegible]] [illegible] *hj* (quamquam littera ultima in uerbo secundo inc. *j*) | [illegible]] [illegible] *f* | [illegible]] [illegible] *h*
1. [illegible]] [illegible] *hj*
2. [illegible] > *h* | [illegible]] [illegible] *hj*
3. [illegible]] [illegible] *hj*
4. [illegible]] c. sey. *hj* | [illegible]] [illegible] *hj*
5. [illegible]] [illegible] *h*, [illegible] *j* | [illegible]] [illegible] *h* | [illegible]] [illegible] *h*, [illegible] *j* | [illegible]] [illegible] *hj* | [illegible]] [illegible] *j*; + [illegible] *hj*
6. [illegible]] [illegible] *h*, [illegible] *j* | [illegible]] [illegible] *j*mg; [illegible] *f*; [illegible] *j*txt | [illegible]] [illegible] *hj*
7. [illegible]] [illegible] *hj*
9. [illegible]] [illegible] *h*, [illegible] *j* | [illegible]] [illegible] *hj* | [illegible]] c. sey. *hj*; [illegible] *f* | [illegible]] [illegible] *hj* | [illegible]] c. sey. *h* | [illegible]] [illegible] *hj*; [illegible] *a*mg*f*mg (cf. Field)
10. [illegible]] [illegible] *f* | [illegible]] [illegible] *hj* | [illegible]] [illegible] *f* | [illegible]] + [illegible] *hj* | [illegible]] [illegible] *hj*
11. [illegible]] [illegible] *hj* | [illegible]] [illegible] *hj*

VII

12 [illegible]
[illegible]
[illegible]
13 [illegible]
[illegible]
14 [illegible]
[illegible]
15 [illegible]
[illegible]
16 [illegible]
[illegible]
17 [illegible]
[illegible]
VIII [illegible]
[illegible]
1 [illegible]
[illegible]
[illegible]
[illegible]

VIII

2 [illegible]
[illegible]
[illegible]
[illegible]
3 [illegible]
[illegible]
[illegible]
4 [illegible]
[illegible]
[illegible]
5 [illegible]
[illegible]
6 [illegible]
[illegible]
[illegible]
7 [illegible]
[illegible]
8 [illegible]
[illegible]
9 [illegible]
[illegible]

a(bfg) hj

12. [illegible]] [illegible] *hj* | [illegible]] [illegible] *hj* | [illegible] 1° et 2°] [illegible] *f* | [illegible]] [illegible] *f*

13. [illegible]] [illegible] *hj*

14. [illegible]] [illegible] *f hj* | [illegible]] [illegible] *hj* | [illegible]] [illegible] *hj*

15. [illegible]] [illegible] *hj*

16. [illegible]] [illegible] *hj* | [illegible]] [illegible] *hj* | [illegible]] [illegible] *hj*

VIII

Inscr. [illegible]] [illegible] *f*; [illegible] *hj* | [illegible]] [illegible] *f* | [illegible]] s. sey. *f h*

1. [illegible]] [illegible] *f hj* | [illegible]] [illegible] *j* | [illegible]] c. sey. *h*

2. [illegible]] [illegible] *j* | [illegible]] [illegible] *f* | [illegible]] [illegible] *j* | [illegible]] [illegible] *hj* | [illegible]] c. sey. *f* | [illegible]] [illegible] *j*

3. [illegible]] s. sey. *f*; [illegible] *hj* | [illegible]] [illegible] sup. ras. *j* | [illegible]] [illegible] *h* ([illegible] sup. ras.), [illegible] *j*

4. [illegible]] [illegible] *f* | [illegible]] [illegible] *f hj*

5. [illegible]] [illegible] *f hj*

6. [illegible]] [illegible] *hj*

7. [illegible]] [illegible] *hj* | [illegible]] [illegible] *hj*

8. [illegible]] s. sey. *f* | [illegible]] c. sey. *h* | [illegible]] [illegible] *hj* | [illegible]] [illegible] *f hj* | [illegible]] [illegible] *hj*

IX

[illegible]
[illegible]
1 [illegible]
[illegible]
2 [illegible]
[illegible]
3 [illegible]
[illegible]
[illegible]
4 [illegible]
[illegible]
[illegible]
5 [illegible]
[illegible]
[illegible]
6 [illegible]
[illegible]
[illegible]
7 [illegible]
[illegible]
8 [illegible]
[illegible]
9 [illegible]
[illegible]
10 [illegible]
[illegible]
[illegible]
[illegible]
11 [illegible]
[illegible]
12 [illegible]
[illegible]
[illegible]
13 [illegible]
[illegible]
[illegible]
[illegible]
14 [illegible]
[illegible]
[illegible]
15 [illegible]
[illegible]
[illegible]
[illegible]

a(bfg) hj

IX

Insc r. [illegible] *f hj* | [illegible] *f* | [illegible] *f* | [illegible] c. sey. *b h* | [illegible] + [illegible] *f*

1. [illegible] *f*

2. [illegible] *bf hj*

3. [illegible] *hj* | [illegible] *hj*

4. [illegible] *b hj* | [illegible] *hj* | [illegible] (*b* uid.)] + [illegible] *hj*

5. [illegible] (*b* absc.)] [illegible] *j* | [illegible] *f* | [illegible] *hj* | [illegible] *hj* | [illegible] ob. abscond. *b*; s. notis *f hj*

6. [illegible] (*b* inc.)] c. sey. *f* | [illegible] *hj* | [illegible] *hj* | [illegible] *hj*

7. [illegible] *hj*

8. [illegible] *h*ᶜ pr m(tr. *h** [!])*j*

9. [illegible] c. sey. *a**(uid.)

10. [illegible] *hj* | [illegible] *hj* | [illegible] *j*

11. [illegible] *h* | [illegible] *hj*

12. [illegible] *hj* | [illegible] s. sey. *f* | [illegible] *h* | [illegible] *f* | [illegible] sup. ras. *a*; [illegible] *hj*

13. [illegible] *hj*

14. [illegible] *hj*

15. [illegible] *hj* | [illegible] *hj*

IX

16 [illegible]
[illegible]
[illegible]
[illegible]
17 [illegible]
[illegible]
18 [illegible]
[illegible]
[illegible]
19 [illegible]
[illegible]
20 [illegible]
[illegible]
[illegible]
[illegible]
21 [illegible]
[illegible]
[illegible]
22 [illegible]
[illegible]
[illegible]
23 [illegible]
[illegible]
[illegible]
24 [illegible]
[illegible]
[illegible]
[illegible]
25 [illegible]
[illegible]
[illegible]
[illegible]
26 [illegible]
[illegible]
27 [illegible]
[illegible]

[illegible]
28 [illegible]
[illegible]
[illegible]
29 [illegible]
[illegible]
[illegible]
30 [illegible]
[illegible]
31 [illegible]
[illegible]

a(fg) hj

16. [illegible] *hj* | [illegible] s. sey. *f* | [illegible] *h*, [illegible] *j*
17. [illegible] pr. [illegible] *h*, pr. [illegible] *j*
18. [illegible] *hj* | [illegible] *hj*
19. [illegible] > *h**, sed c pr m | [illegible] *hj*
20. [illegible] *h* | [illegible] > *hj*; [illegible] *f*
21. [illegible] *hj* | [illegible] s. sey. *f*
22. [illegible] *hj* | [illegible] *hj* | [illegible] *hj*
23. [illegible] *j* | [illegible] *f* | [illegible] *hj*
24. [illegible] *hj* | [illegible] *hj* | [illegible] *hj*
25. [illegible] *hj* | [illegible] *h*, [illegible] *j* | [illegible] > *hj* | [illegible] *hj* | [illegible] *hj*
27. [illegible] *hj* | [illegible] c. sey. *f* | [illegible] *hj* | [illegible] *f*
28. [illegible] *hj* | [illegible] *hj* | [illegible] s. sey. *hj* | [illegible] *hj*
29. [illegible] *h*, [illegible] *j* | [illegible] *hj* | [illegible] 1° ∩ 2° *j* | [illegible] 1°] [illegible] *h* | [illegible] 2°] [illegible] *hj* | [illegible] *f*mg frt (non *g*)] [illegible] *hj*
30. [illegible] *hj* | [illegible] *hj*
31. [illegible] *hj*

IX

32 [illegible]

33 [illegible]

34 [illegible]

35 [illegible]

36 [illegible]

37 [illegible]

38 [illegible]

X

1 [illegible]

2 [illegible]

3 [illegible]

4 [illegible]

5 [illegible]

6 [illegible]

7 [illegible]

a(cfg) hj

32. [illegible]] [illegible] *hj*
33. [illegible]] [illegible] *f*] [illegible] *g j* | [illegible]] [illegible] *hj* | [illegible]] [illegible] *hj*
34. [illegible]] [illegible] *hj* | [illegible]] [illegible] *hj* | [illegible]] [illegible] *hj* | [illegible]] [illegible] *hj*
35. [illegible]] [illegible] *hj*
36. [illegible]] tr. *hj* | [illegible]] om. metob. *c*; s. notis *f* (non testatur [illegible]) *hj* | [illegible]] [illegible] *hj*
37. [illegible]] [illegible] *hj*
38. [illegible]] [illegible] *hj* | [illegible]] [illegible] *hj*

X

Inscr. [illegible]] [illegible] *f hj* | [illegible] > *h*
1. [illegible]] [illegible] *hj* | [illegible]] [illegible] *hj*
3. [illegible]] s. sey. *f* uid. *g* | [illegible]] [illegible] *hj* | [illegible]] [illegible] *hj*
4. [illegible]] [illegible] *hj*
5. [illegible]] [illegible] *hj*
6. [illegible]] c. sey. *f* | [illegible]] [illegible] *hj* | [illegible]] abest in *f**, sed c pr m | [illegible]] [illegible] *hj*

X

[illegible]
[illegible]
8 [illegible]
[illegible]
[illegible]

XI

[illegible]
[illegible]
1 [illegible]
[illegible]
2 [illegible]
[illegible]
[illegible]
[illegible]
3 [illegible]
[illegible]
[illegible]
4 [illegible]

XI

[illegible]
[illegible]
5 [illegible]
[illegible]
[illegible]
[illegible]
[illegible]
6 [illegible]
[illegible]
[illegible]
7 [illegible]
[illegible]
8 [illegible]
[illegible]
[illegible]

ac(fg) hj

8. [illegible] > *hj* | [illegible] s. sey. *c* | [illegible] *f hj* | [illegible] *cf* | [illegible] *hj*

XI

Inscr. [illegible] *f*; [illegible] *h*; [illegible] *j*

1. [illegible] *hj* | [illegible] s. sey. *cf hj*

2. [illegible] *f* | [illegible] *c*; [illegible] *hj*

3. [illegible] *f*; [illegible] *hj* | [illegible] *cf* | [illegible] *hj*

4. [illegible] *hj* | [illegible] 1° *f* | [illegible] *hj* | [illegible] *hj*

5. [illegible] c. sey. *f* | [illegible] *g*] [illegible] > *f** (qua manu correctum est inc.) | [illegible] *c*, [illegible] *f*, [illegible] *hj* | [illegible] *hj*

6. [illegible] *h*([illegible] inc.)*j* | [illegible] *hj* | [illegible] *hj*

7. [illegible] *hj* | [illegible] *hj*

8. [illegible] *hj*

XIII

[illegible]
1 [illegible]
2 [illegible]
3 [illegible]

XII

[illegible]
1 [illegible]
2 [illegible]
3 [illegible]
4 [illegible]
5 [illegible]
6 [illegible]

ac(fg) (h)j

XII

Insc. [illegible] *f*; [illegible] *hj* | [illegible]
+ [illegible] *f*

1. [illegible] sup. ras. et [illegible] sequitur in margine (primo u. 1b ad [illegible] scriptus est uid., deinde c pr m) *j* | [illegible] *h* | [illegible] *h*

2. [illegible] 1° [illegible] *hj* | [illegible] s. sey. *cf*; [illegible] *hj* | [illegible] *hj* | [illegible] *j*

3. [illegible] *j* | [illegible] *j* | [illegible] *j*

4. [illegible] *f* | [illegible] *j* | [illegible] *c*

6. [illegible] *f*mg* (*g* non testatur)

XIII

Insc. [illegible] *f*; [illegible] *j*

1. [illegible] *c* | [illegible] *j* | [illegible] + [illegible] *j*

2. [illegible] s. sey. *f*

3. [illegible] *j* | [illegible] 2° > *j* | [illegible] c. sey. *c* | [illegible] *f* non testatur | [illegible] *j* | [illegible] *j* | [illegible] (sic) *j* | [illegible] *j* | [illegible] *j* | [illegible] *j* | [illegible] *c*; [illegible] *j* | [illegible] *j*

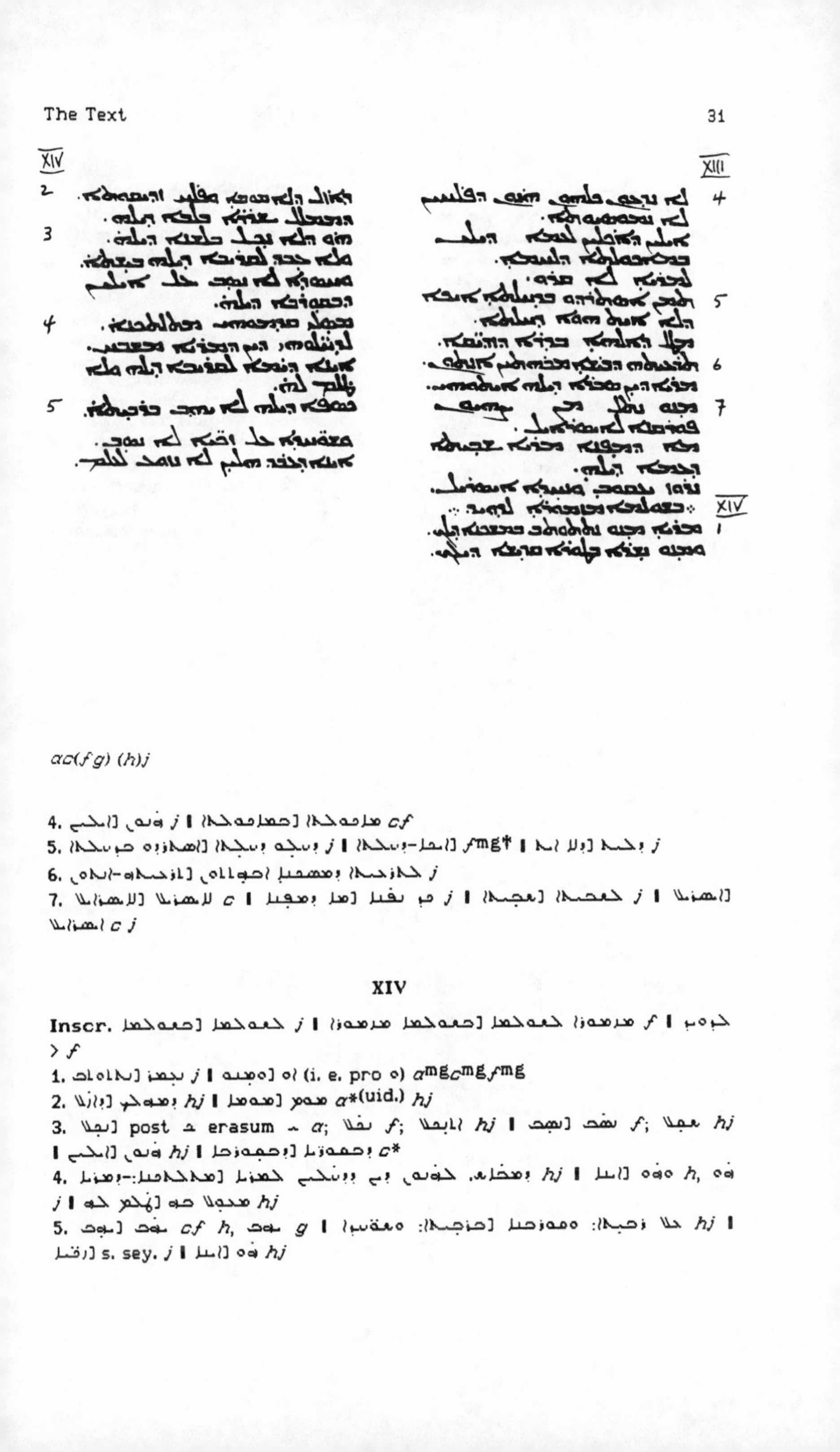

XIII

4 [illegible]
[illegible]
[illegible]
[illegible]
[illegible]
5 [illegible]
[illegible]
[illegible]
6 [illegible]
[illegible]
7 [illegible]
[illegible]
[illegible]
[illegible]
[illegible]

XIV

1 [illegible]
[illegible]

XIV

2 [illegible]
[illegible]
3 [illegible]
[illegible]
[illegible]
[illegible]
4 [illegible]
[illegible]
[illegible]
[illegible]
5 [illegible]
[illegible]
[illegible]

ac(fg) (h)j

4. [illegible] *j* | [illegible] *cf*
5. [illegible] *j* | [illegible] *f*mg* | [illegible] *j*
6. [illegible] *j*
7. [illegible] *j* | [illegible] *j* | [illegible] *c* | [illegible] *c j*

XIV

Inscr. [illegible] *j* | [illegible] *f* | [illegible] > *f*
1. [illegible] *j* | [illegible] (i. e. pro [illegible]) *a*mg *c*mg *f*mg
2. [illegible] *hj* | [illegible] *a**(uid.) *hj*
3. [illegible] post [illegible] erasum [illegible] *a*; [illegible] *f*; [illegible] *hj* | [illegible] *f*; [illegible] *hj* | [illegible] *c** | [illegible] *hj* |
4. [illegible] *hj* | [illegible] *h*, [illegible] *j* | [illegible] *hj*
5. [illegible] *cf h*, [illegible] *g* | [illegible] *hj* | [illegible] s. sey. *j* | [illegible] *hj*

XV

[illegible]
1 [illegible]
2 [illegible]
[illegible]
[illegible]
3 [illegible]
[illegible]
4 [illegible]
[illegible]
[illegible]
[illegible]
[illegible]
5 [illegible]
[illegible]
6 [illegible]
[illegible]
[illegible]

XV

7 [illegible]
[illegible]
[illegible]
8 [illegible]
[illegible]
[illegible]
[illegible]
9 [illegible]
[illegible]
[illegible]
10 [illegible]
[illegible]
[illegible]
[illegible]
11 [illegible]
[illegible]
[illegible]

a(b)c(f g) hj

XV

Insc. [illegible]] [illegible] *h*

2. [illegible]] [illegible] *hj* | [illegible]] [illegible] *h*, [illegible] *j*

3. [illegible]] [illegible] *hj*

4. [illegible]] [illegible] *hj* | [illegible]] [illegible] s. sey. *f* | [illegible]] [illegible] *hj* | [illegible]] s. sey. *f* | [illegible]] [illegible] *hj*

5. [illegible]] [illegible] *hj*

6. [illegible]] [illegible] *c hj* | [illegible]] [illegible] *hj* | [illegible]] [illegible] *hj*

7. [illegible]] [illegible] *hj* | [illegible]] [illegible] *hj*

8. [illegible] (*b* absc.)] [illegible] *hj* | [illegible] > *hj* | [illegible] (*b* absc.)] pr. [illegible] *hj* | [illegible] > *j*

9. [illegible] (*b* absc.)] [illegible] | [illegible] *h*, [illegible] *j* | [illegible] (*b* inc.)] [illegible] *hj*

11. [illegible]] [illegible] *cf hj* | [illegible]] [illegible] *h* uid. *j* | [illegible]] [illegible] *hj*

XVI

[illegible]
1 [illegible]
[illegible]
[illegible]
[illegible]
2 [illegible]
[illegible]
3 [illegible]
[illegible]
4 [illegible]
[illegible]
[illegible]
[illegible]
5 [illegible]
[illegible]

XVI

6 [illegible]
[illegible]
7 [illegible]
[illegible]
[illegible]
8 [illegible]
[illegible]
9 [illegible]
[illegible]
[illegible]
10 [illegible]
[illegible]
11 [illegible]
[illegible]
[illegible]

abc(efg) hj

XVI 5. [illegible] partes inferiores horum uerborum resectae in *a*, sed *ce* hab. uerba integra ([illegible] absc. in *b*)

XVI

Inscr. [illegible] *c*

1. [illegible] *hj* | [illegible] *hj* | [illegible] *hj* | [illegible] *f j* | [illegible] *hj*

2. [illegible] > *j**, sed c pr m uid. | [illegible] *h*uid.(quamquam sey. inc.)*j*

3. [illegible] *h*uid.(punctum inc.)*j* | [illegible] *hj* | [illegible] *hj* | [illegible] (*b* absc.) [illegible] *hj*

4. [illegible] + [illegible] *hj*

5. [illegible] *hj* | [illegible] *hj*

6. [illegible] (*b* absc.) [illegible] *hj* | [illegible] > *e** sed c pr m

7. [illegible] *hj* | [illegible] + [illegible] *hj* | [illegible] *hj* | [illegible] *hj* | [illegible] *hj*

9. [illegible] (*b* absc.) > *hj* | [illegible] *hj* | [illegible] (*b*inc.) [illegible] *hj* | [illegible] *hj*

10. [illegible] (*b*inc.) [illegible] *hj* | [illegible] *e* | [illegible] *hj*

11. [illegible] *hj* | [illegible] puncta sey. aut omissa sunt aut perierunt *b*; s. sey. *f* | [illegible] *hj*

XVI

[Syriac] 12
[Syriac]
[Syriac] 13
[Syriac]
[Syriac]
[Syriac]
[Syriac] 14
[Syriac]
[Syriac]
[Syriac]
[Syriac]
[Syriac]
[Syriac] 15
[Syriac]
[Syriac]
[Syriac]
[Syriac] XVII
[Syriac]
[Syriac]
[Syriac]

XVII

[Syriac]
[Syriac]
1 [Syriac]
2 [Syriac]
[Syriac]
[Syriac]
[Syriac]
[Syriac]
3 [Syriac]
[Syriac]
4 [Syriac]
[Syriac]
5 [Syriac]
[Syriac]
6 [Syriac]
[Syriac]
[Syriac]
[Syriac]
[Syriac]
[Syriac]

abce(fg) hj

XVII 6. [Syriac]] haec uerba ad imam paginam absc. *a*, sed hab. *be*

12. [Syriac]] [Syriac] *hj* | [Syriac] > *j** sed c pr m | [Syriac]] + [Syriac] *hj* | [Syriac]] [Syriac] (sic) *hj*

13. [Syriac]] [Syriac] *f* | [Syriac]] [Syriac] *hj* | [Syriac]] [Syriac] *hj* | [Syriac] (*e*inc.)] c. sey. *c h**(punctum alterum aut periit aut erasum est)

14. [Syriac]] *c* punctum superius habebat, sed nunc ut lemma est; [Syriac] *e*; [Syriac] *hj* | [Syriac] 2° > *hj* | [Syriac] (*b*uid.)] [Syriac] *hj* | [Syriac] (*f*uid., *g* deest; *b* absc.)] [Syriac] *e* (nullum pronomen solutum possessiuum apparet, quamquam Ms nocitum est aliquantum) | [Syriac]] s. sey. *c* | [Syriac] > *hj*

15. [Syriac]] [Syriac] *hj* | [Syriac] (*b*uid.)] [Syriac] *hj* | [Syriac] (*f*inc., *g* deest)] [Syriac] *hj*

XVII

Inscr. [Syriac]] [Syriac] *hj* | [Syriac]] [Syriac] *hj* | [Syriac]] [Syriac] *hj* | [Syriac]] [Syriac] *j*

2. [Syriac]] [Syriac] *e**, sed c pr m | [Syriac]] [Syriac] *hj* | [Syriac]] [Syriac] *c* | [Syriac]] [Syriac] *hj* | [Syriac]] [Syriac] *hj*

3. [Syriac]] [Syriac] *hj*

4. [Syriac]] [Syriac] *h*, [Syriac] *j* | [Syriac]] [Syriac] *hj* | [Syriac]] [Syriac] *hj*

5. [Syriac]] c. sey. *c*; [Syriac] *h*, [Syriac] *j* | [Syriac]] [Syriac] *bc* | [Syriac]] s. sey. *c*

6. [Syriac]] [Syriac] *hj* | [Syriac]] tr. *c* | [Syriac]] [Syriac] *e*

XVII

[illegible] 7
[illegible]
[illegible]
[illegible]
[illegible] 8
[illegible]
[illegible]
[illegible] 9
[illegible]
[illegible] 10
[illegible]
[illegible] 11
[illegible]
[illegible]
[illegible] 12
[illegible]
※[illegible]
[illegible] 13
[illegible]

XVII

14 [illegible]
[illegible]
15 [illegible]
[illegible]
[illegible]
[illegible]
16 [illegible]
[illegible]
17 [illegible]
[illegible]
18 [illegible]
[illegible]
19 [illegible]
[illegible]
[illegible]
20 [illegible]
[illegible]
[illegible]

abce(fg) hj

7. [illegible] *hj* | [illegible] bis scr. (!) *e* | [illegible] s. sey. *b*; [illegible] *hj* | [illegible] s. sey. *h*; [illegible] *c*

8. [illegible] *e*; [illegible] *hj* | [illegible] *h*, [illegible] *j*

9. [illegible] s. sey. *c hj* | [illegible] (*b* absc.)] [illegible] *h*, [illegible] *j*

10. [illegible] (*b* inc.)] [illegible] *hj* | [illegible] s. sey. *ce hj*

11. [illegible] (*b* absc.)] [illegible] *hj* | [illegible] *hj* | [illegible] *e*, [illegible] *h*, [illegible] *j*

12. [illegible] s. notis *e hj*

15. [illegible] *bef* | [illegible] *hj* | [illegible] *hj* | [illegible] *hj*

16. [illegible] *hj* | [illegible] *h*; [illegible] *j*

17. [illegible] *hj* | [illegible] *hj* | [illegible] *hj* | [illegible] *g*] [illegible] *f**, sed c pr m | [illegible] pr. [illegible] *hj*

18. [illegible] *be h* | [illegible] 1° ∩ 2° *c* ([illegible] 1° et [illegible] absc. *b*)

19. [illegible] (*b* absc.)] [illegible] *hj* | [illegible] 2° ([illegible] absc. *b*)] *f* mg† | [illegible] (*b* absc.)] [illegible] *hj*

20. [illegible] > *j*

XVII

[illegible] 21
[illegible]
[illegible] 22
[illegible]
[illegible] 23
[illegible]
[illegible] 24
[illegible]
[illegible]
[illegible] 25
[illegible]
[illegible] 26
[illegible]
[illegible] 27
[illegible]
[illegible] 28
[illegible]
[illegible]
[illegible] 29
[illegible]
[illegible]

30 [illegible]
[illegible]
[illegible]
[illegible]
31 [illegible]
[illegible]
32 [illegible]
[illegible]
33 [illegible]
[illegible]
34 [illegible]
[illegible]
35 [illegible]
[illegible]
[illegible]
[illegible]
36 [illegible]
[illegible]
37 [illegible]
[illegible]
38 [illegible]
[illegible]
39 [illegible]
[illegible]
[illegible]

a(b)c(efg) hj

22. [illegible]] [illegible] *c*

23. [illegible]] [illegible] *hj* | [illegible]] [illegible] *hj*

24. [illegible]] [illegible] *c*

25. [illegible]] [illegible] *hj*

26. [illegible]] [illegible] *hj* | [illegible]] [illegible] *ce j*, [illegible] *h*

27. [illegible]] [illegible] *hj*

28. [illegible]] [illegible] *hj*

29. [illegible]] [illegible] *hj* | [illegible]] [illegible] *f* | [illegible]] [illegible] *hj*

30. [illegible]] [illegible] *c* | [illegible]] [illegible] *bcef* | [illegible]] [illegible] *hj* | [illegible]] [illegible] *hj* | [illegible]] [illegible] *hj* | [illegible]] [illegible] *hj*

31. [illegible] 1° > *j*

32. [illegible]] [illegible] *hj* | [illegible]] [illegible] *hj*

33. [illegible]] [illegible] *c*, [illegible] *f*; [illegible] *j* | [illegible]] [illegible] *hj*

35. [illegible]] [illegible] *hj* | [illegible]] [illegible] *f* | [illegible]] [illegible] *h*, [illegible] *j* | [illegible]] [illegible] *hj* | [illegible] *g*] [illegible] *f**, sed c pr m | [illegible]] [illegible] *hj*

36. [illegible]] [illegible] *hj*

37. [illegible]] [illegible] *hj*

38. [illegible]] [illegible] *hj*

39. [illegible] *f*] [illegible] *g*, [illegible] *hj* | [illegible]] [illegible] *hj* | [illegible]] [illegible] *hj*

XVII

40 [illegible]

[illegible]

41 [illegible]

[illegible]

42 [illegible]

[illegible]

[illegible]

43 [illegible]

[illegible]

[illegible]

[illegible]

44 [illegible]

[illegible]

45 [illegible]

[illegible]

46 [illegible]

[illegible]

47 [illegible]

[illegible]

XVII

48 [illegible]

[illegible]

[illegible]

49 [illegible]

[illegible]

50 [illegible]

[illegible]

[illegible]

XVIII

[illegible]

1 [illegible]

[illegible]

[illegible]

2 [illegible]

[illegible]

3 [illegible]

[illegible]

4 [illegible]

[illegible]

[illegible]

[illegible]

ac(fg) hj

40. [illegible] < *hj* | [illegible] [illegible] *hj*
41. [illegible] pr. [illegible] *hj* | [illegible] (*f* uid.)] [illegible] *g* (cf. Pesh); [illegible] *hj*
42. [illegible] [illegible] *hj* | [illegible] [illegible] *hj* | [illegible] [illegible] *cf*; [illegible] *hj*
43. [illegible] [illegible] *h*, [illegible] *j**; [illegible] *j*c | [illegible] [illegible] *hj* | [illegible] [illegible] *h*, [illegible] *j* | [illegible] [illegible] *hj* | [illegible] [illegible] *f* | [illegible] < *hj*
44. [illegible] (*f* uid.)] [illegible] (sic) *g*; [illegible] *h*, [illegible] *j*
45. [illegible] (*f* inc., *g* deest)] [illegible] *hj* | [illegible] s. sey. *f*
46. [illegible] 1° > *hj* | [illegible] [illegible] *hj*
48. [illegible] [illegible] *f*; [illegible] *hj* | [illegible] [illegible] *hj* | [illegible] [illegible] *hj* | [illegible] c. sey. *c*
49. [illegible] [illegible] *c*, [illegible] *hj*
50. [illegible] s. sey. *c*; [illegible] *hj* | [illegible] [illegible] *h*

XVIII

Inscr. [illegible] [illegible] *f hj*
1. [illegible] s. sey. *c hj* | [illegible] [illegible] *f*; [illegible] *hj* | [illegible] [illegible] *hj**
2. [illegible] [illegible] *hj* | [illegible] [illegible] *hj*
3. [illegible] [illegible] *hj* | [illegible] [illegible] *c*; [illegible] *h*, [illegible] *j* | [illegible] [illegible] *hj* | [illegible] [illegible] *hj*(s. puncto)
4. [illegible] [illegible] *hj* | [illegible] [illegible] *hj*

XVIII

5 [illegible]
[illegible]
6 [illegible]
[illegible]
[illegible]
[illegible]
[illegible]
7 [illegible]
[illegible]
[illegible]
[illegible]
8 [illegible]
[illegible]
9 [illegible]
[illegible]
[illegible]

10 [illegible]
[illegible]
[illegible]
11 [illegible]
[illegible]
12 [illegible]
[illegible]
13 [illegible]
[illegible]
[illegible]
[illegible]
14 [illegible]
[illegible]
[illegible]
[illegible]

XIX
1 [illegible]
[illegible]

ac(fg) hj

5. [illegible] *hj* | [illegible] *cf*

6. [illegible] *c* | [illegible] *hj* | [illegible] *c* | [illegible] *h**, [illegible] *h*ᶜ pr m*j* | [illegible] *f* ([illegible] insertatum est [pr m] inter [illegible] et [illegible]); [illegible] *hj*

7. [illegible] *hj* | [illegible] *hj*

8. [illegible] c. sey. *c*; [illegible] *hj* | [illegible] *f*] [illegible] *c*, [illegible] *g*; [illegible] *h*, [illegible] *j* | [illegible] *hj*

9. [illegible] *hj* | [illegible] *cf* | [illegible] *hj*

10. [illegible] c. sey. *c*; [illegible] *h*, [illegible] *j* | [illegible] *hj* | [illegible] > *c* | [illegible] *hj* | [illegible] *hj*

11. [illegible] *hj* | [illegible] c. sey. *f*

12. [illegible] *f hj*

13. [illegible] *hj* | [illegible] *f* | [illegible] *hj* | [illegible] *hj*

14. [illegible] *hj* | [illegible] c. sey. *c*; [illegible] *hj* | [illegible] *c*

XIX

Inscr. [illegible] *f hj* | [illegible] > *f*

1. [illegible] *f*] [illegible] *g*; [illegible] *hj*

XIX

2 [illegible]
[illegible]
3 [illegible]
[illegible]
[illegible]
4 [illegible]
[illegible]
5 [illegible]
[illegible]
[illegible]
6 [illegible]
[illegible]
[illegible]
[illegible]
7 [illegible]
[illegible]
[illegible]
8 [illegible]

[illegible]
9 [illegible]
[illegible]
[illegible]

XX

[illegible]
1 [illegible]
[illegible]
2 [illegible]
[illegible]
[illegible]
3 [illegible]
[illegible]
[illegible]
[illegible]
4 [illegible]
[illegible]
5 [illegible]
[illegible]
[illegible]
[illegible]

ac(efg) hj

3. [illegible] *hj* | [illegible] c. sey. *cf j* | [illegible] (*f* uid.)] pr. ※ (s. metob.) *c*; pr. ο *g*; [illegible] *hj*
4. [illegible] *hj*
5. [illegible] *hj* | [illegible] *a**(uid.), sed c pr m | [illegible] *hj*
6. [illegible] *hj* | [illegible] *hj*
7. [illegible] *hj* | [illegible] *hj*
8. [illegible] *c*; [illegible] *e*
9. [illegible] *h*, [illegible] *j*

XX

Inscr. [illegible] *f*; [illegible] *hj* | [illegible] > *hj*
2. [illegible] *hj* | [illegible] *hj* | [illegible] *c*mg *f*mg, etiam *a*mg quamquam perperam pro [illegible] | [illegible] *hj* | [illegible] *a**(uid.) *cf*mg *j*, [illegible] *e*, [illegible] *h*
3. [illegible] *c hj* | [illegible] *f* | [illegible] *hj*
4. [illegible] *hj*(s. puncto) | [illegible] (*e* uid.)] [illegible] *hj* | [illegible] *e*
5. [illegible] ([illegible] absc. *e*)] [illegible] *hj* | [illegible] pr. ο *j*

XX

6 [illegible]
[illegible]
[illegible]
7 [illegible]
[illegible]
8 [illegible]
[illegible]
[illegible]
9 [illegible]
[illegible]
[illegible]
[illegible]
10 [illegible]

[illegible]
11 [illegible]
[illegible]
[illegible]
12 [illegible]
[illegible]
[illegible]
13 [illegible]
[illegible]

XXI

[illegible]
[illegible]
1 [illegible]
[illegible]
[illegible]
[illegible]
2 [illegible]
[illegible]
[illegible]

ae(fg) hj

6. [illegible] (*e* absc.)] [illegible] *hj*

7. [illegible] (*e* absc.)] [illegible] *hj* | [illegible] *f* (*e* absc.)] > *g*; [illegible] *hj*

8. [illegible] *e hj* | [illegible] *hj*

9. [illegible] 1° > *j**, sed c pr m | [illegible] *hj* | [illegible] *hj* | [illegible] *e*

10. [illegible] c. sey. *f* | [illegible] *hj* | [illegible] s. sey. *ef hj*

11. [illegible] *hj* | [illegible] *hj* | [illegible] *f* | [illegible] *hj* | [illegible] *hj*; [illegible] *f*

12. [illegible] *f*

13. [illegible] s. sey. *f*

XXI

Inscr. [illegible] *f*; [illegible] *hj* | [illegible] > *f* | [illegible] > *f*

1. [illegible] 1°] [illegible] *hj* | [illegible] *hj* | [illegible] *hj* | [illegible] > *j**, sed c pr m

2. [illegible] *hj* | [illegible] *hj*

XXI

3 [illegible]

[illegible]

4 [illegible]

[illegible]

5 [illegible]

[illegible]

6 [illegible]

[illegible]

7 [illegible]

[illegible]

8 [illegible]

[illegible]

9 [illegible]

[illegible]

[illegible]

10 [illegible]

11 [illegible]

[illegible]

12 [illegible]

[illegible]

13 [illegible]

14 [illegible]

[illegible]

[illegible]

[illegible]

15 [illegible]

[illegible]

[illegible]

16 [illegible]

[illegible]

[illegible]

αe(fg) hj

3. [illegible]] [illegible] *hj* | [illegible]] *e**(uid.) [illegible] *e*ᶜ

4. [illegible]] [illegible] *hj* | [illegible]] [illegible] *hj*

5. [illegible]] [illegible] *hj*

6. [illegible]] [illegible] *hj* | [illegible]] [illegible] *h*

7. [illegible]] [illegible] *hj* | [illegible] + [illegible] *hj* | [illegible]] [illegible] *hj* | [illegible]] [illegible] *e* [illegible]] [illegible] *hj*

8. [illegible]] [illegible] *hj* | [illegible]] [illegible] *hj* | [illegible] (abscond. *f*)] [illegible] (sic) *g* | [illegible] ⟩ *hj*

9. [illegible]] [illegible] *h*, [illegible] *j*

11. [illegible]] s. sey. *hj* | [illegible]] c. sey. *g* (in *f* hoc uerbum fere perditum, quamquam puncta sey. apparent); [illegible] *hj* | [illegible]] pr. [illegible] *hj*

12. [illegible]] [illegible] *e*; [illegible] *hj* | [illegible]] [illegible] *hj* | [illegible]] [illegible] (sic) *hj* | [illegible]] [illegible] *h*, [illegible] *j*

13. [illegible]] [illegible] *hj*

14. [illegible]] [illegible] *h*

15. [illegible]] [illegible] *ef hj* | [illegible]] [illegible] *hj*, etiam *e**(uid.) sed c pr m (quamquam restat punctum inferius) | [illegible]] [illegible] *hj*

16. [illegible]] [illegible] *hj* | [illegible]] [illegible] *h*, [illegible] *j* | [illegible]] [illegible] *hj*

XXI

17 [illegible]

18 [illegible]

19 [illegible]

20 [illegible]

21 [illegible]

22 [illegible]

23 [illegible]

24 [illegible]

XXI

25 [illegible]

26 [illegible]

27 [illegible]

28 [illegible]

29 [illegible]

30 [illegible]

31 [illegible]

a(c)e(fg) hj

17. [illegible]] [illegible] *hj* | [illegible]] [illegible] *e*; [illegible] *hj*

18. [illegible]] [illegible] *f*

20. [illegible]] [illegible] *hj* | [illegible]] [illegible] *hj* | [illegible]] [illegible] *f*

21. [illegible]] [illegible] *hj* (praeter *h* hab. [illegible])

23. [illegible]] [illegible] *hj* | [illegible]] [illegible] *f*; [illegible] *hj*(hab. ⟦[illegible]⟧[illegible]) | [illegible]] [illegible] *h*, ⟦[illegible]⟧[illegible] *j* | [illegible]] [illegible] *hj* | [illegible]] [illegible] *e hj*

24. [illegible]] [illegible] *hj* | [illegible]] [illegible] *h*, [illegible] *j* | [illegible]] [illegible] *hj* | [illegible]] [illegible] *h*, [illegible] *j*

25. [illegible]] pr. [illegible] *hj* | [illegible]] [illegible] *hj* | [illegible]] [illegible] *a**(uid.), sed c pr m

26. [illegible]] [illegible] *a*mg *f*mg *j*mg | [illegible]] [illegible] *hj* | [illegible] *f*] coniunxit c. [illegible] *g*; c. sey. *e*

27. [illegible]] [illegible] *hj* | [illegible]] [illegible] *hj* | [illegible]] [illegible] *ef*; [illegible] *hj* | [illegible]] [illegible] *hj*

28. [illegible] > *hj*

29. [illegible]] [illegible] *hj* | [illegible]] [illegible] *hj*

30. [illegible] 1°] [illegible] *cf* | [illegible]] [illegible] *hj* | [illegible] > *hj* | [illegible]] [illegible] *hj* | [illegible]] pr. [illegible] *hj*

31. [illegible]] [illegible] *hj* | [illegible]] [illegible] *hj* | [illegible]] [illegible] *hj*c pr m (> *j**) | [illegible]] [illegible] *j*

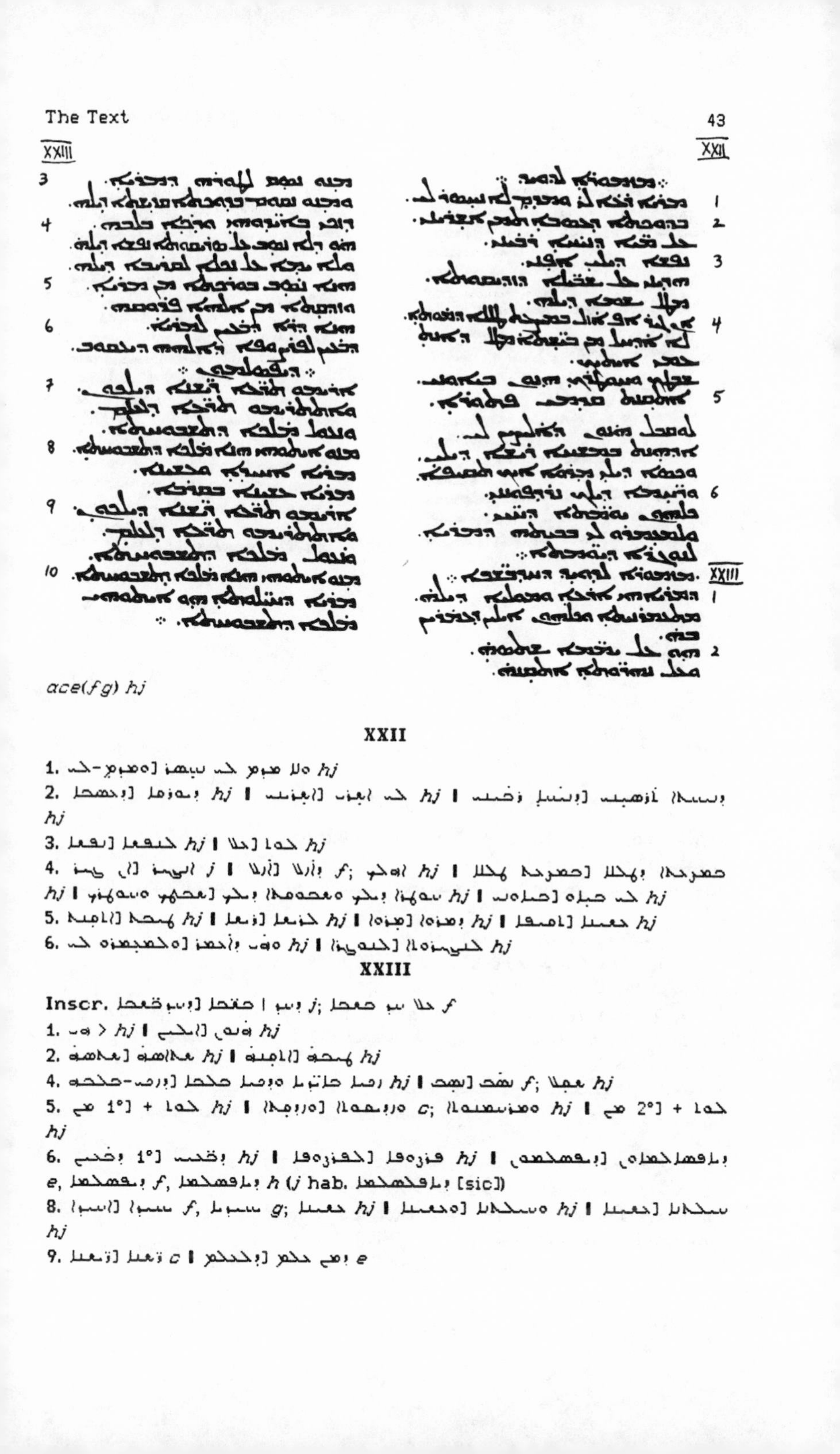

XXII

[illegible]

1 [illegible]

2 [illegible]

3 [illegible]

4 [illegible]

5 [illegible]

6 [illegible]

XXIII

[illegible]

1 [illegible]

2 [illegible]

3 [illegible]

4 [illegible]

5 [illegible]

6 [illegible]

7 [illegible]

8 [illegible]

9 [illegible]

10 [illegible]

ace(fg) hj

XXII

1. [illegible] *hj*
2. [illegible] *hj* | [illegible] *hj* | [illegible] *hj*
3. [illegible] *hj* | [illegible] *hj*
4. [illegible] *j* | [illegible] *f*; [illegible] *hj* | [illegible] *hj* | [illegible] *hj* | [illegible] *hj*
5. [illegible] *hj* | [illegible] *hj* | [illegible] *hj* | [illegible] *hj*
6. [illegible] *hj* | [illegible] *hj*

XXIII

Inscr. [illegible] *j*; [illegible] *f*

1. [illegible] > *hj* | [illegible] *hj*
2. [illegible] *hj* | [illegible] *hj*
4. [illegible] *hj* | [illegible] *f*; [illegible] *hj*
5. [illegible] 1°] + [illegible] *hj* | [illegible] *c*; [illegible] *hj* | [illegible] 2°] + [illegible] *hj*
6. [illegible] 1°] [illegible] *hj* | [illegible] *hj* | [illegible] *e*, [illegible] *f*, [illegible] *h* (*j* hab. [illegible] [sic])
8. [illegible] *f*, [illegible] *g*; [illegible] *hj* | [illegible] *hj* | [illegible] *hj*
9. [illegible] *c* | [illegible] *e*

XXIV

[illegible]
1 [illegible]
2 [illegible]
[illegible]
[illegible]
3 [illegible]
[illegible]
[illegible]
4 [illegible]
[illegible]
5 [illegible]
[illegible]
[illegible]
[illegible]
6 [illegible]
[illegible]
7 [illegible]
[illegible]
[illegible]

[illegible]
8 [illegible]
[illegible]
[illegible]
9 [illegible]
[illegible]
10 [illegible]
[illegible]
[illegible]
[illegible]
11 [illegible]
[illegible]
[illegible]
12 [illegible]
[illegible]
[illegible]
13 [illegible]
[illegible]

ace(fg) hj

XXIV

2. [illegible]] ad u. 1 trahit *e*; + [illegible] *hj* | [illegible]] [illegible] *hj* | [illegible]] [illegible] *hj*
3. [illegible] 1° et 2°] [illegible] *hj*
4. [illegible]] [illegible] *hj* | [illegible]] [illegible] *hj* | [illegible]] [illegible]
hj
5. [illegible]] [illegible] *h*, [illegible] *j* | [illegible]] [illegible] *hj*
6. [illegible]] [illegible] *e* | [illegible] *f*] s. sey. *g*; [illegible] *hj*
7. [illegible]] [illegible] *hj* | [illegible]] [illegible] *cf*
8. [illegible] > *hj* | [illegible]] [illegible] *a**, sed c pr m | [illegible]] [illegible] *c*; *f* testatur [illegible] tantum; [illegible] *h*, [illegible] *j* | [illegible]] [illegible] *cf* | [illegible]] [illegible] *hj*
9. [illegible] 1°] [illegible] *hj* | [illegible]] [illegible] *j* | [illegible] 2°] [illegible] *hj*
10. [illegible]] [illegible] *hj* | [illegible]] [illegible] *ef*; [illegible] *hj* | [illegible]] [illegible] *hj*
11. [illegible]] [illegible] *hj*
12. [illegible]] [illegible] *j* | [illegible]] [illegible] *hj* | [illegible]] [illegible] *hj*
13. [illegible]] s. sey. *g* (*f* hab. sey. uid. quamquam punctum alterum languet) | [illegible]] [illegible] *e*

XXIV

14 ܠܡܦܩܐ ܗܘ ܡܪܢܐ ܕܐܫܠܡ
ܕܡܫܠܡ ܠܗ.
ܘܬܫܒܘܚܬܐ ܕܝܠܗ ܠܡܘܕܝܘ ܠܗܘܢ.
15 ܟܠ ܟܠܗܘܢ ܠܘܬ ܡܪܢܐ.
ܡܛܠ ܕܗܘ ܢܦܩ ܡܢ ܦܘܡܐ ܕܟܠ.
16 ܚܙܘ ܒܗ ܘܦܪܘܩ ܟܠ.
ܡܛܠ ܕܡܫܝܚܐ ܘܡܪܢܐ ܐܝܬܘܗܝ ܗܘ.
17 ܐܘܠܨܢܐ ܕܠܟܐ ܕܝܠܗ ܡܢܗ.
ܡܢ ܐܢܫܘܬܐ ܕܝܠܗ ܐܬܦܢܝ.
18 ܚܙܝ ܒܡܫܡܫܢܘܬܗ ܠܫܘܒܚܐ ܕܝܠܗ.
ܘܡܘܕܐ ܟܠܗܘܢ ܒܢܝ̈ܗܘܢ.
19 ܚܙܝ ܠܦܠܚ̈ܘܗܝ ܕܗܒܝܒ.
ܘܠܐܝܢܐ ܕܫܘܝܢ ܩܢܘܡܗܘܢ.
20 ܢܬܪ ܠܢܦܫܐ ܕܝܠܗ ܘܦܪܩܗܘܢ.
ܠܐ ܐܬܒܛܠ ܡܛܠ ܕܦܪܩܬ ܠܗ.
21 ܠܡܫܒܚܘ ܐܠܗܘܬܐ ܕܚܫܡ ܗܘܐ ܠܟ.
ܡܛܠ ܕܦܪܩܬ ܠܗ ܡܪܢܐ.

XXIV

22 ܦܪܘܩ ܐܠܗܐ ܠܡܫܝܚܟ.
ܡܢ ܟܠܗܘܢ ܐܘܠܨܢܐ ܕܝܠܗ.

XXV

÷ ܕܕܘܝܕ ÷

1 ܕܐܝܠܝ ܡܪܢܐ ܡܛܠ ܕܐܬܝܠܝ
ܒܡܫܡܫܢܘܬܟ ܦܪܘܩ.
ܡܛܠ ܟܠ ܐܠܗܐ ܕܝܠܟ ܡܫܒܚܝܢ ܐܢܫܐ
ܠܐ ܐܬܬܠܝܬ.
2 ܒܟܠ ܡܪܢܐ ܫܡܥܝ.
ܒܚܘܪ ܒܦܘܠܚܢܐ ܕܝܠܟ ܡܠܟܐ.
3 ܡܛܠ ܕܐܬܚܫܒ ܠܗܘܐ ܟܠ ܐܬܥܒܕܘܢ.
ܘܬܦܪܘܩ ܒܐܝܪܐ ܕܝܠܗ.
4 ܠܐ ܬܬܒܥ ܒܒܥܐ ܒܡܘܬܐ ܕܚܘܫܒܢܐ.
ܡܢ ܚܙܝ ܟܠ ܢܦܫܐ ܠܐ ܐܬܟܠ.
5 ܦܪܘܩ ܒܪܘܚܐ ܕܫܠܡܘܬܟ.
ܡܢ ܕܫܡܥܝ ܠܐ ܐܬܚܒ.
6 ܐܫܬܠܡ ܦܘܪܩܢܐ ܐܝܬܝ.
ܘܐܬܒܪܟ ܠܡܫܒܚܘ ܡܪܢܐ.

a(b)ce(fg) hj

14. ܘܬܫܒܘܚܬܐ] ܬܫܒܘܚܬܐ *hj* | ܗܘ > *hj* | ܕܐܬܠܝܡ] ܕܝܠܗ *hj* | ܘܐܫܠܡܬ] ܘܐܫܠܡ *ef*; ܘܐܫܠܡ *hj*
15. ܢܦܩ] ܢܦܩܘ *hj* | ܦܘܡܐ] c. sey. *c*; ras. sup. ܝ uid., erat frt sey. *j* | ܕܟܠ] ܕܝܠܗ ܟܠܗܘܢ *hj*
16. ܚܙܘ ܒܗ] ܚܙܘ ܒܗ ܐܢܫܐ *hj* | ܘܦܪܘܩ] ܦܪܘܩ *j**(uid.), sed c pr m | ܘܡܪܢܐ] ܘܡܫܝܚܐ *hj*
17. ܐܘܠܨܢܐ] ܐܘܠܨܢܗ *e*, ܐܘܠܨܢܘܗܝ *f*, ܐܘܠܨܢܐ *hj*
18. ܒܡܫܡܫܢܘܬܗ] ܡܫܡܫܢܘܬܐ *a**(uid.), sed c pr m uid.; ܡܫܡܫܢܘܬܐ ܕܝܠܗ *hj* | ܘܡܘܕܐ] ܘܡܘܕܝܢ *hj*
19. ܩܢܘܡܗܘܢ] ܩܢܘܡܗ *e*
20. ܢܬܪ] ܢܛܪ *hj* | ܘܦܪܩܗܘܢ] ܘܦܪܩ *hj* | ܠܗ] ܠܟܠܗܘܢ *hj*
21. ܕܚܫܡ] ܕܚܫܡܬ *hj*

XXV

1. ܕܐܝܠܝ] ܕܐܝܠܝܢ *hj* | ܐܠܗܐ] ܡܪܢܐ *hj* | ܕܝܠܟ > *hj* | ܐܬܬܠܝܬ] ܐܬܬܠܝ *f*
2. ܦܘܠܚܢܐ] ܦܘܠܚܢܐ *hj* | ܘܒܚܘܪ] ܘܒܚܘܪ ܕܝܠܟ *hj*
4. ܒܚܘܫܒܢܐ] ܚܘܫܒܢܐ ܕܝܠܗ *hj* | ܡܘܬܐ] ܡܘܬܐ *c* | ܬܬܒܥ ܟܠ] ܬܬܒܥܘܢ ܕܡܫܒܚܝܢ ܗܘܝ ܡܢ ܟܠ *hj* (ܗܘܝ > *j**, sed c pr m)
5. ܕܫܠܡܘܬܟ] ܕܫܠܡܘܬܐ *hj*
6. ܦܘܪܩܢܐ] ܦܘܪܩܢܐ *hj* | ܐܝܬܝ] s. sey. *e*

XXVI

[illegible]
[illegible]
3 [illegible]
[illegible]
[illegible]
[illegible]
4 [illegible]
[illegible]
[illegible]
[illegible]
[illegible]
5 [illegible]
[illegible]
[illegible]
[illegible]
6 [illegible]
[illegible]
[illegible]
[illegible]
[illegible]
[illegible]
7 [illegible]
[illegible]

XXV

7 [illegible]
[illegible]
8 [illegible]
[illegible]
[illegible]
9 [illegible]
[illegible]
[illegible]
10 [illegible]
[illegible]
[illegible]
11 [illegible]
[illegible]
12 [illegible]
[illegible]
[illegible]

XXVI

1 [illegible]
[illegible]
[illegible]
[illegible]
2 [illegible]
[illegible]

abce(fg) hj

8. [illegible]] [illegible] *cf hj* | [illegible]] [illegible] *hj*c pr m ([illegible] > *j**[uid.] [ǁ], sed c pr m)
9. [illegible]] tr. *hj* | [illegible]] [illegible] *hj*
10. [illegible]] [illegible] *hj* | [illegible]] [illegible] *hj* | [illegible]] [illegible] *c*; [illegible] *h*; [illegible] *j* | [illegible]] [illegible] *j* | [illegible]] c. sey. *hj*
11. [illegible]] [illegible] *hj*
12. [illegible]] s. sey. *cf* | [illegible]] [illegible] *a**(uid.), sed c pr m; [illegible] *hj* | [illegible]] [illegible] *hj*

XXVI

Inscr. [illegible]] [illegible] *f*
1. [illegible]] [illegible] *hj* | [illegible]] [illegible] *hj* | [illegible]] [illegible] *hj* | [illegible]] [illegible] *hj*
2. [illegible]] [illegible] *hj* | [illegible]] [illegible] *hj* | [illegible]] [illegible] *hj* | [illegible]] [illegible] *hj*
3. [illegible]] [illegible] *e*
4. [illegible]] + [illegible] *hj* | [illegible]] [illegible] *h* | [illegible]] [illegible] *hj* | [illegible]] [illegible] *hj*
5. [illegible]] [illegible] (sic) *hj*
6. [illegible]] [illegible] *b*; [illegible] *hj* | [illegible] 1°] [illegible] *c* | [illegible]] [illegible] *hj*
7. [illegible]] [illegible] *e*; [illegible] *hj* | [illegible]] [illegible] *hj*

XXVII

[illegible]

2 [illegible]

3 [illegible]

4 [illegible]

5 [illegible]

6 [illegible]

7 [illegible]

XXVI

8 [illegible]

9 [illegible]

10 [illegible]

11 [illegible]

12 [illegible]

13 [illegible]

14 [illegible]

XXVII

1 [illegible]

abce(fg) hj

8. [illegible]] bis scr. (l) *h*
9. [illegible]] [illegible] *hj* | [illegible]] + [illegible] *f* | [illegible]] [illegible] *hj*
11. [illegible] > *j**, sed c pr m | [illegible]] [illegible] *h*, [illegible] *j* | [illegible]] c. sey. *j*
12. [illegible]] [illegible] *hj*
14. [illegible]] [illegible] *e*, [illegible] *j*

XXVII

1. [illegible] 1° ∩ 2° *j**, sed c pr m | [illegible]] [illegible] *hj* | [illegible]] [illegible] *c*
2. [illegible]] [illegible] *hj* | [illegible]] [illegible] *h*, [illegible] *j* | [illegible]] [illegible] *hj*
3. [illegible]] [illegible] *h* | [illegible]] [illegible] *b*, [illegible] *c* | [illegible]] [illegible] *hj* | [illegible]] s. sey. *j*
4. [illegible]] *f*mg† (sey. apud [illegible] inc., s. sey. *g*mg†; principio omittebantur uerba [illegible] [homtel.], sed c pr m uid.; hab. [illegible]) | [illegible]] [illegible] *hj* | [illegible]] [illegible] *hj*
5. [illegible]] [illegible] *f* | [illegible]] [illegible] *h*
6. [illegible] > *hj* | [illegible]] [illegible] *hj*
7. [illegible]] [illegible] *f*

XXVII

8 ܡܪܝܐ ܚܣܝܢܐ ܕܥܡܗ ܗܘ ܥܘܕܪܢܗܘܢ·
ܘܡܬܚܡܣܢܐ ܕܦܘܪܩܢܐ ܕܡܫܝܚܐ
ܗܘ ܥܘܕܪܢܗ·
9 ܦܪܘܩ ܠܥܡܟ ܘܒܪܟ ܡܪܝܐ·
ܡܪܝܐ ܠܝܪܬܘܬܟ·
ܪܥܝ ܐܢܘܢ ܘܐܪܝܡ ܐܢܘܢ ܥܕܡܐ ܠܥܠܡ·

XXVIII

ܡܙܡܘܪܐ ܠܕܘܝܕ· ܕܫܘܠܡܐ ܕܡܫܟܢܐ·
1 ܐܝܬܘ ܠܡܪܝܐ ܒܢܝܐ ܕܐܠܗܐ·
ܐܝܬܘ ܠܡܪܝܐ ܒܢܝܐ ܕܕܟܪ̈ܐ·
ܐܝܬܘ ܠܡܪܝܐ ܫܘܒܚܐ ܘܐܝܩܪܐ·
2 ܐܝܬܘ ܠܡܪܝܐ ܫܘܒܚܐ ܠܫܡܗ ܕܝܠܗ·
ܣܓܘܕܘ ܠܡܪܝܐ ܒܕܪܬܐ ܩܕܝܫܬܐ ܕܝܠܗ·
3 ܩܠܗ ܕܡܪܝܐ ܥܠ ܡ̈ܝܐ·
ܐܠܗܐ ܕܫܘܒܚܬܐ ܐܪܥܡ·
ܡܪܝܐ ܥܠ ܡ̈ܝܐ ܣܓܝ̈ܐܐ·
4 ܩܠܗ ܕܡܪܝܐ ܒܚܝܠܐ·
ܩܠܗ ܕܡܪܝܐ ܒܪܒܘܬ ܦܐܝܘܬܐ·
5 ܩܠܗ ܕܡܪܝܐ ܕܡܬܒܪ ܐܪ̈ܙܐ·
ܘܢܬܒܪ ܡܪܝܐ ܠܐܪ̈ܙܐ ܕܠܒܢܢ·
6 ܘܢܕܩ ܐܢܘܢ ܐܝܟ ܥܓܠܐ ܠܠܒܢܢ·
ܘܚܒܝܒܐ ܐܝܟ ܒܪܐ ܕܪ̈ܝܡܐ·
7 ܩܠܗ ܕܡܪܝܐ ܕܦܣܩ ܫܠܗܒܝܬܐ ܕܢܘܪܐ·
8 ܩܠܗ ܕܡܪܝܐ ܕܡܙܝܥ ܡܕܒܪܐ ܡܕܒܪܝܐ·
ܘܢܙܝܥ ܡܕܒܪܐ ܡܪܝܐ ܡܕܒܪܐ ܕܩܕܫ·

XXVIII

9 ܩܠܗ ܕܡܪܝܐ ܕܡܬܩܢ ܠܐܝ̈ܠܐ·
ܘܢܓܠܐ ܥܒ̈ܐ·
ܘܒܗܝܟܠܗ ܟܠܢܫ ܐܡܪ ܫܘܒܚܐ·
10 ܡܪܝܐ ܒܡܡܘܠܐ ܢܥܡܪ·
ܘܢܬܒ ܡܪܝܐ ܡܠܟܐ ܠܥܠܡ·
11 ܡܪܝܐ ܚܝܠܐ ܠܥܡܗ ܕܝܠܗ ܢܬܠ·
ܡܪܝܐ ܢܒܪܟ ܠܥܡܗ ܕܝܠܗ ܒܫܠܡܐ·

XXIX ܡܙܡܘܪܐ ܕܬܫܒܘܚܬܐ ܕܚܘܕܬܐ
ܕܒܝܬܐ ܠܕܘܝܕ ∴
1 ܐܪܝܡܟ ܡܪܝܐ ܕܩܒܠܬܢܝ·
ܘܠܐ ܚܕܝܬ ܠܒܥܠܕܒܒ̈ܝ ܥܠܝ·
2 ܡܪܝܐ ܐܠܗܝ ܩܥܝܬ ܠܘܬܟ ܘܐܣܝܬܢܝ·
3 ܡܪܝܐ ܐܣܩܬܗ ܡܢ ܫܝܘܠ ܠܢܦܫܐ ܕܝܠܝ·
ܦܪܩܬܢܝ ܡܢ ܗܢܘܢ ܕܢܚܬܝܢ ܠܓܘܒܐ·
4 ܙܡܪܘ ܠܡܪܝܐ ܙܕ̈ܝܩܐ ܕܝܠܗ·
ܘܐܘܕܘ ܠܥܘܗܕܢܐ ܕܩܕܝܫܘܬܐ ܕܝܠܗ·
5 ܡܛܠ ܕܪܘܓܙܐ ܒܚܡܬܗ ܘܚ̈ܝܐ ܒܨܒܝܢܗ·
ܒܪܡܫܐ ܢܒܘܬ ܒܟܝܐ·
ܘܒܨܦܪܐ ܚܕܘܬܐ·
6 ܐܢܐ ܕܝܢ ܐܡܪܬ ܒܫܠܝܘܬܝ ܠܐ
ܐܙܘܥ ܠܥܠܡ·
7 ܡܪܝܐ ܒܨܒܝܢܟ ܝܗܒ ܠܫܘܦܪܐ ܕܝܠܝ
ܚܝܠܐ·
ܐܗܦܟܬ ܕܝܢ ܦܪ̈ܨܘܦܝܟ ܘܗܘܝܬ ܡܬܕܠܚܐ·
8 ܠܘܬܟ ܡܪܝܐ ܐܩܥܐ·
ܘܠܘܬ ܐܠܗܐ ܕܝܠܝ ܐܬܟܫܦ·

abce(fg) hj

XXVIII

Insr. ܡܙܡܘܪܐ] ܕܡܙܡܘܪܐ *f*; > *j*

1. ܐܝܬܘ-ܠܡܪܝܐ 1°] in linea Pesh, sed sequitur adnotatio ܗܢܐ ܦܣܘܩܐ ܠܝܬܘܗܝ ܒܫܒܥܝܢ *f*

2. ܠܫܡܗ 1° > *j**, sed c pr m uid. | ܣܓܘܕܘ] ܘܣܓܘܕܘ *bce hj*

3. ܕܫܘܒܚܬܐ] ܡܫܒܚܐ *e**, sed c pr m

5. ܐܪ̈ܙܐ] ܐܪܙܐ *hj*

6. ܕܪ̈ܝܡܐ] s. sey. *cf*

9. ܕܡܬܩܢ] ܕܡܬܩܢ *f* | ܠܐܝ̈ܠܐ] ܠܐܝܠܐ *g* (fin. abscond. *f*); ܠܐ (prbl.) *j*

XXIX

Insr. ܕܚܘܕܬܐ] ܚܘܕܬܐ ܗܠܐ *f* | ܠܕܘܝܕ] ܕܕܘܝܕ *f*

5. ܪܘܓܙܐ] ܪܘܓܙܐ *f*

6. ܒܫܠܝܘܬܝ] ܒܫܠܝܘܬܐ *f* | ܠܥܠܡ > *hj*

8. ܐܩܥܐ] ܐܩܪܐ *f* | ܘܠܘܬ] ܘܠܘܬܟ *e*

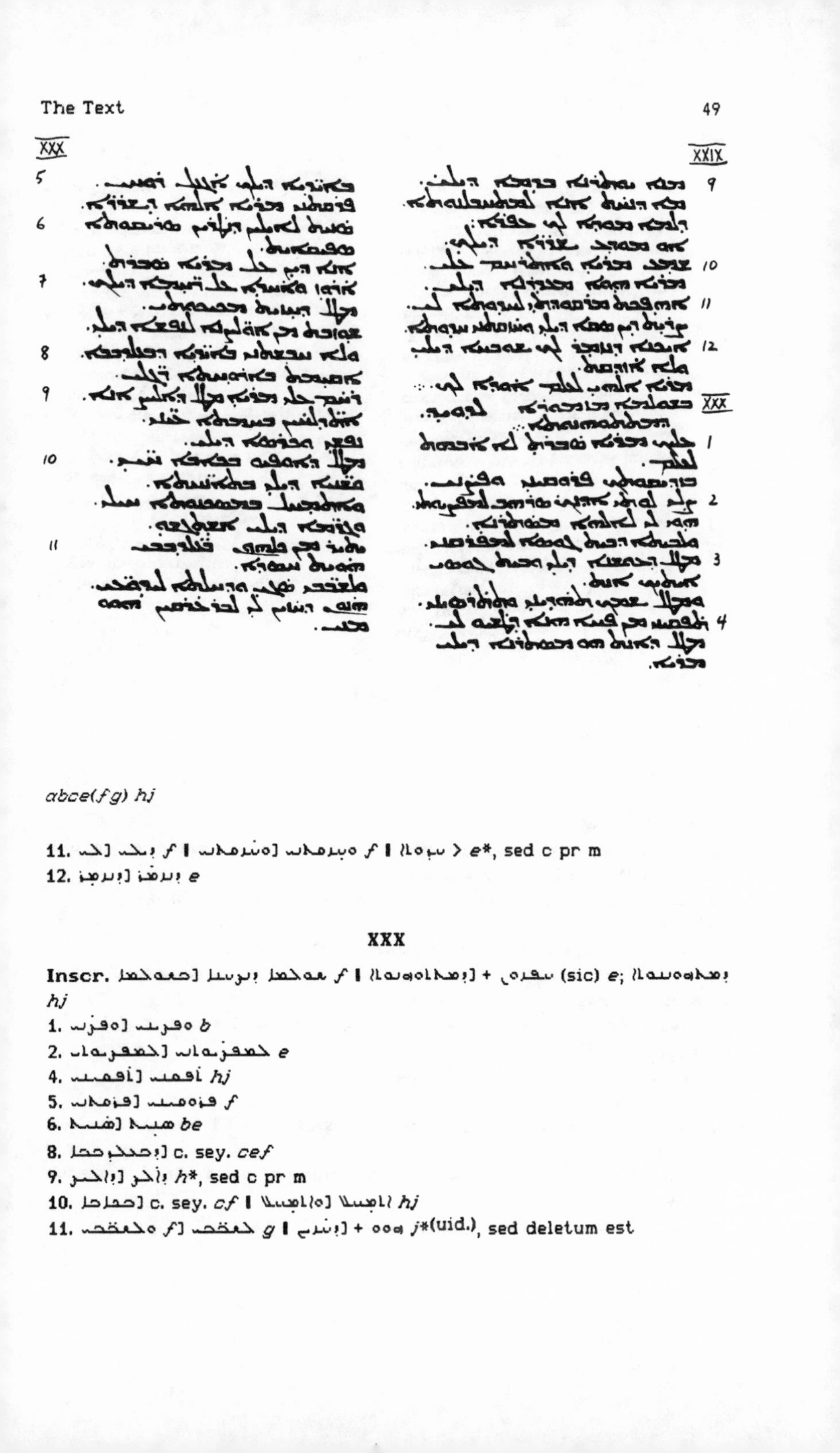

XXIX

9 [illegible]

10 [illegible]

11 [illegible]

12 [illegible]

XXX [illegible]

1 [illegible]

2 [illegible]

3 [illegible]

4 [illegible]

XXX

5 [illegible]

6 [illegible]

7 [illegible]

8 [illegible]

9 [illegible]

10 [illegible]

11 [illegible]

abce(fg) hj

11. [illegible]] [illegible] *f* | [illegible]] [illegible] *f* | [illegible] > *e**, sed c pr m
12. [illegible]] [illegible] *e*

XXX

Insc r. [illegible]] [illegible] *f* | [illegible]] + [illegible] (sic) *e*; [illegible] *hj*
1. [illegible]] [illegible] *b*
2. [illegible]] [illegible] *e*
4. [illegible]] [illegible] *hj*
5. [illegible]] [illegible] *f*
6. [illegible]] [illegible] *be*
8. [illegible]] c. sey. *cef*
9. [illegible]] [illegible] *h**, sed c pr m
10. [illegible]] c. sey. *cf* | [illegible]] [illegible] *hj*
11. [illegible] *f*] [illegible] *g* | [illegible]] + [illegible] *j**(uid.), sed deletum est

XXX

12 [illegible]
[illegible]
13 [illegible]
[illegible]
[illegible]
[illegible]
14 [illegible]
[illegible]
15 [illegible]
[illegible]
[illegible]
16 [illegible]
[illegible]
17 [illegible]
[illegible]
18 [illegible]
[illegible]
[illegible]
[illegible]
[illegible]

XXX

19 [illegible]
[illegible]
[illegible]
[illegible]
[illegible]
20 [illegible]
[illegible]
[illegible]
[illegible]
21 [illegible]
[illegible]
22 [illegible]
[illegible]
[illegible]
[illegible]
[illegible]
23 [illegible]
[illegible]
[illegible]
[illegible]
24 [illegible]
[illegible]

abce(fg) hj

12. [illegible]] [illegible] *e*

13. [illegible]] sup. ras., sed pr m *j* | [illegible]] [illegible] > *j**, sed c pr m uid. | [illegible]] tr. *h* | [illegible]] [illegible] *f*

14. [illegible] ∩ [illegible] u. 15 *j**, sed c pr m (hab. [illegible] sicut *h*)

16. [illegible]] [illegible] *c*

17. [illegible] *g*] [illegible] *c h*, [illegible] *e*, [illegible] *f j*

18. [illegible]] [illegible] sup. ras. *a*; [illegible] *bcef* | [illegible]] c. sey. *e*; [illegible] sup. ras. *j*

19. [illegible]] [illegible] *e* | [illegible] *f*] [illegible] *g*, [illegible] *h* | [illegible]] sup. ras. *j* | [illegible]] s. sey. *bcf*(*g* inc.) *hj*

20. [illegible]] [illegible] *f* | [illegible]] + [illegible] *f*

21. [illegible]] [illegible] *bce hj*

22. [illegible]] [illegible] *h* (in *j* uerbum prius est [illegible]) | [illegible]] [illegible] *f*

23. [illegible]] *e* hab. ÷ apud [illegible] solum; s. notis *f*(non testatur [illegible]) *hj*

24. [illegible]] [illegible] *e* (deest punctum [illegible])

XXXI

ܠܕܘܝܕ ܕܣܘܟܠܬܢܘܬܐ ܀

1 ܛܘܒܝܗܘܢ ܗܢܘܢ ܕܐܫܬܒܩܘ ܠܗ
ܥܘܠܘܬܗܘܢ .
ܘܗܢܘܢ ܕܐܬܟܣܝܘ ܚܛܗܝܗܘܢ .
2 ܛܘܒܝܗ ܗܘ ܓܒܪܐ ܗܘ ܕܠܐ
ܢܚܫܘܒ ܠܗ ܡܪܝܐ ܚܛܝܬܐ .
ܘܠܐ ܐܝܬ ܒܦܘܡܗ ܢܟܠܐ .
3 ܡܛܠ ܕܫܬܩܬ ܒܠܝܘ ܓܪܡܝ .
ܡܢ ܗܘ ܕܩܥܝܐ ܐܢܐ ܟܠܗ ܝܘܡܐ .
4 ܡܛܠ ܕܐܝܡܡܐ ܘܠܠܝܐ ܝܩܪܬ
ܥܠܝ ܐܝܕܟ .
ܐܬܗܦܟܬ ܠܕܘܘܢܘܬܐ ܕܥܠܝ ܟܕ
ܐܬܢܩܒ ܒܝ ܟܘܒܐ .
5 ܚܛܝܬܐ ܕܝܠܝ ܝܕܥܬ ܠܟ .
ܘܠܐ ܥܘܠܘܬܐ ܕܝܠܝ ܟܣܝܬ .
ܐܡܪܬ ܐܘܕܐ ܥܠ ܠܗ
ܥܘܠܘܬܐ ܕܝܠܝ ܠܡܪܝܐ .
ܘܐܢܬ ܫܒܩܬ ܠܛܒܝܬܐ ܕܚܛܝܬܐ ܕܝܠܝ .

XXXI

6 ܚܠܦ ܗܕܐ ܢܨܠܐ ܠܘܬܟ ܟܠ ܚܣܝܐ
ܒܥܕܢܐ ܦܪܝܫܐ .
ܒܪܡ ܒܡܒܘܠܐ ܕܡܝܐ ܣܓܝܐܐ
ܠܘܬܗ ܠܐ ܢܬܩܪܒܘܢ .
7 ܐܢܬ ܗܘ ܒܝܬ ܓܘܣܐ ܕܝܠܝ ܡܢ ܐܘܠܨܢܐ
ܕܡܟܪܟ ܠܝ .
ܚܕܘܬܐ ܕܝܠܝ ܦܪܘܩܝܢܝ ܡܢ ܗܠܝܢ ܕܚܕܪܘܢܝ .
8 ܐܣܟܠ ܐܢܐ ܠܟ ܘܐܚܘܐ ܐܢܐ ܠܟ
ܒܐܘܪܚܐ ܗܕܐ ܕܬܐܙܠ ܐܢܬ .
ܐܫܪܪ ܥܠܝܟ ܥܝܢܝ .
9 ܠܐ ܬܗܘܘܢ ܐܝܟ ܣܘܣܝܐ ܘܐܝܟ
ܟܘܕܢܝܐ ܗܢܘܢ ܕܠܝܬ ܠܗܘܢ
ܣܘܟܠܬܢܘܬܐ .
ܒܙܡܐܡܐ ܘܒܦܓܘܕܐ ܦܟܘܗܝ
ܠܡܚܢܩܘ .
ܕܗܢܘܢ ܠܐ ܩܪܒܝܢ ܠܘܬܟ .
10 ܣܓܝܐܝܢ ܡܚܘܬܗ ܕܚܛܝܐ .
ܠܗܘ ܕܝܢ ܕܡܣܒܪ ܥܠ ܡܪܝܐ
ܛܝܒܘܬܐ ܬܚܕܪܝܘܗܝ .
11 ܚܕܘ ܒܡܪܝܐ ܘܪܘܙܘ ܙܕܝܩܐ .
ܘܐܫܬܒܗܪܘ ܟܠܟܘܢ ܬܪܝܨܝ ܠܒܐ .

abce(fg) hj

XXXI

Insc. ܠܕܘܝܕ] ܡܙܡܘܪܐ *c* ‖ ܕܣܘܟܠܬܢܘܬܐ] ܕܣܘܟܠܬܢܘܬܐ ܐܘܟܝܬ ܗܘܠܐ ܥܠ *f*
2. ܐܦܠܐ] ܐܦ ܠܐ *c*
4. fin.] + ܕܐܦܣܠܡܐ *hj*
5. ܠܐ 2° > *h* (l) ‖ fin.] + ܕܦܣܠܡܘܣ *a*^mg^*c*, + ܕܐܦܣܠܡܘܣ *b*, + ܕܐܦܣܠܡܘܣ *e*, + ܕܐܦܣܠܡܐ *h*
6. ܠܘܬܟ] ܠܘܬܗ *f*
7. ܕܚܕܪܘܢܝ] ܕܚܕܪܘܢ *f* ‖ fin.] + ܕܐܦܣܠܡܐ *hj*
8. ܕܬܐܙܠ > *e** (l), sed c pr m ‖ ܥܝܢܝ ܥܠܝܟ] tr. *c*
9. ܕܠܝܬ ܠܗܘܢ] ܕܠܐ ܡܣܬܟܠܝܢ *j**(uid.) (cf. Pesh), sed c pr m (praeter om. ܕ uid.) ‖ ܘܒܦܓܘܕܐ] ܘܦܓܘܕܐ *e* ‖ ܠܡܚܢܩܘ] ܠܡܚܢܩܘ *h*, ܠܡܚܢܩܘ *j*
10. ܡܚܘܬܗ] c. sey. *bce* ‖ ܬܚܕܪܝܘܗܝ] ܬܚܕܪܝܘܗܝ *j*^mg^; ܬܚܕܪܝܘܗܝ *h*; ܬܚܕܪܝܘܗܝ *j*^txt^
11. ܘܐܫܬܒܗܪܘ] ܘܐܫܬܒܗܪܘ *e**, sed c pr m ‖ ܬܪܝܨܝ] ܟܠ ܬܪܝܨܝ *e*

XXXII

ܡܙܡܘܪܐ ܠܕܘܝܕ. ܕܠܝܬ ܠܗ ܪܘܫܡܐ
ܠܥܠ ܒܥܒܪܝܐ. ∴
1 ܪܘܙܘ ܙܕܝܩܐ ܒܡܪܝܐ.
ܠܬܪ̈ܝܨܐ ܦܐܝܐ ܬܫܒܘܚܬܐ.
2 ܐܘܕܘ ܠܡܪܝܐ ܒܟܢܪܐ.
ܒܩܝܬܪܐ ܕܥܣ̈ܪ ܢܩܫܝܢ ܙܡܪܘ ܠܗ.
3 ܙܡܪܘ ܠܗ ܙܡܝܪܬܐ ܚܕܬܐ.
ܫܦܝܪ ܙܡܪܘ ܒܝܒܒܐ.
4 ܡܛܠ ܕܬܪܝܨܐ ܗܝ ܡܠܬܗ ܕܡܪܝܐ.
ܘܟܠܗܘܢ ܥܒ̈ܕܘܗܝ ܒܗܝܡܢܘܬܐ.
5 ܪܚܡ ܡܪܚܡܢܘܬܐ ܘܕܝܢܐ ܡܪܝܐ.
ܡܢ ܪ̈ܚܡܘܗܝ ܕܡܪܝܐ ܡܠܝܐ ܐܪܥܐ.
6 ܒܡܠܬܗ ܕܡܪܝܐ ܫܡ̈ܝܐ ܐܫܬܪܪܘ.
ܘܒܪܘܚܐ ܕܦܘܡܗ ܟܠܗܘܢ
ܚܝܠܘܬܐ ܕܝܠܗܘܢ.
7 ܕܟܢܫ ܐܝܟ ܙܩܐ ܡ̈ܝܐ ܕܝܡܐ.
ܗܘ ܕܝܗܒ ܒܣܝ̈ܡܬܐ ܬܗܘ̈ܡܐ.
8 ܬܕܚܠ ܡܢ ܡܪܝܐ ܟܠܗ ܐܪܥܐ.
ܡܢܗ ܕܝܢ ܢܙܘܥܘܢ ܟܠܗܘܢ ܗܢܘܢ
ܕܥܡܪܝܢ ܒܬܒܝܠ.
9 ܡܛܠ ܕܗܘ ܐܡܪ ܘܗܘܘ.
ܗܘ ܦܩܕ ܘܐܬܒܪܝܘ.
10 ܡܪܝܐ ܡܒܛܠ ܡܚܫ̈ܒܬܐ ܕܥܡ̈ܡܐ.
ܒܛܠ ܕܝܢ ܡܚܫ̈ܒܬܐ ܕܥܡ̈ܡܐ.
ܘܣܠܐ ܡܬܪ̈ܥܝܬܐ ܕܪ̈ܫܢܐ.
11 ܡܬܪܥܝܬܗ ܕܝܢ ܕܡܪܝܐ ܠܥܠܡ ܩܝܡܐ.
ܡܚܫ̈ܒܬܐ ܕܠܒܗ ܠܕܪܐ ܘܠܕܪܐ.
12 ܛܘܒܝܗ̇ ܠܐܡܬܐ ܗܝ ܕܐܝܬܝܗ̇ ܗܘ
ܕܐܝܬܘܗܝ ܡܪܝܐ ܐܠܗܐ ܕܝܠܗ.
ܥܡܐ ܗܘ ܕܓܒܝܘܗܝ ܠܝܪܬܘܬܐ ܠܗ.
13 ܡܢ ܫܡܝܐ ܚܪ ܡܪܝܐ.
ܚܙܐ ܠܟܠܗܘܢ ܒܢ̈ܝ ܐ̈ܢܫܐ.
14 ܡܢ ܡܛܝܒܘܬܐ ܕܡܘܬܒܐ ܕܝܠܗ.
ܚܪ ܒܟܠܗܘܢ ܗܢܘܢ ܕܥܡܪܝܢ ܒܐܪܥܐ.
15 ܗܘ ܕܓܒܠ ܠܚܘܕܐܝܬ ܠܒ̈ܘܬܐ ܕܟܠܗܘܢ.
ܗܘ ܕܡܣܬܟܠ ܒܟܠܗܘܢ ܥܒ̈ܕܝܗܘܢ.
16 ܠܐ ܡܬܦܪܩ ܡܠܟܐ ܡܛܠ
ܣܘܓܐ ܚܝܠܐ.
ܘܓܢܒܪܐ ܠܐ ܢܬܦܪܩ ܒܣܘܓܐܐ
ܕܚܝܠܘܬܐ ܕܝܠܗ.
17 ܕܓܠ ܗܘ ܣܘܣܝܐ ܠܦܘܪܩܢܐ.
ܒܣܘܓܐܐ ܕܝܢ ܕܚܝܠܗ ܠܐ
ܢܬܦܪܩ.
18 ܗܐ ܥܝ̈ܢܘܗܝ ܕܡܪܝܐ ܥܠ ܕܚ̈ܠܘܗܝ.
ܐܝܠܝܢ ܕܡܣܟܝܢ ܥܠ ܪ̈ܚܡܘܗܝ.

ab(c)e(fg) hj

XXXII 9. ܦܩܕ] ܦܩܕ (sic) *a*

XXXII

Inscr. ܠܕܘܝܕ > *f*
1. ܒܡܪܝܐ] ܒ sup. ras. *a*; ܠܡܪܝܐ *c*
2. ܐܘܕܘ] ܐܘܕܝ *f* | ܒܟܢܪܐ] ܘܒܟܢܪܐ *a**, sed c pr m | ܕܥܣ̈ܪ] s. sey. *c h* | ܙܡܪܘ] ܙܡܪܘ *c* | ܠܗ ∩ ܠܗ u. 3 *j**, sed c pr m uid.
3. ܙܡܪܘ 2°] ܙܡܪܘ *b hj*
4. ܗܝ > *hj*
6. ܚܝܠܘܬܗ] ܚܝܠܘܬܐ *f hj* | ܕܡܪܝܐ] ܕܦܘܡܗ *f* | ܫܡ̈ܝܐ] s. sey. *cf hj*
7. ܕܡܟܢܫ] ܘܡܟܢܫ *h* | ܙܩܐ] c. sey. *cf* | ܕܝܡܐ] ܕܝ̈ܡܐ *hj*
8. ܒܬܒܝܠ] ܕܬܒܝܠ *e* | ܗܢܘܢ] ܐܝܠܝܢ *cf*
10. ܕܥܡ̈ܡܐ] ܕܥܡܡܐ *bc*
11. ܡܚܫ̈ܒܬܐ] s. sey. *h* | ܠܕܪܐ ܘܠܕܪܐ] c. sey. *cf*
13. ܚܪ] ܚܙܐ *f* | ܚܙܐ] ܚܪ *f* | ܕܐ̈ܢܫܐ] s. sey. *ef hj*
18. ܕܚ̈ܠܘܗܝ] ܠܗܘܢ ܕܕܚܠܝܢ ܠܗ *hj*

XXXII

19 ܠܡܦܪܩܘ ܡܢ ܡܘܬܐ ܢܦ̈ܫܬܐ ܕܝܠܗܘܢ.
ܘܠܡܬܪܣܝܘ ܐܢܘܢ ܒܟܦܢܐ.
20 ܢܦܫܢ ܕܝܠܢ ܡܣܟܝܐ ܠܡܪܝܐ.
ܡܛܠ ܕܡܥܕܪܢܢ ܘܡܬܪܣܝܢܢ ܕܝܠܢ
ܐܝܬܘܗܝ.
21 ܡܛܠ ܕܒܗ ܢܚܕܘܢ ܠܒܢ.
ܘܒܫܡܗ ܩܕܝܫܐ ܬܟܝܠܝܢ.
22 ܢܗܘܘܢ ܡܪܝܐ ܪ̈ܚܡܝܟ ܥܠܝܢ.
ܐܝܟܢܐ ܕܡܣܟܝܢ ܠܟ. ⁘

XXXIII ܠܕܘܝܕ ܐܡܬܝ ܕܫܢܝ ܦܪܨܘܦܐ
ܕܝܠܗ ܩܕܡ ܐܒܝܡܠܟ. ܘܫܒܩܗ
ܘܐܙܠ. ⁘
1 ܐܒܪܟܝܘܗܝ ܠܡܪܝܐ ܒܟܠܙܒܢ.
ܒܟܠܙܒܢ ܬܫܒܘܚܬܗ ܒܦܘܡܝ.
2 ܒܡܪܝܐ ܬܫܬܒܗܪ ܢܦܫܐ ܕܝܠܝ.
ܢܫܡܥܘܢ ܡܟ̈ܝܟܐ ܘܢܚܕܘܢ.
3 ܐܘܪܒܘ ܠܡܪܝܐ ܥܡܝ.
ܘܢܪܘܡܡ ܫܡܗ ܐܟܚܕܐ.
4 ܒܥܝܬ ܠܡܪܝܐ ܘܥܢܢܝ.
ܘܡܢ ܟܠܗܘܢ ܐܘܠܨ̈ܢܝ ܦܪܩܢܝ.
5 ܐܬܦܢܝܘ ܠܘܬܗ ܘܐܬܢܗܪܘ.
ܘܐܦ̈ܝܟܘܢ ܕܝܠܟܘܢ ܠܐ ܢܒܗܬܘܢ.
6 ܗܢܐ ܒܝܫܐ ܩܪܐ ܘܡܪܝܐ ܫܡܥܗ.
ܘܡܢ ܟܠܗܘܢ ܐܘܠܨ̈ܢܘܗܝ ܦܪܩܗ.
7 ܢܛܪܐ ܡܠܐܟܗ ܕܡܪܝܐ ܒܚܘܕܪܐ

XXXIII

ܕܕܚܠܝܢ ܠܗ ܘܦܪܩ ܐܢܘܢ.
8 ܛܥܡܘ ܘܚܙܘ ܕܒܣܝܡܐ ܗܘ ܡܪܝܐ.
ܛܘܒܘܗܝ ܠܓܒܪܐ ܗܘ ܐܝܢܐ
ܕܡܣܒܪ ܒܗ.
9 ܕܚܠܘ ܡܢ ܡܪܝܐ ܟܠܗܘܢ ܩܕ̈ܝܫܘܗܝ.
ܡܛܠ ܕܠܐ ܐܝܬ ܚܣܝܪܘܬܐ
ܠܐܝܠܝܢ ܕܕܚܠܝܢ ܡܢܗ.
10 ܥܬܝܪ̈ܐ ܐܬܡܣܟܢܘ ܘܟܦܢܘ.
ܐܝܠܝܢ ܕܝܢ ܕܒܥܝܢ ܠܡܪܝܐ ܠܐ
ܢܚܣܪܘܢ ܡܢ ܟܠ ܛܒܬܐ. ⁘
⁘ ܕܚܫܚܚܘܢ ⁘
11 ܬܘ ܒܢ̈ܝܐ ܫܡܥܘܢܝ.
ܕܚܠܬܗ ܕܡܪܝܐ ܐܠܦܟܘܢ.
12 ܡܢܘ ܐܝܬܘܗܝ ܒܪܢܫܐ ܗܘ ܕܪܚܡ
ܚ̈ܝܐ.
ܕܪܚܝܡ ܠܝܘܡܬܐ ܘܢܚܙܐ ܛܒ̈ܬܐ.
13 ܢܛܪ ܠܫܢܟ ܡܢ ܒܝܫܬܐ.
ܘܣܦܘ̈ܬܟ ܕܠܐ ܢܡܠܠܢ ܢܟܠܐ.
14 ܐܬܦܢܝ ܡܢ ܒܝܫܬܐ ܘܥܒܕ ܛܒܬܐ.
ܒܥܝ ܫܠܡܐ ܘܪܕܘܦܝܗܝ.
15 ܥܝܢܘܗܝ ܕܡܪܝܐ ܥܠ ܙܕ̈ܝܩܐ.
ܘܐܕ̈ܢܐ ܕܝܠܗ ܠܒܥܘܬܗܘܢ.

abe(fg) hj

XXXIII

Insc. ܕܝܠܗ ܦܪܨܘܦܐ] ܦܪܨܘܦܗ *f* | ܘܫܒܩܗ] ܘܫܕܪܗ *f hj*
1. ܒܟܠܙܒܢ 1°] ܒܟܠ ܙܒܢ *b*; ܒܟܠ ܥܕܢ *hj*
2. ܬܫܬܒܗܪ] ܬܫܬܒܚ *e* | ܢܫܡܥܘܢ] ܢܫܡܥܘܢ *e hj* | ܘܢܚܕܘܢ] ܘܚܕܘܢ *hj*
3. ܐܘܪܒܘ] ܐܪܒܘ *hj*
4. ܐܘܠܨ̈ܢܝ] ܟܠܗ ܐܘܠܨܢܝ *hj*
8. ܕܡܣܒܪ] ܕܡܣܟܐ *f*
9. ܕܚܠܘ-ܡܢܗ] *f*mg†
10. ܕܚܫܚܚܘܢ] ܕܐܚܫܚܚܢ *b hj*, ܕܐܚܫܚܚܘܢ *e*, ܕܚܫܚܚܢ *f*
12. ܕܪܚܝܡ-ܛܒ̈ܬܐ] ܘܪܚܝܡ ܠܝܘܡܬܐ ܣܓܝܐܐ *f*
13. ܒܝܫܬܐ] c. sey. *e*
15. ܘܐܕ̈ܢܐ] s. sey. *f*

XXXIII

16 [illegible]

17 [illegible]

18 [illegible]

19 [illegible]

20 [illegible]

21 [illegible]

22 [illegible]

XXXIV

1 [illegible]

2 [illegible]

3 [illegible]

XXXIV

4 [illegible]

5 [illegible]

6 [illegible]

7 [illegible]

8 [illegible]

9 [illegible]

10 [illegible]

ab(c)e(fg) hj

18. [illegible]] [illegible] *hj*

19. [illegible]] s. sey. *f hj*

21. [illegible]] [illegible] *f* | [illegible]] c. sey. *f* | [illegible]] [illegible] *f*; [illegible] *j*

22. [illegible]] [illegible] *j*

XXXIV

Inscr. [illegible]] [illegible] *h*

3. [illegible]] [illegible] *a**(uid.), sed c pr m | [illegible]] [illegible] *f*

4. [illegible] > *e**, sed c pr m uid. | [illegible]] [illegible] *e hj* | [illegible]] [illegible] *g j*, [illegible] *f*

5. [illegible]] [illegible] erat > *a**(uid.), sed c pr m

6. [illegible]] c. sey. *f*

7. [illegible]] [illegible] *b* | [illegible] *f*] [illegible] *c*, [illegible] *g*

8. [illegible]] [illegible] sup. ras. *j*

9. [illegible]] tr. *e* | [illegible]] [illegible] *e* | [illegible]] [illegible] *e*

10. [illegible]] [illegible] *f*

XXXIV

11 [illegible]
12 [illegible]
13 [illegible]
14 [illegible]
15 [illegible]
16 [illegible]
17 [illegible]
18 [illegible]

XXXIV

19 [illegible]
20 [illegible]
21 [illegible]
22 [illegible]
23 [illegible]
24 [illegible]
25 [illegible]
26 [illegible]

abce(fg) hj

11. [illegible] > *j**, sed c pr m
13. [illegible] 1°] [illegible] *c* | [illegible]] [illegible] *e*
14. [illegible]] [illegible] *f*
15. [illegible]] + [illegible] *f*; [illegible] *g*
16. [illegible]] [illegible] *e*
17. [illegible]] [illegible] *fg*c pr m, [illegible] *g**
19. [illegible] 1° > *e**, sed scriptum est int. | [illegible]] [illegible] *cef hj* | [illegible]] c. sey. *e* (primo deerat [illegible], deinde c pr m) | [illegible]] [illegible] *cef j*, [illegible] *h*
22. [illegible]] [illegible] *e* ([illegible] frt principio [illegible], sed [illegible] pr m) | [illegible] 1°] [illegible] *hj*
23. [illegible]] [illegible] *cf*
26. [illegible]] tr. *hj*

XXXIV

27 [illegible]

28 [illegible]

XXXV

1 [illegible]

2 [illegible]

3 [illegible]

4 [illegible]

5 [illegible]

6 [illegible]

7 [illegible]

8 [illegible]

9 [illegible]

10 [illegible]

11 [illegible]

12 [illegible]

XXXVI

1 [illegible]

2 [illegible]

3 [illegible]

4 [illegible]

abce(fg) hj

27. [illegible]] [illegible] *a**(uid.)(sed c pr m) *h**(uid.); [illegible] *h*c*j*

XXXV

Insor. [illegible]] [illegible] *f*

1. [illegible]] [illegible] *hj*

2. [illegible]] [illegible] *f*

3. [illegible] (*b* absc.)] [illegible] *e*, [illegible] *h*

5. [illegible] > *j** (l), sed c pr m

6. [illegible]] [illegible] | [illegible] *j* | [illegible]] s. sey. *ce*(*e* etiam s. puncto [illegible]) *h*

7. [illegible]] ras. sup. [illegible], frt habebat sey. *j*

8. [illegible]] s. sey. *a*mg*b*mg, item et txt et mg *cf*

10. [illegible]] [illegible] *hj*

12. [illegible]] [illegible] *hj* | [illegible]] [illegible] *f hj* | [illegible]] [illegible] *b*, [illegible] *ef*

XXXVI

Insor. [illegible]] [illegible] *a**(uid.)(sed c pr m)*f*

1. [illegible]] [illegible] *cf j* | [illegible] *g*] c. sey. *f*uid.

3. [illegible]] [illegible] *c*

XXXVI

5 [illegible]

6 [illegible]

7 [illegible]

8 [illegible]

9 [illegible]

10 [illegible]

11 [illegible]

12 [illegible]

13 [illegible]

14 [illegible]

15 [illegible]

16 [illegible]

17 [illegible]

18 [illegible]

19 [illegible]

20 [illegible]

21 [illegible]

22 [illegible]

23 [illegible]

24 [illegible]

a(b)ce(fg) hj

6. [illegible]] c. sey. *c*
7. [illegible]] [illegible] *j**(uid.), sed [illegible] deleta est | [illegible]] [illegible] *f*mg*
9. [illegible] *f*] [illegible] *g*
10. [illegible]] [illegible] *j*
13. [illegible]] [illegible] *f*
14. [illegible]] [illegible] *e**, sed [illegible] inserta est (pr m) inter litteras [illegible] quamquam [illegible] restant
15. [illegible]] [illegible] *h*, [illegible] *j*
17. [illegible]] [illegible] *j*
18. [illegible]] [illegible] *hj* | [illegible] *f*] [illegible] *g*
22. [illegible]] [illegible] *hj*
23. [illegible]] manuscriptum sartum est, scriptio est pr m uid. *j*
24. [illegible]] [illegible] (sic) *j*

XXXVI

[illegible] 25
[illegible]
[illegible]
[illegible] 26
[illegible]
[illegible] 27
[illegible]
[illegible] 28
[illegible]
[illegible]
[illegible]
[illegible]
[illegible] 29
[illegible]
[illegible] 30
[illegible]
[illegible]
[illegible] 31
[illegible]
[illegible] 32
[illegible]
[illegible] 33
[illegible]
[illegible]
[illegible] 34
[illegible]
[illegible]

XXXVI

35 [illegible]
[illegible]
[illegible]
36 [illegible]
[illegible]
[illegible]
37 [illegible]
[illegible]
[illegible]
38 [illegible]
[illegible]
39 [illegible]
[illegible]
[illegible]
40 [illegible]
[illegible]
[illegible]

XXXVII

1 [illegible]
[illegible]
[illegible]
2 [illegible]
[illegible]
3 [illegible]
[illegible]
[illegible]
[illegible]

ace(fg) hj

25. [illegible]] [illegible] *h* | [illegible]] s. sey. *j*
27. [illegible]] s. sey. *cf hj*
29. [illegible]] c. sey. *e*
30. [illegible]] c. sey. *j*
31. [illegible]] [illegible] *a**(uid.), sed c pr m
33. [illegible]] [illegible] *c h*
36. [illegible]] [illegible] *f* | [illegible]] [illegible] *e*, [illegible] *f*, [illegible] *hj*
37. [illegible]] [illegible] *f*
38. [illegible]] s. sey. *f h*
39. [illegible]] s. sey. *e*
40. [illegible]] [illegible] (sic) *j*

XXXVII

Inscr. [illegible]] [[illegible]] [illegible] *f* | [illegible]] s. notis *cf hj*
1. [illegible]] [illegible] *ce h* | [illegible]] [illegible] *e* | [illegible]] [illegible] *c j*, [illegible] *h*
3. [illegible] 2° > *hj* (probabiliter prbl. de [illegible])

XXXVII

[illegible] 4
[illegible]
[illegible]
[illegible] 5
[illegible]
[illegible] 6
[illegible]
[illegible]
[illegible]
[illegible] 7
[illegible]
[illegible] 8
[illegible]
[illegible] 9
[illegible]
[illegible] 10
[illegible]
[illegible]
[illegible] 11
[illegible]
[illegible]
[illegible] 12
[illegible]
[illegible]
[illegible]

XXXVII

[illegible]
13 [illegible]
[illegible]
[illegible]
14 [illegible]
[illegible]
[illegible]
15 [illegible]
[illegible]
16 [illegible]
[illegible]
[illegible]
[illegible]
17 [illegible]
[illegible]
18 [illegible]
[illegible]
[illegible]
[illegible]
19 [illegible]
[illegible]
20 [illegible]

[illegible]
[illegible]
[illegible]

ace(fg) hj

4. [illegible]] [illegible] *hj* | [illegible]] [illegible] *e hj*; [illegible] *f* | [illegible]] [illegible] *c* | [illegible]] [illegible] *f j*, [illegible] *h*
5. [illegible] *j**] [illegible] *f hj*c (pr m?)
6. [illegible]] [illegible] erat [illegible] *a**(uid.)
7. [illegible]] [illegible] *a*mg*c*mg*f*mg (i. e. pro [illegible])
8. [illegible]] [illegible] *f* | [illegible]] [illegible] *h*, [illegible] *j*
9. [illegible] *f*] c. sey. *g* (cf. Pesh) | [illegible] 2°] [illegible] *e*
10. [illegible] *g*] [illegible] *c*, [illegible] *f*, [illegible] *h*
12. [illegible]] c. sey. *e*; [illegible] *f* | [illegible]] s. sey. *hj*
13. [illegible] > *j*
14. [illegible]] [illegible] *cef hj* | [illegible] > *j*
16. [illegible] > *j**, sed c pr m
18. [illegible]] [illegible] *e*, [illegible] *f j*, [illegible] *h*
19. [illegible]] [illegible] *hj* | [illegible]] s. sey. *f j* | [illegible]] tr. *f*
20. [illegible] *f*] [illegible] *cg*, [illegible] *hj* | [illegible]] > *e*; *g*mg† (sed [illegible], et [illegible] pro [illegible] uid.), *f*mg† non apparet

XXXVII

21 [illegible]

22 [illegible]

XXXVIII

1 [illegible]

2 [illegible]

3 [illegible]

4 [illegible]

5 [illegible]

XXXVIII

6 [illegible]

7 [illegible]

8 [illegible]

9 [illegible]

10 [illegible]

11 [illegible]

12 [illegible]

ace(fg) hj

XXXVIII

Insc. [illegible] *f* | [illegible] *e*txt*f*, [illegible] *e*mg

1. [illegible] *c hj* | [illegible] *f*

2. [illegible] s. sey. *c*

3. [illegible] *e*

4. [illegible] *h* | [illegible] *f*

5. [illegible] *h* | [illegible] *f* | [illegible] *e* | [illegible] *e*, [illegible] *f*, [illegible] *hj*

6. [illegible] *c* | [illegible] *c*

7. [illegible] *f*mg*

8. [illegible] *hj* | [illegible] pr. [illegible] *e** (I), sed deletum est uid. | [illegible] *f* | [illegible] c. sey. *f*

10. [illegible] s. sey. *g* (cf. Pesh; *f* hab. sey. uid. quamquam puncta aliquantulum languent) | [illegible] > *e**, sed c pr m

11. [illegible] *f* | [illegible] *e* | [illegible] *e*, [illegible] *h*, [illegible] *j*

XXXVIII

[illegible]
13 [illegible]
[illegible]

XXXIX

1 [illegible]
2 [illegible]
3 [illegible]
4 [illegible]
5 [illegible]

XXXIX

6 [illegible]
7 [illegible]
8 [illegible]
9 [illegible]
10 [illegible]
11 [illegible]
12 [illegible]

a(*b*)*ce*(*fg*) (*h*)*j*

12. [illegible] > *j**, sed c pr m | [illegible] *hj* (primo *j* omittebat [illegible], deinde c pr m)
13. [illegible] *cf h*, [illegible] *e*, [illegible] *g*, [illegible] *j*

XXXIX

Inscr. [illegible] *f* | [illegible] tr. *f*
2. [illegible] *e j*, [illegible] *h* | [illegible] *f j*, [illegible] *h*
5. [illegible] pr. ras., erat frt o uel ; *a* | [illegible] *hj* | [illegible] *h*; [illegible] *j*mg | [illegible] *f*
6. [illegible] *f*
7. [illegible] *b*
9. [illegible] *j*
10. [illegible] *e**(uid.) (prbl., cf. u. 11), sed c pr m
11. [illegible] *f*, [illegible] *j* (*h* hab. [illegible]) | [illegible] *f*
12. [illegible] *c hj* | [illegible] *c*; [illegible] *f* | [illegible] *h* | [illegible] *hj* | [illegible] *cef hj* | [illegible] *f*; [illegible] *j* | [illegible] s. sey. *c j* | [illegible] *b*

XXXIX

13 [illegible]
[illegible]
14 [illegible]
[illegible]
[illegible]
[illegible]
15 [illegible]
[illegible]
16 [illegible]
[illegible]
[illegible]
[illegible]
17 [illegible]
[illegible]
[illegible]
[illegible]
[illegible]

XL

1 [illegible]
[illegible]
[illegible]
2 [illegible]
[illegible]
[illegible]
[illegible]

XL

3 [illegible]
[illegible]
[illegible]
4 [illegible]
[illegible]
5 [illegible]
[illegible]
6 [illegible]
[illegible]
[illegible]
[illegible]
[illegible]
7 [illegible]
[illegible]
[illegible]
8 [illegible]
[illegible]
[illegible]
9 [illegible]
[illegible]
[illegible]
[illegible]
10 [illegible]

a(b)ce(fg) j

13. [illegible]] [illegible] *j**(uid.) (homarch.), sed c pr m uid. | [illegible]] [illegible] *e* | [illegible] *f*(s. puncto diacritico)] [illegible] *g*
14. [illegible]] [illegible] *f*
15. [illegible] 2°] [illegible] *j**, sed c pr m uid.
16. fin.] + [illegible] *j*
17. [illegible]] [illegible] *f*, [illegible] *g*

XL

Insor. [illegible]] [illegible] *f*
2. [illegible]] [illegible] *c* | [illegible]] om. et Pesh et SyrPs *f**, sed tota linea e Pesh et uerba [[illegible]] [illegible] e SyrPs (hab. *g*) relata sunt (pr m) | [illegible]] [illegible] *c*, [[illegible]] [illegible] *j*
3. [illegible]] [illegible] *e* | [illegible]] c. sey. *f* uid. (alterum punctum sey. languet, sed *g* hab. sey.) | [illegible]] [illegible] *e** sed add. [illegible] pr m (l), [illegible] *j*
6. [illegible]] [illegible] *ce* | [illegible]] [illegible] *j*
9. [illegible]] [illegible] *f*

XL

[illegible]
11 [illegible]
[illegible]
12 [illegible]
[illegible]
13 [illegible]
[illegible]

XLI

[illegible]
[illegible]
1 [illegible]
[illegible]
[illegible]
[illegible]
2 [illegible]
[illegible]
[illegible]
3 [illegible]
[illegible]
[illegible]
[illegible]
4 [illegible]
[illegible]
[illegible]
[illegible]

[illegible]
[illegible]
5 [illegible]
[illegible]
[illegible]
[illegible]
6 [illegible]
[illegible]
[illegible]
[illegible]
[illegible]
7 [illegible]
[illegible]
[illegible]
[illegible]
8 [illegible]
[illegible]
[illegible]
[illegible]
9 [illegible]
[illegible]
[illegible]
[illegible]
10 [illegible]
[illegible]

a(b)ce(fg) (h)j

10. [illegible]] [illegible] *j*

11. [illegible]] [illegible] *j**(uid.) (= Pesh), sed c pr m **I** [illegible]] [illegible] *f*

13. [illegible]] [illegible] *e*, [illegible] *hj*

XLI

Inscr. [illegible]] [illegible] *f* **I** [illegible]] [illegible] *e*

1. [illegible]] s. sey. *f* **I** [illegible]] [illegible] *e j**(sed - 2° partim deleta est)
2. [illegible]] [illegible] *f h*; > *j**, sed c pr m
3. [illegible]] [illegible] *e* **I** [illegible] > *e**, sed c pr m uid.
4. [illegible]] [illegible] *f* **I** [illegible]] [illegible] *b hj* **I** [illegible]] [illegible] *f* **I** [illegible]] c. sey. *f*
5. [illegible]] > *c*; [illegible] *j* **I** [illegible] *fg*c pr m] [illegible] *bcg* j* **I** [illegible]] [illegible] *b* **I** [illegible]] *e** inc., sed c pr m
6. [illegible]] [illegible] *f* **I** [illegible]] [illegible] (sic) *e* **I** [illegible]] [illegible] *e j*
7. [illegible]] [illegible] *e*, [illegible] *f*
8. [illegible]] [illegible] *f*

XLI

[illegible]
[illegible]
11 [illegible]
[illegible]
[illegible]
[illegible]
[illegible]

XLII

1 [illegible]
[illegible]
[illegible]
2 [illegible]
[illegible]
[illegible]
[illegible]
3 [illegible]
[illegible]
[illegible]
4 [illegible]
[illegible]
[illegible]
[illegible]
5 [illegible]
[illegible]
[illegible]
[illegible]

XLIII

[illegible]
[illegible]
1 [illegible]
[illegible]
[illegible]
[illegible]
2 [illegible]
[illegible]
3 [illegible]
[illegible]
[illegible]
[illegible]
[illegible]
[illegible]
4 [illegible]
[illegible]
5 [illegible]
[illegible]
[illegible]
6 [illegible]
[illegible]
7 [illegible]
[illegible]
8 [illegible]
[illegible]
[illegible]
9 [illegible]

a(b)ce(fg) hj

10. [illegible] + [illegible] *c*

11. [illegible] [illegible] *j* | [illegible] [illegible] *ce j* | [illegible] [illegible] *bcef hj* | [illegible]※] s. notis *e*uid.(quamquam puncta occulta ante et post uerbum) *hj*, *c* om. metob. uel euanuit | [illegible] [illegible] *f* | [illegible]※] s. notis *e hj* (*hj* hab. [illegible])

XLII

2. [illegible] + [illegible] *f*
4. [illegible] 2°] [illegible] *j*
5. [illegible] [illegible] *c* | [illegible]※] s. notis *e hj*

XLIII

Inscr. [illegible] *f*
3. [illegible] [illegible] *e hj*
4. [illegible] s. sey. *cf*
6. [illegible] 1° et 2°] [illegible] *f* | [illegible] [illegible] *f*
7. [illegible] [illegible] *j*
8. [illegible] [illegible] *e*, [illegible] *f*, [illegible] *hj*
9. [illegible] [illegible] pro [illegible] *a**(uid.), sed c pr m

XLIII

ܘܠܐ ܢܦܩ ܐܢܬ ܒܚܝܠܘܬܢ ܐܠܗܢ·
ܐܗܦܟܬ ܠܢ ܠܒܣܬܪܐ ܡܢ ܩܕܡ 10
ܒܥܠܕܒܒܝܢ·
ܘܣܢܐܝܢ ܕܒܙܙܝܢ ܗܘܘ ܠܢ ܒܙܘ ܠܗܘܢ·
ܝܗܒܬ ܠܢ ܐܝܟ ܥܢܐ ܠܡܐܟܘܠܬܐ· 11
ܘܒܥܡܡܐ ܒܕܪܬ ܠܢ·
ܙܒܢܬ ܠܥܡܟ ܕܠܐ ܕܡܝܐ ܘܠܐ ܣܓܝܬ· 12
ܠܐ ܐܣܓܝܬܗܘܢ ܗܘܐ ܡܣܟܢܘܬܐ
ܒܫܘܚܠܦܐ ܕܝܠܟ·
ܣܡܬܢ ܚܣܕܐ ܠܫܒܒܝܢ· 13
ܡܘܩܐ ܘܓܘܚܟܐ ܠܕܚܕܪ̈ܝܢ·
ܣܡܬܢ ܠܡܬܠܐ ܒܥܡ̈ܡܐ· 14
ܢܝܕܐ ܕܪܝܫܐ ܒܐܘܡ̈ܘܬܐ·
ܟܠܗ ܝܘܡܐ ܒܘܣܪܐ ܕܝܠܝ ܩܕܡܝ 15
ܐܝܬܘܗܝ·
ܘܒܗܬܬܐ ܕܦܪ̈ܨܘܦܐ ܕܝܠܝ ܚܦܬܢܝ·
ܡܢ ܩܠܐ ܕܚܣܕܐ ܕܡܚܣܕܢܐ ܘܡܓܕܦ· 16
ܡܢ ܦܪ̈ܨܘܦܐ ܕܒܥܠܕܒܒܐ ܘܡܬܒܥܢܐ·
ܗܠܝܢ ܟܠܗܝܢ ܐܬܝ̈ ܥܠܝܢ ܘܠܐ ܛܥܝܢܟ· 17
ܘܠܐ ܐܫܩܪܢ ܒܕܝܬܩܐ ܕܝܠܟ·
ܘܠܐ ܐܗܦܟ ܠܒܣܬܪܐ ܠܒܢ ܕܝܠܢ· 18
ܘܐܣܛܝܬ ܥܩܒܬܢ ܡܢ ܐܘܪܚܐ ܕܝܠܟ·
ܡܛܠ ܕܡܟܟܬ ܠܢ ܒܕܘܟܬܐ ܕܡܘ̈ܟܟܐ· 19
ܘܚܦܝܬ ܠܢ ܛܠܠܐ ܕܡܘܬܐ·
ܐܢ ܛܥܝܢ ܫܡܗ ܕܐܠܗܢ· 20
ܘܐܢ ܦܫܛܢ ܐܝܕ̈ܝܢ ܕܝܠܢ ܠܘܬ
ܐܠܗܐ ܢܘܟܪܝܐ·
ܠܐ ܐܠܗܐ ܒܥܐ ܗܠܝܢ· 21
ܗܘ ܓܝܪ ܝܕܥ ܕܟܣ̈ܝܬܗ ܕܠܒܐ·
ܡܛܠ ܕܡܛܠܬܟ ܡܬܩܛܠܝܢ 22
ܟܠܗ ܝܘܡܐ·
ܐܬܚܫܒܢ ܐܝܟ ܥܢܐ ܕܠܢܟܣܬܐ·
ܐܬܬܥܝܪ ܠܡܢܐ ܕܡܟ ܐܢܬ 23
ܡܪܝܐ·
ܥܘܪ ܘܠܐ ܬܪܚܩ ܠܢ ܠܓܡܪ·
ܠܡܢܐ ܦܪ̈ܨܘܦܟ ܡܟܣܐ ܐܢܬ 24
ܘܛܥܐ ܐܢܬ ܠܡܣܟܢܘܬܢ ܘܠܐܘܠܨܢܢ ܕܝܠܢ·
ܡܛܠ ܕܐܬܡܟܟܬ ܠܥܦܪܐ ܢܦܫܐ ܕܝܠܢ· 25
ܘܕܒܩܬ ܒܐܪܥܐ ܟܪܣܢ·
ܩܘܡ ܡܪܝܐ ܥܕܪ ܠܢ· 26
ܘܦܪܘܩ ܠܢ ܡܛܠ ܚܣܕܐ ܕܝܠܟ· ܀

XLIV

ܒܫܘܠܡܐ ܥܠܦ ܙܡܪܐ
ܕܡܫܬܠܦܝܢ· ܠܒܢ̈ܝܐ ܕܩܘܪܚ
ܒܣܘܟܠܘܬܐ ܡܫܒܚܬܐ·
ܥܠ ܡܫܝܚܐ· ܀
1 ܪܘܚܐ ܠܒܝ ܡܠܬܐ ܛܒܬܐ·
ܐܡܪ ܐܢܐ ܐܢܐ ܥܒܕ̈ܝ ܠܡܠܟܐ·
ܠܫܢܝ ܩܢܝܐ ܕܤܦܪܐ ܕܥܒܕ ܩܠܝܠܐܝܬ·
2 ܫܦܝܪܐ ܒܫܘܦܪܐ ܝܬܝܪ ܡܢ ܒܢ̈ܝ ܐܢܫܐ·
ܐܬܐܫܕܬ ܛܝܒܘܬܐ ܒܣܦܘܬܐ ܕܝܠܟ·
ܡܛܠ ܗܢܐ ܒܪܟܟ ܐܠܗܐ ܠܥܠܡ·
3 ܐܣܘܪ ܣܝܦܟ ܥܠ ܚܨܟ ܓܢܒܪܐ·
4 ܒܫܘܒܚܟ ܘܒܫܘܦܪܐ ܕܝܠܟ·

ace(fg) hj

10. ܘܣܢܐܝܢ-ܠܗܘܢ] *fmg** (sed hab. ܡܣܩܘܢ pro ܡܣܢܩܝܢ, cf. ܡܣܩܘܢ in *c*)
11. ܒܕܪܬ] ܒܕܪܬ *ef*, ܒܕܪܬ *h*, ܒܕܪܬ *j*
12. ܕܡܝܐ] ܕܡܝܐ *c* | ܘܠܐ-ܗܘܐ] ܘܠܐ ܗܘܐ *hj* | ܒܫܘܚܠܦܐ] ܒܫܘܚܠܦ *hj*
13. ܠܚܕܪ̈ܝܢ] ܠܚܕܪܝܢ *f*
14. ܡܬܠܐ] ܡܬܠܐ *j*
15. ܩܕܡܝ] ܩܕܡܘܗܝ *e**(uid.), sed c pr m uid.
17. ܒܕܝܬܩܟ] ܒܕܝܬܩܐ *ef j*, ܒܕܝܬܩܟ *h*
18. ܠܒܢ > *j**, sed c pr m
20. ܠܐܠܗܢ] c. sey. *c*
21. ܗܠܝܢ > *c* | ܡܛܫܝܬܗ ܕܠܒܐ > *h** (!), sed c pr m (praeter hab. ܡܛܫܝܬܗ sicut *ef j*)
23. ܕܡܟ-ܡܪܝܐ] s. notis *ef hj*
24. ܘܠܐܘܠܨܢܢ] c. sey. *cf j*
25. ܐܬܡܟܟܬ] ܐܬܡܟܟܬ *f*, ܐܬܡܟܟ *h*

XLIV

Inscr. ܥܠ ܡܫܝܚܐ] ܡܫܝܚܐ *c*
2. ܐܢܫܐ] s. sey. *ef hj*

XLIV

[illegible]
[illegible]
[illegible]
[illegible] 5
[illegible]
[illegible]
[illegible] 6
[illegible]
[illegible] 7
[illegible]
[illegible]
[illegible]
[illegible] 8
[illegible]
[illegible]
[illegible]
[illegible] 9
[illegible]
[illegible]
[illegible]
[illegible]

XLIV

10 [illegible]
[illegible]
11 [illegible]
[illegible]
[illegible]
12 [illegible]
[illegible]
[illegible]
13 [illegible]
[illegible]
14 [illegible]
[illegible]
[illegible]
15 [illegible]
[illegible]
16 [illegible]
[illegible]
[illegible]
17 [illegible]
[illegible]
[illegible]

ace(fg) hj

4. [illegible] *g*] [illegible] *cef h*
5. [illegible] [illegible] *e hj*
6. [illegible] [illegible] *e*
7. ab [illegible] ad [illegible] (i. e. [illegible]) manuscriptum *j* sartum est, et scriptio est fere pr m quamquam scribendi genus uerborum [illegible] et [illegible] (cf. infra) aliquantulum inusitatum est | [illegible] [illegible] *f* | [illegible] [illegible] *hj*(cf. supra) | [illegible] *c* | [illegible] *hj*
8. [illegible] c. sey. *cf*, [illegible] *g*
9. [illegible] 1° > *e* | [illegible] c. sey. *cf*, [illegible] *g* | [illegible] s. sey. *f* | [illegible] s. sey. *f hj*
10. [illegible] [illegible] *e j*
11. [illegible] [illegible] *hj*
12. [illegible] s. notis *cef j* | [illegible] bis scr. *e**, sed scriptio 2° deleta est
14. [illegible] [illegible] *f hj*
15. [illegible] [illegible] *e*, [illegible] *f hj*
16. [illegible] [illegible] *ef hj*
17. [illegible] > *hj* | [illegible] c. sey. *f*

XLV

[illegible]
[illegible]
1 [illegible]
[illegible]
[illegible]
2 [illegible]
[illegible]
[illegible]
3 [illegible]
[illegible]
[illegible]
4 [illegible]
[illegible]
5 [illegible]
[illegible]

XLV

6 [illegible]
[illegible]
7 [illegible]
[illegible]
8 [illegible]
[illegible]
9 [illegible]
[illegible]
[illegible]
[illegible]
10 [illegible]
[illegible]
[illegible]
11 [illegible]
[illegible]

ace(fg) hj

XLV

Insor. [illegible]] [illegible] *f* | [illegible] 2°] [illegible] *f* | [illegible]] [illegible] *e* | [illegible]] s. sey. *ce hj*

1. [illegible]] [illegible] *f* | [illegible]] s. sey. *f*

2. [illegible]] [illegible] *e h*, [illegible] *j*

3. [illegible]] [illegible] *e*, [illegible] *f j*, [illegible] *h*

5. [illegible]] [illegible] *e*

6. [illegible]] [illegible] *ce*; [illegible] *f* | [illegible]] [illegible] *c*, [illegible] *f*

7. [illegible] > *e**, sed c pr m | [illegible]] + [illegible] *h*, + [illegible] *j*

8. [illegible]] [illegible] *f*

9. [illegible]] c. sey. *h* | [illegible]] [illegible] *f* | [illegible]] s. sey. *c*

10. [illegible] 1°] [illegible] *hj*(s. puncto diacritico) | [illegible] 2°] [illegible] *cf*; [illegible] *h*, [illegible] *j*

XLVI

ܠܫܘܠܡܐ ܚܠܦ ܒܢܝ̈ܐ ܕܩܘܪܚ
ܡܙܡܘܪܐ. ÷
1 ܟܠܗܘܢ ܥܡܡ̈ܐ ܢܩܫܘ ܐܝ̈ܕܝܐ.
ܝܒܒܘ ܠܐܠܗܐ ܒܩܠܐ ܕܪܘܙܘܬܐ.
2 ܡܛܠ ܕܡܪܝܐ ܡܪܝܡܐ ܕܚܝܠܐ.
ܡܠܟܐ ܪܒܐ ܥܠ ܟܠܗ ܐܪܥܐ.
3 ܫܥܒܕ ܠܢ ܥܡܡ̈ܐ ܘܐܡܘ̈ܬܐ
ܬܚܝܬ ܪ̈ܓܠܝܢ.
4 ܓܒܐ ܠܢ ܝܪܬܘܬܐ ܕܝܠܗ.
ܠܫܘܦܪܗ ܕܝܥܩܘܒ ܗܘ ܕܐܚܒ.
5 ܣܠܩ ܐܠܗܐ ܒܝܒܒܐ.
ܡܪܝܐ ܒܩܠܐ ܕܫܝܦܘܪܐ.
6 ܙܡܪܘ ܠܐܠܗܢ ܙܡܪܘ.
ܙܡܪܘ ܠܡܠܟܢ ܙܡܪܘ.
7 ܡܛܠ ܕܡܠܟܐ ܕܟܠܗ ܐܪܥܐ ܐܠܗܐ.
ܙܡܪܘ ܡܣܬܟܠܐܝܬ.
8 ܐܡܠܟ ܐܠܗܐ ܥܠ ܥܡܡ̈ܐ.
ܐܠܗܐ ܝܬܒ ܥܠ ܟܘܪܣܝܐ ܩܕܝܫܐ ܕܝܠܗ.

XLVI

9 ܪ̈ܫܢܐ ܕܥܡܡ̈ܐ ܐܬܟܢܫܘ
ܥܡ ܐܠܗܗ ܕܐܒܪܗܡ.
ܡܛܠ ܕܕܐܠܗܐ ܐܚ̈ܝܕܐ ܥܠ
ܐܪܥܐ ܛܒ ܐܫܬܩܠܘ. ÷

XLVII ܬܫܒܘܚܬܐ ܕܡܙܡܘܪܐ ܠܒܢ̈ܝܐ
ܕܩܘܪܚ ܒܬܪ̈ܝܢ ܒܫܒܐ. ÷
1 ܪܒ ܡܪܝܐ ܘܡܫܒܚ ܛܒ.
ܒܡܕܝܢܬܐ ܕܐܠܗܢ ܒܛܘܪܐ ܩܕܝܫܐ
ܕܝܠܗ.
2 ܕܫܦܝܪܐ ܒܪ̈ܘܙܘܬܐ ܕܟܠܗ ܐܪܥܐ.
ܛܘܪܐ ܕܨܗܝܘܢ ܣܛܪ̈ܐ ܕܓܪܒܝܐ.
ܡܕܝܢܬܗ ܕܡܠܟܐ ܪܒܐ.
3 ܐܠܗܐ ܒܡܣܬܪ̈ܬܐ ܕܝܠܗ ܡܬܝܕܥ
ܡܐ ܕܡܣܬܥܕ ܠܗ.
4 ܡܛܠ ܕܗܐ ܡܠ̈ܟܐ ܐܬܟܢܫܘ
ܥܒܪܘ ܐܟܚܕܐ.
5 ܗܢܘܢ ܟܕ ܚܙܘ ܗܟܢܐ ܐܬܕܡܪܘ.

ace(fg) hj

XLVI

Insc. ܠܫܘܠܡܐ] ܠܫܘܠܡܐ ܕܢܘܨܚܐ *f*
1. ܕܪܘܙܘܬܐ] ܕܪܘܙܬܐ *ef j*
4. ܗܘ] ܗܘ *f* | ܕܐܚܒ] + ܕܐܬܦܫܛܠܗ *hj*
6. ܙܡܪܘ 2°] ܘܙܡܪܘ *c*, ܘܙܡܪܘ *f* | ܙܡܪܘ 2° ∩ 4° *h** sed c pr m uid., praeter hab. ܠܡܠܟܢ ܕܝܠܢ sicut *j* (non apparet punctum diacriticum apud utrumlibet ܘܙܡܪܘ in *h*, quamquam atramentum palluit) | ܙܡܪܘ 4°] ܘܙܡܪܘ *f*
8. ܝܬܒ] ܝܬܒ *j*
9. ܐܚ̈ܝܕܐ] ܐܚ̈ܝܕܢܐ *cef hj* | ܥܠ > *e** (!), sed c pr m

XLVII

Insc. ܕܡܙܡܘܪܐ] c. sey. *c* | ܠܒܢ̈ܝܐ ܕܩܘܪܚ] ܠܒܢ̈ܝ ܩܘܪܚ *f* |
÷ܒܬܪ̈ܝܢ ܒܫܒܐ] s. notis *hj*; ܒܬܪ ܚܕ ܒܫܒܐ *f* (s. notis)
2. ܒܪ̈ܘܙܘܬܐ] s. sey. *h*, ܒܪܘܙܘܬܐ *e*, ܒܪܘܙܘܬܐ *f j*; ܒܪ̈ܘܙܘܬܐ *c* | ܣܛܪ̈ܐ] s. sey. *cf*
4. ܐܟܚܕܐ] ܐܝܟ ܚܕܐ *hj*

XLVII

6 [illegible]

7 [illegible]

8 [illegible]

9 [illegible]

10 [illegible]

11 [illegible]

12 [illegible]

13 [illegible]

14 [illegible]

XLVIII

1 [illegible]

2 [illegible]

3 [illegible]

4 [illegible]

5 [illegible]

ace(fg) hj

6. [illegible]] [illegible] *e*, [illegible] *f*, [illegible] *h* | [illegible]] [illegible] *e*
7. [illegible]] [illegible] *f*, [illegible] *g* | [illegible] (*c* absc.)] s. sey. *f*
8. [illegible]] [illegible] *hj* | [illegible]] [illegible] *e*, [illegible] *f*, [illegible] *h*; > *j**, sed [[illegible]] *j*c pr m
10. [illegible]] [illegible] *f*
11. [illegible]] [illegible] *a**, sed c pr m uid.
12. [illegible]] [illegible] *c* | [illegible]] [illegible] *f*; [illegible] *j**(uid.) (= Pesh), sed c pr m
13. [illegible]] [illegible] *e*, [illegible] *f*mg, [illegible] *h*, [[illegible]] *j*
14. [illegible]] c. sey. *e*

XLVIII

1. [illegible]] [illegible] *f*mg (adsignatur [illegible])
2. [illegible]] [illegible] *hj* | [illegible]] [illegible] *f* | [illegible]] s. sey. *e hj* | [illegible]] c. sey. *c hj* | [illegible]] c. sey. *c j*
4. [illegible]] [illegible] *c*
5. [illegible]] [illegible] *h*, [illegible] *j*

XLVIII

6 [illegible]
7 [illegible]
8 [illegible]
9 [illegible]
10 [illegible]
11 [illegible]
12 [illegible]

XLVIII

13 [illegible]
14 [illegible]
15 [illegible]
16 [illegible]
17 [illegible]
18 [illegible]
19 [illegible]
20 [illegible]

ace(fg) hj

6. [illegible]] [illegible] *f*

7. [illegible] 1° > *j* (homtel.) | [illegible] 2°] *f*mg† | [illegible] > *j*

9. [illegible]] [illegible] *j* | [illegible]] [illegible] *cef* | [illegible]※] s. notis *f j*

10. [illegible]] c. sey. *f*

11. [illegible]] s. notis *ef* (*f* non testatur [illegible]) *hj*; om. metob. *c* | [illegible]] c. sey. *f*

12. [illegible]] [illegible] *hj* | [illegible]] [illegible] *h*

13. [illegible]] [illegible] *e*, [illegible] *f*mg *j*, [illegible] *h*

14. [illegible]] [illegible] *j* | [illegible]] [illegible] *h*, [illegible] *j* | [illegible]] punctum sup. [illegible] *a**(uid.), sed deletum est (quod est sub [illegible], pr m est)

15. [illegible]] [illegible] *e*, [illegible] *f j**, [illegible] *hj*c pr m

17. [illegible]] *f* testatur tantum [illegible] quamquam [illegible] sequitur in linea Pesh supra | [illegible] > *j**(uid.) (homtel.?), sed c pr m

18. [illegible]] [illegible] *e*

20. [illegible]] [illegible] | [illegible] *h* | [illegible]] [illegible] *hj* | [illegible]] s. sey. *f* | [illegible]] [illegible] *c*, [illegible] *h*

XLIX

ܡܙܡܘܪܐ ܕܐܣܦ

1 ܐܠܗܐ ܕܐܠܗ̈ܐ ܡܪܝܐ ܡܠܠ
ܘܩܪܐ ܠܐܪܥܐ.
ܡܢ ܡܕܢܚ̈ܝ ܫܡܫܐ ܘܥܕܡܐ
ܠܡܥܪ̈ܒܘܗܝ.
2 ܡܢ ܨܗܝܘܢ ܫܘܡܠܝ ܫܘܒܚܬܐ
ܕܫܘܦܪܗ.
3 ܐܠܗܐ ܓܠܝܐܝܬ ܢܐܬܐ.
ܐܠܗܢ ܘܠܐ ܢܫܬܘܩ.
ܢܘܪܐ ܩܕܡܘܗܝ ܬܐܟܘܠ.
ܘܚܕܪ̈ܘܗܝ ܥܠܥܠܐ ܬܩܝܦ.
4 ܩܪܐ ܠܫܡܝܐ ܠܥܠ.
ܘܠܐܪܥܐ ܠܡܦܪܫܘ ܠܥܡܗ ܕܝܠܗ.
5 ܟܢܫܘ ܠܗ ܚܣܝ̈ܕܘܗܝ ܕܝܠܗ.
ܗܢܘܢ ܕܩܝܡܝܢ ܩܝܡܗ ܕܝܠܗ ܥܠ ܕܒ̈ܚܐ.
6 ܢܚܘܘܢ ܫܡܝܐ ܙܕܝܩܘܬܗ.
ܡܛܠ ܕܐܠܗܐ ܕܝܢܐ ܐܝܬܘܗܝ.
ܕܦܘܫܠܡܬܐ
7 ܫܡܥ ܥܡܐ ܕܝܠܝ ܘܐܡܠܠ.
ܐܝܣܪܝܠ ܘܐܣܗܕ ܒܟ ܐܢܐ ܠܟ.
ܐܠܗܐ ܐܠܗܟ ܐܢܐ ܐܢܐ.

XLIX

8 ܠܘ ܥܠ ܕܒ̈ܚܝܟ ܐܟܣܢܟ.
ܩܘܪ̈ܒܢܝܟ ܕܝܢ ܥܠܘ̈ܬܟ ܩܕܡܝ
ܐܝܬܝܗܘܢ ܟܠܝܘܡ.
9 ܠܐ ܐܣܒ ܡܢ ܒܝܬܟ ܬܘܪ̈ܐ.
ܘܐܦܠܐ ܡܢ ܡܪ̈ܥܝܬܟ ܥܬܘܕ̈ܐ.
10 ܕܝܠܝ ܓܝܪ ܐܢܘܢ ܟܠܗܘܢ
ܚܝܘܬ ܚܩܠܐ ܕܒܪܐ.
ܒܥܝܪ̈ܐ ܕܒܛܘܪ̈ܐ ܘܬܘܪ̈ܐ.
11 ܝܕܥܬ ܟܠܗܘܢ ܦܪ̈ܚܬܐ ܕܫܡܝܐ.
ܘܫܘܦܪܬܐ ܕܚܩܠܐ ܥܡܝ ܐܝܬܝܗ.
12 ܐܢ ܟܦܢܬ ܠܐ ܐܡܪ ܠܟ.
ܕܝܠܝ ܓܝܪ ܐܝܬܝܗ ܬܒܝܠ ܘܡܫܡܠܝܘܬܗ
ܘܡܠܝܐ ܕܝܠܗ.
13 ܠܡܐ ܐܟܘܠ ܒܣܪܐ ܕܬܘܪ̈ܐ.
ܐܘ ܕܡܐ ܕܬܝܫ̈ܐ ܐܫܬܐ.
14 ܕܒܘܚ ܠܐܠܗܐ ܕܒܚܬܐ ܕܬܘܕܝܬܐ:
ܘܦܪܘܥ ܠܡܪܝܡܐ ܢܕܪ̈ܝܟ.
15 ܘܩܪܝܢܝ ܒܝܘܡܐ ܕܐܘܠܨܢܟ.
ܘܐܦܨܝܟ ܘܬܫܒܚܢܝ.
ܕܦܘܫܠܡܬܐ

ace(fg) hj

XLIX

Insor. ܕܐܣܦ] ܠܐܣܦ *f*

1. ܘܩܪܐ] ܩܪܐ *j* | ܡܕܢܚ̈ܝ] ܡܕܢܚܝ *e**, sed c pr m

3. ܢܫܬܘܩ] s. sey. *e h*

4. ܩܪܐ] ܢܩܪܐ *a*mg*c*mg | ܠܥܡܗ] ܠܥܡܐ *e**(uid.), sed c pr m; ܠܥܡܗ *f*

5. ܟܢܫܘ] ܟܢܫܘ *cg* (*f* hab. ܟܢܫܘ) | ܕܝܠܗ] ܕܝܠܗ *ef j*, ܕܝܠܗ *h*

6. ܫܡܝܐ] c. sey. *e j* | ܕܦܘܫܠܡܬܐ] ܕܦܘܫܠܡܬܐ *e*, ܕܦܘܫܠܡܬܐ *f j*, ܕܦܘܫܠܡܬܐ *h*

7. ܐܝܣܪܝܠ] ܐܝܣܪܝܠ *cf hj*, ܐܝܣܪܝܠ *e* | ܐܢܐ-ܐܠܗܐ > *e**, sed c pr m

8. ܐܝܬܝܗܘܢ] ܝ 2° erat ܘ, sed correcta est (qua manu inc.) *a*

9. ܡܢ 2°] + ܒܝܬܟ *j*

10. ܚܝܘܬ] s. sey. *c hj* | ܒܥܝܪ̈ܐ] s. sey. *f*

11. ܦܪ̈ܚܬܐ] c. sey. *j* | ܘܫܘܦܪܬܐ] ܘܫܘܦܪܐ *j**(uid.), sed c pr m | ܥܡܝ] pr. ܕ *j**, sed deleta est praeter punctum

14. ܕܒܚܬܐ] ܕܒܚܬܐ *e* | ܕܬܘܕܝܬܐ] ܕܬܘܕܝܬܐ *j**(uid.), sed c pr m uid. (i. e. [[ܕܬܘ]]ܕܝܬܐ) | ܠܡܪܝܡܐ] ܠܡܪܝܡܐ *h**, sed uncus (= ܡ?) adfixus est ad imam lineam inter ܠ (qua manu inc.) | ܢܕܪ̈ܝܟ] ܢܕܪܝܟ *hj*

15. ܕܦܘܫܠܡܬܐ] ܕܦܘܫܠܡܬܐ *e*, ܕܦܘܫܠܡܬܐ *f*, ܕܦܘܫܠܡܬܐ *hj*

XLIX

16 ܠܚܛܝܐ ܕܝܢ ܐܡܪ ܐܠܗܐ.
ܠܡܢܐ ܐܢܬ ܡܫܬܥܐ ܐܢܬ ܕܘܩܕܢܝ.
ܘܫܩܠ ܐܢܬ ܕܝܬܩܐ ܕܝܠܝ ܥܠ
ܦܘܡܟ.
17 ܐܢܬ ܕܝܢ ܣܢܝܬ ܡܪܕܘܬܐ.
ܘܐܪܡܝܬ ܡ̈ܠܝ ܠܒܣܬܪܟ.
18 ܐܢ ܚܙܝܬ ܗܘܝܬ ܓܢܒܐ ܪܗܛܬ
ܗܘܝܬ ܥܡܗ.
ܘܥܡ ܓܝܪ̈ܐ ܡܢܬܟ ܣܐܡ ܗܘܝܬ.
19 ܦܘܡܟ ܐܣܓܝ ܒܒܝܫܬܐ.
ܘܠܫܢܟ ܡܓܕܠ ܗܘܐ ܢܟܠܐ.
20 ܟܕ ܝܬܒ ܐܢܬ ܥܠ ܐܚܘܟ ܡܡܠܠ
ܗܘܝܬ.
ܘܥܠ ܒܪܗ ܕܐܡܟ ܣܐܡ ܗܘܝܬ
ܟܫܠܐ.
21 ܗܠܝܢ ܥܒܕܬ ܘܫܬܩܬ.
ܣܒܪܬ ܠܗ ܠܐܢܡܘܣܘܬܐ.
ܕܐܗܘܐ ܕܡܐ ܐܢܐ ܠܟ.
ܐܟܣܢܟ ܘܐܩܝܡ ܩܕܡ ܦܪܨܘܦܟ
ܚ̈ܛܗܝܟ ܕܝܠܟ.

XLIX

22 ܐܣܬܟܠܘ ܕܝܢ ܗܠܝܢ ܟܠܟܘܢ ܐܝܠܝܢ
ܕܛܥܝܢ ܠܐܠܗܐ.
ܕܠܡܐ ܢܚܛܘܦ ܐܝܟ ܐܪܝܐ ܘܠܐ
ܢܗܘܐ ܡܢ ܕܦܪܘܩ.
23 ܕܒܚܐ ܕܬܫܒܘܚܬܐ ܢܫܒܚܢܢܝ.
ܘܬܡܢ ܐܘܪܚܐ ܗܝ ܕܐܚܘܝܘܗܝ
ܠܗܘܢ ܦܘܪܩܢܗ ܕܐܠܗܐ.:

L ܠܫܘܠܡܐ ܡܙܡܘܪܐ ܠܕܘܝܕ. ܟܕ
ܐܬܐ ܠܘܬܗ ܢܬܢ ܢܒܝܐ.
ܐܡܬܝ ܕܥܠ ܠܘܬ ܒܬܫܒܥ:
1 ܪܚܡ ܥܠܝ ܐܠܗܐ ܐܝܟ ܪܒܐ
ܚܢܢܐ ܕܝܠܟ.
ܘܐܝܟ ܣܘܓܐܐ ܕܡܪ̈ܚܡܢܘܬܐ ܕܚܢܢܝܟ
ܥܛܝ ܥܘܠܐ ܕܝܠܝ.
2 ܝܬܝܪܐܝܬ ܐܫܝܓܝܢܝ ܡܢ
ܠܐܢܡܘܣܘܬܐ ܕܝܠܝ.
ܘܡܢ ܚܛܝܬܐ ܕܝܠܝ ܕܟܝܢܝ.
3 ܡܛܠ ܕܠܐܢܡܘܣܘܬܐ ܕܝܠܝ ܐܢܐ
ܝܕܥ ܐܢܐ.

ace(fg) hj

16. ܠܚܛܝܐ] ܕܠܚܛܝܐ *ef j*, ܕܚܛܝܐ *h*
18. ܓܢܒܐ] s. sey. *h* | ܪܗܛܬ] ܪܗܛܬܝ *f*
20. ܥܠ] ܥܡ *cef* | ܘܥܠ] ܘܥܡ *c*
21. ܘܫܬܩܬ] primo ܠܟ post ܘܫܬܩܬ uid. (= Pesh), deinde c pr m *j* | ܠܐ] sup. ras. (pr m) *j* | ܠܐܢܡܘܣܘܬܐ] ܠܐܢܡܘܣܘܬ *f* | ܕܐܗܘܐ *f*(s. puncto diacritico)] ܕܐܗܘܐ *g* | ܦܪܨܘܦܟ] ܦܪܨܘܦܐ *f*
22. ܘܠܐ *f*] ܐܠܐ *g*
23. ܠܗܘܢ] ܒܗܘܢ *h*

L

Inscr. ܠܫܘܠܡܐ] ܠܫܘܠܡܐ ܕܙܡܝܪܐ *f* | ܠܗ > *f* | ܐܬܐ ܠܘܬܗ] ܥܠ ܠܘܬ *f* | ܒܬܫܒܥ] ܒܪ ܫܒܥ *e hj*
1. ܕܚܢܢܝܟ] ܕܚܢܢܟ *f*
2. ܐܫܝܓܝܢܝ] ܐܫܝܓܢܝ *e*

L

[illegible]
4 [illegible]
[illegible]
[illegible]
[illegible]
5 [illegible]
[illegible]
[illegible]
6 [illegible]
[illegible]
[illegible]
7 [illegible]
[illegible]
8 [illegible]
[illegible]
9 [illegible]
[illegible]
10 [illegible]
[illegible]
11 [illegible]
[illegible]
12 [illegible]

L

[illegible]
13 [illegible]
[illegible]
14 [illegible]
[illegible]
[illegible]
15 [illegible]
[illegible]
16 [illegible]
[illegible]
[illegible]
17 [illegible]
[illegible]
[illegible]
18 [illegible]
[illegible]
19 [illegible]
[illegible]
[illegible]

ace(fg) hj

4. [illegible]] [illegible] *f**(uid.) (cf. σ′: Field u. 6), sed [illegible] tantum correctum est (qua manu inc.): *g* etiam hab. [illegible] | [illegible]] [illegible] *j*mg

5. [illegible]] s. sey. *f h* | [illegible]] [illegible] *h*, [illegible] *j*

6. [illegible] > *e*

7. [illegible]] [illegible] *a**(uid.), sed c pr m

8. [illegible]] [illegible] *f*mg (adsignatur [illegible]); [illegible] *h* (de *j* cf. infra) | [illegible] > *j*txt, [illegible] *j*mg (pr m) sed deinde [illegible] inductum est uid. | [illegible]] [illegible] *f* *j*mg(cf. sup.) | [illegible]] [illegible] *cf* *j*mg

9. [illegible]] [illegible] *c* (principio [illegible] bis scr., sed 1° inducta est)

10. [illegible] = *c*c pr m, *c** inc. | [illegible]] [illegible] *f hj*

11. [illegible] 1°] [illegible] *hj* | [illegible]] [illegible] *h*

12. [illegible]] [illegible] *f j* | [illegible]] [illegible] *h*, [illegible] *j* | [illegible]] [illegible] *e hj*; [illegible] *f*

13. [illegible]] [illegible] (sic) *f*

18. [illegible]] [illegible] *c** sed punctum inferius inductum est uid., [illegible] *ef*, [illegible] *hj* | [illegible]] [illegible] *e*, [illegible] *j*

19. [illegible]] s. sey. *ce hj* | [illegible]] c. sey. *cf* | [illegible]] [illegible] *e h*, [illegible] *c j*

LI

ܒܫܘܠܡܐ ܕܡܣܬܟܠܢܘܬܐ ܠܕܘܝܕ.
ܟܕ ܐܬܐ ܕܘܐܝܓ ܐܕܘܡܝܐ ܘܐܡܪ
ܠܫܐܘܠ ܘܐܡܪ ܠܗ. ܐܬܐ ܕܘܝܕ
ܠܒܝܬܗ ܕܐܒܝܡܠܟ ܀
1 ܡܢܐ ܡܫܬܒܗܪ ܐܢܬ ܒܒܝܫܘܬܐ ܚܝܠܬܢܐ.
ܠܐ ܢܡܘܣܐ ܟܠܗ ܝܘܡܐ.
2 ܥܘܠܐ ܐܬܚܫܒ ܠܫܢܟ.
ܐܝܟ ܡܣܦܬܐ ܠܛܫܐ ܥܒܕܬ ܢܟܠܐ.
3 ܐܚܒܬ ܒܝܫܬܐ ܝܬܝܪ ܡܢ ܛܒܬܐ.
ܕܝܐܦܣܠܡܐ ܀
ܥܘܠܐ ܝܬܝܪ ܡܢ ܕܬܡܠܠ ܙܕܝܩܘܬܐ.
ܕܝܐܦܣܠܡܐ ܀
4 ܐܚܒܬ ܟܠܗܘܢ ܡܠܐ ܕܛܘܒܥܐ.
ܠܫܢܐ ܢܟܠܢܝܐ.

5 ܡܛܠ ܗܢܐ ܐܠܗܐ ܢܣܚܦܝܟ ܠܙܒܢܐ.
ܢܣܠܩܟ ܘܢܫܢܝܟ ܡܢ ܡܫܟܢܟ.
ܘܥܩܪܟ ܡܢ ܐܪܥܐ ܕܚܝܐ.
ܕܝܐܦܣܠܡܐ ܀
6 ܘܢܚܙܘܢ ܙܕܝܩܐ ܘܢܕܚܠܘܢ.
ܘܥܠܘܗܝ ܢܓܚܟܘܢ ܘܢܐܡܪܘܢ.
7 ܗܐ ܓܒܪܐ ܗܘ ܕܠܐ ܣܡ
ܠܐܠܗܐ ܡܥܕܪܢܐ ܕܝܠܗ.
ܐܠܐ ܬܟܠ ܥܠ ܣܘܓܐܐ ܕܥܘܬܪܗ.
ܘܐܬܚܝܠ ܒܣܪܝܩܘܬܐ ܕܝܠܗ.
8 ܐܢܐ ܕܝܢ ܐܝܟ ܙܝܬܐ
ܦܐܪܢܐ ܒܒܝܬܗ ܕܐܠܗܐ.
ܣܒܪܬ ܥܠ ܚܢܢܗ ܕܐܠܗܐ ܠܥܠܡ
ܘܠܥܠܡ ܥܠܡܝܢ.
9 ܐܘܕܐ ܠܟ ܠܥܠܡ ܡܛܠ ܕܥܒܕܬ.
ܘܐܣܒܪ ܠܫܡܟ ܡܛܠ ܕܛܒ
ܩܕܡ ܙܕܝܩܐ ܕܝܠܟ ܀

abc(efg) hj

LI

Inscr. ܠܕܘܝܕ > *f*; ܕܕܘܝܕ ܠܕ *h* | ܠܫܐܘܠ] ܠܫܐܘܠ *j* | ܐܬܐ 2° *g*] > *f**, sed ܐܬܐ scriptum est (pr m) | ܕܘܝܕ] ܕܘܝܕ *f* | ܠܒܝܬܗ ܕܐܒܝܡܠܟ] ܕܐܒܝܡܠܟ *f*; ܐܒܝܡܠܟ (pro ܕܐܒܝܡܠܟ) *a*mg *b*mg *c*mg *j*mg

1. ܚܝܠܬܢܐ] + ܐܢܬ *hj*

3. ܕܝܐܦܣܠܡܐ 1°] ܕܝܐܦܣܠܡܐ *b h*, ܕܝܐܦܣܠܡܐ *f*mg *j* | ܕܝܐܦܣܠܡܐ 2°] ܕܝܐܦܣܠܡܐ *b h*, ܕܝܐܦܣܠܡܐ *f j*

4. ܢܟܠܢܝܐ] c. sey. (sic) *h*

5. ܢܣܚܦܝܟ] ܢܣܚܦܟ *h* | ܘܢܫܢܝܟ] ܘܢܫܢܟ *j* | ܡܫܟܢܟ] + ܕܝܠܟ *hj* | ܘܥܩܪܟ] ܘܢܥܩܪܟ *cf* | ܕܝܐܦܣܠܡܐ] ܕܝܐܦܣܠܡܐ *b h*, ܕܝܐܦܣܠܡܐ *f j*

6. ܘܢܕܚܠܘܢ] ܘܢܕܚܠܘܢ *hj* | ܢܓܚܟܘܢ] ܢܓܚܟܘܢ *f*, ܢܓܚܟܘܢ *g*

7. ܗܘ *f*] ܗܘ *g**(uid.) (cf. Pesh), sed ܝ erasa est

8. ܒܒܝܬܗ] ܒܒܝܬܐ *a**(uid.), sed ܗ pr m

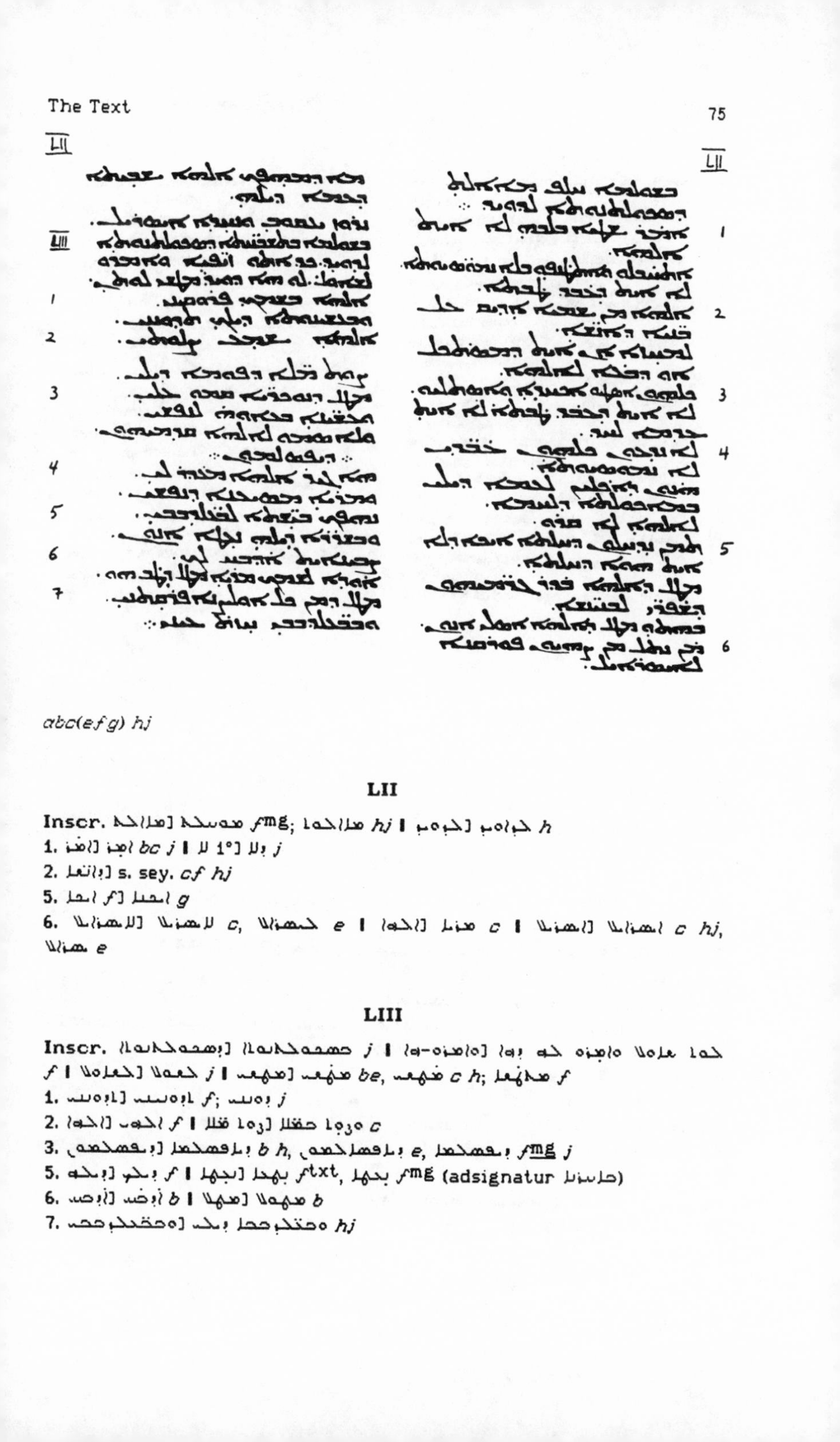

LII

[illegible]

1 [illegible]

2 [illegible]

3 [illegible]

4 [illegible]

5 [illegible]

6 [illegible]

[illegible]

LIII

[illegible]

1 [illegible]

2 [illegible]

3 [illegible]

4 [illegible]

5 [illegible]

6 [illegible]

7 [illegible]

abc(efg) hj

LII

Insor. [illegible]] [illegible] *fmg*; [illegible] *hj* | [illegible]] [illegible] *h*

1. [illegible]] [illegible] *bc j* | [illegible] 1°] [illegible] *j*

2. [illegible]] s. sey. *cf hj*

5. [illegible] *f*] [illegible] *g*

6. [illegible]] [illegible] *c*, [illegible] *e* | [illegible]] [illegible] *c* | [illegible]] [illegible] *c hj*, [illegible] *e*

LIII

Insor. [illegible]] [illegible] *j* | [illegible]] [illegible] *f* | [illegible]] [illegible] *j* | [illegible]] [illegible] *be*, [illegible] *c h*; [illegible] *f*

1. [illegible]] [illegible] *f*; [illegible] *j*

2. [illegible]] [illegible] *f* | [illegible]] [illegible] *c*

3. [illegible]] [illegible] *b h*, [illegible] *e*, [illegible] *fmg j*

5. [illegible]] [illegible] *f* | [illegible]] [illegible] *ftxt*, [illegible] *fmg* (adsignatur [illegible])

6. [illegible]] [illegible] *b* | [illegible]] [illegible] *b*

7. [illegible]] [illegible] *hj*

LIV

[illegible]
[illegible]
1 [illegible]
[illegible]
2 [illegible]
[illegible]
[illegible]
3 [illegible]
[illegible]
[illegible]
[illegible]
4 [illegible]
[illegible]
5 [illegible]
[illegible]
6 [illegible]
[illegible]
[illegible]
7 [illegible]
[illegible]
[illegible]

8 [illegible]
[illegible]
[illegible]
9 [illegible]
[illegible]
[illegible]
10 [illegible]
[illegible]
[illegible]
[illegible]
[illegible]
11 [illegible]
[illegible]
12 [illegible]
[illegible]
[illegible]
[illegible]
13 [illegible]
[illegible]
14 [illegible]
[illegible]
[illegible]

abce(fg) hj

LIV

Insc. [illegible] > *f* | [illegible] *e*mg | [illegible] *h*

3. [illegible] s. sey. *f* | [illegible] *a*mg*b*mg*c*mg*f*

4. [illegible] *g*] [illegible] *ef*, [illegible] *h*

6. [illegible] s. sey. *f* | fin.] + [illegible] *hj*

7. [illegible] *bf*, [illegible] *e*, [illegible] *hj*; [illegible] *c* | [illegible] *b*, [illegible] *e*; om. hic sed cf. u. 6 *hj*

8. [illegible] bis scr. *j*

9. [illegible] *hj*

10. [illegible] *b*, [illegible] *e*, [illegible] *h* | [illegible] *f*mg‡ | [illegible] *hj* | [illegible] *c* (cf. *f*mg‡ supra)

12. [illegible] *b*, [illegible] *e* | [illegible] s. sey. *c*

14. [illegible] *f* | [illegible] > *e** (l), sed c pr m

LIV

15 [illegible]

16 [illegible]

17 [illegible]

18 [illegible]

19 [illegible]

20 [illegible]

21 [illegible]

22 [illegible]

23 [illegible]

LV

1 [illegible]

2 [illegible]

abce(fg) hj

15. [illegible]] [illegible] *cf hj*, [illegible] *e* | [illegible]] [illegible] *c*, [illegible] *e hj* | [illegible]] s. sey. *e hj* | [illegible]] s. sey. *cf*

18. [illegible]] [illegible] *hj* | [illegible]] [illegible] *e*

19. [illegible]] [illegible] *b h*, [illegible] *e*, [illegible] *f j*

20. [illegible]] [illegible] *c* | [illegible]] sup. ras. (pr m uid.) *j* | [illegible]] [illegible] *ef j*, [illegible] *h* | [illegible] > *j**, sed c pr m

21. [illegible]] [illegible] *b*c pr m([illegible] *b**[uid.]) *hj* | [illegible] *g*] [illegible] *f* | [illegible]] c. sey. *ce*

22. [illegible]] [illegible] *j**, sed c pr m

23. [illegible]] [illegible] *c* | [illegible]] s. sey. *f* | [illegible]] [illegible] *hj*

LV

Inscr. [illegible]] haec inscr. in *f*mg ([illegible] pro [illegible]; [illegible] [*g*mg hab. [illegible]]) et ascripta est α′ (non in *g*mg), dum sunt lectiones uerae (c. uar.) ex α′ (s. ascriptione) et σ′ in textu (cf. Field) | [illegible]] s. sey. *j*

1. [illegible]] [illegible] *b* | [illegible]] [illegible] *h*

2. [illegible] 1° > *e*; *f*mg* quamquam post [illegible] lectio periit | [illegible] 1°] s. sey. *h* | [illegible]] c. sey. *bce* | [illegible] 2°] tr. *f***g*, sed lectio in *f* correcta est uid. (tria puncta sup. [illegible], qua manu inc.) | [illegible] 2° > *e*

LV

3 [illegible]
[illegible]
4 [illegible]
[illegible]
[illegible]
5 [illegible]
[illegible]
6 [illegible]
[illegible]
[illegible]
7 [illegible]
[illegible]
8 [illegible]
[illegible]
[illegible]
9 [illegible]
[illegible]
[illegible]
10 [illegible]
[illegible]

LV

11 [illegible]
[illegible]
12 [illegible]
[illegible]
13 [illegible]
[illegible]
[illegible]

LVI [illegible]
[illegible]
[illegible]
[illegible]
1 [illegible]
[illegible]
[illegible]
[illegible]
2 [illegible]
[illegible]
[illegible]
3 [illegible]
[illegible]
[illegible]
[illegible]

abce(fg) hj

3. [illegible]] [illegible] *bce hj*
4. [illegible]] [illegible] *f* [illegible] *g* | [illegible]] [illegible] *j*; [illegible] *h* | [illegible]] [illegible] *j**(uid.) (cf. Pesh), sed c pr m uid.
5. [illegible]] [illegible] *h*
6. [illegible]] [illegible] *c* | [illegible]] [illegible] *ef j*, [illegible] *g* | [illegible]] [illegible] *e**, sed c pr m
7. [illegible]] [illegible] *f*
8. [illegible]] [illegible] *f hj*
9. [illegible]] *f*mg† | [illegible] > *c*
10. [illegible] 1°] *f*mg† | [illegible] 2° ∩ [illegible] u. 11 *hj* | [illegible] 2°] [illegible] *e*
13. [illegible]] c. sey. *cf*; [illegible] *hj* | [illegible]] [illegible] sup. ras. (qua manu inc.) *a*

LVI

Inscr. [illegible]] [illegible] *e* | [illegible]] [illegible] *j*
1. [illegible]] [illegible] *f*, [illegible] *g*; [illegible] *e* | [illegible] > *e*
2. [illegible]] [illegible] *b hj*, [illegible] *e*, [illegible] *f*mg
3. [illegible]] [illegible] *f* | [illegible]] [illegible] *b hj*, [illegible] *e*, [illegible] *f*

LVI

4 [illegible]

5 [illegible]

6 [illegible]

7 [illegible]

8 [illegible]

9 [illegible]

10 [illegible]

11 [illegible]

LVII

1 [illegible]

2 [illegible]

3 [illegible]

4 [illegible]

5 [illegible]

abce(fg) hj

4. [illegible]] [illegible] *j**, sed c pr m
5. [illegible]] [illegible] erat [illegible], sed correcta est (qua manu inc.) *a* ❙ [illegible]] s. sey. *c h*
6. [illegible]] [illegible] *b hj*, [illegible] *e*, [illegible] *f*
7. [illegible]] [illegible] *j*
8. [illegible]] [illegible] *c*, [illegible] *j* ❙ [illegible] 1°] [illegible] *c* ❙ [illegible] 2°] [illegible] *bce*
9. [illegible]] punctum deletum est sub [illegible], sed de superiore non liquet a qua manu sit *a*; [illegible] *j*
10. [illegible]] c. sey. *be h*
11. [illegible]] s. sey. *h*

LVII

1. [illegible]] c. sey. *bc j*
3. [illegible]] [illegible] *e*, [illegible] *f*
5. [illegible]] [illegible] *e* ❙ [illegible]] s. sey. *c*

LVII

6 [Syriac]
[Syriac]
[Syriac]
7 [Syriac]
[Syriac]
[Syriac]
8 [Syriac]
[Syriac]
[Syriac]
9 [Syriac]
[Syriac]
[Syriac]
[Syriac]
10 [Syriac]
[Syriac]

11 [Syriac]
[Syriac]
[Syriac]
[Syriac]
[Syriac]

LVIII

[Syriac]
[Syriac]
[Syriac]
1 [Syriac]
[Syriac]
2 [Syriac]
[Syriac]
[Syriac]
3 [Syriac]
[Syriac]
[Syriac]
[Syriac]
4 [Syriac]
[Syriac]

abce(fg) hj

6. [Syriac]] [Syriac] *f* | [Syriac]] [Syriac] *f*

9. [Syriac]] [Syriac] *a**(uid.) (non liquet qua manu correctum est) *hj* | [Syriac]] c. sey. *h* | [Syriac]] c. sey. *c* | [Syriac]] [Syriac] *bcef hj* | [Syriac]] [Syriac] *e*[c] (a 1° deleta est)

10. [Syriac]] [Syriac] *hj** (non liquet qua manu correctum est *j*) | [Syriac]] c. sey. *f hj* | [Syriac]] c. sey. *hj*

11. [Syriac]] [Syriac] *j**(uid.) (= Pesh), sed c pr m uid.

LVIII

Inscr. [Syriac]] [Syriac] *j* | [Syriac]] [[Syriac]] [Syriac] *h*

2. [Syriac]] s. sey. *f*

3. [Syriac]] [Syriac] *e**(uid.), sed c pr m

LVIII

12 ܢܛܝܪܬܐ ܕܦܘܩܕܢܝܟ ܡܠܟܬܐ
ܕܦܘܩܕܢܝܟ.
ܘܢܬܢܛܪܘܢ ܒܦܘܩܕܢܝܟ.
ܘܡܢ ܠܡܛܪܐ ܘܡܛܠܬܐ ܢܛܪܢ
ܠܡܪܝܐ.
13 ܠܡܪܝܐ ܒܪܝܟܐ ܕܡܪܝܐ
ܡܠܟܐ ܢܫܒܚܘܢ.
ܘܢܒܪܟܘܢ ܕܐܠܗܐ ܥܠܝܐ ܟܠ
ܒܫܡܗ ܘܟܠ ܒܪܝܬܐ ܕܐܪܥܐ.
ܕܫܠܡܘܬܐ ܀
14 ܢܫܒܚܘܢ ܙܕܝܩܐ ܘܢܘܕܘܢ
ܐܝܟ ܦܠܚܐ.
ܘܢܬܦܪܥܘܢ ܒܡܢܝܢܘܬܐ.
15 ܚܝܘ ܢܬܕܟܪܘܢ ܠܡܪܝܐ.
ܘܐܝܟ ܠܐ ܢܬܟܠܘܢ ܐܦ ܢܬܠܘܢ.
16 ܐܝܟܐ ܕܝܢ ܐܘܪܚܐ ܠܡܫܝܚܝܗ.
ܘܐܘܪܚܐ ܕܟܐܢܘܬܐ ܠܡܫܝܚܝܗ.
ܘܟܠ ܕܒܝܬ ܡܫܝܚܐ ܕܝܠܗ.
ܘܒܝܬ ܠܗܘܢ ܒܡܫܝܚܐ ܕܐܬܡܫܚ ܠܗ.
17 ܡܬܩܪܐ ܐܬܠܝܬ ܠܗ ܐܘܪܚܐ.
ܐܠܗܐ ܕܡܫܝܚܐ ܐܝܬ.
ܐܠܗܐ ܦܪܘܩܐ ܕܝܠܗ ܀

ܐܬܬܚܝܪ ܠܡܦܪܩܢܐ ܕܝܠܗ ܘܗܝ.
5 ܘܐܘܕܐ ܡܪܝܐ ܐܠܗܐ ܕܫܘܠܡܬܐ
ܐܠܗܐ ܕܦܘܪܩܢܝ.
ܘܠܐ ܐܚܫܒܬܢܝ ܠܟܠܗܘܢ ܚܛܝܐ.
ܠܐ ܬܫܒܘܩ ܠܟܠܗܘܢ ܐܠܗܝ
ܕܒܥܝܢ ܠܐ ܢܚܫܘܒܘܢܢܝ.
ܕܫܠܡܘܬܐ ܀
6 ܢܫܒܚܘܢ ܙܕܝܩܐ ܘܢܘܕܘܢ ܐܝܟ
ܦܠܚܐ.
ܘܢܬܦܪܥܘܢ ܒܡܢܝܢܘܬܐ.
7 ܗܐ ܚܝܘ ܢܬܟܠܘܢ ܒܫܡܗ.
ܘܫܡܗ ܒܡܫܒܚܘܬܗ ܡܟܠ
ܕܒܝܬ ܥܡܟ.
8 ܘܐܝܬ ܡܪܝܐ ܕܝܢܝ ܟܠܗܘܢ
ܫܡܥܬ ܠܟܠܗܘܢ ܒܪܫܝܬܐ.
9 ܫܘܒܚܐ ܕܝܠܗ ܠܡܫܝܚܐ ܐܝܟ
ܟܠ ܕܐܝܬ ܐܠܗܐ ܕܡܫܝܚܐ ܐܝܬ.
10 ܐܠܗܐ ܕܝܠܗ ܕܫܘܒܚܐ ܢܫܬܒܚܘܢ.
ܐܠܗܐ ܕܝܠܗ ܫܡܗ ܠܗ ܒܟܠܗܘܢ.
11 ܠܐ ܬܬܢܫܐ ܐܝܟ ܕܠܒܐ ܠܢܦܫܗ
ܠܥܠܡܐ ܕܝܠܗ.
ܗܪܟܐ ܐܝܟ ܒܫܠܡܐ.
ܘܐܝܬ ܐܝܟ ܕܡܫܝܚܘܬܐ ܕܝܠܗ
ܡܪܝܐ.

ab(c)e(fg) hj

5. ܕܐܬܦܨܝܬ] ܕܐܬܦܨܝܬܢܝ *bc hj*, ܕܦܨܝܬ (sic) *e* | ܒܡܫܬܠܡܢܘܬܐ] ܕܡܫܬܠܡܢܐ *b h*, ܕܡܫܬܠܡܢܘܬܐ *e*, ܕܡܫܬܠܡܢܐ *f*mg; *j* hab. litteras ܕܡܫ, contractio pro uel ܕܡܫܬܠܡܢܐ uel ܕܡܫܬܠܡܢܐ

6. ܡܠܟܐ] c. sey. *hj* | ܘܢܬܦܪܥܘܢ] ܘܢܬܦܪܥܘܢ *b*, ܘܢܬܦܪܥܘܢ *j*

8. ܠܫܡܐ *g*] ܠܫܡܐ *b h*, ܠܫܡܐ *e*, ܠܫܡܐ *f*

9. ܐܦܝܢ] ܒܐܦܝܢ *cf* | ܐܝܟ] ܐܝܟܢ *hj*

10. ܐܠܗܐ 2° - ܡܫܒܚܝܢ > *hj* (homarch.) | ܡܫܒܚܝܢ] ܡܫܒܚܝܢ *cf*

11. ܠܥܠܡܐ] ܥܠܡܐ *e*

12. ܒܦܘܩܕܢܝܟ] ܒܦܘܩܕܢܟ *c* | ܘܡܢ > *j** (!), sed c pr m uid. | ܘܡܛܠܬܐ] ܡܛܠܬܐ *j* | ܠܡܪܝܐ] ܠܡܪܝܐ *e*

13. ܠܡܪܝܐ] s. sey. *cf hj*; > *e* | ܒܫܡܗ] ܕܫܠܡܘܬܐ *b h*, ܕܫܠܡܘܬܗ *e*, ܕܫܠܡܘܬܐ *f j*

14. ܡܠܟܐ] c. sey. *hj* | ܘܢܬܦܪܥܘܢ] ܘܢܬܦܪܥܘܢ *e j*

15. ܠܡܪܝܐ] ܠܡܪܝܐ *e*c pr m(ܠܡܪܝܐ *e**[uid.]) *hj* | ܐܝܟ] ܐܝܟ *be h*

16. ܐܘܪܚܐ] ܐܘܪܚܐ *f*, ܐܘܪܚܐ *j*

17. ܐܘܪܚܐ] ܐܘܪܚܐ *j* | ܐܝܬ] ܐܝܬܝܗ *hj* | ܐܠܗܐ] ܐܠܗܐ *e**(uid.), sed c pr m

LIX

[illegible]
[illegible]
[illegible]
[illegible]
[illegible]
[illegible]
1 [illegible]
[illegible]
2 [illegible]
[illegible]
3 [illegible]
[illegible]
4 [illegible]
[illegible]
[illegible]
5 [illegible]
[illegible]

LIX

6 [illegible]
[illegible]
[illegible]
7 [illegible]
[illegible]
[illegible]
8 [illegible]
[illegible]
[illegible]
[illegible]
9 [illegible]
[illegible]
10 [illegible]
[illegible]
11 [illegible]
[illegible]
12 [illegible]
[illegible]

ab(d)e(fg) hj

LIX

Inscr. [illegible] *f* | [illegible] s. sey. *f j* | [illegible] *e*, [illegible] *f*, [illegible] *j* | [illegible] *e* | [illegible] s. sey. *ef h*

1. [illegible] 2° > *j** (l), sed c pr m

2. [illegible] *hj*

4. [illegible] + [illegible] *hj* | [illegible] duae litterae inter [illegible] et [illegible] uid., sed incertae sunt *d* | [illegible] *b*, [illegible] *e*; > *d hj*(de *hj* cf. supra)

5. [illegible] *b*, [illegible] *ef j*

6. [illegible] *d*

7. [illegible] *e* | [illegible] *d* | [illegible] *b*, [illegible] *d*

8. [illegible] *f* | [illegible] *h* | [illegible] c. sey. *e* | [illegible] (sic) *d*

9. [illegible] (sic, praeter s. puncto [illegible]) *d*; [illegible] *j*mg

11. [illegible] > *j*

12. [illegible] *f*mg† | [illegible] *h*

LX

[illegible]

1 [illegible]

[illegible]

2 [illegible]

[illegible]

[illegible]

3 [illegible]

[illegible]

[illegible]

4 [illegible]

[illegible]

[illegible]

5 [illegible]

[illegible]

6 [illegible]

[illegible]

[illegible]

[illegible]

7 [illegible]

[illegible]

8 [illegible]

[illegible]

LXI

[illegible]

[illegible]

1 [illegible]

[illegible]

[illegible]

2 [illegible]

[illegible]

[illegible]

3 [illegible]

[illegible]

[illegible]

[illegible]

[illegible]

4 [illegible]

[illegible]

[illegible]

[illegible]

[illegible]

[illegible]

ab(c)de(fg) hj

LXI 4. [illegible]] litterae [illegible] partim perditae ex contactu paginae prioris apud 57:5 [illegible] *a*

LX

Insc. > *d*

2. [illegible]] [illegible] *d*

3. [illegible]] [illegible] *b h*, [illegible] *de*, [illegible] *f* (quamquam *g* hab. [illegible], itaque frt punctum superius periit in *f*)

4. [illegible]] [illegible] *hj* (quamquam *j** om. uerbum prius [!], sed c pr m) ‖ [illegible]] c. sey. *be* ‖ [illegible]] [illegible] *b*, [illegible] *e*, [illegible] *f*; > *d hj*(de *hj* cf. prope) ‖ fin.] + [illegible] *hj*

5. [illegible]] [illegible] *hj*

6. [illegible]] [illegible] *a**, sed c pr m ‖ [illegible] *d*[c] pr m] [illegible] *bd*e hj*; c. sey. *f*

7. [illegible]] [illegible] *hj*

8. [illegible]] [illegible] *d j* ‖ [illegible]] c. sey. *e* ‖ [illegible]] [illegible] *f*

LXI

Insc. > *d* ‖ [illegible]] [illegible] *f* ‖ [illegible]] [illegible] *hj*

2. [illegible]] [illegible] *j* ‖ [illegible]] [illegible] *j*

4. [illegible] > *d* ‖ [illegible]] [illegible] *f* ‖ [illegible]] [illegible] *b*, [illegible] *e*, [illegible] *f*[mg] *hj*; > *d*

LXI

5 [illegible]
[illegible]
[illegible]
6 [illegible]
[illegible]
7 [illegible]
[illegible]
[illegible]
[illegible]
8 [illegible]
[illegible]
[illegible]
[illegible]
9 [illegible]
[illegible]
[illegible]

[illegible]
10 [illegible]
[illegible]
[illegible]
[illegible]
11 [illegible]
[illegible]
12 [illegible]
[illegible]
[illegible]
[illegible]

LXII

[illegible]
[illegible]
1 [illegible]
[illegible]
[illegible]
[illegible]
[illegible]

abcde(fg) hj

5. [illegible]] [illegible] *c*; [illegible] *hj**, sed *j* c pr m uid.
6. [illegible]] [illegible] *d**, sed c pr m
8. [illegible]] [illegible] *b*, [illegible] *e*, [illegible] *hj*; > *d*
9. [illegible]] s. sey. *bcf hj* | [illegible] 1°] s. sey. *bcef hj* | [illegible]] c. sey. *ce* | [illegible] 2°] s. sey. *bcef hj* | [illegible] *g*] [illegible] *f*
10. [illegible] *f*] [illegible] *c*, [illegible] *g h* | [illegible]] [illegible] *d*, [illegible] *e* | [illegible]] [illegible] *d* | [illegible] *b**] [illegible] *b*c pr m uid.*e*
11. [illegible]] s. sey. *e*
12. [illegible]] [illegible] *cef j*

LXII

Inscr. > *d* | [illegible]] [illegible] *e*
1. [illegible]] [illegible] *d**, sed c pr m (s. puncto diacritico) | [illegible]] s. sey. *j* | [illegible]] [illegible] *j* | [illegible]] [illegible] *cde**(sed c pr m) *hj*

LXII

2 [illegible]
[illegible]
3 [illegible]
[illegible]
[illegible]
4 [illegible]
[illegible]
5 [illegible]
[illegible]
[illegible]
6 [illegible]
[illegible]
[illegible]
7 [illegible]
[illegible]
8 [illegible]
[illegible]
9 [illegible]
[illegible]
[illegible]
10 [illegible]
[illegible]

11 [illegible]
[illegible]
[illegible]
[illegible]

LXIII

[illegible]
1 [illegible]
[illegible]
[illegible]
2 [illegible]
[illegible]
[illegible]
3 [illegible]
[illegible]
[illegible]
[illegible]
4 [illegible]
[illegible]
[illegible]
[illegible]
5 [illegible]
[illegible]
[illegible]
6 [illegible]
[illegible]

a(b)c(d)e(f g) hj

2. [illegible]] [illegible] *cf*
3. [illegible]] [illegible] *bce*, [illegible] *d** sed alterum punctum sey. deletum est (frt pr m) | [illegible]] [illegible] *b*
5. [illegible]] [illegible] *de* | [illegible]] [illegible] *b*
6. [illegible]] s. sey. *cf hj*
7. [illegible]] + [illegible] *j* | [illegible]] s. sey. *bcd*uid. (o uid. perdita) *ef hj* | [illegible]] [illegible] *hj*
9. [illegible]] [illegible] *f*
10. [illegible]] [illegible] *e*, [illegible] *h*, [illegible] *j* | [illegible]] [illegible] *a**, sed c pr m
11. [illegible]] [illegible] *hj*

LXIII

1. [illegible]] c. sey. *cf*
2. [illegible]] [illegible] *b*, [illegible] *c j*
4. [illegible]] [illegible] *hj* | [illegible]] [illegible] (sic) *hj*
5. [illegible]] [illegible] *j*

LXIII

[illegible]
7 [illegible]
[illegible]
8 [illegible]
[illegible]
9 [illegible]
[illegible]
10 [illegible]
[illegible]

LXIV

[illegible]
1 [illegible]
2 [illegible]
3 [illegible]
4 [illegible]
5 [illegible]
[illegible]
6 [illegible]
7 [illegible]
8 [illegible]
[illegible]
9 [illegible]
[illegible]
10 [illegible]
[illegible]

a(b)ce(fg) hj

7. [illegible]] c. sey. *f hj*
9. [illegible]] [illegible] *e* | [illegible]] [illegible] *hj* | [illegible] *f*] [illegible] *g*, [illegible] *j*

LXIV

Insc. [illegible] > *h* | [illegible]] tr. *f* | [illegible]] s. notis *ef hj*(> *hj*)
1. [illegible]] [illegible] *e*
2. [illegible]] [illegible] *ce hj*
3. [illegible]] [illegible] *f*
4. [illegible]] s. sey. *j*
5. [illegible]] + [illegible] *j* | [illegible] > *j*
6. [illegible] *f*] [illegible] *ce*, [illegible] *g*, [illegible] *h*
8. [illegible]] c. sey. *e* | [illegible]] [illegible] *f*
9. [illegible]] [illegible] *e*; [illegible] *h**, [illegible] *h*c (qua manu inc.) | [illegible]] [illegible] *cf*
10. [illegible]] s. sey. *f*

LXIV

11 [illegible]

12 [illegible]

13 [illegible]

LXV

1 [illegible]

2 [illegible]

3 [illegible]

4 [illegible]

5 [illegible]

6 [illegible]

7 [illegible]

8 [illegible]

9 [illegible]

10 [illegible]

11 [illegible]

12 [illegible]

13 [illegible]

abce(fg) hj

12. [illegible]] [illegible] (sic) *c*

LXV

1. [illegible]] [illegible] *f*

2. [illegible]] [illegible] *c*, [illegible] *e*

3. [illegible]] [illegible] (sic) *c*

4. [illegible] 2° > *j**, sed c pr m uid. | [illegible]] [illegible] *hj*c pr m ([illegible] *j**[uid.]) | [illegible]] [illegible] *b hj*uid.(*j* hab. [[illegible]]), [illegible] *e*, [illegible] *f*

5. [illegible]] s. sey. *hj*; [illegible] *c* | [illegible]] [illegible] *a**, sed c pr m; [illegible] *c hj* | [illegible]] s. sey. *b*c*e*

7. [illegible]] [illegible] *c* | [illegible] > *j** (l) (cf. Pesh), sed c pr m | [illegible]] [illegible] *b h*, [illegible] *e*, [illegible] *f*mg *j*

9. [illegible]] [illegible] *b*c, [illegible] *hj*

11. [illegible]] c. sey. *f*

12. [illegible]] [illegible] *e* | [illegible]] [illegible] *b* | [illegible]] litterae partim perierunt, sed etiamnunc apparent *a* | [illegible]] [illegible] *e* (ras. inter [illegible] et [illegible]) | [illegible]] [illegible] (sic) *c*

13. [illegible]] [illegible] *f**, sed [illegible] inducta est (in atramento inscriptionium); [illegible] *g** (cf. Pesh), sed [illegible] inducta est (in atramento inscriptionium)

LXV

14 [illegible]
[illegible]
[illegible]
15 [illegible]
[illegible]
[illegible]
[illegible]
[illegible]
16 [illegible]
[illegible]
[illegible]
17 [illegible]
[illegible]
18 [illegible]
[illegible]
19 [illegible]
[illegible]
20 [illegible]
[illegible]
[illegible]

LXVI [illegible]
[illegible]

LXVI

1 [illegible]
[illegible]
[illegible]
2 [illegible]
[illegible]
3 [illegible]
[illegible]
4 [illegible]
[illegible]
[illegible]
[illegible]
5 [illegible]
[illegible]
6 [illegible]
[illegible]
7 [illegible]
[illegible]

LXVII [illegible]
[illegible]
1 [illegible]
[illegible]
[illegible]
[illegible]

abce(fg) hj

14. [illegible]] [illegible] *c*
15. [illegible]] [illegible] *b h*, [illegible] *e*, [illegible] *f j*
16. [illegible]] [illegible] *hj* | [illegible]] [illegible] *hj*
18. [illegible]] [illegible] *f*, [illegible] *g j*
19. [illegible]] [illegible] *f*

LXVI

Inscr. [illegible]] [illegible] *f*
1. [illegible] *g*] [illegible] *b*, [illegible] *e*, [illegible] *f*, [illegible] *hj* | [illegible]] [illegible] *e*, [illegible] *c hj*; [illegible] *f*, [illegible] *g* ([illegible] haud dubie corruptio est pro [illegible]) | [illegible]] [illegible] *b hj*, [illegible] *e*
4. [illegible]] [illegible] *b h*, [illegible] *e*, [illegible] *j*
6. [illegible]] c. sey. *cf h*

LXVII

Inscr. [illegible] > *j*
1. [illegible]] [illegible] *hj*

LXVII

2 [illegible]

3 [illegible]

4 [illegible]

5 [illegible]

6 [illegible]

7 [illegible]

8 [illegible]

9 [illegible]

10 [illegible]

abce(fg) hj

2. [illegible]] om. ob. sed hab. metob. *c*; in *e*, [illegible] (et [illegible]) tantum sub ob. (cf. MT et Pesh); s. notis *f hj*
3. [illegible]] [illegible] *c* | [illegible] > *e* (sed spatium aut ras. e duabus uel tribus litteris in latitudine post [illegible]) | [illegible]] [illegible] *b*, [illegible] *cef*
4. [illegible]] [illegible] *e*, [illegible] *hj* | [illegible]] [illegible] *cef* | [illegible]] [illegible] *g* (*f* hab. [illegible]) | [illegible]] c. sey. *e* | [illegible]] [illegible] *c**, sed [illegible] scripta est in margine (qua manu inc.) | [illegible]] *f*mg† (praeter hab. [illegible])
6. [illegible]] [illegible] *b j*, [illegible] *cef h* | [illegible]] c. sey. *ce*; [illegible] *j**, sed nunc hab. lemma (qua manu inc.) | [illegible]] sup. ras. (pr m uid.) *j* | [illegible]] [illegible] > *j**(uid.), sed c pr m | [illegible]] s. sey. *cf*
7. [illegible]] [illegible] *b h*, [illegible] *e*, [illegible] *f*mg *j*
8. [illegible] > *j**, sed c pr m uid. | [illegible]] s. sey. *j* | [illegible]] c. sey. *b hj*; > *e* | [illegible]] [illegible] *h*, [illegible] *j* | [illegible]] [illegible] *e* | [illegible]] [illegible] *e* | [illegible]] [illegible] *c*, [illegible] *e*, [illegible] *h*
10. [illegible]] [illegible] *hj*c pr m ([illegible] > *j** [!])

LXVII

11 [illegible]
[illegible]
12 [illegible]
[illegible]
[illegible]
13 [illegible]
[illegible]
[illegible]
[illegible]
14 [illegible]
[illegible]
15 [illegible]
[illegible]
16 [illegible]
[illegible]
[illegible]
[illegible]
[illegible]
17 [illegible]
[illegible]
[illegible]
18 [illegible]
[illegible]
[illegible]
[illegible]
19 [illegible]
[illegible]
[illegible]
20 [illegible]
[illegible]
21 [illegible]
[illegible]
[illegible]
[illegible]

abce(fg) hj

11. [illegible]] [illegible] *j*

12. [illegible]] c. sey. *c* | [illegible] 2° > *e* | [illegible]] c. sey. *hj*

13. [illegible]] [illegible] *c*ftxt, [illegible] *f*mg (adsignatur [illegible]); > *e* | [illegible]] [illegible] (sic) *c*, [illegible] *f* | [illegible]] [illegible] *b h*, [illegible] *e*, [illegible] *j*; > *c*

14. [illegible]] s. sey. *c* | [illegible]] [illegible] *b* ([illegible] partim sup. ras., sed pr m)

15. [illegible] 1° ∩ 2° *hj*

16. [illegible] > *j** (l), sed c pr m

17. [illegible]] s. sey. *b j* | [illegible]] c. sey. *ce* | [illegible] > *h*

18. [illegible]] [illegible] *c* | [illegible] *f*] [illegible] *g* | [illegible]] [illegible] *f hj*

19. [illegible] *g*] [illegible] *b*, [illegible] *e*, [illegible] *f*, [illegible] *hj* | [illegible]] s. sey. *cf* | [illegible]] [illegible] *b*, [illegible] *e*, [illegible] *f*mg *hj*

20. [illegible]] [illegible] *e* | [illegible]] + [illegible] *e*; [illegible] scripta est (pr m) pro [illegible] *e*mg

21. [illegible]] [illegible] *e hj*

LXVII

22 [illegible]
[illegible]
23 [illegible]
[illegible]
24 [illegible]
[illegible]
[illegible]
25 [illegible]
[illegible]
26 [illegible]
[illegible]
27 [illegible]
[illegible]
[illegible]
28 [illegible]
[illegible]
29 [illegible]
[illegible]
30 [illegible]
[illegible]

LXVII

[illegible]
[illegible]
[illegible]
[illegible]
31 [illegible]
[illegible]
[illegible]
32 [illegible]
[illegible]
33 [illegible]
[illegible]
[illegible]
34 [illegible]
[illegible]
[illegible]
35 [illegible]
[illegible]
[illegible]
[illegible]

abce(fg) hj

22. [illegible]] [illegible] *e*, [illegible] *f*
23. [illegible]] [illegible] *e*; [illegible] *j*
24. [illegible]] [illegible] *f* | [illegible]] [illegible] *f*
25. [illegible]] [illegible] *bc* | [illegible]] [illegible] *cf*
26. [illegible]] s. sey. *f* | [illegible]] [illegible] *e*, [illegible] *h*
27. [illegible] 1° et 2°] [illegible] *b* | [illegible]] [illegible] *ce hj* | [illegible] 3°] [illegible] *b*
28. [illegible]] [illegible] *hj*ᶜ ([illegible] pro uerbo priore *j**(uid.) [cf. Pesh], sed qua manu correctum est inc.) | [illegible]] [illegible] *j** (cf. Pesh)
29. [illegible]] [illegible] *c*, [illegible] *e*, [illegible] *j*
30. [illegible]] s. sey. *cf* | [illegible] > *e**, sed c pr m | [illegible]] [illegible] *hj* | [illegible]] c. sey. *e*
31. [illegible]] [illegible] *e* | [illegible]] > *a**, sed c pr m; [illegible] *b*, [illegible] *e*, [illegible] *f hj*
32. [illegible]] [illegible] *c*, [illegible] *e* | [illegible]] [illegible] *c*, [illegible] *ef*
33. [illegible]] c. sey. *cf*
34. [illegible]] [illegible] *e*, [illegible] *f hj*
35. [illegible]] [illegible] *e*, [illegible] *hj*

LXVIII

[illegible]
[illegible]
1 [illegible]
[illegible]
2 [illegible]
[illegible]
[illegible]
[illegible]
3 [illegible]
[illegible]
[illegible]
4 [illegible]
[illegible]
[illegible]
[illegible]
[illegible]
5 [illegible]
[illegible]
6 [illegible]
[illegible]
[illegible]
[illegible]

LXVIII

7 [illegible]
[illegible]
8 [illegible]
[illegible]
9 [illegible]
[illegible]
10 [illegible]
[illegible]
11 [illegible]
[illegible]
12 [illegible]
[illegible]
[illegible]
[illegible]
13 [illegible]
[illegible]
[illegible]
14 [illegible]
[illegible]
[illegible]
[illegible]
15 [illegible]
[illegible]
[illegible]

abce(fg) hj

LXVIII

2. [illegible]] [illegible] *b*, [illegible] *c*, [illegible] *ef* uid. *j*, [illegible] *g* | [illegible]] [illegible] *j** (= Pesh), sed c pr m

3. [illegible]] [illegible] *f*, [illegible] *hj*

4. [illegible]] sup. ras. (pr m) *a* | [illegible]] s. sey. *b**(frt)*c* | [illegible]] [illegible] *b*c uid. ([illegible] frt erat [illegible] quamquam punctum [illegible] pr m; primo [illegible] antecedebat [illegible] uid., deinde erasa est)

5. [illegible]] [illegible] *f* | [illegible]] [illegible] *g* | [illegible]] [illegible] *f*

6. [illegible] 1° > *j* | [illegible]] [illegible] *bc*, [illegible] *e*, [illegible] *h*

9. [illegible]] s. sey. *c*

10. [illegible]] [illegible] *a**(sed c pr m frt)*ef*

12. [illegible]] [illegible] *hj* | [illegible]] [illegible] *h* | [illegible]] [illegible] *f*

14. [illegible]] [illegible] sup. ras., sed pr m uid. *a*; [illegible] *c**(uid.)([illegible] *c*c pr m), [illegible] *e* | [illegible]] c. sey. *h*

15. [illegible] 1°] [illegible] | [illegible] *h* | [illegible] 2°] [illegible] *c* | [illegible]] [illegible] *e*

LXVIII

16 [illegible]
[illegible]
17 [illegible]
[illegible]
18 [illegible]
[illegible]
19 [illegible]
[illegible]
[illegible]
20 [illegible]
[illegible]
[illegible]
[illegible]
[illegible]
21 [illegible]
[illegible]
22 [illegible]
[illegible]
[illegible]
23 [illegible]
[illegible]
24 [illegible]

LXVIII

[illegible]
25 [illegible]
[illegible]
26 [illegible]
[illegible]
[illegible]
27 [illegible]
[illegible]
[illegible]
28 [illegible]
[illegible]
29 [illegible]
[illegible]
30 [illegible]
[illegible]
[illegible]
31 [illegible]
[illegible]
[illegible]
32 [illegible]
[illegible]

abce(fg) hj

LXVIII 23. [illegible]] s. sey. *a*

16. [illegible]] c. sey. *c* | [illegible]] [illegible] *f* | [illegible]] [illegible] *e*
17. [illegible]] [illegible] *b*, [illegible] *c*, [illegible] *e hj*
20. [illegible]] [illegible] *f*
22. [illegible]] c. sey. *a**(uid.)
23. [illegible]] [illegible] *c*
24. [illegible]] [illegible] *c*; [illegible] *e*
25. [illegible]] [illegible] *h*
26. [illegible]] [illegible] *h* | [illegible]] s. sey. *f*
27. [illegible] *g**(uid.)] [illegible] *efg*c pr m uid. | [illegible]] [illegible] *hj*
28. [illegible]] [illegible] *f*; [illegible] *h*, [illegible] *j* | [illegible] > *h** (l), sed [illegible] additum est (qua manu inc.)
29. [illegible]] [illegible] *e* | [illegible]] [illegible] *b*, [illegible] *c hj*
30. [illegible]] [illegible] *f*
31. [illegible]] [illegible] (sic) *e*
32. [illegible]] [illegible] *ce*, [illegible] *f*mg (s. puncto *g*mg; utraque adsignatur [illegible]), [illegible] *h*; [illegible] *f*txt (s. puncto *g*txt)

LXVIII

33 [illegible]
34 [illegible]
35 [illegible]
36 [illegible]

LXIX

1 [illegible]
2 [illegible]
3 [illegible]

LXIX

4 [illegible]
5 [illegible]

LXX

1 [illegible]
2 [illegible]
3 [illegible]
4 [illegible]

abce(fg) hj

33. [illegible]] [illegible] *c**([illegible] *c*^c pr m)*f*
34. [illegible]] s. sey. *hj* | [illegible]] [illegible] *f* | [illegible]] [illegible] *f*
35. [illegible]] [illegible] *b*
36. [illegible]] *f*mg†; > *hj* | [illegible]] [illegible] *h*

LXIX

1. [illegible]] c. sey. uid. nisi punctum minus sup. [illegible] macula est *b*
3. [illegible]] [illegible] *e hj*

LXX

Insc*r*. [illegible] > *f* | [illegible]] [illegible] *ce* | fin.] + [illegible] *e*
4. [illegible] 2°] [illegible] *b* | [illegible]] [illegible] *h*

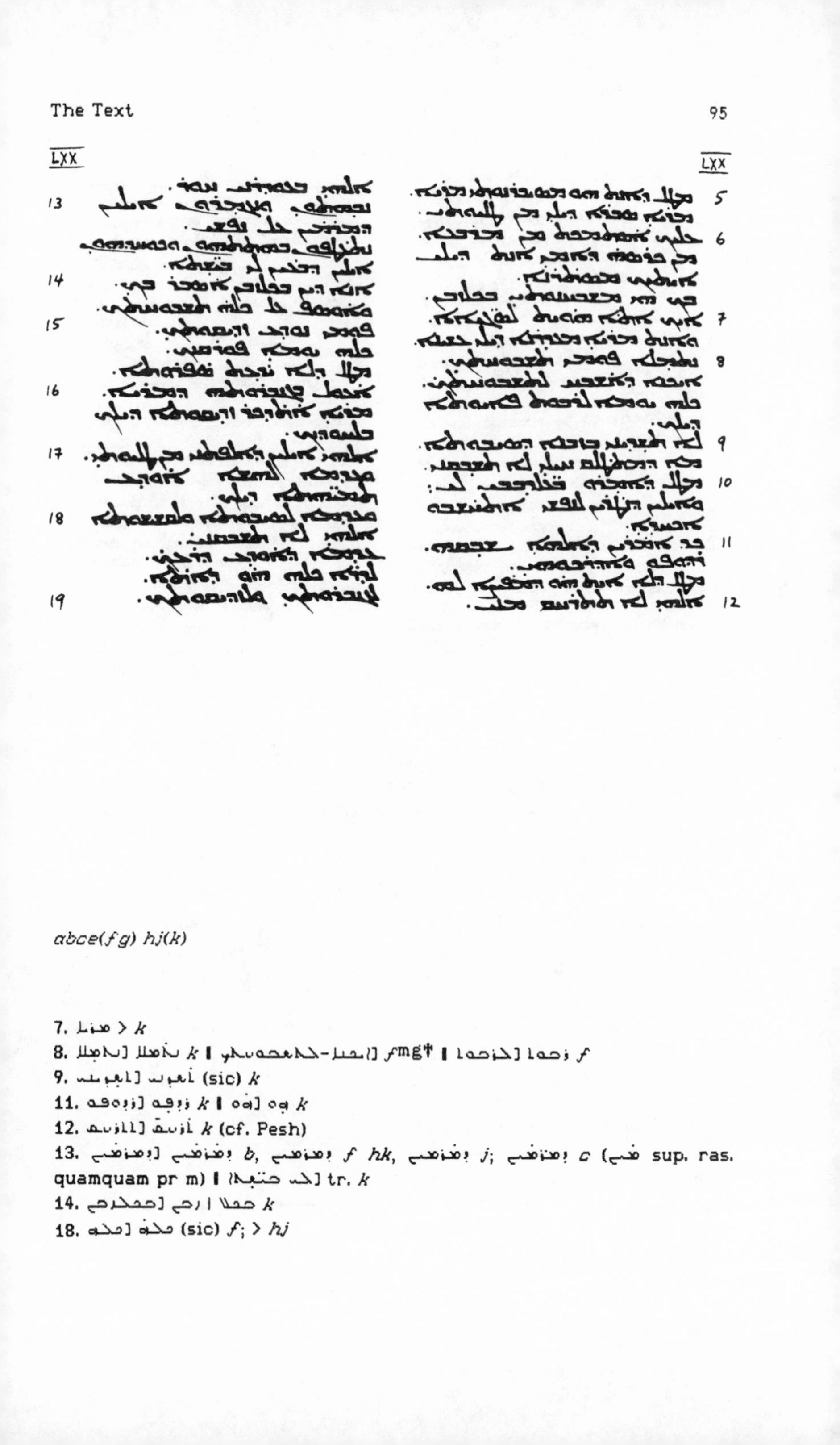

LXX

5 [illegible]
[illegible]
6 [illegible]
[illegible]
[illegible]
[illegible]
7 [illegible]
[illegible]
8 [illegible]
[illegible]
[illegible]
[illegible]
9 [illegible]
[illegible]
10 [illegible]
[illegible]
[illegible]
11 [illegible]
[illegible]
[illegible]
12 [illegible]

LXX

[illegible]
13 [illegible]
[illegible]
[illegible]
[illegible]
14 [illegible]
[illegible]
15 [illegible]
[illegible]
[illegible]
16 [illegible]
[illegible]
[illegible]
17 [illegible]
[illegible]
[illegible]
18 [illegible]
[illegible]
[illegible]
[illegible]
[illegible]
19 [illegible]

abce(fg) hj(k)

7. [illegible] > *k*
8. [illegible]] [illegible] *k* | [illegible]] *f* mg† | [illegible]] [illegible] *f*
9. [illegible]] [illegible] (sic) *k*
11. [illegible]] [illegible] *k* | [illegible]] [illegible] *k*
12. [illegible]] [illegible] *k* (cf. Pesh)
13. [illegible]] [illegible] *b*, [illegible] *f hk*, [illegible] *j*; [illegible] *c* ([illegible] sup. ras. quamquam pr m) | [illegible]] tr. *k*
14. [illegible]] [illegible] *k*
18. [illegible]] [illegible] (sic) *f*; > *hj*

LXX

[illegible]
[illegible]
[illegible]
20 [illegible]
[illegible]
[illegible]
[illegible]
[illegible]
21 [illegible]
[illegible]
[illegible]
[illegible]
22 [illegible]
[illegible]
[illegible]
[illegible]
23 [illegible]
[illegible]
24 [illegible]
[illegible]
[illegible]
[illegible]

LXXI

[illegible]
1 [illegible]
[illegible]

LXXI

2 [illegible]
[illegible]
3 [illegible]
[illegible]
4 [illegible]
[illegible]
[illegible]
5 [illegible]
[illegible]
6 [illegible]
[illegible]
[illegible]
7 [illegible]
[illegible]
[illegible]
8 [illegible]
[illegible]
[illegible]
9 [illegible]
[illegible]
10 [illegible]
[illegible]
[illegible]
[illegible]

a(b)ce(fg) hj

20. [illegible] > *j* | [illegible] s. sey. *f* | [illegible] *f*
21. [illegible] haec uerba absunt in *f*txt quamquam erant in *f*mg* uid. (index est in textu, sed margo sinister absc.); haec uerba item absunt in *g*
22. [illegible] *b j*, [illegible] *e*, [illegible] *h*

LXXI

Inscr. [illegible] *e*(ܠ scripta est [pr m] pro ܕ *e*mg)*f*
3. [illegible] *j**(uid.) (= Pesh), sed correctum est (qua manu inc.) | [illegible] + [illegible] *j**(uid.) (cf. Pesh), sed [illegible] refictum est ad [illegible] (pr m uid.)
4. [illegible] *c* | [illegible] *cf* | [illegible] c. sey. *h*; [illegible] *c*
5. [illegible] s. sey. *ef*
6. [illegible] *a*mg*c*mg*e*f*mg*
7. [illegible] *e* | [illegible] *j*
8. [illegible] 1° > *j** (!), sed c pr m
9. [illegible] *c*c pr m, [illegible] *hj*
10. [illegible] *c*, [illegible] (sic) *f* | [illegible] 1° ∩ 2° *hj* | [illegible] *ef*

LXXI

11 ܢܣܓܕܘܢ ܠܗ ܟܠܗܘܢ ܡ̈ܠܟܐ
ܕܐܪܥܐ.
ܟܠܗܘܢ ܥܡ̈ܡܐ ܢܦܠܚܘܢ
ܒܫܥܒܕܐ ܠܗ.
12 ܡܛܠ ܕܦܪܩ ܠܒܝܫܐ ܡܢ ܚܣܝܢܐ.
ܘܡܣܟܢܐ ܗܘ ܕܠܐ ܥܕܝܪ ܗܘܐ
ܠܗ ܡܥܕܪܢܐ.
13 ܢܚܘܣ ܥܠ ܒܝܫܐ ܘܡܣܟܢܐ.
ܘܢܦܫ̈ܬܐ ܕܡܣܟ̈ܢܐ ܢܦܪܘܩ.
14 ܡܢ ܪܒܝܬܐ ܘܡܢ ܥܘܠܐ ܢܦܪܘܩ
ܢܦܫ̈ܬܗܘܢ.
ܘܝܩܝܪ ܫܡܗܘܢ ܩܕܡܘܗܝ.
15 ܘܢܚܐ ܘܢܬܝܗܒ ܠܗ ܡܢ
ܕܗܒܐ ܕܐܪܒܝܐ.
ܘܢܨܠܘܢ ܡܛܠܬܗ ܒܟܠܙܒܢ.
ܟܠܗ ܝܘܡܐ ܢܒܪܟܘܢܗ.
16 ܢܗܘܐ ܣܡܟܐ ܒܐܪܥܐ ܥܠ
ܪ̈ܫܐ ܕܛܘܪ̈ܐ.
ܢܬܬܪܝܡ ܝܬܝܪ ܡܢ ܠܒܢܢ
ܦܐܪܐ ܕܝܠܗ.

LXXI

ܘܢܦܪܚܘܢ ܡܢ ܡܕܝܢܬܐ ܐܝܟ
ܥܣܒܐ ܕܐܪܥܐ.
17 ܢܗܘܐ ܫܡܗ ܡܒܪܟ ܠܥܠܡܝܢ.
ܩܕܡ ܫܡܫܐ ܢܩܘܡ ܫܡܗ.
ܘܢܬܒܪܟܘܢ ܒܗ ܟܠܗܝܢ ܫܪ̈ܒܬܐ
ܕܐܪܥܐ.
ܟܠܗܘܢ ܥܡ̈ܡܐ ܛܘܒܐ ܢܬܠܘܢ ܠܗ.
18 ܒܪܝܟ ܗܘ ܡܪܝܐ ܐܠܗܐ ܕܐܝܣܪܐܝܠ.
ܗܘ ܕܥܒܕ ܬܕܡܪ̈ܬܐ ܒܠܚܘܕܘܗܝ.
19 ܘܒܪܝܟ ܫܡܐ ܕܬܫܒܘܚܬܐ ܕܝܠܗ.
ܠܥܠܡ ܘܠܥܠܡ ܕܥܠܡܐ.
ܘܬܬܡܠܐ ܡܢ ܬܫܒܘܚܬܗ ܟܠܗ
ܐܪܥܐ ܬܗܘܐ ܬܗܘܐ.

20 ܐܫܬܠܡܘ ܬܫܒܚܬܐ ܕܕܘܝܕ
ܒܪܗ ܕܐܝܫܝ.

a(b)ce(fg) hj

LXXI 11. ܥܡܡܐ] s. sey. *a*

11. ܢܦܠܚܘܢ] + ܠܗ *f*
12. ܕܦܪܩ] ܕܦܪܩ *e hj* | ܘܡܣܟܢܐ] ܘܠܡܣܟܢܐ *c hj* | ܥܕܝܪ] ܥܕܝܪ *h* (linea sub ܒ, significatio inc.)
15. ܘܢܚܐ] ܘܢܐܚܐ *f* | ܕܐܪܒܝܐ] ܕܐܪܐܒܝܐ *e*, ܕܐܪܐܒܝܐ *f* | ܒܟܠܙܒܢ] ܒܟܠ | ܙܒܢ *j*
16. ܪ̈ܫܐ] ܪܫܐ *cf*, ܪ̈ܫܐ *e hj*
17. ܠܥܠܡܝܢ] ܠܥܠܡ *e**, sed c pr m | ܩܕܡ-ܫܡܫܐ] *f*mg‡ (praeter ܫܡܫ pro ܫܡܫܐ); > *e* | ܘܢܬܒܪܟܘܢ] *e** inc., sed c pr m uid. (s. puncto diacritico); ܢܬܒܪܟܘܢ *cf* | ܟܠܗܝܢ] bis scr. *e**(uid.) (!), sed 2° erasum est
18. ܕܐܝܣܪܐܝܠ] ܕܐܝܣܪܝܠ *e*, ܕܐܝܣܪܐܝܠ *hj*
19. ܘܒܪܝܟ] + ܗܘ *c hj* | ܠܥܠܡ 1°] ܘܠܥܠܡ *h* | ܠܥܠܡ 2°] ܘܠܥܠܡ *hj*
20. ܐܫܬܠܡܘ (*b* uid.)] ܐܫܬܠܡ *f* | ܕܐܝܫܝ] ܕܐܝܫܝ *e*

LXXII

[illegible]

1 [illegible]

2 [illegible]

3 [illegible]

4 [illegible]

5 [illegible]

6 [illegible]

7 [illegible]

8 [illegible]

9 [illegible]

LXXII

10 [illegible]

11 [illegible]

12 [illegible]

13 [illegible]

14 [illegible]

15 [illegible]

16 [illegible]

17 [illegible]

18 [illegible]

ab(c)e(fg) hj

LXXII

1. [illegible]] [illegible] *e*
2. [illegible]] ܕ sup. lin. pr m uid. (frt principio uerbum erat [illegible]) *j* | [illegible]] [illegible] *hj*
3. [illegible]] + [illegible] *j*
5. [illegible]] [illegible] *b j*(l) | [illegible]] [illegible] *e*
6. [illegible]] [illegible] *j*
9. [illegible]] [illegible] *f*, [illegible] *j*
10. [illegible]] [illegible] *ef*
11. [illegible]] [illegible] *bef hj*
12. [illegible]] c. sey. *e*, [illegible] *f*
13. [illegible]] [illegible] *f*
14. [illegible]] s. sey. *f j* (sey. inc. *h*)
15. [illegible]] [illegible] *f*, [illegible] *g j*; [illegible] *e* | [illegible]] *f*mg† | [illegible]] [illegible] *hj*
17. [illegible]] s. sey. *f hj*
18. [illegible]] s. sey. *f* ([illegible] [sic] *g*) | [illegible]] [illegible] *e*c pr m uid. *f h* | [illegible]] c. sey. *e*

LXXII

19 [illegible]

20 [illegible]

21 [illegible]

22 [illegible]

23 [illegible]

24 [illegible]

25 [illegible]

26 [illegible]

27 [illegible]

28 [illegible]

LXXII

LXXIII

1 [illegible]

2 [illegible]

3 [illegible]

4 [illegible]

5 [illegible]

6 [illegible]

7 [illegible]

8 [illegible]

9 [illegible]

abe(fg) hj(k)

23. ܠܥܠܡ ܥܠܡܝܢ] ܠܥܠܡ ܥܠܡ- ܘܠܥ- *f* mg* | ܘܠܥܠܡ ܥܠܡܝܢ *b*

26. ܠܒܝ > *a**, sed c pr m

27. ܕܢܦܩܘ] ܕܢܦܩܘ *f*

28. ܘܐܫܝܡ] ܘܐܫܝܡ *a**(uid.), sed ܘ 1° reficta est ad ܪ (qua manu inc.) | ܬܫܒܚܬܟ] post ܬ linea, magnam partem sub lin., pro ܝ (significatio lineae inc.) *e*

LXXIII

Insc. ܕܡܫܡܠܝܘܬܐ] ܠܐܣܦ tr. *j*

1. ܕܢܣܒܬ] ܕܢܣܒܬ *f*

2. ܐܬܪܦܝ] ܐܬܪܦܝ *e h* | ܐܬܗܦܟ] ܐܬܗܦܟ *f*

3. ܫܠܡܘܬܐ] s. sey. *h* | ܕܐܬܟܠܝ] ܕܐܬܟܠܝ *b*, ܕܐܬܟܠܝ *hj*

4. ܒܪܐ] c. sey. *f*

5. ܕܒܣܡܝܢܐ] c. sey. *f*

6. ܕܡܬܗܠ] s. sey. *h* | ܚܣܘܟܘ] ܚܣܘܟܘ *k*

8. ܐܬܪܥܝܘ] s. sey. *f jk* | ܬܘܩܦܐ] s. sey. *hjk* | ܘܐ > *e* | ܘܐܬܟܠܘ] ܘܐܬܟܠܘ *j*, ܘܐܬܟܠܘ *k*; ܢܬܟܠܘ *f*, ܢܬܟܠܘ *g* | ܒܬܫܘܥܬܗ] ܒܬܫܘܥܬܗ *hjk*

9. ܢܫܝܢ] ܢܫܝܢ *f*

LXXIII

10 [illegible]

11 [illegible]

12 [illegible]

13 [illegible]

14 [illegible]

15 [illegible]

16 [illegible]

17 [illegible]

18 [illegible]

19 [illegible]

20 [illegible]

21 [illegible]

22 [illegible]

23 [illegible]

abe(fg) hj(k)

11. [illegible]] [illegible] *ef j*, [illegible] *h*, [illegible] *k* | [illegible] > *k* | fin.] + [illegible] *k*
12. [illegible]] [illegible] *j**, sed - erasa est | [illegible]] [illegible] *hjk*
13. [illegible]] [illegible] *b* | [illegible]] [illegible] *e* | [illegible]] [illegible] *j** (= Pesh), sed [illegible] scriptum est sup. [illegible] (pr m uid.)
14. [illegible]] [illegible] *b*
15. [illegible]] c. sey. *a*mg*b*mg*ef hj* | [illegible] 2°] sub ※ *b* | [illegible]] [illegible] *e*, [illegible] *hj*
17. [illegible]] [illegible] *f* | [illegible]] [illegible] *e j*(s. punctis diacriticis)
18. [illegible]] [illegible] *e*
19. [illegible]] [illegible] *h*, [illegible] *j* | [illegible]] s. sey. *f*
20. [illegible]] [illegible] *ef j*, [illegible] *h* | [illegible]] [illegible] *b* | [illegible] > *e**, sed c pr m uid. | [illegible]] c. sey. *be hj*
21. [illegible]] [illegible] *e*, [illegible] *h*, [illegible] *j*
22. [illegible]] [illegible] *e*
23. [illegible]] [illegible] *e* | [illegible] > *e*

LXXIV

[illegible]

[illegible]

1 [illegible]

2 [illegible]

3 [illegible]

4 [illegible]

5 [illegible]

6 [illegible]

7 [illegible]

8 [illegible]

[illegible]

9 [illegible]

10 [illegible]

LXXV

[illegible]

1 [illegible]

2 [illegible]

3 [illegible]

4 [illegible]

5 [illegible]

6 [illegible]

a(b)e(fg) hj

LXXIV

Inscr. [illegible] *f*

2. [illegible] > *a**, sed c pr m | [illegible] > *e*

3. [illegible] *be* | [illegible] *bef hj* | [illegible] *b h*, [illegible] *f*, [illegible] *j*

5. [illegible] *j**(uid.) (= Pesh), sed c pr m

6. [illegible] *ef hj* | [illegible] sup. ras. (qua manu inc.) *j* | [illegible] *f*

8. [illegible] *f*

10. [illegible] c. sey. *j*; [illegible] (sic) *h*

LXXV

Inscr. [illegible] > *e** (l), sed c pr m

1. [illegible] bis scr. (l) *j**(uid.), sed 2° erasum est | [illegible] *e*, [illegible] *hj*

3. [illegible] *e hj* | [illegible] *e*, [illegible] *hj*

5. [illegible] *h*, [illegible] *j* | [illegible] fere totum sup. ras. (pr m) *a* | [illegible] 2°] litterae [illegible] refictae sunt (pr m?) *j*

LXXV

[Syriac]
7 [Syriac]
[Syriac]
[Syriac]
8 [Syriac]
[Syriac]
9 [Syriac]
[Syriac]
[Syriac]
10 [Syriac]
[Syriac]
[Syriac]
11 [Syriac]
[Syriac]
[Syriac]
12 [Syriac]
[Syriac]

LXXVI

[Syriac]
[Syriac]
1 [Syriac]
[Syriac]
2 [Syriac]

LXXVI

[Syriac]
[Syriac]
[Syriac]
[Syriac]
3 [Syriac]
[Syriac]
[Syriac]
4 [Syriac]
[Syriac]
5 [Syriac]
[Syriac]
[Syriac]
6 [Syriac]
[Syriac]
7 [Syriac]
[Syriac]
8 [Syriac]
[Syriac]
9 [Syriac]
[Syriac]
10 [Syriac]
[Syriac]

a(b)e hj

6. [Syriac]] [Syriac] *h*, [Syriac] *j*

7. [Syriac] > *e*

8. [Syriac]] [Syriac] *h*, [Syriac] *j*; [Syriac] *e*

9. [Syriac]] [Syriac] *j* | [Syriac]] [Syriac] *e* | [Syriac]] [Syriac] *b h*, [Syriac] *e*, [Syriac] *j*

10. [Syriac]] [Syriac] *be hj* | [Syriac]] [Syriac] *hj*

11. [Syriac]] [Syriac] *hj* (primo [Syriac] bis scr. uid. *j* [1], deinde 2° erasum est) | [Syriac]] [Syriac] *hj*

12. [Syriac] 1° > *e* | [Syriac]] [Syriac] *hj* | [Syriac]] [Syriac] *b* | [Syriac] 2°] [Syriac] *e*

LXXVI

Inscr. [Syriac]] [Syriac] *e*txt, [Syriac] *e*mg (adsignatur [[Syriac]]), [Syriac] *hj*

2. [Syriac]] [Syriac] *e**(sed c pr m) *j**(sed c pr m uid.) | [Syriac]] [Syriac] (sic) *j*

3. [Syriac]] [Syriac] *b* | [Syriac]] [Syriac] *b*, [Syriac] *h*, [Syriac] *e*, [Syriac] *j*

7. [Syriac]] c. sey. *be*

9. [Syriac]] [Syriac] *j**, sed correctum est (qua manu inc.) | [Syriac]] [Syriac] *be*

LXXVII

[Syriac] ⁘
1 [Syriac]
[Syriac]
2 [Syriac]
[Syriac]
3 [Syriac]
[Syriac]
4 [Syriac]
[Syriac]
[Syriac]
[Syriac]
[Syriac]
5 [Syriac]
[Syriac]
[Syriac]
[Syriac]
6 [Syriac]
[Syriac]
[Syriac]
[Syriac]
7 [Syriac]
[Syriac]
[Syriac]
[Syriac]

LXXVI

[Syriac] 11
[Syriac]
[Syriac]
[Syriac] 12
[Syriac]
[Syriac] 13
[Syriac]
[Syriac] 14
[Syriac]
[Syriac]
[Syriac] 15
[Syriac]
[Syriac] ⁘
[Syriac] 16
[Syriac]
[Syriac] 17
[Syriac]
[Syriac]
[Syriac]
[Syriac] 18
[Syriac]
[Syriac]
[Syriac] 19
[Syriac]
[Syriac]
[Syriac] 20
[Syriac] ⁘

a(b)e(fg) hj

11. [Syriac]] [Syriac] *e*, [Syriac] *j* | [Syriac]] pars inferior [Syriac] et [Syriac] totum sup. ras. (pr m uid.) *a* | [Syriac]] [Syriac] (*b*uid.) *hj*

14. [Syriac] > *e*

15. [Syriac]] [Syriac] *e*, [Syriac] *h*, [Syriac] *j*

16. [Syriac] 1° et 2°] [Syriac] *e*

17. [Syriac]] [Syriac] *e*, [Syriac] *h*, [Syriac] *j*

18. [Syriac] > *j** (l), sed uerba [Syriac] (= *h*) addita sunt pr m | [Syriac]] [Syriac] *e*

LXXVII

1. [Syriac]] [Syriac] *f*

3. [Syriac]] [Syriac] *e*; [Syriac] *f hj* | [Syriac]] s. sey. *e hj* | [Syriac]] [Syriac] *h* | [Syriac]] [Syriac] *j*

4. [Syriac]] [Syriac] *f* | [Syriac]] [Syriac] *a*mg*f*mg | [Syriac]] [Syriac] *e* | [Syriac]] [Syriac] sup. ras. (qua manu inc.) *a*; [Syriac] *f*; [Syriac] *h**, sed [Syriac] inserta est (pr m) inter [Syriac] et [Syriac]; [Syriac] *j*

5. [Syriac]] [Syriac] *f* | [Syriac]] [Syriac] *e* | [Syriac]] [Syriac] *f* | [Syriac]] s. sey. *e hj*

6. [Syriac]] s. sey. *e hj*

LXXVII

8 [illegible]
9 [illegible]
10 [illegible]
11 [illegible]
12 [illegible]
13 [illegible]
14 [illegible]
15 [illegible]
16 [illegible]
17 [illegible]
18 [illegible]
19 [illegible]

20 [illegible]
21 [illegible]
22 [illegible]
23 [illegible]
24 [illegible]
25 [illegible]
26 [illegible]
27 [illegible]
28 [illegible]
29 [illegible]
30 [illegible]

a(b)e(fg) hj(k)

8. [illegible]] ras. litterae unae inter [illegible] *e* | [illegible] 2°] [illegible] *h* | [illegible]] [illegible] *f*
10. [illegible]] [illegible] *ef j*, [illegible] *h*
11. [illegible]] s. sey. *f hj* | [illegible]] [illegible] *f* | [illegible]] [illegible] *b*
12. [illegible]] [illegible] *f j**(uid.)(qua manu correctum est inc.)
18. [illegible]] [illegible] *j*
20. [illegible] > *j*
21. [illegible]] [illegible] *j* | [illegible]] [illegible] *a*mg *b*mg *f*mg, [illegible] *g*mg | [illegible]] [illegible] *e*
23. [illegible]] [illegible] *f*
27. [illegible] > *j**, sed c pr m
28. [illegible]] c. sey. *f*, [illegible] *hjk* | [illegible]] s. sey. *k*
30. [illegible]] [illegible] *hjk*

LXXVII

31 [illegible]

32 [illegible]

33 [illegible]

34 [illegible]

35 [illegible]

36 [illegible]

37 [illegible]

38 [illegible]

39 [illegible]

40 [illegible]

41 [illegible]

42 [illegible]

43 [illegible]

44 [illegible]

45 [illegible]

46 [illegible]

47 [illegible]

48 [illegible]

49 [illegible]

50 [illegible]

51 [illegible]

a(b)e(f g) hj(k)

31. [illegible] *f* | [illegible] *e*, [illegible] *hjk*

33. [illegible] *j**, sed o inserta est (pr m uid.) inter [illegible] | [illegible] (sic) *k*

37. [illegible] > *k* | [illegible] *f*, [illegible] *j*; [illegible] *h*, [illegible] *k* | [illegible] *ef j*, [illegible] *hk*

38. [illegible] *g*] [illegible] *e h*, [illegible] *f j* | [illegible] > *j**, sed c pr m uid.

39. [illegible] *h*

40. [illegible] s. sey. *j* | [illegible] *hj*

41. [illegible] *e*, [illegible] *hj*

42. [illegible] *hj* | [illegible] c. sey. *f*

43. [illegible] *h*

44. [illegible] *hj* ([illegible] > *j** [l], sed c pr m); [illegible] *f*

45. [illegible] c. sey. *e hj* | [illegible] *h*, [illegible] *j*

46. [illegible] c. sey. *hj*

47. [illegible] *hj* | [illegible] *hj* | [illegible] *e j*

48. [illegible] *hj*

49. [illegible] *f*

50. [illegible] *f*

LXXVII

[illegible]
[illegible]
52 [illegible]
[illegible]
[illegible]
53 [illegible]
[illegible]
54 [illegible]
[illegible]
55 [illegible]
[illegible]
[illegible]
[illegible]
[illegible]
[illegible]
56 [illegible]
[illegible]
57 [illegible]
[illegible]
58 [illegible]
[illegible]
59 [illegible]
[illegible]
60 [illegible]
[illegible]

61 [illegible]
[illegible]
62 [illegible]
[illegible]
63 [illegible]
[illegible]
64 [illegible]
[illegible]
65 [illegible]
[illegible]
[illegible]
66 [illegible]
[illegible]
67 [illegible]
[illegible]
68 [illegible]
[illegible]
69 [illegible]
[illegible]
70 [illegible]
[illegible]
71 [illegible]
[illegible]
[illegible]
72 [illegible]

abe(fg) hj

51. [illegible]] [illegible] *ef hj* | [illegible]] c. sey. *j*; [illegible] *f*

52. [illegible]] [illegible] *hj*

53. [illegible]] [illegible] *f*

55. [illegible]] [illegible] *b**(sed correctum est per rasuram)*f* | [illegible]] c. sey. *f* | [illegible]] [illegible] *hj* | [illegible]] [illegible] *e*, [illegible] *h*

59. [illegible]] [illegible] *e*

60. [illegible]] [illegible] *e*

61. [illegible]] [illegible] *f* | [illegible]] [illegible] *hj* | [illegible]] c. sey. *ef*

63. [illegible]] [illegible] (sic) *j*txt, sed [illegible] (= *h*) scriptum est (pr m) in mg pro uerbo priore

64. [illegible] *g*] c. sey. *f*

65. [illegible]] [illegible] *j**, sed [illegible] inserta est inter [illegible] (qua manu inc.) | [illegible]] [illegible] *e*, [illegible] *f*, [illegible] *h*; [illegible] *j*

66. [illegible]] [illegible] *hj*

69. [illegible]] [illegible] *j**, sed c pr m uid. | [illegible]] [illegible] *h*

70. [illegible] > *j** (!), sed c pr m | [illegible]] s. sey. *f*

71. [illegible] *g*] [illegible] *bf*, [illegible] *e j* | [illegible]] [illegible] *e*

LXXVII

ܘܒܣܘܟܠܬܘܬܐ ܕܐܝܕܘܗܝ
ܕܒܪ ܐܢܘܢ. ܀

LXXVIII

ܡܙܡܘܪܐ ܕܐܣܦ ܀

1 ܐܠܗܐ ܥܠܘ ܥܡܡܐ ܠܝܪܬܘܬܟ
ܘܛܡܘ ܗܝܟܠܐ ܩܕܝܫܐ ܕܝܠܟ.
ܣܡܘ ܠܐܘܪܫܠܡ ܠܚܘܪܒܐ.
2 ܣܡܘ ܫܠܕܐ ܕܥܒ̈ܕܝܟ.
ܡܐܟܘܠܬܐ ܠܦܪ̈ܚܬܐ ܕܫܡܝܐ.
ܠܒܣܪܐ ܕܚܣ̈ܝܐ ܕܝܠܟ ܠܚܝܘܬ
ܒܪܐ ܕܐܪܥܐ.
3 ܐܫܕܘ ܕܡܗܘܢ ܐܝܟ ܡ̈ܝܐ.
ܚܕ̈ܪܝ ܐܘܪܫܠܡ ܘܠܐ ܐܝܬ
ܗܘܐ ܕܩܒܪ.
4 ܗܘܝܢ ܚܣܕܐ ܠܫ̈ܒܒܝܢ.
ܡܘܡܝܩܐ ܘܡܘܝܩܐ ܠܕܚܕ̈ܪܝܢ.
5 ܥܕܡܐ ܠܐܡܬܝ ܡܪܝܐ ܬܪܓܙ
ܠܓܡܪ.
ܬܐܩܕ ܐܝܟ ܢܘܪܐ ܚܣܡܟ.
6 ܐܫܘܕ ܚܡܬܟ ܥܠ ܥܡ̈ܡܐ
ܐܝܠܝܢ ܕܠܐ ܝܕܥܘܢ ܠܟ.
ܘܥܠ ܡܠܟܘ̈ܬܐ ܐܝܠܝܢ ܕܒܫܡܟ
ܠܐ ܩܪܘ.
7 ܡܛܠ ܕܐܟܠܘ ܠܝܥܩܘܒ ܘܠܕܘܟܬܗ
ܐܚܪܒܘ.
8 ܠܐ ܬܬܕܟܪ ܠܢ ܣܟ̈ܠܘܬܐ
ܕܝܠܢ ܩܕ̈ܡܝܬܐ.
ܥܓܠ ܢܩܕܡܘܢ ܠܐܦܝܢ ܪ̈ܚܡܝܟ ܡܪܝܐ.
ܡܛܠ ܕܐܬܡܣܟܢܢ ܛܒ.
9 ܥܕܪ ܠܢ ܐܠܗܢ ܦܪܘܩܢ.
ܡܛܠ ܫܘܒܚܐ ܕܫܡܟ ܡܪܝܐ.
ܦܪܘܩ ܠܢ.
ܘܫܒܘܩ ܥܠ ܚܛܗ̈ܝܢ ܡܛܠ ܫܡܟ.
10 ܕܠܡܐ ܢܐܡܪܘܢ ܥܡ̈ܡܐ
ܐܝܟܐ ܐܝܬܘܗܝ ܐܠܗܗܘܢ ܕܝܠܗܘܢ.
ܘܢܬܝܕܥ ܒܥܡ̈ܡܐ ܩܕܡ ܥܝܢ̈ܝܢ ܕܝܠܢ.
ܬܒܥܬܐ ܕܕܡܐ ܕܥܒ̈ܕܝܟ ܗܘ ܕܐܬܐܫܕ.
11 ܬܥܘܠ ܩܕܡܝܟ ܬܢܚܬܐ
ܕܐܣܝܪ̈ܐ ܕܟܦ̈ܝܦܝܢ.
ܐܝܟ ܪܒܘܬܐ ܕܕܪܥܟ.
ܫܒܘܩ ܠܒ̈ܢܝܐ ܕܩܛܝ̈ܠܐ ܕܡܚܝܠܝܢ.
12 ܦܪܘܥ ܠܫܒ̈ܒܝܢ ܫܒܥ ܥܦ̈ܝܦܐ
ܒܥܘܒܗܘܢ.
ܚܣܕܗܘܢ ܗܘ ܕܚܣܕܘܟ ܡܪܝܐ..
13 ܚܢܢ ܕܝܢ ܥܡܐ ܕܝܠܟ ܘܥܢ̈ܐ
ܕܪܥܝܬܐ ܕܝܠܟ.
ܢܘܕܐ ܠܟ ܐܠܗܐ ܠܥܠܡ.
ܠܕܪܐ ܘܠܕܪܐ ܢܫܬܥܐ ܬܫܒܘܚܬܟ ܀

LXXIX

ܒܫܠܡܐ ܫܠܡ [illegible]
ܬܫܒܘܚܬܐ. ܠܐܣܦ ܡܙܡܘܪܐ ܀

a(b)e(f g) hj

72. ܘܒܣܘܟܠܬܘܬܐ] s. sey. *f*

LXXVIII

1. ܘܛܡܘ] ܘܛܡܘ *b*, ܘܛܡܘ *e*, ܘܛܡܘ *h* | ܣܡܘ] ܣܡܘ *h*; ܘܣܡܘ *j* | ܠܐܘܪܫܠܡ] ܠܐܘܪܫܠܡ *e*, ܠܐܘܪܫܠܡ *j*
2. ܕܥܒ̈ܕܝܟ] s. sey. *f* | ܚܣܝܐ] c. sey. *e*
3. ܐܘܪܫܠܡ] ܐܘܪܫܠܡ *e*, ܐܘܪܫܠܡ *j*
4. ܘܡܘܝܩܐ] ܘܡܝܩܐ *be**(sed ܘ inserta est [pr m uid.] inter ܡܝ) *hj*
5. ܬܪܓܙ ܠܓܡܪ] tr. *a**, sed c pr m | ܠܓܡܪ] ܠܓܡܪ *f*
8. ܠܐܦܝܢ] ܠܐܦܝܢ *b*(etiam punctum paruum sup. ܠ 1°, frt macula est), ܠܐܦ̈ܝܢ *h* | ܕܐܬܡܣܟܢܢ] ܕܐܬܡܣܟܢܢ *h*
11. ܬܥܘܠ] ܬܥܘܠ *e*, ܬܥܘܠ *j* | ܬܢܚܬܐ] c. sey. *f* | ܕܐܣܝܪܐ 1°] ܕܐܣܝܪ̈ܐ *e hj* | ܕܩܛܝ̈ܠܐ] c. sey. *e*
12. ܕܚܣܕܘܟ] ܕܚܣܕܘܟ *e*
13. ܢܫܬܥܐ] ܢܫܬܥܐ *h*, ܢܫܬܥܐ *j*

LXXIX

Insc. ܡܙܡܘܪܐ *f*] > *g**, sed c pr m

LXXIX

[illegible] 1
[illegible]
[illegible]
[illegible] 2
[illegible]
[illegible] 3
[illegible]
[illegible] 4
[illegible]
[illegible]
[illegible] 5
[illegible]
[illegible] 6
[illegible]
[illegible] 7
[illegible]
[illegible]
[illegible] 8
[illegible]
[illegible] 9
[illegible]
[illegible] 10
[illegible]
[illegible] 11
[illegible]
[illegible] 12
[illegible]

13 [illegible]
[illegible]
14 [illegible]
[illegible]
[illegible]
15 [illegible]
[illegible]
[illegible]
16 [illegible]
[illegible]
17 [illegible]
[illegible]
[illegible]
18 [illegible]
[illegible]
[illegible]
[illegible]
19 [illegible]
[illegible]

LXXX [illegible]
[illegible]
1 [illegible]
[illegible]
[illegible]
2 [illegible]
[illegible]
3 [illegible]

ae(fg) hj(k)

1. [illegible]] [illegible] *ef hj* | [illegible]] c. sey. *f*
2. [illegible]] [illegible] *h*
5. [illegible]] [illegible] *f*
7. [illegible]] [illegible] *e*, [illegible] *f h*, [illegible] *j*
8. [illegible]] [illegible] sup. ras. (pr m uid.) *j*
10. [illegible]] primo *e* testabatur lemma, deinde [illegible] adfixa est uid. (pr m) | [illegible]] [illegible] *e* ([illegible] sup. ras., frt pr m); [illegible] *hjk*
12. [illegible]] [illegible] *h*
13. [illegible]] [illegible] *k* | [illegible]] [illegible] *j**(uid.) (cf. Pesh), sed c pr m | [illegible]] [illegible] *k* | [illegible]] [illegible] *f*; [illegible] *hjk*; [illegible] (pro [illegible]) *a*mg*f*mg (frt lectio ε': cf. Field)
14. [illegible]] [illegible] *e* | [illegible]] + [illegible] *k* | [illegible]] [illegible] (sic) *k*
16. [illegible]] [illegible] *hjk* ([illegible] pro [illegible] *j**[uid.], sed c pr m uid.)
17. [illegible]] [illegible] *hj* | [illegible] > *h* (!)
18. [illegible] > *e*

LXXX

3. [illegible]] c. sey. *hj* | [illegible]] c. sey. *f*

LXXX

[illegible]
4 [illegible]
[illegible]
5 [illegible]
[illegible]
[illegible]
6 [illegible]
[illegible]
7 [illegible]
[illegible]
[illegible]
[illegible]
8 [illegible]
[illegible]
9 [illegible]
[illegible]
10 [illegible]
[illegible]
[illegible]
11 [illegible]
[illegible]
12 [illegible]
[illegible]
[illegible]
13 [illegible]
[illegible]
14 [illegible]
[illegible]
[illegible]
[illegible]
15 [illegible]
[illegible]
16 [illegible]
[illegible]

ae(fg) hj

4. [illegible]] [illegible] *e*, [illegible] *f hj*
5. [illegible]] [illegible] *h*
6. [illegible]] [illegible] *hj* | [illegible]] [illegible] *f*
7. [illegible]] [illegible] *f* (*g* hab. [illegible]) | [illegible]] [illegible] *e*, [illegible] *f j*, [illegible] *h*
8. [illegible]] [illegible] *f* (macula antecedit [illegible], sed nullum uestigium litterae apparet) | [illegible]] [illegible] *e* | [illegible]] [illegible] *h*
10. [illegible]] [illegible] *e hj*; [illegible] *g* ([illegible] tantum apparet in *f*)
11. [illegible]] [illegible] *e*, [illegible] *h*
12. [illegible]] [illegible] *f* ([illegible] *g*) | [illegible]] [illegible] *hj*
13. [illegible]] [illegible] *e*, [illegible] *g hj* | [illegible] *g**(uid.)] [illegible] *g*c pr m uid.
14. [illegible]] [illegible] *hj*

LXXXI

[illegible]
1 [illegible]
[illegible]
2 [illegible]
[illegible]
[illegible]
[illegible]
3 [illegible]
[illegible]
4 [illegible]
[illegible]
5 [illegible]
[illegible]
[illegible]
6 [illegible]
[illegible]
7 [illegible]
[illegible]

[illegible]
8 [illegible]
[illegible]

LXXXII

[illegible]
1 [illegible]
[illegible]
2 [illegible]
[illegible]
3 [illegible]
[illegible]
4 [illegible]
[illegible]
[illegible]
5 [illegible]
[illegible]
6 [illegible]
[illegible]

αe(fg) hj

LXXXI

Inscr. ܡܙܡܘܪܐ ܠܐܣܦ] tr. *j*

1. [illegible]] [illegible] sup. ras. *e*; [illegible] *j**(uid.), sed c pr m | [illegible]] [illegible] *g j*, [illegible] *h*

2. [illegible]] c. sey. *eg h* | [illegible]] [illegible] *e*, [illegible] *g j*, [illegible] *h*

3. [illegible]] [illegible] *g*

4. [illegible]] [illegible] *g* | [illegible]] [illegible] (sic) *g*

5. [illegible]] [illegible] *j* | [illegible]] [illegible] *j**(uid.) (= Pesh), sed c pr m

7. [illegible]] [illegible] *j*

8. [illegible]] [illegible] *hj* | [illegible]] [illegible] *e*

LXXXII

Inscr. [illegible]] s. sey. *ef j* (littera paenultima in *h* hab. nec punctum [illegible] nec sey.)

1. [illegible]] litterae [illegible] sup. ras. (pr m uid.) *j* | [illegible]] [illegible] *f* | [illegible]] [illegible] *ef* uid. (punctum languet, sed hab. *g*), [illegible] *j*

3. [illegible]] [illegible] *j**, sed [illegible] adfixa est (pr m uid.)

4. [illegible]] [illegible] *f* | [illegible]] [illegible] (sic) *e* | [illegible]] [illegible] *e h*, [illegible] *j*

5. [illegible]] [illegible] *ef j*, [illegible] *h*

6. [illegible]] [illegible] *ef*

LXXXII

7 [illegible]

8 [illegible]

9 [illegible]

10 [illegible]

11 [illegible]

12 [illegible]

13 [illegible]

14 [illegible]

15 [illegible]

16 [illegible]

17 [illegible]

18 [illegible]

LXXXIII

1 [illegible]

2 [illegible]

3 [illegible]

4 [illegible]

ae(fg) hj

7. [illegible]] [illegible] *e*txt, [illegible] *e*mg (adsignatur [illegible]), [illegible] *j*

8. [illegible]] [illegible] *e*, [illegible] *f hj*

9. [illegible]] [illegible] *e* | [illegible]] [illegible] *g*([illegible] *f*) *h*

10. [illegible]] [illegible] *e*

11. [illegible]] [illegible] *a**(sed c pr m) *j**(qua manu correctum est inc.) | [illegible] 2° *f*] [illegible] *g*

16. [illegible]] [illegible] *j* (uerbum prius c. sey. in *h*)

17. [illegible]] [illegible] *hj*

LXXXIII

Inscr. [illegible]] [illegible] *j**, sed c pr m | [illegible]] [illegible] *e*

1. [illegible]] s. sey. *hj* | [illegible] > *e** (!), sed c pr m

2. [illegible] *f*] [illegible] *eg**(uid.)(sed c pr m uid.) | [illegible]] s. sey. *f*

3. [illegible]] [illegible] *e*

4. [illegible]] s. sey. *f*; [illegible] *hj* | [illegible]] [illegible] *j**(uid.), sed [illegible] erasum est et [illegible] refictum est (pr m uid.) ad [illegible] ([illegible] *h*) | [illegible]] s. sey. *eg* ([illegible] *f*) | [illegible]] s. sey. *g*(sey. inc. in *f*) *hj* | [illegible]] [illegible] *e*, [illegible] *f*mg; [illegible] u. 4 ∩ u. 8 praeter hab. [illegible] *hj*

LXXXIII

5 ܛܘܒܘܗܝ ܗܘ ܠܓܒܪܐ ܗܘ
ܕܐܝܬܘܗܝ ܡܥܕܪܢܘܬܗ ܠܘܬܟ.
ܡܣܩ̈ܢܘܬܐ ܒܠܒܗ ܣܡ.
6 ܗܘܝܘ ܕܥܒܪܝܢ ܒܥܘܡܩܐ
ܕܒܟܝܬܐ ܠܐܬܪܐ ܗܘ ܕܣܡܗ.
ܐܦ ܓܝܪ ܒܘܪ̈ܟܬܐ ܢܬܠ ܗܘ
ܕܣܐܡ ܢܡܘܣܐ.
7 ܢܐܙܠܘܢ ܡܢ ܚܝܠܐ ܠܚܝܠܐ.
ܢܬܚܙܐ ܐܠܗܐ ܕܐܠܗ̈ܐ ܒܨܗܝܘܢ.
8 ܡܪܝܐ ܐܠܗܐ ܕܚܝ̈ܠܘܬܐ.
ܫܡܥ ܨܠܘܬܝ ܕܝܠܝ.
ܨܘܬ ܐܠܗܗ ܕܝܥܩܘܒ.
ܕܫܘܠܡܗܘܢ ⁘
9 ܡܣܬܬܪܢܐ ܕܝܠܢ ܚܙܝ ܐܠܗܐ.
ܘܚܘܪ ܒܦܪܨܘܦܗ ܕܡܫܝܚܟ.
10 ܡܛܠ ܕܡܫܒܚ ܝܘܡܐ ܚܕ
ܒܕܪ̈ܬܟ ܛܒ ܡܢ ܐ̈ܠܦܐ.
ܓܒܝܬ ܠܡܫܬܕܝܘ ܒܒܝܬܗ
ܕܐܠܗܐ ܕܝܠܝ ܝܬܝܪܐܝܬ.
ܐܘ ܕܐܥܡܪ ܒܡܫܟܢ̈ܐ ܕܚܛܝ̈ܐ.
11 ܡܛܠ ܕܪ̈ܚܡܬܐ ܘܫܪܪܐ ܪܚܡ
ܡܪܝܐ ܐܠܗܐ.
ܛܝܒܘܬܐ ܘܫܘܒܚܐ ܢܬܠ ܐܠܗܐ.
ܡܪܝܐ ܠܐ ܢܟܠܐ ܛܒ̈ܬܐ ܠܗܠܝܢ
ܕܪܕܝܢ ܒܬܡܝܡܘܬܐ.
12 ܡܪܝܐ ܐܠܗܐ ܕܚܝ̈ܠܘܬܐ.
ܛܘܒܝܗ ܗܘ ܠܓܒܪܐ ܕܡܣܒܪ ܒܟ ⁘

LXXXIV

ܠܡܫܠܡܢܘܬܐ ܠܒܢ̈ܝܐ ܕܩܘܪܚ ܡܙܡܘܪܐ ⁘
1 ܐܨܛܒܝܬ ܡܪܝܐ ܒܐܪܥܐ ܕܝܠܟ.
ܐܦܢܝܬ ܫܒܝܬܗ ܕܝܥܩܘܒ.
2 ܫܒܩܬ ܠܗ ܠܥܘܠܘ̈ܬܐ
ܕܥܡܐ ܕܝܠܟ.
ܚܦܝܬ ܟܠܗܘܢ ܚܛܗ̈ܝܗܘܢ.
ܕܫܘܠܡܗܘܢ ⁘
3 ܫܠܝܬ ܟܠܗ ܪܘܓܙܟ.

ae(fg) hj

6. ܗܘܝܘ] ܗܘܝ *e*^c pr m uid. (erat ܗܘܝܘ) | ܕܢܬܠ] ܕܢܬܠܘܢ *ef* | ܕܗܘܝܘ] ܕܗܘܝ *e*^c pr m (erat ܕܗܘܝܘ)
8. ܕܫܘܠܡܗܘܢ] tantum hab. ܕ (?) s. puncto *e*; ܕܫܘܠܡܐ *g* (tantum litterae ܕܫ apparent in *f*); de *hj* cf. u. 4
10. ܚܘܒܐ] ܘ sup. ras. (pr m uid.) *j*

LXXXIV

Inscr. ܕܩܘܪܚ] ܕܩܘܪܚܝ *e*
2. ܒܐܪܥܐ] ܠܐܪܥܐ *hj* | ܫܒܝܬܗ] ܫܒܝܬ *f j*, ܫܒܝܬ *h* | ܠܥܘܠܘ̈ܬܐ] ܥܘܠܘ̈ܬܐ *j* | ܕܫܘܠܡܗܘܢ] ܕܦܘܫܠܡܗܘܢ *e*, ܕܦܘܫܠܡܐ *h*, ܕܫܘܠܡܐ *j*
3. ܟܠܗ] ܟܠܗ *ef hj*

LXXXIV

[illegible]
4 [illegible]
[illegible]
5 [illegible]
[illegible]
6 [illegible]
[illegible]
[illegible]
7 [illegible]
[illegible]
8 [illegible]
[illegible]
[illegible]
[illegible]
[illegible]
[illegible]
9 [illegible]
[illegible]
10 [illegible]
[illegible]
11 [illegible]
[illegible]
12 [illegible]
[illegible]
13 [illegible]
[illegible]

LXXXV

[illegible]
1 [illegible]
[illegible]
[illegible]
2 [illegible]
[illegible]
[illegible]
3 [illegible]
[illegible]
4 [illegible]
[illegible]
5 [illegible]
[illegible]
[illegible]
6 [illegible]
[illegible]
7 [illegible]
[illegible]
8 [illegible]
[illegible]
9 [illegible]
[illegible]
[illegible]
10 [illegible]
[illegible]
[illegible]

a(b)e(fg) hj

4. [illegible]] [illegible] *g* (macula antecedit [illegible] in *f*, itaque [illegible] inc.)
9. [illegible]] [illegible] *ef hj*
10. [illegible]] [illegible] *f*
12. [illegible] > *j* | [illegible]] [illegible] *f* | [illegible]] [illegible] *e*
13. [illegible]] [illegible] *e*; > *j**, sed [illegible] additum est (pr m uid.) | [illegible]] [illegible] *e j*(s. puncto diacritico) | [illegible]] [illegible] *e*

LXXXV

3. [illegible]] [illegible] *be hj*
10. [illegible]] + [illegible] *hj* | [illegible]] [illegible] *hj*

LXXXV

11 [illegible]
[illegible]
[illegible]
12 [illegible]
[illegible]
13 [illegible]
[illegible]
[illegible]
14 [illegible]
[illegible]
[illegible]
[illegible]
15 [illegible]
[illegible]
[illegible]
16 [illegible]
[illegible]
[illegible]
17 [illegible]
[illegible]
[illegible]

LXXXVI

[illegible]
[illegible]
1 [illegible]
2 [illegible]
[illegible]
[illegible]
3 [illegible]
[illegible]
[illegible]
4 [illegible]
[illegible]
[illegible]
[illegible]
5 [illegible]
[illegible]
[illegible]
6 [illegible]
[illegible]
[illegible]
7 [illegible]
[illegible]

abe(fg) hj

11. [illegible]] [illegible] *a*mg *b*mg (uerbum prius c. puncto superiore) *f*mg
12. [illegible]] [illegible] *hj* ([illegible] > *j** [I], sed c pr m)
13. [illegible]] s. sey. *f hj*
14. [illegible]] [illegible] *e*; [illegible] *hj*
15. [illegible]] [illegible] *f j**(uid.)(sed c pr m)
16. [illegible]] [illegible] *f*

LXXXVI

Inscr. [illegible]] [illegible] *e*
3. [illegible]] [illegible] *e**(uid.), sed c pr m | [illegible]] [illegible] *b h*, [illegible] *e*, [illegible] *f j*
4. [illegible]] [illegible] *e* | [illegible]] [illegible] *e j* | [illegible] *a*mg *b*mg
5. [illegible]] [illegible] *a*mg *b*mg (adsignatur [illegible]); [illegible] *f*mg (adsignatur [illegible]) | [illegible]] [illegible] *e* | [illegible]] [illegible] *hj* | [illegible]] [illegible] *hj*
6. [illegible]] [illegible] *bef j* | [illegible]] [illegible] *ef* c pr m uid. *hj*, [illegible] *f**(sed [illegible] uid. [quamquam punctum non apparet] inserta est inter [illegible]) *g* | [illegible]] [illegible] *f*; [illegible] *hj* | [illegible]] [illegible] *b*txt ([illegible] [sic] *h*), [illegible] *e*, [illegible] *f*mg *j*; [illegible] *a*mg *b*mg
7. [illegible]] [illegible] *f* | [illegible]] [illegible] *bef*uid. ([illegible], *g* hab. [illegible]) *hj* | [illegible]] c. sey. *e j*

LXXXVII

[illegible]
[illegible]
[illegible]
[illegible]
[illegible] 1
[illegible]
[illegible] 2
[illegible]
[illegible] 3
[illegible]
[illegible] 4
[illegible]
[illegible] 5
[illegible]
[illegible]
[illegible]
[illegible] 6
[illegible]
[illegible] 7
[illegible]

LXXXVII

8 [illegible]
[illegible]
[illegible]
9 [illegible]
[illegible]
[illegible]
10 [illegible]
[illegible]
[illegible]
11 [illegible]
[illegible]
12 [illegible]
[illegible]
13 [illegible]
[illegible]
14 [illegible]
[illegible]

abe(fg) hj

LXXXVII

Inscr. [illegible] *e* | [illegible] > *j**, sed c pr m | [illegible] *e* (littera secunda breuis est plus solito et littera alia erat uid., sed qua manu reficta est inc.), [illegible] *hj* | [illegible] *e*, [illegible] *f* | [illegible] *a*mg*b*mg, [illegible] *e* | [illegible] *b* inter textum et marginem in manu seriore | [illegible] *e*

1. [illegible] ∩ [illegible] u. 2 *e**, sed uerba [illegible] inserta sunt (pr m)

2. [illegible] *j*; de *e* cf. supra

4. [illegible] *j* | [illegible] *b*

5. [illegible] *b* | [illegible] *f*; [illegible] *be hj* | [illegible] *f* | [illegible] *h*

6. [illegible] *a*mg*b*mg*e*fmg *hj* | [illegible] *ef h*, [illegible] *j*

7. [illegible] *a*mg*b*mg*f*mg(praeter punctum uel macula sup. [illegible], sed puncta sey. apparent nec in *f*mg nec in *g*mg) | fin.] + [illegible] *f*, + [illegible] *hj*

8. [illegible] *f*

10. [illegible] *e* | [illegible] *b h*, [illegible] *e*, [illegible] *f*mg(in textu *g*) *j*

11. [illegible] c. sey. *j**(uid.) (cf. Pesh), sed punctum alterum apud [illegible] erasum est

13. [illegible] *j**(uid.) (cf. Pesh), sed refictum est (pr m) ad [illegible] | [illegible] tr. *e*

14. [illegible] *f*, [illegible] *g*

LXXXVII

[illegible] 15
[illegible]
[illegible]
[illegible]
[illegible] 16
[illegible]
[illegible] 17
[illegible]
[illegible] 18
[illegible]

LXXXVIII

[illegible]
[illegible]
[illegible] 1
[illegible]
[illegible]
[illegible] 2
[illegible]
[illegible]

LXXXVIII

3 [illegible]
[illegible]
4 [illegible]
[illegible]
[illegible]
5 [illegible]
[illegible]
6 [illegible]
[illegible]
[illegible]
7 [illegible]
[illegible]
[illegible]
[illegible]
8 [illegible]
[illegible]
[illegible]
9 [illegible]
[illegible]
[illegible]

abe(fg) hj

15. [illegible] s. sey. *f* | [illegible] tr. *a**, sed c pr m | [illegible] *f*] [illegible] (sic) *g*
16. [illegible] *hj**(sed c pr m) | [illegible] *h*, [illegible] *j* | [illegible] (sic) in linea *f*, sed [illegible] sub lin. (pr m uid.) | [illegible] *e*, [illegible] *f j*
18. [illegible] s. sey. *h* | [illegible] > *e*

LXXXVIII

Inscr. [illegible] *e*
1. [illegible] c. sey. *f*
2. [illegible] *j**(uid.) (= Pesh), sed c pr m | [illegible] c. sey. *e* | [illegible] *e*; [illegible] *h*; [illegible] *j* | [illegible] (sic notae) *e*; [illegible] *hj*
3. [illegible] *ef j*, [illegible] *h* | [illegible] s. sey. *f*
4. [illegible] *e* (punctum superius minus est quam punctum inferius), [illegible] *j* | [illegible] *b* | [illegible] *b h*, [illegible] *e*, [illegible] *f j*
5. [illegible] s. sey. *hj* | [illegible] sup. ras., sed pr m *a* | [illegible] *e*
6. [illegible] *a*mg*b*mg, [illegible] (sic) *f*mg | [illegible] c. sey. *f*
7. [illegible] s. sey. *b*txt*e hj*; [illegible] *f*txt; [illegible] *a*mg*b*mg*f*mg; [illegible] *f*mg (adsignatur [illegible]) | [illegible] *hj* | [illegible] *be hj* | [illegible] s. sey. *h*

LXXXVIII

10 [illegible]

11 [illegible]

12 [illegible]

13 [illegible]

14 [illegible]

15 [illegible]

16 [illegible]

17 [illegible]

LXXXVIII

[illegible]

18 [illegible]

19 [illegible]

20 [illegible]

21 [illegible]

22 [illegible]

23 [illegible]

24 [illegible]

25 [illegible]

abe(fg) hj

10. [illegible]] c. sey. *f* | [illegible]] c. sey. *g* (in *f* punctum unum apparet sup. [illegible], aliud obscuratur uid. a macula)
11. [illegible]] s. sey. *j* | [illegible]] [illegible] *hj*
12. [illegible]] [illegible] *f*
13. [illegible]] [illegible] *e* | [illegible]] [illegible] *e*; [illegible] *hj*
14. [illegible]] ras. post lemma (ex uestigiis erat frt [illegible]) *j*
17. [illegible]] [illegible] *e*
18. [illegible]] [illegible] *e*, [illegible] *hj*
19. [illegible]] [illegible] *a*mg*b*mg*ef*mg(adsignatur α'σ', sed cf. "Appendix: C.") *hj*
20. [illegible]] [illegible] *b j*, [illegible] *e h*
21. [illegible]] [illegible] (sic) *h*; *j* nunc hab. lemma (s. puncto diacritico), sed litterae [illegible] partim sup. ras. uid. et [illegible] uid. erasa est apud initium uerbi
23. [illegible]] [illegible] *f* | [illegible]] [illegible] *j*
24. [illegible]] [illegible] *e*
25. [illegible]] [illegible] *h*

LXXXVIII

[illegible]
26 [illegible]
[illegible]
27 [illegible]
[illegible]
28 [illegible]
[illegible]
29 [illegible]
[illegible]
30 [illegible]
[illegible]
31 [illegible]
[illegible]
32 [illegible]
[illegible]
[illegible]
33 [illegible]
[illegible]
34 [illegible]
[illegible]
[illegible]
35 [illegible]
[illegible]
36 [illegible]
[illegible]

37 [illegible]
[illegible]
38 [illegible]
[illegible]
39 [illegible]
[illegible]
40 [illegible]
[illegible]
41 [illegible]
[illegible]
42 [illegible]
[illegible]
43 [illegible]
[illegible]
44 [illegible]
[illegible]
45 [illegible]
[illegible]
[illegible]
46 [illegible]
[illegible]
[illegible]
47 [illegible]
[illegible]
[illegible]
[illegible]

abe(fg) hj

26. [illegible]] [illegible] *h*, [illegible] *j*

28. [illegible]] [illegible] *ef j*, [illegible] *h* | [illegible]] [illegible] *f*

29. [illegible] *g*(s. puncto)] [illegible] *f**, sed *l* inserta est pr m uid.

31. [illegible]] *f*mg†([illegible] [sic] pro [illegible] *g*mg†)

32. [illegible]] [illegible] *j* | [illegible]] [illegible] *h* (in *j* uerbum prius c. sey.)

33. [illegible]] [illegible] *hj*

34. [illegible]] [illegible] *ef j*, [illegible] *h*

35. [illegible]] [illegible] *b* | [illegible]] [illegible] *f*

36. [illegible]] [illegible] *hj*

37. [illegible]] + [illegible] *h*, + [illegible] *j*

39. [illegible]] [illegible] *ef j*, [illegible] *h*

41. [illegible]] [illegible] sup. ras. pr m *a*; [illegible] *hj*

42. [illegible] > *e** (homtel.), sed c pr m

44. [illegible]] [illegible] *b*, [illegible] *ef h*, [illegible] *j* | [illegible] > *e** (l), sed c pr m

45. [illegible]] [illegible] *e**(uid.), sed c pr m | [illegible]] [illegible] *b j*, [illegible] *e*, [illegible] *f*mg *h*

46. [illegible] > *j** (l), sed c pr m

47. [illegible]] [illegible] *e* | [illegible]] [illegible] *j* | [illegible]] c. sey. *be*

LXXXVIII

48 [illegible]
[illegible]
[illegible]
49 [illegible]
[illegible]
[illegible]
50 [illegible]
[illegible]
[illegible]
51 [illegible]
[illegible]
[illegible]
52 [illegible]
[illegible]

LXXXIX

1 [illegible]
[illegible]
2 [illegible]
[illegible]
[illegible]
3 [illegible]
[illegible]
4 [illegible]
[illegible]
[illegible]
5 [illegible]
[illegible]
[illegible]
6 [illegible]
[illegible]
7 [illegible]
[illegible]
8 [illegible]
[illegible]
9 [illegible]
[illegible]
[illegible]
[illegible]

abe(fg) hj

48. [illegible]] [illegible] *j* | [illegible]] [illegible] *b h*, [illegible] *e*, [illegible] *f j*
50. [illegible]] [illegible] *e*, [illegible] *hj*
52. [illegible] 2°] [illegible] *hj*

LXXXIX

1. [illegible]] [illegible] *f*
2. [illegible]] [illegible] *bef*, [illegible] *h*, [illegible] *j* | [illegible]] [illegible] *e*; [illegible] *j*
3. [illegible]] [illegible] *b*, [illegible] *f*, [illegible] *h*; [illegible] (sic) *j**, sed [illegible] addita est sup. [illegible] et punctum sup. [illegible] (qua manu inc.); [illegible] *e**, sed c pr m | [illegible]] [illegible] *h*, [illegible] *j* | [illegible]] [illegible] *h* | [illegible]] c. sey. *be*
4. [illegible]] [illegible] *e hj* | [illegible]] [illegible] *hj*
5. [illegible]] s. sey. *f* | [illegible]] [illegible] *b hj*, [illegible] *e*, [illegible] *f* | [illegible]] [illegible] *e*; [illegible] *hj*
6. [illegible]] [illegible] *j*
9. [illegible]] [illegible] e^{c} (qua manu inc.)

LXXXIX

[illegible] 10
[illegible]
[illegible]
[illegible]
[illegible]
[illegible] 11
[illegible]
[illegible] 12
[illegible]
[illegible] 13
[illegible]
[illegible] 14
[illegible]
[illegible] 15
[illegible]
[illegible] 16
[illegible]

LXXXIX

17 [illegible]
[illegible]
[illegible]

XC [illegible]

1 [illegible]
[illegible]
2 [illegible]
[illegible]
[illegible]
3 [illegible]
[illegible]
[illegible]
4 [illegible]
[illegible]
[illegible]
5 [illegible]
[illegible]

abe(fg) hj

10. [illegible]] + [illegible] *bef hj* | [illegible]] c. sey. *e* | [illegible] *f j* | [illegible]] [illegible] *e* | [illegible]] [illegible] *e*; [illegible] *j* (in *h* uerbum prius est [illegible])
11. [illegible]] [illegible] *e*
12. [illegible]] [illegible] *e* | [illegible]] [illegible] *f* | [illegible]] [illegible] *ef*, [illegible] *hj*
13. [illegible]] [illegible] (sic) *e*
14. [illegible]] + [illegible] *e*mg | [illegible]] punctum superius reprobatum est pr m *a* | [illegible]] + [illegible] *e*c pr m | frt erant duo stichi in *e* (sicut in lemmate: cf. Rahlfs), sed nunc sunt tres ([illegible] ad [illegible] [cf. sup.], [illegible] ad [illegible] u. 15)
17. [illegible]] c. sey. *hj*

XC

Inscr. [illegible]] [illegible] *f*
1. [illegible]] [illegible] *f*
4. [illegible] (inc.)] [illegible] *ef* | [illegible]] [illegible] *e h*
5. [illegible]] [illegible] *e* | [illegible] 2°] [illegible] *e*

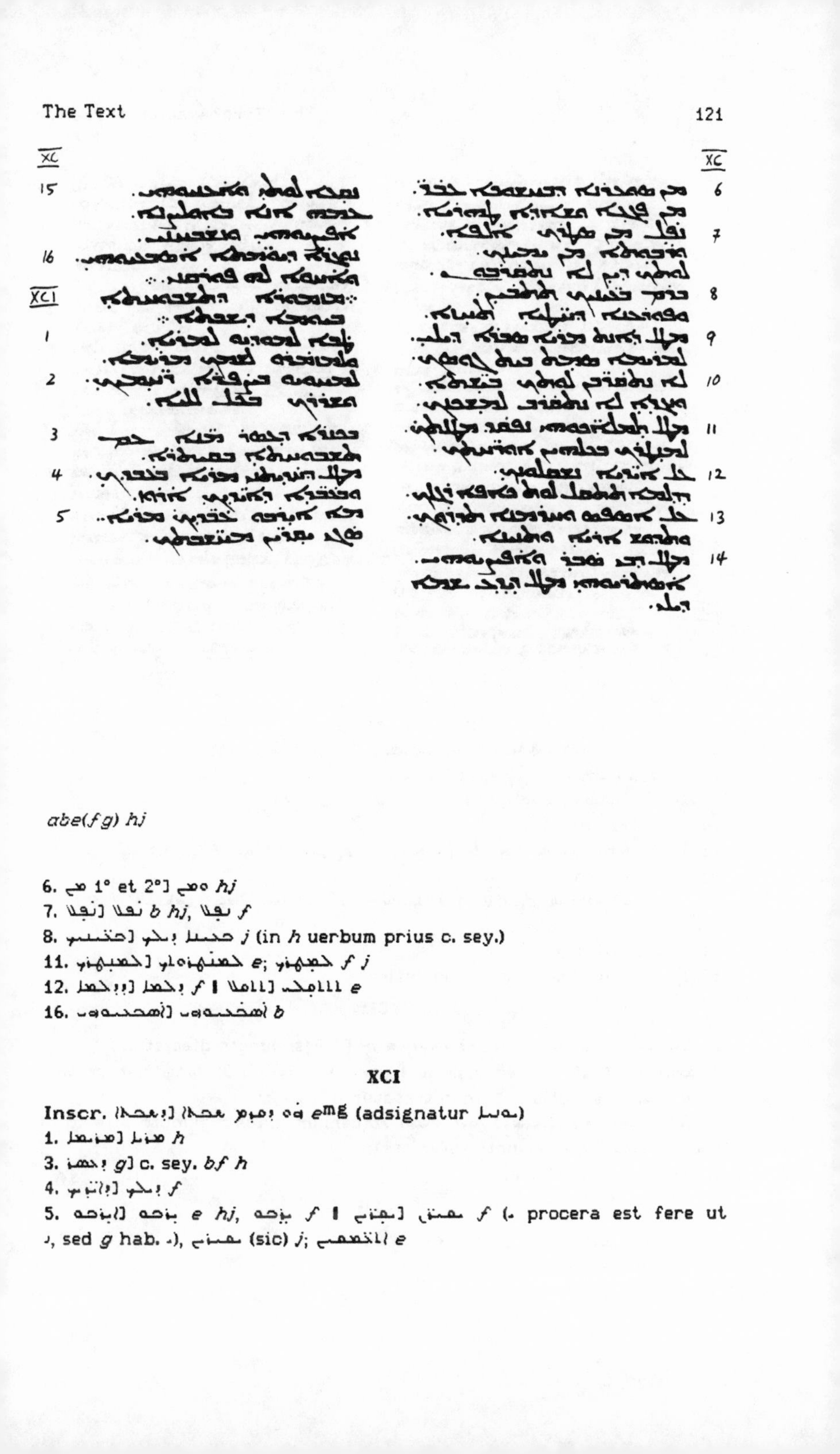

XC

6 [illegible]
[illegible]
7 [illegible]
[illegible]
[illegible]
8 [illegible]
[illegible]
9 [illegible]
[illegible]
10 [illegible]
[illegible]
11 [illegible]
[illegible]
12 [illegible]
[illegible]
13 [illegible]
[illegible]
14 [illegible]
[illegible]
[illegible]

15 [illegible]
[illegible]
[illegible]
16 [illegible]
[illegible]

XCI [illegible]
[illegible]
1 [illegible]
[illegible]
2 [illegible]
[illegible]
3 [illegible]
[illegible]
4 [illegible]
[illegible]
5 [illegible]
[illegible]

abe(fg) hj

6. [illegible] 1° et 2°] [illegible] *hj*
7. [illegible]] [illegible] *b hj*, [illegible] *f*
8. [illegible]] [illegible] *j* (in *h* uerbum prius c. sey.)
11. [illegible]] [illegible] *e*; [illegible] *f j*
12. [illegible]] [illegible] *f* | [illegible]] [illegible] *e*
16. [illegible]] [illegible] *b*

XCI

Insc. [illegible]] [illegible] *e*mg (adsignatur [illegible])
1. [illegible]] [illegible] *h*
3. [illegible] *g*] c. sey. *bf h*
4. [illegible]] [illegible] *f*
5. [illegible]] [illegible] *e hj*, [illegible] *f* | [illegible]] [illegible] *f* ([illegible] procera est fere ut [illegible], sed *g* hab. [illegible]), [illegible] (sic) *j*; [illegible] *e*

XCI

6 [illegible]
[illegible]
7 [illegible]
[illegible]
[illegible]
[illegible]
8 [illegible]
[illegible]
9 [illegible]
[illegible]
[illegible]
[illegible]
10 [illegible]
[illegible]
11 [illegible]
[illegible]
[illegible]
12 [illegible]
[illegible]
13 [illegible]
[illegible]
14 [illegible]
[illegible]

15 [illegible]
[illegible]

XCII

[illegible]
[illegible]
[illegible]
1 [illegible]
[illegible]
[illegible]
[illegible]
[illegible]
2 [illegible]
[illegible]
3 [illegible]
[illegible]
* [illegible]
4 [illegible]
[illegible]
[illegible]
5 [illegible]
[illegible]
[illegible]

XCIII

[illegible]
[illegible]
[illegible]

abe(fg) hj

6. [illegible]] [illegible] *e* | [illegible]] [illegible] *e*, [illegible] *j* | [illegible]] [illegible] *hj*
7. [illegible]] [illegible] *b*, [illegible] *ef* | [illegible]] c. sey. *f*
9. [illegible]] [illegible] *b*, [illegible] *hj* | [illegible]] c. sey. *f*
10. [illegible]] [illegible] *e*
11. [illegible]] [illegible] *b*, [illegible] *e*; [illegible] *f*; [illegible] *hj* | [illegible]] [illegible] *e*
12. [illegible]] [illegible] *e*; [illegible] *h* | [illegible]] [illegible] *f* (cf. u. 13)
14. [illegible]] [illegible] *e*
15. [illegible]] [illegible] *hj*(s. puncto diacritico)

XCII

1. [illegible]] [illegible] *hj* | [illegible] *j**] [illegible] *e jc* pr m(s. puncto diacritico)
3. [illegible] 1° ∩ 2° *h**, sed c pr m | [illegible]] *b* etiam hab. metob. post [illegible]; s. notis *ef*(*f* non testatur [illegible]) *hj*
4. [illegible]] s. sey. *j* | [illegible]] [illegible] *hj*(uerbum prius c. puncto inferiore) | [illegible]] [illegible] *hj*(c. puncto inferiore)
5. [illegible]] [illegible] (sic) *h*

XCIII

Inscr. [illegible]] c. sey. *be* | [illegible]] [illegible] *f*

XCIII

1 [illegible]

2 [illegible]

3 [illegible]

4 [illegible]

5 [illegible]

6 [illegible]

7 [illegible]

8 [illegible]

9 [illegible]

10 [illegible]

11 [illegible]

12 [illegible]

13 [illegible]

14 [illegible]

15 [illegible]

16 [illegible]

17 [illegible]

18 [illegible]

abe(fg) hj

4. [illegible] *g*] [illegible] *b*, [illegible] *f* uid. (punctum sup. [illegible] in macula), [illegible] *hj*
5. [illegible]] [illegible] *e*
6. [illegible]] [illegible] *f j** (qua manu correctum est inc.) | [illegible]] c. sey. *f*; in *j*, [illegible] fere abolita (seu consulto seu forte) quamquam *j** habebat lemma | [illegible]] s. puncto in *f*, sed hab. uocalem [illegible] apud [illegible], itaque Pa'el est
7. [illegible]] [illegible] *j** (uid.) (= Pesh), sed littera prima erasa est
8. [illegible]] [illegible] *hj* | [illegible] 2° *f*] [illegible] *g*, [illegible] *j*; [illegible] *e*
9. [illegible]] c. sey. *hj*
11. [illegible]] [illegible] *e*
12. [illegible] (*b* uid.)] [illegible] *j* | [illegible]] [illegible] *hj*
13. [illegible]] [illegible] *e*; [illegible] *hj* (s. puncto) | [illegible]] c. sey. *f* uid. (puncta sey. languent, sed hab. *g*) *hj*
15. [illegible]] [illegible] *e* | [illegible]] [illegible] (sic) *e* | [illegible]] [illegible] *j** (= Pesh), sed c pr m uid. | [illegible]] [illegible] *b h*, [illegible] *e*, [illegible] (sic) *j*
16. [illegible]] [illegible] *b*, [illegible] *hj*
17. [illegible]] [illegible] *a**, sed c pr m | [illegible]] [illegible] *e hj*
18. [illegible] *f*] [illegible] *g** (cf. Pesh), sed [illegible] inducta est uid. (qua manu inc.) | [illegible]] [illegible] *f* | [illegible] > *hj*

XCIII

19 [illegible]
20 [illegible]
21 [illegible]
22 [illegible]
23 [illegible]

XCIV

1 [illegible]
2 [illegible]
3 [illegible]
4 [illegible]
5 [illegible]
6 [illegible]
7 [illegible]
8 [illegible]
9 [illegible]
10 [illegible]
11 [illegible]

XCV

1 [illegible]
2 [illegible]
3 [illegible]

a(b)e(fg) hj

19. ܒܐܪܥܐ] s. sey. *f* | ܒܣܘܓܐ] ܒܣܘܓܐ ܕܚܘܫܒܝ *j* (uerbum prius c. sey. *h*)
20. ܕܝܚܠܐ] ܕܝܚܒܐ *f*
23. ܘܢܦܪܘܥ] ܘܦܪܘܥ *f*

XCIV

4. ܘܪ̈ܘܡܐ] ܘܪܘܡܐ *e*, ܘܪ̈ܘܡܐ *f*
8. ܐܦܘܗܝ] ܠܐܦܘܗܝ *f* | ܒܬܘܕܝܬܐ] ܒܬܘܕܝܬܐ *j** (= Pesh), sed qua manu correctum est inc.
9. ܐܝܟ] ܐܝܟܢܐ *hj*
10. ܟܠܗܘܢ] ܟܠܟܠ *hj*

XCV

Inscr. ܬܫܒܚܐ] ܬܫܒܘܚܬܐ *h* | ܠܕܘܝܕ > *f*
2. ܘܒܪܟܘ] ܒܪܟܘ *e*^c (ܘ uid. erasa est) | ܝܘܡܐ ܡܢ] tr. *h* | ܦܘܪܩܢܗ] ܕܦܘܪܩܢܐ ܕܝܠܗ *hj*^c pr m(uerbum prius refictum est, sed lectio principalis inc.)
3. ܐܘܕܥܘ-ܬܕܡܪ̈ܬܗ > *j*

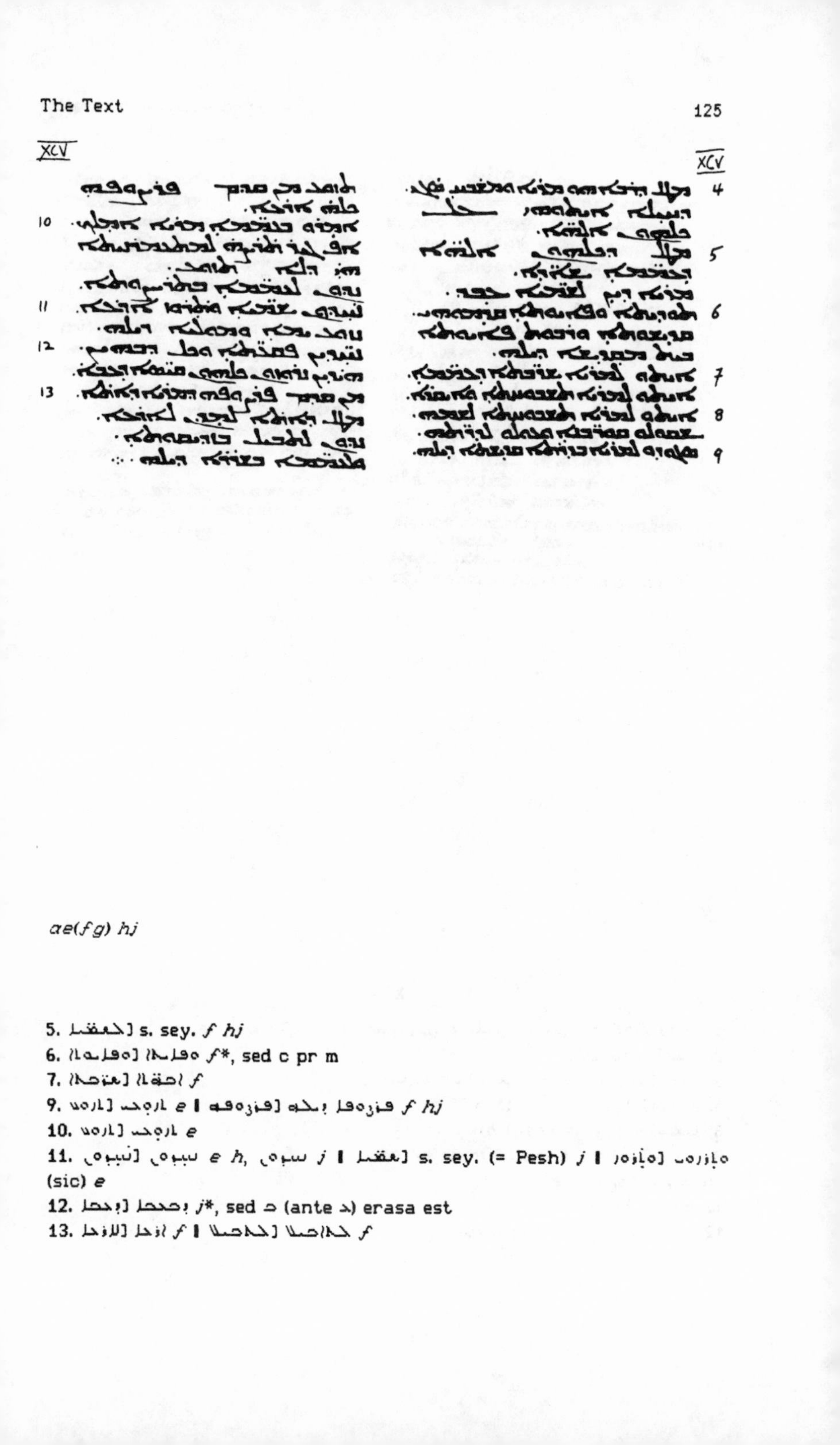

XCV

4 [illegible]
[illegible]
[illegible]
5 [illegible]
[illegible]
[illegible]
6 [illegible]
[illegible]
[illegible]
7 [illegible]
[illegible]
8 [illegible]
[illegible]
9 [illegible]
[illegible]
[illegible]
10 [illegible]
[illegible]
[illegible]
[illegible]
11 [illegible]
[illegible]
12 [illegible]
[illegible]
13 [illegible]
[illegible]
[illegible]
[illegible]

ae(fg) hj

5. [illegible]] s. sey. *f hj*
6. [illegible]] [illegible] *f**, sed c pr m
7. [illegible]] [illegible] *f*
9. [illegible]] [illegible] *e* | [illegible]] [illegible] *f hj*
10. [illegible]] [illegible] *e*
11. [illegible]] [illegible] *e h*, [illegible] *j* | [illegible]] s. sey. (= Pesh) *j* | [illegible]] [illegible] (sic) *e*
12. [illegible]] [illegible] *j**, sed [illegible] (ante [illegible]) erasa est
13. [illegible]] [illegible] *f* | [illegible]] [illegible] *f*

XCVI

܀ܠܕܘܝܕ. ܐܡܬܝ ܕܐܪܥܐ
ܕܠܗ ܡܬܩܢܐ ܀
1 ܡܪܝܐ ܐܡܠܟ ܬܪܘܙ ܐܪܥܐ.
ܢܬܒܣܡܢ ܓܙܪܬܐ ܣܓܝܐܬܐ.
2 ܥܢܢܐ ܘܥܪܦܠܐ ܚܕܪܘܗܝ.
ܙܕܝܩܘܬܐ ܘܕܝܢܐ ܬܘܪܨܐ
ܕܟܘܪܣܝܗ.
3 ܢܘܪܐ ܩܕܡܘܗܝ ܬܗܠܟ ܘܬܘܩܕ.
ܚܕܪܢܐܝܬ ܠܒܥܠܕܒܒܘܗܝ.
4 ܐܢܗܪܘ ܒܪܩܘܗܝ ܠܬܒܝܠ.
ܚܙܬ ܘܙܥܬ ܐܪܥܐ.
5 ܛܘܪܐ ܐܝܟ ܩܘܪܐ ܐܬܬܫܝܚܘ
ܡܢ ܩܕܡ ܦܪܨܘܦܗ ܕܡܪܝܐ.
ܡܢ ܩܕܡ ܦܪܨܘܦܗ ܕܡܪܝܐ ܕܟܠܗ
ܐܪܥܐ.
6 ܚܘܝܘ ܫܡܝܐ ܙܕܝܩܘܬܗ.
ܘܚܙܘ ܟܠܗܘܢ ܥܡܡܐ ܫܘܒܚܗ.
7 ܢܒܗܬܘܢ ܟܠܗܘܢ ܐܝܠܝܢ
ܕܣܓܕܝܢ ܠܓܠܝܦܐ.
ܐܝܠܝܢ ܕܡܫܬܒܗܪܝܢ ܒܦܬܟܪܝܗܘܢ.
ܣܓܘܕܘ ܠܗ ܟܠܗܘܢ ܡܠܐܟܘܗܝ.
8 ܫܡܥܬ ܘܚܕܝܬ ܨܗܝܘܢ.
ܘܪܘܙܝ ܒܢܬܗ ܕܝܗܘܕܐ:
ܡܛܠ ܕܝܢܝܟ ܡܪܝܐ.
9 ܡܛܠ ܕܐܢܬ ܡܪܝܐ ܡܪܝܡܐ
ܥܠ ܟܠܗ ܐܪܥܐ.
ܛܒ ܥܠܝܬ ܐܬܬܪܝܡܬ ܥܠ
ܡܢ ܟܠܗܘܢ ܐܠܗܐ.
10 ܐܝܠܝܢ ܕܡܚܒܝܢ ܠܡܪܝܐ ܣܢܘ ܒܝܫܬܐ.
ܢܛܪ ܡܪܝܐ ܢܦܫܬܐ ܕܚܣܝܐ ܕܝܠܗ.
ܡܢ ܐܝܕܐ ܕܚܛܝܐ ܢܦܨܐ ܐܢܘܢ.
11 ܢܘܗܪܐ ܕܢܚ ܠܙܕܝܩܐ.
ܘܠܬܪܝܨܝ ܠܒܐ ܚܕܘܬܐ.
12 ܚܕܘ ܙܕܝܩܐ ܒܡܪܝܐ.
ܘܐܘܕܘ ܠܥܘܗܕܢܐ ܕܩܕܝܫܘܬܐ ܕܝܠܗ ܀

XCVII

܀ܡܙܡܘܪܐ ܠܕܘܝܕ ܀
1 ܫܒܚܘ ܠܡܪܝܐ ܬܫܒܘܚܬܐ ܚܕܬܐ.
ܡܛܠ ܕܬܕܡܘܪܬܐ ܥܒܕ ܡܪܝܐ.

ae(fg) hj

XCVI

1. ܬܪܘܙ] ܪܘܙ *e* | ܢܬܒܣܡܢ] ܬܬܒܣܡ *e h*, ܢܬܒܣܡ *j* | ܓܙܪܬܐ] ܓܙܝܪܬܐ (sic) *f*
2. ܥܢܢܐ] c. sey. *hj*
3. ܘܬܘܩܕ] ܬܘܩܕ *e* | ܠܒܥܠܕܒܒܘܗܝ] ܘܠܒܥܠܕܒܒܘܗܝ *e*
5. ܐܬܬܫܝܚܘ] ܐܬܫܝܚܘ *e* | ܡܢ 1° ∩ 2° *e*
6. ܫܡܝܐ] s. sey. (= Pesh) *hj*
8. ܘܚܕܝܬ] ܘܚܕܬ *f* | ܕܝܗܘܕܐ] ܕܝܗܘܕ *ef hj*
10. ܕܚܣܝܐ] s. sey. *e*
11. ܠܙܕܝܩܐ] c. sey. *h*
12. ܕܩܕܝܫܘܬܐ ܕܝܠܗ] ܕܩܕܝܫܘܬܗ *hj*

XCVII

[Syriac text]
2 [Syriac text]
3 [Syriac text]
4 [Syriac text]
5 [Syriac text]
6 [Syriac text]
7 [Syriac text]
8 [Syriac text]
9 [Syriac text]

XCVIII

1 [Syriac text]
2 [Syriac text]
3 [Syriac text]
4 [Syriac text]
5 [Syriac text]
6 [Syriac text]
7 [Syriac text]
8 [Syriac text]
9 [Syriac text]

ae(fg) hj

XCVII

1. [Syriac]] sup. ras. (qua manu inc.) *j* | [Syriac]] uerbum principale inc., sed partes erasae sunt relinquere lemma *j*
3. [Syriac]] [Syriac] *e h*, [Syriac] *j* | [Syriac] 1°] sup. ras. (pr m) *a* | [Syriac]] [Syriac] *e*
5. [Syriac] (*h* absc.)] [Syriac] *e* | [Syriac] 1°] c. sey. *hj*
7. [Syriac]] [Syriac] *h*
8. [Syriac]] [Syriac] *e*
9. [Syriac]] [Syriac] *hj* | [Syriac]] [Syriac] *f*

XCVIII

1. [Syriac]] [Syriac] *ef*, [Syriac] *h*; [Syriac] *j* | [Syriac]] [Syriac] *e*
4. [Syriac]] [Syriac] *e**(sed c pr m) *h*uid.(litterae [Syriac] praeter partem puncti uni sey. uid. absc.)*j*
6. [Syriac]] [Syriac] *j* (uerbum prius in *h* est [Syriac]) | [Syriac]] [Syriac] *j* (uerbum prius in *h* est [Syriac])
7. [Syriac]] [Syriac] *j*

XCVIII

[Syriac manuscript text]

XCIX

1 [Syriac manuscript text]

2 [Syriac manuscript text]

3 [Syriac manuscript text]

4 [Syriac manuscript text]

5 [Syriac manuscript text]

C

1 [Syriac manuscript text]

2 [Syriac manuscript text]

3 [Syriac manuscript text]

4 [Syriac manuscript text]

5 [Syriac manuscript text]

6 [Syriac manuscript text]

7 [Syriac manuscript text]

8 [Syriac manuscript text]

a(b)e(fg) hj

XCIX

Insc. ܡܙܡܘܪܐ] pr. ܕܕܘܝܕ e^c (qua manu inc.; a manu eadem iterum scriptum est in mg) | ܒܬܘܕܝܬܐ] ܕܬܘܕܝܬܐ *ef*

2. ܒܚܕܘܬܐ] ܒܠܚܕܘܬܐ *hj*

3. ܗܘܝܘ ܕܥܒܕܢ] ܗܘ *e* (ras. antecedit ܗܘ, erat uid. ܕ ܥܒܕܢ)

C

1. ܐܙܡܪ] ܐܙܡܪ *e*(uocalis ܙܩܦܐ apud ܐ et ܦܬܚܐ apud ܡ, itaque uerbum Pe'al est), ܐܙܡܪ *j*; ܐܡܪ *h**, sed ܙ inserta est pr m

2. ܐܙܡܪ] ܐܙܡܪ *e*, ܐܙܡܪ *f*, ܐܙܡܪ *h*, ܐܙܡܪ *j* | ܐܡܬܝ] ܐܡܬܝ *e*

3. ܕܒܓܢ] ܕܒܓܢ *e*(macula uel punctum paruum [frt serius additum est, pr m?] sub lin.) *j*, ܕܒܓܢ *f*

5. ܕܐܟܠܩܪܨܐ] ܩܪܨܐ ܕܐܟܠ *e hj* (*f* hab. ܕܐܟܠ, sed non testatur ܩܪܨܐ quod est in linea Pesh) | ܘܕܪܘܪܒܝ] ܘܕܪܘܪܒܝ *ef*(s. puncto diacritico); ܕܪܘܪܒܝ[ܘ] *j*

6. ܬܡܝܡܐ] ܬܡܝܡܐ ܕܐܝܟ *h* (in *j* uerbum prius c. sey.) | ܡܗܝܡܢܐ] ܡܗܝܡܢܐ *e*

7. ܥܒܕ] ܕܥܒܕ *hj* | ܢܟܠܐ] ܢܟܠܐ *hj*(c. puncto superiore)

8. ܒܨܦܪܐ] sey. sup. ras., sed pr m uid. *a*; s. sey. *hj*

CI

[illegible]
[illegible]
1 [illegible]
[illegible]
2 [illegible]
[illegible]
[illegible]
[illegible]
3 [illegible]
[illegible]
4 [illegible]
[illegible]
5 [illegible]
[illegible]
6 [illegible]
[illegible]
7 [illegible]
[illegible]
8 [illegible]
[illegible]
[illegible]
9 [illegible]
[illegible]
[illegible]

CI

10 [illegible]
[illegible]
[illegible]
11 [illegible]
[illegible]
12 [illegible]
[illegible]
13 [illegible]
[illegible]
[illegible]
14 [illegible]
[illegible]
15 [illegible]
[illegible]
16 [illegible]
[illegible]
17 [illegible]
[illegible]
18 [illegible]
[illegible]
19 [illegible]
[illegible]
[illegible]

ab(d)e(fg) hj

CI

Inscr. [illegible] (*b*inc.)] [illegible] *e*, [illegible] *hj*

2. [illegible] (*b* absc.)] [illegible] *de*, [illegible] *h* | [illegible] (*b* absc.)] [illegible] *h*, [illegible] *j*

3. [illegible] (*b* absc.)] [illegible] *hj* | [illegible] (*b* absc., *d*inc.)] [illegible] *e*; [illegible] *j*(cf. α′ in Field [u. 4]) | [illegible] (*b* absc.)] [illegible] *j*(cf. α′ in Field [u. 4])

4. [illegible]] [illegible] *f*

5. [illegible] (*b* absc.)] [illegible] *hj* | [illegible] (*b*inc.)] c. sey. *f* | [illegible]] c. sey. (sic) *f*

8. [illegible] (*b*uid.)] [illegible] *hj*

9. [illegible] 2° (*b*uid.*d*uid.)] + [illegible] *f*

10. [illegible] (*b*inc.)] [illegible] *h*, [illegible] *j*

11. [illegible] (*b*inc.)] c. sey. *e hj*

13. [illegible]] + [illegible] *d**, sed erasum est | [illegible]] [illegible] *f*

15. [illegible]] primo [illegible] scripta est post [illegible], deinde c pr m ad [illegible] *j* | [illegible]] + [illegible] *e* | [illegible]] [illegible] *e*

17. [illegible]] bis scr. (l) *e*

18. [illegible]] [illegible] *b*; [illegible] *e*

CI

20 [illegible]

21 [illegible]

22 [illegible]

23 [illegible]

24 [illegible]

25 [illegible]

26 [illegible]

27 [illegible]

28 [illegible]

CII

1 [illegible]

2 [illegible]

3 [illegible]

4 [illegible]

5 [illegible]

6 [illegible]

7 [illegible]

8 [illegible]

9 [illegible]

10 [illegible]

11 [illegible]

a(b)de(fg) hj

20. [illegible] c. sey. *h*; [illegible] *j*

21. [illegible] [illegible] *e*, [illegible] *j*

23. [illegible] > *e* | [illegible] [illegible] *e*; [illegible] *hj* ([illegible] > *j** [(], sed c pr m)

24. [illegible] [illegible] *hj* | [illegible] s. sey. *bf h*

25. [illegible] > *hj* | [illegible] [illegible] *hj*(s. puncto) | [illegible] s. sey. *d* | [illegible] s. sey. (sic) *d*

26. [illegible] [illegible] *h*

28. [illegible] + [illegible] *d* | [illegible] > *d** (l), sed c pr m

CII

Insc. > *d* | [illegible] + [illegible] *e*

1. [illegible] [illegible] *hj*

3. [illegible] [illegible] *hj*

5. [illegible] [illegible] *e* | [illegible] > *e**, sed c pr m

6. [illegible] [illegible] *j*

7. [illegible] [illegible] *f* | [illegible] [illegible] *df hj*, [illegible] *e* | [illegible] s. sey. *f*

10. [illegible] [illegible] *h* (in *j* uerbum prius c. sey.)

11. [illegible] [illegible] *hj*

CII

12 [illegible]
[illegible]
13 [illegible]
[illegible]
14 [illegible]
[illegible]
15 [illegible]
[illegible]
16 [illegible]
[illegible]
[illegible]
17 [illegible]
[illegible]
[illegible]
18 [illegible]
[illegible]
19 [illegible]
[illegible]
20 [illegible]
[illegible]
[illegible]

21 [illegible]
[illegible]
22 [illegible]
[illegible]
[illegible]

CIII

[illegible]
[illegible]
[illegible]
1 [illegible]
[illegible]
[illegible]
2 [illegible]
[illegible]
[illegible]
3 [illegible]
[illegible]
[illegible]
4 [illegible]
[illegible]
5 [illegible]
[illegible]

a(d)e(fg) hj

12. [illegible] (*d* inc.)] c. sey. *e* | [illegible] (*d* uid.)] c. sey. *e*
13. [illegible]] bis scr. (l) *e*
14. [illegible] > *d**, sed insertum est a manu seriore | [illegible]] [illegible] *e* | [illegible]] [illegible] (sic) *d*
15. [illegible]] [illegible] *e** (= Pesh), sed c pr m uid.
16. [illegible] > *d* | [illegible]] [illegible] *d**(uid.), [illegible] *d*c pr m uid. | [illegible]] [illegible] *e*
18. [illegible]] [illegible] *ef j*, [illegible] *h*

CIII

Inscr. [illegible]] [illegible] *f* | [illegible]] pr. [[illegible]] [illegible] *f* (*g* hab. [illegible])

1. [illegible]] [illegible] > *ef hj*
4. [illegible]] [illegible] *f hj*
5. [illegible]] [illegible] *hj*

CIII

6 [illegible]
[illegible]
7 [illegible]
[illegible]
8 [illegible]
[illegible]
9 [illegible]
[illegible]
[illegible]
10 [illegible]
[illegible]
11 [illegible]
[illegible]
12 [illegible]
[illegible]
13 [illegible]
[illegible]
14 [illegible]
[illegible]
[illegible]

15 [illegible]
[illegible]
[illegible]
16 [illegible]
[illegible]
17 [illegible]
[illegible]
18 [illegible]
[illegible]
[illegible]
19 [illegible]
[illegible]
20 [illegible]
[illegible]
21 [illegible]
[illegible]
[illegible]
22 [illegible]
[illegible]
23 [illegible]
[illegible]
24 [illegible]
[illegible]
[illegible]

ae(fg) hj

8. [illegible]] [illegible] *hj*(c. puncto superiore) | [illegible]] [illegible] *hj*(s. ullo puncto diacritico)

11. [illegible]] [illegible] *f* | [illegible]] [illegible] (sic) *h* | [illegible]] c. sey. *h*

13. [illegible]] s. sey. *h* | [illegible]] [illegible] *e*

16. [illegible]] [illegible] *e*; [illegible] *j*

18. [illegible]] [illegible] *f*; [illegible] ([illegible] apud ï et [illegible] apud [illegible]) *e*; [illegible] *hj* | [illegible] > *e*

19. [illegible]] [illegible] *e*; [illegible] *j* | [illegible]] [illegible] *e hj* | [illegible]] [illegible] *hj* ([illegible] sup. ras., sed pr m uid. *j*)

21. [illegible]] [illegible] *f*

22. [illegible]] [illegible] *f*

23. [illegible] > *e** (l), sed c pr m

24. [illegible]] *l* > *ef hj* | [illegible]] [illegible] *j*

CIII

25 ܗܢܐ ܝܡܐ ܪܒܐ ܘܪܘܝܚܐ.
ܬܡܢ ܪ̈ܚܫܐ ܕܡܫܬܠܦܬܐ ܕܠܝܬ ܡܢܝܢܐ.
ܚܝ̈ܘܬܐ ܙܥܘܪ̈ܬܐ ܥܡ ܪ̈ܘܪܒܬܐ.
26 ܬܡܢ ܐܠܦ̈ܐ ܡܗܠܟ̈ܢ.
ܬܢܝܢܐ ܗܢܐ ܕܒܪܝܬ ܠܡܓܚܟܘ ܒܗ.
27 ܟܠܗܘܢ ܠܘܬܟ ܡܣܟܝܢ.
ܠܡܬܠ ܣܝܒܪܬܗܘܢ ܒܥܕܢܗ ܘܒܙܒܢܐ.
28 ܡܐ ܕܝܗܒܬ ܠܗܘܢ ܢܠܩܛܘܢ.
ܡܐ ܕܦܬܚܬ ܐܝܕ ܐܝܕܟ ܕܡܠܝܐ.
ܟܠ ܡܬܡܠܝܢ ܒܛܝܒܘܬܐ.
29 ܡܐ ܕܐܗܦܟܬ ܡܢ ܦܪܨܘܦܟ ܢܬܕܠܚܘܢ.
ܬܣܒ ܐܢܬ ܪܘܚܗܘܢ ܘܢܦܩܘܢ.
ܘܠܥܦܪܗܘܢ ܢܬܦܢܘܢ.
30 ܬܫܕܪ ܪܘܚܟ ܘܢܬܒܪܘܢ.
ܘܬܚܕܬ ܦܪܨܘܦܗ ܕܐܪܥܐ.
31 ܢܗܘܐ ܫܘܒܚܗ ܕܡܪܝܐ ܠܥܠܡܝܢ.
ܘܢܚܕܐ ܡܪܝܐ ܒܥܒܕ̈ܘܗܝ.
32 ܗܘ ܕܚܐܪ ܒܐܪܥܐ ܘܡܙܝܥ ܠܗ ܠܐܪܥܐ.
ܗܘ ܕܩܪܒ ܠܛܘܪ̈ܐ ܘܡܬܬܢܢܝܢ.
33 ܐܫܒܚ ܠܡܪܝܐ ܒܚܝܝ.
ܐܙܡܪ ܠܐܠܗܝ ܥܕܡܐ ܕܐܝܬܝ.
34 ܢܫܦܪ ܠܐܠܗܐ ܬܫܒܘܚܬܐ ܕܝܠܝ.
ܐܢܐ ܕܝܢ ܐܚܕܐ ܒܡܪܝܐ.
35 ܢܦܣܩܘܢ ܚܛܝܐ ܡܢ ܐܪܥܐ.
ܘܠܐ ܢܬܩܝܡܘܢ ܐܝܟܢܐ ܕܠܐ ܢܗܘܘܢ.
ܒܪܟܝ ܢܦܫܝ ܠܡܪܝܐ ⁘

CIV

⁘ ܗܠܠܘܝܐ ⁘
1 ܐܘܕܘ ܠܡܪܝܐ ܘܩܪܘ ܒܫܡܗ.
ܐܘܕܥܘ ܒܥܡܡ̈ܐ ܥܒ̈ܕܘܗܝ.
2 ܫܒܚܘ ܠܗ ܘܙܡܪܘ ܠܗ.
ܐܫܬܥܘ ܒܟܠܗܘܢ ܬܕܡܪ̈ܬܗ.
3 ܐܫܬܒܗܪܘ ܒܫܡܗ ܩܕܝܫܐ.
ܢܚܕܐ ܠܒܗܘܢ ܕܐܝܠܝܢ ܕܒܥܝܢ ܠܡܪܝܐ.
4 ܒܥܘ ܠܡܪܝܐ ܘܐܬܥܫܢܘ.
ܒܥܘ ܦܪܨܘܦܗ ܒܟܠܙܒܢ.
5 ܐܬܕܟܪܘ ܬܕܡܪ̈ܬܗ ܕܥܒܕ.
ܐܬܘܬܐ ܕܝܠܗ ܘܕܝ̈ܢܐ ܕܦܘܡܗ.

a(b)e(fg) hj

27. ܣܝܒܪܬܗܘܢ] ܠܗܘܢ ܣܝܒܪܬܐ *hj*
31. ܠܥܠܡܝܢ *g*] c. sey. *e* (*f* hab. lineam sup. ܡ, frt habebat ibi sey.)
32. ܘܡܬܬܢܢܝܢ] ܘܡܬܬܢܢܝܢ (sic) *hj*
33. ܐܙܡܪ (*b* inc.)] ܐܙܡܪ *h*, ܐܙܡܪ *j* | ܒܚܝܝ] ܒܚܝܐ ܕܝܠܝ *hj* (in *j* uerbum secundum erat ܕܝܠܗ uid., sed correctum est per rasuram) | ܐܙܡܪ (*b* inc.)] ܐܙܡܪ *e*(sed punctum inferius frt deletum est pr m), ܐܙܡܪ *f*, ܐܙܡܪ *h*, ܐܙܡܪ *j*
34. ܢܫܦܪ (*b* inc.)] ܢܫܦܪ *ef hj* | ܠܐܠܗܐ] ܠܗ *e* | ܬܫܒܘܚܬܝ] ܒ sup. ras. (pr m uid.) *e*
35. ܢܗܘܘܢ] + ܐܢܘܢ *hj*

CIV

Inscr. ܗܠܠܘܝܐ] ܗܠܠܘܝܗ *e*
1. ܠܡܪܝܐ] ܪܝ sup. ras. (pr m) *j* | ܘܩܪܘ (*b* absc.)] ܘ 1° sup. ras. (pr m) *j*
2. ܐܫܬܥܘ *f*] ܐܫܬܥܝܘ *e j*, ܐܫܬܥܘ *g*
3. ܐܫܬܒܗܪܘ] ܐܫܬܒܗܪܘ *j*
5. ܘܕܝܢܐ (*b* inc.)] s. sey. *j*

CIV

[illegible] 6
[illegible]
[illegible] 7
[illegible]
[illegible] 8
[illegible]
[illegible] 9
[illegible]
[illegible] 10
[illegible]
[illegible] 11
[illegible]
[illegible] 12
[illegible]
[illegible] 13
[illegible]
[illegible] 14
[illegible]
[illegible] 15
[illegible]
[illegible] 16
[illegible]
[illegible] 17
[illegible]
[illegible] 18

CIV

[illegible]
19 [illegible]
[illegible]
20 [illegible]
[illegible]
21 [illegible]
[illegible]
22 [illegible]
[illegible]
[illegible]
23 [illegible]
[illegible]
[illegible]
24 [illegible]
[illegible]
[illegible]
25 [illegible]
[illegible]
[illegible]
26 [illegible]
[illegible]
27 [illegible]
[illegible]
28 [illegible]
[illegible]
29 [illegible]
[illegible]

abe(fg) hj

6. [illegible] > *j**, sed c pr m

8. [illegible] *b*, [illegible] *e* | [illegible] *ef j*, [illegible] *h* | [illegible] > *e** (l), sed [illegible] relatum est pr m *e* | [illegible] *e hj*

9. [illegible] s. sey. *b*

10. [illegible] *f* | [illegible] *h* | [illegible] *e*, [illegible] *f hj* | [illegible] *e*, [illegible] *hj*; [illegible] *f*

11. [illegible] *e**(frt) (= Pesh), sed c pr m | [illegible] c. sey. *e*

12. [illegible] (*b*inc.)] s. sey. *h*

14. [illegible] ras. sub [illegible] 1° *a*; [illegible] *b*, [illegible] *e*

15. [illegible] 1°] [illegible] *j* | [illegible] 1° > *h*

20. [illegible] *b* | [illegible] *e**, sed [illegible] inserta est pr m inter [illegible] quamquam litterae [illegible] non erasae sunt

21. [illegible] *hj*(c. puncto inferiore) | [illegible] *b* | [illegible] *hj*

23. [illegible] *b hj*, [illegible] *e*

25. [illegible] *f*] [illegible] *g hj*c pr m([illegible] *j**[uid.] [cf. Pesh])

27. [illegible] *e* | [illegible] *f* | [illegible] *j* (in *h* uerbum prius est [illegible])

28. [illegible] *a*mg*b*mg*f*mg, item *hj* praeter [illegible] pro [illegible] | [illegible] *f*

CIV

[illegible] 30
[illegible]
[illegible] 31
[illegible]
[illegible] 32
[illegible]
[illegible] 33
[illegible]
[illegible] 34
[illegible]
[illegible] 35
[illegible]
[illegible] 36
[illegible]
[illegible] 37
[illegible]
[illegible] 38
[illegible]
[illegible] 39
[illegible]
[illegible] 40
[illegible]
[illegible] 41
[illegible]
[illegible] 42

[illegible]
43 [illegible]
[illegible]
44 [illegible]
[illegible]
45 [illegible]
[illegible]

CV

[illegible]
1 [illegible]
[illegible]
2 [illegible]
[illegible]
3 [illegible]
[illegible]
4 [illegible]
[illegible]
[illegible]
5 [illegible]
[illegible]
[illegible]
6 [illegible]
[illegible]
7 [illegible]
[illegible]
[illegible]
[illegible]

abe(fg) hj

30. [illegible]] [illegible] *f* | [illegible]] [illegible] *ef h*, [illegible] *j*

31. [illegible]] [illegible] *j* | [illegible]] s. sey. *hj*

32. [illegible]] [illegible] *hj*

34. [illegible]] [illegible] *hj*

35. [illegible] 2° > *j*(prbl. uid., quamquam cf. Rahlfs)

36. [illegible]] [illegible] *hj*c pr m uid., [illegible] *j** | [illegible]] [illegible] *ef hj* | [illegible]] [illegible] *hj*

37. [illegible]] [illegible] *f*

43. [illegible]] [illegible] *h*

44. [illegible]] [illegible] *h* | [illegible]] [illegible] *g**(uid.), sed [illegible] inducta est (pr m uid.; *f* hab. [illegible]) | [illegible]] s. sey. *e*

CV

Inscr. [illegible] 1°] [illegible] *e*

1. [illegible]] [illegible] *f*

2. [illegible]] [illegible] *b*

3. [illegible]] [illegible] *hj* | [illegible] *e**(uid.)] [illegible] *e*c pr m; [illegible] *hj* | [illegible]] [illegible] *j*

4. [illegible]] [illegible] *e* (praeter punctum [illegible] omissum est)

5. [illegible]] [illegible] *f* | [illegible]] [illegible] sup. ras. pr m *a*

CV

8 ܘܦܪܩ ܐܢܘܢ ܡܛܠ ܫܡܗ.
ܠܡܘܕܥܘ ܓܢܒܪܘܬܗ.
9 ܘܟܐܐ ܒܝܡܐ ܣܘܡܩܐ ܘܝܒܫ.
ܘܕܒܪ ܐܢܘܢ ܒܬܗܘܡܐ ܐܝܟ
ܕܒܡܕܒܪܐ.
10 ܘܐܦܨܝ ܐܢܘܢ ܡܢ ܐܝܕܐ ܕܣܢܝܐ.
ܘܦܪܩ ܐܢܘܢ ܡܢ ܐܝܕܐ ܕܒܥܠܕܒܒܐ.
11 ܘܚܦܘ ܡܝܐ ܠܐܠܘܨܝܗܘܢ.
ܚܕ ܡܢܗܘܢ ܠܐ ܐܫܬܚܪ.
12 ܘܗܝܡܢܘ ܒܡܠܘܗܝ.
ܘܫܒܚܘ ܬܫܒܘܚܬܗ.
13 ܘܐܣܪܗܒܘ ܛܥܘ ܥܒܕܘܗܝ.
ܠܐ ܩܘܘ ܠܡܠܟܗ.
14 ܘܪܓܒܘ ܪܓܬܐ ܒܡܕܒܪܐ.
ܘܢܣܝܘ ܠܐܠܗܐ ܒܐܬܪܐ ܕܠܐ ܡܝܐ.
15 ܘܝܗܒ ܠܗܘܢ ܫܐܠܬܗܘܢ.
ܘܫܕܪ ܣܒܥܬܐ ܒܢܦܫܬܗܘܢ.
16 ܘܐܚܡܬܘ ܠܡܘܫܐ ܒܡܫܪܝܬܐ.
ܠܐܗܪܘܢ ܩܕܝܫܗ ܕܡܪܝܐ.
17 ܐܬܦܬܚܬ ܐܪܥܐ ܘܒܠܥܬ ܠܕܬܢ.
ܘܟܣܬ ܥܠ ܟܢܘܫܬܐ ܕܐܒܝܪܘܢ.
18 ܘܝܩܕܬ ܢܘܪܐ ܒܟܢܘܫܬܗܘܢ.
ܘܫܠܗܒܝܬܐ ܐܘܩܕܬ ܠܚܛܝܐ.
19 ܘܥܒܕܘ ܥܓܠܐ ܒܚܘܪܒ.
ܘܣܓܕܘ ܠܦܬܟܪܐ.

20 ܘܚܠܦܘ ܬܫܒܘܚܬܗܘܢ.
ܒܕܡܘܬܐ ܕܥܓܠܐ ܕܐܟܠ ܥܣܒܐ.
21 ܘܛܥܘ ܠܐܠܗܐ ܗܘ ܕܦܪܩ ܠܗܘܢ.
ܗܘ ܕܥܒܕ ܪ̈ܘܪܒܬܐ ܒܡܨܪܝܢ.
22 ܬܕܡܪ̈ܬܐ ܒܐܪܥܐ ܕܚܡ.
ܘܕܚܝܠܬܐ ܥܠ ܝܡܐ ܣܘܡܩܐ.
23 ܘܐܡܪ ܠܡܘܒܕܘ ܐܢܘܢ.
ܐܠܘ ܠܐ ܡܘܫܐ ܓܒܝܗ.
ܩܡ ܒܬܒܪܬܐ ܩܕܡܘܗܝ.
ܠܡܗܦܟܘ ܚܡܬܗ.
ܕܠܐ ܢܚܒܠ ܐܢܘܢ.
24 ܘܐܫܬܛܘ ܠܐܪܥܐ ܪ̈ܓܝܓܬܐ.
ܠܐ ܗܝܡܢܘ ܠܡܠܬܗ.
25 ܘܪܛܢܘ ܒܡܫܟܢܝܗܘܢ +
ܠܐ ܫܡܥܘ ܩܠܗ ܕܡܪܝܐ.
26 ܘܐܪܝܡ ܐܝܕܗ ܥܠܝܗܘܢ.
ܠܡܪܡܝܘ ܐܢܘܢ ܒܡܕܒܪܐ.
27 ܘܠܡܪܡܝܘ ܙܪܥܗܘܢ ܒܥܡ̈ܡܐ.
ܘܠܡܒܕܪܘ ܐܢܘܢ ܒܐܬܪ̈ܘܬܐ.
28 ܘܐܫܬܡܠܝܘ ܠܒܥܠ ܦܥܘܪ.
ܘܐܟܠܘ ܕܒܚܐ ܕܡܝ̈ܬܐ.
29 ܘܐܪܓܙܘܗܝ ܒܡܥܒܕܝܗܘܢ.
ܘܣܓܝܬ ܒܗܘܢ ܡܚܘܬܐ.
30 ܘܩܡ ܦܝܢܚܣ ܘܦܝܣ.

a(b)e(fg) hj

9. ܒܡܕܒܪܐ] s. sey. *e*
10. ܕܣܢܝܐ] ܕܣܢܝܢ ܠܗܘܢ *hj* | ܕܒܥܠܕܒܒܐ] c. sey. *j*
11. ܠܐܠܘܨܝܗܘܢ] ܠܐܠܨܝܗܘܢ *f hj*
13. ܩܘܘ-ܠܡܠܟܗ > *e** (homtel.?), sed c pr m
17. ܘܟܣܬ] ܘܚܦܬ *hj* | ܟܢܘܫܬܐ] ܟܢܘܫܬܗ *h* (= Pesh) | ܕܐܒܝܪܘܢ] ܐܒܝܪܘܢ (pro ܕܐܒܝܪܘܢ) *e*mg (adsignatur [[ܠܗ]]ܘ)
18. ܒܟܢܘܫܬܗܘܢ] ܒܟܢܘܫܬܐ ܕܝܠܗܘܢ *hj* | ܠܚܛܝܐ] ܠܚܛܝ̈ܐ *j**(uid.) (= Pesh), sed c pr m
21. ܕܦܪܩ] ܕܦܪܩ *j*
23. ܐܠܘ ܠܐ] ܐܠܘܠܐ *hj*
25. ܘܪܛܢܘ] ܘܪܛܢܘ *e*
29. ܒܡܥܒܕܝܗܘܢ] ܒܡܥܒܕܐ ܕܝܠܗܘܢ *hj*c pr m uid.(uerbum prius erat ܒܡܥܒܕܐ *j**; litterae ܘܢ abscond. *j*); + ܘܒܡܦܩܢܘܬܗܘܢ ܐܬܗܦܟܘ *e*mg (e Pesh a manu seriore)

CV

[illegible]

31 [illegible]

32 [illegible]

33 [illegible]

34 [illegible]

35 [illegible]

36 [illegible]

37 [illegible]

38 [illegible]

39 [illegible]

40 [illegible]

41 [illegible]

42 [illegible]

43 [illegible]

44 [illegible]

45 [illegible]

46 [illegible]

47 [illegible]

48 [illegible]

ae(fg) hj

CV 39. [illegible]] primo litterae [illegible] scriptae sunt secundum lemma, deinde inductae sunt pr m et [illegible] scriptum est postea *a*

31. [illegible]] [illegible] *j*
33. [illegible]] [illegible] *f*
36. [illegible]] c. sey. *f*
38. [illegible]] [illegible] *f*; [illegible] *j**, sed c pr m
41. [illegible]] [illegible] *hj*
44. [illegible]] [illegible] *h*
45. [illegible]] [illegible] *e*, [illegible] *hj* | [illegible]] [illegible] *ef*, [illegible] *h*, [illegible] *j*
48. [illegible]] [illegible] *e*, [illegible] *hj* | [illegible]] [illegible] *a**, sed c pr m | [illegible] 2°] [illegible] *h*

CVI

[illegible]
1 [illegible]
2 [illegible]
3 [illegible]
4 [illegible]
5 [illegible]
6 [illegible]
7 [illegible]
8 [illegible]
9 [illegible]
10 [illegible]
11 [illegible]

CVI

[illegible]
12 [illegible]
13 [illegible]
14 [illegible]
15 [illegible]
16 [illegible]
17 [illegible]
18 [illegible]
19 [illegible]
20 [illegible]

ae(fg) hj

CVI

Insсr. ܗܠܠܘܝܐ] ܗܠܠܘܝܗ *e*; > *f*
1. ܕܒܣܝܡܐ] ܕܒܣܝܡ *f hj*
2. ܕܒܥܠܕܒܒܘܗܝ] ܕܒܥܠܕܒܒܐ *e j*; ܕܒܥܠܕܒܒܐ *h*
6. ܡܢ ܐܘܠܨܢܝܗܘܢ] ܡܢ ܐ̈ܘܠܨܢܝܗܘܢ *h*
7. ܘܕܒܪ] ܕܒܪ *f*
8. ܪ̈ܚܡܘܗܝ] ܪ̈ܚܡܘܗܝ *f*txt, ܪ̈ܚܡܘܗܝ *g*txt; ܕܚ̈ܢܢܘܗܝ *f*mg (adsignatur ܐܢܫܐ)
10. ܒܟܒ̈ܠܐ] ܒܟܒܠܐ *f*, ܒܟܒ̈ܠܐ *hj* | ܘܛܠܠܐ] c. sey. *j*
12. ܘܐܬܡܟܟ] ܘܐܬܡܟܟ *h*
13. ܡܢ ܐܘܠܨܢܝܗܘܢ] ܡܢ ܐ̈ܘܠܨܢܝܗܘܢ *h* | ܘܦܪܩ-ܐܢܘܢ > *e** (l), sed c pr m | ܐܢܘܢ] bis scr. (l) *j*
14. ܘܛܠܠܐ] ܘܡܢ ܛܠܠܐ *j**(uid.) (cf. Pesh), sed ܡܢ erasum est
15. ܪ̈ܚܡܘܗܝ] ܪ̈ܚܡܘܗܝ *f*, ܪ̈ܚܡܘܗܝ *g* | ܕܐ̈ܢܫܐ *f*] c. sey. *g*
17. ܡܥܘ̈ܠܬܗܘܢ] ܡܥܘܠܬܗ ܕܐܘܪܚܗܘܢ *j* (in *h* uerbum prius est [[ܐ]]ܡܥܘܠܬܗ) | ܡܥܘ̈ܠܬܗܘܢ] s. sey. *f*
19. ܠܘܬ ܡܪܝܐ] ܠܡܪܝܐ *j**, sed c pr m
20. ܘܦܨܝ] ܘܦܪܩ *j**(uid.) (cf. Pesh), sed c pr m | ܡܢ ܚܒ̈ܠܝܗܘܢ] s. sey. *f*

CVI

31 ܢܘܕܘܢ ܠܡܪܝܐ ܛܝܒܘܬܗ.
ܘܬܕܡܪܬܗ ܠܒܢܝ ܐܢܫܐ.
32 ܢܪܝܡܘܢܝܗܝ ܒܟܢܘܫܬܐ ܕܥܡܐ.
ܘܥܠ ܡܘܬܒܐ ܕܩܫܝܫܐ ܢܫܒܚܘܢܝܗܝ.
33 ܣܡ ܢܗܪܘܬܐ ܠܡܕܒܪܐ.
ܘܡܒܘܥܐ ܕܡܝܐ ܠܨܗܝܐ.
34 ܐܪܥܐ ܕܥܒܕܐ ܦܐܪܐ ܠܡܠܝܚܬܐ.
ܡܢ ܒܝܫܘܬܐ ܕܥܡܘܪܝܗ ܒܗ.
35 ܣܡ ܡܕܒܪܐ ܠܡܒܘܥܐ ܕܡܝܐ.
ܘܐܪܥܐ ܨܗܝܬܐ ܠܡܦܩܢܐ ܕܡܝܐ.
36 ܘܐܘܬܒ ܬܡܢ ܟܦܢܐ.
ܘܬܩܢܘ ܡܕܝܢܬܐ ܠܡܥܡܪܗܝܢ.
37 ܘܙܪܥܘ ܚܩܠܬܐ ܘܢܨܒܘ ܟܪܡܐ.
ܘܥܒܕܘ ܦܐܪܐ ܕܥܠܠܬܐ.
38 ܘܒܪܟ ܐܢܘܢ ܘܣܓܝܘ ܛܒ.
ܘܒܥܝܪܗܘܢ ܠܐ ܐܒܨܪ.
39 ܘܒܨܪܘ ܘܐܬܡܟܟܘ.
ܡܢ ܐܘܠܨܢܐ ܕܒܝܫܬܐ
ܘܕܟܘܪܗܢܐ.
40 ܐܫܕ ܫܛܝܬܐ ܥܠ
ܪܘܫܢܐ.
ܘܐܛܥܝ ܐܢܘܢ ܒܡܕܒܪܐ
ܕܠܐ ܐܘܪܚܐ.

CVI

21 ܢܘܕܘܢ ܠܡܪܝܐ ܛܝܒܘܬܗ.
ܘܬܕܡܪܬܗ ܠܒܢܝ ܐܢܫܐ.
22 ܘܢܕܒܚܘܢ ܠܗ ܕܒܚܐ ܕܬܘܕܝܬܐ.
ܘܢܫܬܥܘܢ ܥܒܕܘܗܝ ܒܬܫܒܘܚܬܐ.
23 ܢܚܬܘ ܝܡܐ ܒܐܠܦܐ:
ܥܒܕܝܢ ܥܒܕܐ ܒܡܝܐ ܣܓܝܐܐ.
24 ܗܢܘܢ ܚܙܘ ܥܒܕܘܗܝ ܕܡܪܝܐ.
ܘܬܕܡܪܬܗ ܒܥܘܡܩܐ.
25 ܐܡܪ ܘܩܡܬ ܪܘܚܐ ܕܥܠܥܠܐ.
ܘܐܬܪܝܡܘ ܓܠܠܘܗܝ.
26 ܣܠܩܝܢ ܠܫܡܝܐ ܘܢܚܬܝܢ
ܠܥܘܡܩܐ.
ܘܢܦܫܗܘܢ ܒܒܝܫܬܐ ܡܬܡܣܝܐ.
27 ܐܫܬܓܫܘ ܘܙܥܘ ܐܝܟ ܪܘܝܐ.
ܘܟܠܗ ܚܟܡܬܗܘܢ ܐܬܒܠܥܬ.
28 ܘܩܪܘ ܠܡܪܝܐ ܟܕ ܐܠܝܨ ܠܗܘܢ.
ܘܡܢ ܐܘܠܨܢܗܘܢ ܦܪܩ ܐܢܘܢ.
29 ܘܐܩܝܡ ܥܠܥܠܐ ܘܩܡܬ ܠܕܡܝܟܬܐ
ܘܫܠܝܘ
ܓܠܠܘܗܝ.
30 ܘܚܕܝܘ ܟܕ ܫܠܝܘ.
ܘܕܒܪ ܐܢܘܢ ܠܢܡܝܐ ܕܨܒܝܢ.

αe(fg) hj

21. ܛܝܒܘܬܗ] ܛܝܒܘܬܗ *f*

22. ܕܒܚܐ] c. sey. *hj* | ܕܬܘܕܝܬܐ] ܕܬܘܕܝܬܐ *ef*

23. ܝܡܐ] ܠܝܡܐ *hj* | ܥܒܕܝܢ] ܘܥܒܕܝܢ *hj*

25. ܘܐܬܪܝܡܘ] ܘܐܬܪܝܡ *e* | ܓܠܠܘܗܝ] ܓܠܠܐ *hj*

26. ܠܫܡܝܐ 1°] bis scr. uid. (l), sed c pr m uid. *j*

27. ܐܫܬܓܫܘ *g*] ܐܫܬܓܫܘ *ef hj* | ܐܝܟ ܪܘܝܐ] ܐܝܟ ܪܘܝܐ *j**(frt) (= Pesh), sed c pr m

28. ܐܘܠܨܢܗܘܢ] ܐܘܠܨܢܗܘܢ *h*

29. ܠܕܡܝܟܬܐ] ܕܡܝܟܬܐ *hj*

30. ܓܠܠܘܗܝ] s. sey. *ef hj*

31. ܛܝܒܘܬܗ] ܛܝܒܘܬܗ *f*, ܛܝܒܘܬܗ *g* | ܠܒܢܝ ܐܢܫܐ *f*] c. sey. *g**(uid.), sed puncta sey. inducta sunt pr m

32. ܢܪܝܡܘܢܝܗܝ] ܢܪܝܡܘܢܝܗܝ (sic) *f j*

34. ܐܪܥܐ > *e**, sed c pr m

36. ܟܦܢܐ] ܟܦܢܐ *hj* | ܠܡܥܡܪܗܝܢ] ܠܡܥܡܪܗܝܢ *hj*

38. ܘܒܥܝܪܗܘܢ] ܘܒܥܝܪܗܘܢ *hj* | ܘܣܓܝܘ] ܘܣܓܝܘ *f*

39. ܘܕܟܘܪܗܢܐ] > *e*; ܟܘܪܗܢܐ *j*

40. ܫܛܝܬܐ] ܫܛܝܬܐ *f hj* | ܪܘܫܢܐ] ܪܘܫܢܐ *f* | ܒܡܕܒܪܐ] ܒܡܕܒܪܐ *j* | ܐܘܪܚܐ] ܐܘܪܚܐ *hj*

CVI

[illegible] 41
[illegible]
[illegible] 42
[illegible]
[illegible]
[illegible] 43
[illegible]

CVII

[illegible]
[illegible]
[illegible] 1
[illegible]
[illegible]
[illegible] 2
[illegible]
[illegible]
[illegible] 3
[illegible]
[illegible] 4
[illegible]
[illegible]

5 [illegible]
[illegible]
6 [illegible]
[illegible]
7 [illegible]
[illegible]
[illegible]
8 [illegible]
[illegible]
9 [illegible]
[illegible]
[illegible]
[illegible]
10 [illegible]
[illegible]
11 [illegible]
[illegible]
[illegible]
12 [illegible]
[illegible]
13 [illegible]
[illegible]

ae(fg) hj

41. [illegible]] [illegible] *f*, [illegible] *j* | [illegible]] [illegible] *hj*
42. [illegible]] [illegible] *e*
43. [illegible]] [illegible] *ef j* | [illegible]] [illegible] *e*, [illegible] *j* | [illegible]] [illegible] *f*

CVII

Insc. [illegible] > *e j* | [illegible]] [illegible] *e*txt, sed ⁘ pro [illegible] *e*mg
1. [illegible]] [illegible] *f*
2. [illegible]] [illegible] (sic) *hj*
4. [illegible]] c. sey. *e*(sed s. puncto ؛ 1°) *hj* | [illegible]] c. sey. *e*
5. [illegible]] s. sey. *hj*
6. [illegible]] [illegible] *e j*
10. [illegible]] [illegible] *f* | [illegible]] [illegible] *α*mg*e f*mg(adsignatur α′ in *f*mg, sed non uerisimile est: cf. MT)

CVIII

[illegible]

ae(fg) hj

CVIII

Inscr. fin.] + [Syriac] *f* (= α′ in *a*mg *f*mg: cf. Field)

1. [Syriac] [Syriac] *e*c pr m uid. *j*

2. [Syriac]] linea finalis litterae [Syriac] et punctum postea sup. ras. (pr m) *a*; [Syriac] *e*

3. [Syriac]] [Syriac] *e*, [Syriac] *h*

4. [Syriac]] [Syriac] *g* (*f* hab. lemma uid. quamquam [Syriac] partim nocita, punctum est supra) **I** [Syriac]] [Syriac] *hj*

6. [Syriac]] [Syriac] *h*

7. [Syriac]] [Syriac] *e* **I** [Syriac]] [Syriac] *j*

8. [Syriac]] [Syriac] *ef*, [Syriac] *h*c pr m uid. (uerbum prius erat [Syriac]) *j* **I** [Syriac]] [Syriac] *e* **I** [Syriac]] [Syriac] *e**(uid.), sed c pr m

10. abest in *f*txt (= Pesh) quamquam est index, sed mg absc. (item abest in *g*txt, etiam est index, quamquam in mg apparet tantum [Syriac] [pro [Syriac]?]) **I** [Syriac]] [Syriac] *hj*

11. [Syriac]] [Syriac] *ef j* **I** [Syriac]] [Syriac] *e j*(!); *f* testatur tantum [Syriac] quamquam hoc uerbum conexum est ad [Syriac] in linea Pesh sup. id **I** [Syriac]] [Syriac] *ef j*

12. [Syriac]] [Syriac] *a*mg *f*mg **I** [Syriac]] [Syriac] *f*

14. [Syriac]] [Syriac] *f hj*; [Syriac] *e*

16. [Syriac]] [Syriac] *e*, [Syriac] *hj*; [Syriac] *f* **I** [Syriac] (*f*inc., *g* deest)] [Syriac] *h*; [Syriac] *j* **I** [Syriac]] [Syriac] *hj* **I** [Syriac]] [Syriac] *f*

CVIII

17 [illegible]
[illegible]
[illegible]
18 [illegible]
[illegible]
[illegible]
19 [illegible]
[illegible]
[illegible]
20 [illegible]
[illegible]
[illegible]
21 [illegible]
[illegible]
[illegible]
[illegible]
22 [illegible]
[illegible]
[illegible]

CVIII

23 [illegible]
[illegible]
24 [illegible]
[illegible]
25 [illegible]
[illegible]
[illegible]
26 [illegible]
[illegible]
27 [illegible]
[illegible]
28 [illegible]
[illegible]
[illegible]
[illegible]
29 [illegible]
[illegible]
30 [illegible]
[illegible]
31 [illegible]
[illegible]

αe(fg) hj

17. [illegible] *f*] [illegible] *g* | [illegible]] [illegible] *f*; [illegible] *j* | [illegible]] [illegible] *e*; [illegible] *j*

19. [illegible]] [illegible] *e*

20. [illegible]] [illegible] *j**(uid.), sed c pr m et postea sequitur [illegible] sicut in lemmate | [illegible]] s. sey. *g* (*f* inc.)

21. [illegible] 2° > *j* | [illegible]] [illegible] *e*, [illegible] *j*

22. [illegible]] [illegible] *hj*

23. [illegible]] [illegible] *h*, [illegible] *j*

24. [illegible] (*f* inc.)] [illegible] *g*; [illegible] (sic) *j* | [illegible]] [illegible] *j*

25. [illegible] (*j* perditum)] [illegible] *e* | [illegible]] [illegible] (sic) *j*

28. [illegible] > *hj* | [illegible]] haec linea abest in *f*txt (= Pesh) quamquam est index, sed ulla lectio in mg periit (item abest in *g*txt, etiam est index, quamquam non est lectio in mg)

29. [illegible]] [illegible] sup. ras. (pr m uid.) *j*

31. [illegible]] [illegible] *j*

CIX

[illegible]
1 [illegible]
2 [illegible]
3 [illegible]
4 [illegible]
5 [illegible]
6 [illegible]
7 [illegible]

CX

[illegible]

CX

1 [illegible]
2 [illegible]
3 [illegible]
4 [illegible]
5 [illegible]
6 [illegible]
7 [illegible]
8 [illegible]
9 [illegible]
10 [illegible]

αe(fg) hj

CIX

Insc. [illegible]] [illegible] *f*
1. [illegible]] [illegible] *h*
3. [illegible]] s. sey. *h* | [illegible]] [illegible] *hj*
4. [illegible]] [illegible] *e*c(ras. in latitudine e fere tribus litteris, quarum uestigia restant, antecedit hoc uerbum) *hj*; [illegible] *f*
5. [illegible]] [illegible] *e**(uid.), sed c pr m | [illegible]] sup. ras. (sed pr m) *e*
6. [illegible]] + [illegible] *j**(uid.) (cf. Pesh), sed c pr m
7. [illegible]] [illegible] *e* | [illegible]] [illegible] *j**(uid.) (= Pesh), sed c pr m uid. | [illegible]] [illegible] *e hj*

CX

Insc. [illegible]] [illegible] *e* | [illegible]] [illegible] *e*; s. notis *f hj*
1. [illegible]] [illegible] *j**(uid.) (= Pesh), sed c pr m uid. | [illegible]] c. sey. *f* | [illegible]] [illegible] *e*
2. [illegible]] s. sey. *hj* | [illegible]] [illegible] *f*
5. [illegible]] [illegible] *hj* | [illegible]] [illegible] *ef j*, [illegible] *h*
6. [illegible]] s. sey. *α*mg*ef*mg | [illegible]] [illegible] *e hj*
8. [illegible] 1° ∩ 2° *hj* | [illegible]] c. sey. *e*
9. [illegible]] [illegible] *ef j*, [illegible] *h*
10. [illegible]] [illegible] *f*

CXI

[illegible]
[illegible]
1 [illegible]
[illegible]
[illegible]
2 [illegible]
[illegible]
3 [illegible]
[illegible]
4 [illegible]
[illegible]
[illegible]
5 [illegible]
[illegible]
6 [illegible]
[illegible]
7 [illegible]
[illegible]
8 [illegible]
[illegible]
9 [illegible]
[illegible]
[illegible]

10 [illegible]
[illegible]
[illegible]

CXII

[illegible]
1 [illegible]
[illegible]
2 [illegible]
[illegible]
3 [illegible]
[illegible]
[illegible]
4 [illegible]
[illegible]
[illegible]
5 [illegible]
6 [illegible]
[illegible]
7 [illegible]
[illegible]
8 [illegible]
[illegible]
9 [illegible]
[illegible]

αe(fg) hj

CXI

Inscr. [illegible] *e* | [illegible] *e*; s. notis *e*(cf. sup.)*f hj*

3. [illegible] pr. [illegible] *e** (cf. Pesh), sed inductum est (pr m uid.) | [illegible] c. sey. *h*

4. [illegible] > *j* | [illegible] > *e*

5. [illegible] *e*, [illegible] *hj* | [illegible] *h*, [illegible] *j*

6. [illegible] > *j** (!), sed c pr m | [illegible] *ef hj*

7. [illegible] *e j*

8. [illegible] (*j* inc.)] [illegible] *e*

9. [illegible] *e*

10. [illegible] *e*

CXII

Inscr. [illegible] *e*

1. [illegible] *j*

2. [illegible] *e h*, [illegible] *j*

3. [illegible] *hj*

4. [illegible] c. sey. *e*

6. [illegible] *ef hj* | [illegible] *f*

CXIII

⁘ ܗܠܠܘܝܐ ⁘

ܒܡܦܩܗ ܕܐܝܣܪܝܠ ܡܢ ܡܨܪܝܢ: 1
ܘܒܝܬܗ ܕܝܥܩܘܒ ܡܢ ܥܡܐ ܒܪܒܪܝܐ.

ܗܘܬ ܝܗܘܕ ܠܩܘܕܫܗ. 2
ܐܝܣܪܝܠ ܫܘܠܛܢܗ ܕܝܠܗ.
ܝܡܐ ܚܙܐ ܘܥܪܩ. 3
ܘܝܘܪܕܢܢ ܗܦܟ ܠܒܣܬܪܗ.
ܛܘܪܐ ܕܘܨܘ ܐܝܟ ܕܟܪܐ. 4
ܘܪܡܬܐ ܐܝܟ ܐܡܪܐ ܕܥܢܐ.
ܡܢܐ ܠܟ ܐܝܬ ܝܡܐ ܕܥܪܩܬ: 5
ܘܠܟ ܝܘܪܕܢܢ ܕܗܦܟܬ ܠܒܣܬܪܟ:
ܛܘܪܐ ܕܕܘܨܬܘܢ ܐܝܟ ܕܟܪܐ. 6
ܘܪܡܬܐ ܐܝܟ ܐܡܪܐ ܕܥܢܐ.
ܡܢ ܩܕܡ ܦܪܨܘܦܗ ܕܡܪܝܐ 7
ܙܥܬ ܐܪܥܐ.
ܡܢ ܩܕܡ ܦܪܨܘܦܗ ܕܐܠܗܗ ܕܝܥܩܘܒ.
ܗܘ ܕܗܦܟ ܠܫܘܥܐ ܠܐܓܡܐ ܕܡܝܐ. 8
ܘܠܛܪܢܐ ܠܡܒܘܥܐ ܕܡܝܐ.
ܠܐ ܠܢ ܡܪܝܐ ܠܐ ܠܢ. 9(1)
ܐܠܐ ܠܫܡܟ ܗܒ ܫܘܒܚܐ.
ܥܠ ܛܝܒܘܬܟ ܘܩܘܫܬܟ.
ܕܠܡܐ ܢܐܡܪܘܢ ܥܡܡܐ 10(2)
ܐܝܟܐ ܐܝܬܘܗܝ ܐܠܗܗܘܢ.
ܐܠܗܢ ܕܝܢ ܕܠܥܠ ܒܫܡܝܐ. 11(3)
ܒܫܡܝܐ ܘܒܐܪܥܐ.
ܟܠܗܝܢ ܐܝܠܝܢ ܕܨܒܐ ܥܒܕ.
ܦܬܟܪܐ ܕܥܡܡܐ ܣܐܡܐ ܘܕܗܒܐ. 12(4)

ܥܒܕܐ ܕܐܝܕܝܐ ܕܒܢܝܢܫܐ.
13(5) ܦܘܡܐ ܐܝܬ ܠܗܘܢ ܘܠܐ ܡܡܠܠܝܢ.
ܥܝܢܐ ܐܝܬ ܠܗܘܢ ܘܠܐ ܚܙܝܢ.
14(6) ܐܕܢܐ ܐܝܬ ܠܗܘܢ ܘܠܐ ܫܡܥܝܢ.
ܢܚܝܪܐ ܐܝܬ ܠܗܘܢ ܘܠܐ ܡܪܝܚܝܢ.
15(7) ܐܝܕܝܐ ܐܝܬ ܠܗܘܢ ܘܠܐ ܡܓܫܫܝܢ.
ܪܓܠܐ ܐܝܬ ܠܗܘܢ ܘܠܐ ܡܗܠܟܝܢ.
ܠܐ ܢܗܓܘܢ ܒܓܓܪܬܗܘܢ.
16(8) ܕܡܝܢ ܠܗܘܢ ܢܗܘܘܢ ܥܒܘܕܝܗܘܢ.
ܘܟܠܗܘܢ ܐܝܠܝܢ ܕܬܟܝܠܝܢ ܥܠܝܗܘܢ.
17(9) ܒܝܬܗ ܕܐܝܣܪܝܠ ܣܒܪ ܒܡܪܝܐ.
ܡܥܕܪܢܗܘܢ ܘܡܣܬܪܢܐ ܕܝܠܗܘܢ
ܐܝܬܘܗܝ.
18(10) ܒܝܬܐ ܕܐܗܪܘܢ ܣܒܪ ܒܡܪܝܐ.
ܡܥܕܪܢܗܘܢ ܘܡܣܬܪܢܐ ܕܝܠܗܘܢ
ܐܝܬܘܗܝ.
19(11) ܕܕܚܠܝܗܝ ܕܡܪܝܐ ܣܒܪܘ ܒܡܪܝܐ.
ܡܥܕܪܢܗܘܢ ܘܡܣܬܪܢܐ ܕܝܠܗܘܢ
ܐܝܬܘܗܝ.
20(12) ܡܪܝܐ ܕܟܪ. ܐܬܕܟܪܢ ܒܪܟ ܠܢ.
ܒܪܟ ܠܒܝܬܐ ܕܐܝܣܪܝܠ.
ܒܪܟ ܠܒܝܬܐ ܕܐܗܪܘܢ.
21(13) ܒܪܟ ܡܪܝܐ ܠܕܚܠܘܗܝ.
ܠܙܥܘܪܐ ܥܡ ܪܘܪܒܐ.
22(14) ܢܘܣܦ ܡܪܝܐ ܥܠܝܟܘܢ.
ܥܠܝܟܘܢ ܘܥܠ ܒܢܝܐ ܕܝܠܟܘܢ.
23(15) ܡܒܪܟܐ ܐܢܬܘܢ ܠܡܪܝܐ.

ae(fg) hj

CXIII

Insc. ܗܠܠܘܝܐ (*j* perditum)] ܗܠܠܘܝܗ *e*
1. ܕܐܝܣܪܐܝܠ] ܕܐܝܣܪܝܠ *e*, ܕܐܝܣܪܐܝܠ *f h*, ܐܝܠ[ ] *j*
2. ܐܝܣܪܐܝܠ] ܝܣܪܐܝܠ *e*, ܐܝܣܪܐܝܠ *f j*, ܝܣܪܐܝܠ *h*
3. ܠܒܣܬܪܗ] ܠ sup. ras. (sed pr m) *a*
4. ܕܘܨܘ] ܕܘܙܘ *j*
5. ܐܝܬ] ܐܝܬ (sic) *f* | ܘܠܟ] ܘܐ (pro ܘ) *a*mg*f*mg | ܠܒܣܬܪܟ] ܕܗܦܟ ܠܒܣܬܪܟ *hj*; ܠܒܣܬܪܟ *e*
6. ܕܕܘܨܬܘܢ] ܕܕܘܙܬܘܢ *j*
7. ܡܢ 2°] ܘܡܢ *j**(uid.) (= Pesh), sed ܘ erasa est
8. ܘܠܡܒܘܥܐ] c. sey. *j*
11(3). ܒܫܡܝܐ 1° > *e* | ܒܫܡܝܐ ܘܒܐܪܥܐ > *h* | ܡܪܝܐ > *e*
12(4). ܕܗܒܐ] c. sey. *ef* | ܕܒܢܝܢܫܐ] ܕܒܢܝ ܐܢܫܐ *e*
16(8). ܥܒܘܕܝܗܘܢ] ܐܝܠܝܢ ܕܥܒܕܝܢ ܠܗܘܢ *hj*
17(9). ܕܐܝܣܪܐܝܠ] ܕܐܝܣܪܝܠ *e*, ܕܐܝܣܪܐܝܠ *f hj* | ܒܡܪܝܐ] ܥܠ ܡܪܝܐ *hj*
18(10). ܒܡܪܝܐ] ܥܠ ܡܪܝܐ *hj*
19(11). ܣܒܪܘ] ܘ > *e** (sic), sed c pr m uid. | ܒܡܪܝܐ] ܥܠܘܗܝ *hj*
20(12). ܕܐܝܣܪܐܝܠ] ܕܐܝܣܪܝܠ *e*

CXIII

ܗܘ ܕܥܒܕ ܫܡܝܐ ܘܐܪܥܐ.
ܫܡܝ̈ ܫܡܝܐ ܕܡܪܝܐ. 24(16)
ܐܪܥܐ ܕܝܢ ܝܗܒ ܠܒܢܝ̈ ܐܢܫܐ.
ܠܐ ܗܘܘ ܡܝ̈ܬܐ ܢܫܒܚܘܢܟ ܡܪܝܐ. 25(17)
ܐܦܠܐ ܟܠܗܘܢ ܐܝܠܝܢ ܕܢܚܬܝܢ ܠܫܝܘܠ.
ܐܠܐ ܚܢܢ ܚܝ̈ܐ ܢܒܪܟ ܠܡܪܝܐ. 26(18)
ܡܢ ܗܫܐ ܘܥܕܡܐ ܠܥܠܡ ܀

CXIV

܀ ܗܠܠܘܝܐ ܀
ܐܚܒܬ ܡܛܠ ܕܫܡܥ ܡܪܝܐ 1
ܩܠܐ ܕܒܥܘܬܝ.
ܡܛܠ ܕܐܪܟܢ ܐܕܢܗ ܠܝ. 2
ܘܒܝܘܡܬܝ ܐܩܪܝܘܗܝ.
ܣܚܪܘܢܝ ܚܒ̈ܠܐ ܕܡܘܬܐ. 3
ܐܘܠ̈ܨܢܐ ܕܫܝܘܠ ܐܫܟܚܘܢܝ.
ܐܘܠܨܢܐ ܘܟܪܝܘܬܐ ܐܫܟܚܬ.
ܘܠܫܡܗ ܕܡܪܝܐ ܩܪܝܬ. 4
ܐܘ ܡܪܝܐ ܦܨܝܗ ܠܢܦܫܝ.
ܡܪܚܡܢܐ ܡܪܝܐ ܘܙܕܝܩܐ. 5
ܘܐܠܗܢ ܡܪܚܡ.
6 ܢܛܪܐ ܕܛܠܝ̈ܐ ܡܪܝܐ.
ܐܬܡܟܟܬ ܘܦܪܩܢܝ.
7 ܐܬܦܢܝ ܢܦܫܝ ܠܢܝܚܟܝ.
ܡܛܠ ܕܡܪܝܐ ܫܦܪ ܥܒܕ ܠܟܝ.
8 ܡܛܠ ܕܦܨܝܗ ܢܦܫܝ ܡܢ ܡܘܬܐ:
ܠܥܝ̈ܢܝ ܡܢ ܕܡ̈ܥܐ:
ܠܪ̈ܓܠܝ ܡܢ ܫܘܪܥܬܐ.
9 ܐܫܦܪ ܩܕܡ ܡܪܝܐ ܒܐܪܥܐ ܕܚ̈ܝܐ ܀

CXV

܀ ܗܠܠܘܝܐ ܀
1(10) ܗܝܡܢܬ ܥܠ ܗܕܐ ܡܠܠܬ.
ܐܢܐ ܕܝܢ ܐܬܡܟܟܬ ܛܒ.
2(11) ܐܢܐ ܕܝܢ ܐܡܪܬ ܒܬܡܗܘܬܐ
ܕܟܠ ܒܪܢܫܐ ܕܓܠ.
3(12) ܡܢܐ ܐܦܪܘܥ ܠܡܪܝܐ ܡܛܠ
ܟܠܗܝܢ ܐܝܠܝܢ ܕܦܪܥܢܝ.
4(13) ܟܣܐ ܕܦܘܪܩܢܐ ܐܣܒ.
ܘܠܫܡܗ ܕܡܪܝܐ ܐܩܪܐ.
5(14) ܢܕܪ̈ܝ ܠܡܪܝܐ ܐܦܪܘܥ.

ae(fg) hj

24(16). ܫܡܝ̈] s. sey. *e hj* | ܕܐܢܫܐ] c. sey. *e j*
26(18). ܐܠܐ] ܐܦ *f* | ܠܡܪܝܐ] bis scr. *j** (l), sed 2° c pr m ad ܡܢ

CXIV

Insor. ܗܠܠܘܝܐ] ܗܠܠܘܝܗ *e*
1. ܩܠܐ] scriptura (frt ܒ) manus incertae in a^{mg}—uoluitne ܒܩܠܐ scriptor?
2. ܕܐܪܟܢ] ܕܐܪܟܢ *hj*
3. ܡܬܒܪ̈ܘܢܐ] ܡܬܒܪ̈ܢܐ *e*
4. ܦܪܘܩܝܗ] ܦܪܘܩ *hj*
5. ܡܪ̈ܚܡ] ܡܪܚܡ *ef h*, ܡܪܚܡ *j*
6. ܢܛܪܐ] c. sey. (sic) *j*
7. ܐܬܦܢܝ] ܐܬܦܢܝ *e*, ܐܬܦܢܝ *hj*
8. ܠܥܝ̈ܢܝ-ܕܡ̈ܥܐ] f^{mg}† | ܫܘܪܥܬܐ] c. sey. *hj**(sed punctum alterum apud ܪ erasum est)

CXV

Insor. ܗܠܠܘܝܐ] ܗܠܠܘܝܗ *e*; > *f*
1(10). ܥܠ ܗܕܐ] ܒܗܕܐ *ef*
2(11). ܒܬܡܗܘܬܐ] ܒܬܡܗܘܢܘܬܐ $f^{txt}g^{txt*}$, ܒܬܡܗܘܢܘܬܐ (sic) g^{txt} c pr m uid.; ܒܬܡܗܘܬܐ $f^{mg}g^{mg}$ c pr m uid. (ambo adsignant ܟܠܐܢܫ), ܒܬܡܗܬܐ (sic) g^{mg*} | ܕܓܠ] ܕܓܠ *e* | ܒܪܢܫܐ] *f* testatur tantum ܐܢܫܐ sub ܐܢܫ ex ܒܪ ܐܢܫ in linea Pesh
5(14). fin.] + ܩܕܡ ܟܠܗ ܥܡܐ ܕܝܠܗ *e*

CXV

[illegible] 6(15)
[illegible]
[illegible] 7(16)
[illegible]
[illegible]
[illegible] 8(17)
[illegible]
[illegible] 9(18)
[illegible]
[illegible] 10(19)
[illegible]

CXVI

[illegible]
[illegible] 1
[illegible]
[illegible] 2
[illegible]

CXVII

[illegible]
1 [illegible]
[illegible]
2 [illegible]
[illegible]
[illegible]
3 [illegible]
[illegible]
[illegible]
4 [illegible]
[illegible]
[illegible]
5 [illegible]
[illegible]
6 [illegible]
[illegible]

ae(fg) hj

6(15). [illegible]] [illegible] *hj*
7(16). [illegible]] [illegible] *hj*^c(litterae [illegible] sup. ras., sed qua manu correctae sunt inc.) | [illegible]] [illegible] *e* | [illegible]] [illegible] *f*
10(19). [illegible]] [illegible] [illegible] *hj*; [illegible] *f* | [illegible]] [illegible] *e*, [illegible] *j*

CXVI

Inscr. [illegible]] [illegible] *e*
1. [illegible]] [illegible] *e*; [illegible] *hj*
2. [illegible]] [illegible] *f*

CXVII

Inscr. [illegible]] [illegible] *e*
2. [illegible]] [illegible] *f* | [illegible]] [illegible] *e*, [illegible] *f hj* | [illegible]] [illegible] *f*
3. [illegible] 1° > *hj* | [illegible]] [illegible] *f*
4. [illegible] 1° > *hj* | [illegible]] [illegible] *f*
6. [illegible] ⌒ [illegible] u. 7 et textus ad [illegible] ex [illegible] 1° u. 8 scriptus est uid. *j**, sed c pr m

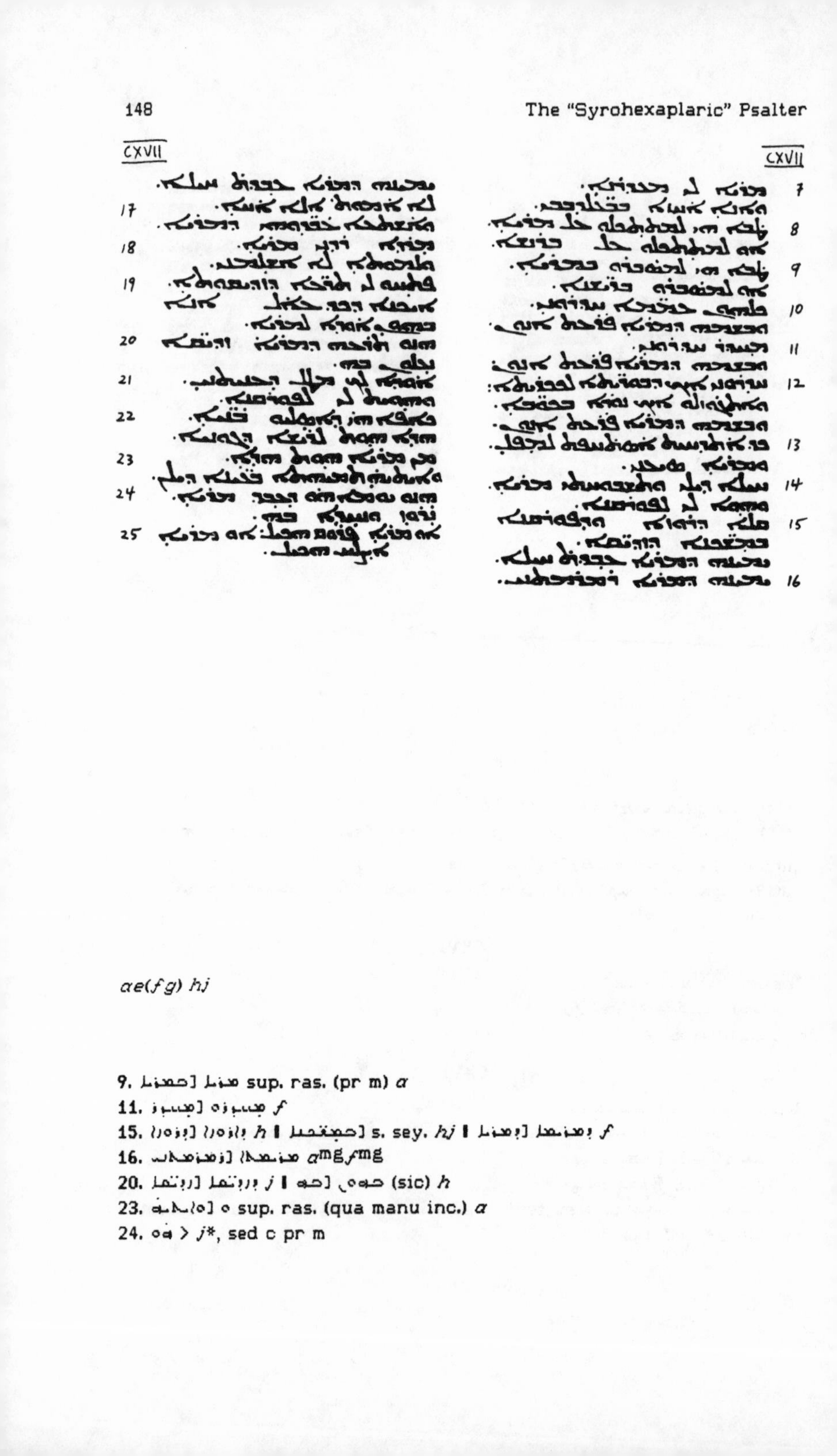

CXVII

7 [illegible]
[illegible]
8 [illegible]
[illegible]
9 [illegible]
[illegible]
10 [illegible]
[illegible]
11 [illegible]
[illegible]
12 [illegible]
[illegible]
[illegible]
13 [illegible]
[illegible]
14 [illegible]
[illegible]
15 [illegible]
[illegible]
[illegible]
16 [illegible]

CXVII

[illegible]
17 [illegible]
[illegible]
18 [illegible]
[illegible]
19 [illegible]
[illegible]
[illegible]
20 [illegible]
[illegible]
21 [illegible]
[illegible]
22 [illegible]
[illegible]
23 [illegible]
[illegible]
24 [illegible]
[illegible]
25 [illegible]
[illegible]

αe(fg) hj

9. [illegible]] [illegible] sup. ras. (pr m) *α*
11. [illegible]] [illegible] *f*
15. [illegible]] [illegible] *h* | [illegible]] s. sey. *hj* | [illegible]] [illegible] *f*
16. [illegible]] [illegible] *α*mg *f*mg
20. [illegible]] [illegible] *j* | [illegible]] [illegible] (sic) *h*
23. [illegible]] ܘ sup. ras. (qua manu inc.) *α*
24. [illegible] > *j**, sed c pr m

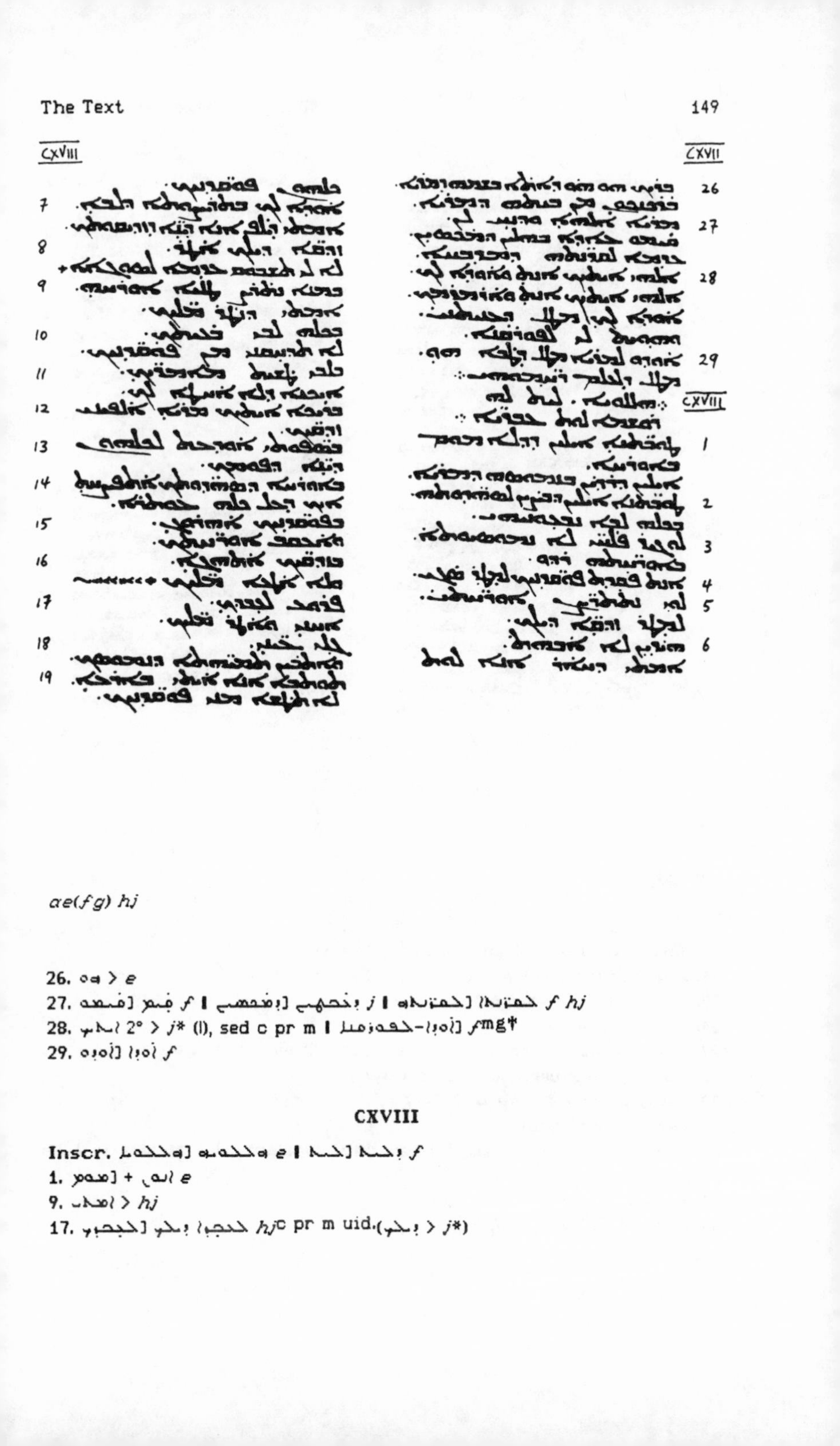

CXVII

26 [illegible]
[illegible]
27 [illegible]
[illegible]
[illegible]
28 [illegible]
[illegible]
[illegible]
[illegible]
29 [illegible]
[illegible]

CXVIII

[illegible]
[illegible]
1 [illegible]
[illegible]
[illegible]
2 [illegible]
[illegible]
3 [illegible]
[illegible]
4 [illegible]
5 [illegible]
[illegible]
6 [illegible]
[illegible]
[illegible]
7 [illegible]
[illegible]
8 [illegible]
[illegible]
9 [illegible]
[illegible]
10 [illegible]
[illegible]
11 [illegible]
[illegible]
12 [illegible]
[illegible]
13 [illegible]
[illegible]
14 [illegible]
[illegible]
15 [illegible]
[illegible]
16 [illegible]
[illegible]
17 [illegible]
[illegible]
18 [illegible]
[illegible]
19 [illegible]
[illegible]

αe(fg) hj

26. [illegible] > *e*
27. [illegible]] [illegible] *f hj* | [illegible]] [illegible] *j* | [illegible]] [illegible] *f*
28. [illegible] 2° > *j** (l), sed c pr m | [illegible]] [illegible] *f* mg*
29. [illegible]] [illegible] *f*

CXVIII

Insc. [illegible]] [illegible] *f* | [illegible]] [illegible] *e*
1. [illegible]] + [illegible] *e*
9. [illegible] > *hj*
17. [illegible]] [illegible] *hj* c pr m uid. ([illegible] > *j**)

CXVIII

20 [illegible]
[illegible]
21 [illegible]
[illegible]
22 [illegible]
[illegible]
23 [illegible]
[illegible]
[illegible]
24 [illegible]
[illegible]
[illegible]
25 [illegible]
[illegible]
26 [illegible]
[illegible]
27 [illegible]
[illegible]
28 [illegible]
[illegible]
29 [illegible]
[illegible]
30 [illegible]
[illegible]
31 [illegible]
[illegible]

CXVIII

32 [illegible]
[illegible]
33 [illegible]
[illegible]
[illegible]
34 [illegible]
[illegible]
35 [illegible]
[illegible]
36 [illegible]
[illegible]
37 [illegible]
[illegible]
[illegible]
38 [illegible]
[illegible]
39 [illegible]
[illegible]
40 [illegible]
[illegible]
41 [illegible]
[illegible]
42 [illegible]
[illegible]
43 [illegible]
[illegible]
[illegible]

ae(fg) hj

20. ܐܬܪܓܪܓܬ] ܐܬܪܓܪܓ *e j* | ܒܟܠܙܒܢ] ܒܟܠ ܙܒܢ *e*
21. ܓܥܪܬ] uocalis ܦܬܚܐ apud ܥ, itaque Pa'el est *e*
22. ܘܡܣܗܕܘܬܟ] ܘܣܗܕܘܬܟ *f h*
24. ܘܡܠܟܝ] c. sey. *e*
27. ܕܦܘܩܕܢܝܟ] spatium pro littera una inter ܕ 2° et ܩ (ras. uid.) *e*;
ܕܝܠܟ ܘܦܘܩܕܢܐ *j* (in *h* uerbum prius est ܦܘܩܕܢܐ)
30. ܕܝܢܝܟ] ܘܕܝܢܝܟ *f* | ܢܛܪܬ ܗܘܝܬ] ܢܛܪܬ *hj*
31. ܐܟܗܦܢܝ] ܐܟܗܦܢ (sic) *j*
32. ܗܘܝܬ] s. puncto (etiam *hj*) sed hab. uocalem ܦܬܚܐ apud ܘ *e*; ܗܘܝܬ *f*
35. ܒܫܒܝܠܐ] c. sey. *j*
36. ܠܡܣܗܕܘܬܟ] ܠܣܗܕܘܬܟ *h*

CXVIII

44 ܘܐܛܪ ܢܡܘܣܟ ܒܟܠܙܒܢ.
ܠܥܠܡ ܥܠܡܝܢ.
45 ܘܐܗܠܟ ܗܘܝܬ ܒܪܘܝܚܘܬܐ.
ܡܛܠ ܕܠܦܘܩܕܢܝܟ ܒܥܝܬ.
46 ܘܡܡܠܠ ܗܘܝܬ ܒܣܗܕܘܬܟ.
ܩܕܡ ܡܠܟܐ ܘܠܐ ܒܗܬ ܗܘܝܬ.
47 ܘܡܬܦܢܩ ܗܘܝܬ ܒܦܘܩܕܢܝܟ
ܗܠܝܢ ܕܐܚܒܬ ܛܒ.
48 ܘܐܪܝܡܬ ܐܝܕܝ ܠܘܬ ܦܘܩܕܢܝܟ
ܗܠܝܢ ܕܐܚܒܬ.
ܘܡܬܗܓܐ ܗܘܝܬ ܒܢܡܘܣܐ ܕܝܠܟ.
49 ܐܬܕܟܪ ܡܠܬܟ ܠܥܒܕܟ ܕܥܠ
ܗܝ ܕܣܒܪܬܢܝ.
50 ܗܝ ܒܘܝܐܬܐ ܒܡܘܟܟܝ.
ܡܛܠ ܕܡܠܬܟ ܐܚܝܬܢܝ.
51 ܘܥܘܠܐ ܒܣܪܝܢ ܗܘܘ ܥܠ
ܢܡܘܣܟ ܒܒܙܚܐ ܠܡܒܙܚܘ.
ܡܢ ܕܝܢ ܢܡܘܣܟ ܠܐ ܐܬܦܢܝܬ.
52 ܐܬܕܟܪܬ ܕܝܢܝܟ ܡܪܝܐ.
ܕܡܢ ܥܠܡ ܘܐܬܒܝܐܬ.
53 ܒܟܪܝܘܬܐ ܐܚܕܬܢܝ ܡܢ ܚܛܝܐ.
ܗܢܘܢ ܕܫܒܩܘ ܢܡܘܣܟ.
54 ܙܡܝܪܬܐ ܠܝ ܙܕܩܐ ܕܝܠܟ ܡܪܝܐ.
ܒܒܝܬܐ ܕܬܘܬܒܘܬܐ ܕܝܠܝ.
55 ܐܬܕܟܪܬ ܒܠܠܝܐ ܫܡܟ.
ܘܢܛܪܬ ܢܡܘܣܟ.
56 ܗܕܐ ܗܘܬ ܠܝ.
ܡܛܠ ܕܙܕܩܐ ܕܝܠܟ ܢܛܪܬ +++
57 ܡܢܬܐ ܕܝܠܝ ܐܢܬ ܡܪܝܐ.
ܐܡܪܬ ܠܡܛܪ ܢܡܘܣܟ.
58 ܒܥܝܬ ܡܢ ܩܕܡ ܐܦܝܟ ܒܟܠܗ ܠܒܝ.
ܪܚܡ ܥܠܝ ܐܝܟ ܡܠܬܟ.
59 ܡܛܠ ܕܐܬܚܫܒܬ ܐܘܪܚܬܟ.
ܘܐܦܢܝܬ ܪܓܠܝ ܠܣܗܕܘܬܟ.
60 ܐܬܛܝܒܬ ܘܠܐ ܐܬܕܘܝܬ.
ܠܡܛܪ ܦܘܩܕܢܝܟ.
61 ܚܒܠܐ ܕܚܛܝܐ ܐܬܟܪܟܘ ܥܠܝ.
ܘܢܡܘܣܟ ܠܐ ܛܥܝܬ.
62 ܒܦܠܓܗ ܕܠܠܝܐ ܡܬܬܥܝܪ
ܗܘܝܬ ܠܡܘܕܝܘ ܠܟ.
ܥܠ ܕܝܢܐ ܕܙܕܝܩܘܬܟ.
63 ܡܫܘܬܦܐ ܐܢܐ ܐܢܘܢ
ܠܟܠܗܘܢ ܕܕܚܠܝܢ.
ܘܠܐܝܠܝܢ ܕܢܛܪܝܢ ܦܘܩܕܢܝܟ.
64 ܛܝܒܘܬܟ ܡܪܝܐ ܡܠܝܐ ܐܪܥܐ.
ܙܕܩܐ ܕܝܠܟ ܐܠܦܢܝ +++
65 ܛܝܒܘܬܐ ܥܒܕܬ ܥܡ ܥܒܕܟ.
ܡܪܝܐ ܐܚܝܢܝ ܐܝܟ ܡܠܬܟ.
66 ܛܝܒܘܬܐ ܘܡܪܕܘܬܐ
ܘܝܕܥܬܐ ܐܠܦܢܝ.
ܡܛܠ ܕܠܦܘܩܕܢܝܟ ܗܝܡܢܬ.
67 ܩܕܡ ܕܐܬܡܟܟ ܐܢܐ ܐܣܟܠܬ.
ܘܡܟܝܠ ܡܠܬܟ ܢܛܪܬ.

ae(fg) hj

45. ܒܪܘܝܚܘܬܐ] ܒܪܘܚܘܬܐ *ef hj*
46. ܒܣܗܕܘܬܟ] s. sey. *f*, ܒܣܗܕܘܬܐ ܕܝܠܟ *hj*
47. ܒܦܘܩܕܢܝܟ] ܒܦ sup. ras. (pr m uid.) *j*
48. ܐܝܕܝ] ܐܝܕܐ *j* (ܐܝܕܐ ܕܝܠܝ *h*)
49. ܣܒܪܬܢܝ] ܕܣܒܪܬܢܝ *e*, ܣܒܪܬܢ *h*
52. ܕܡܢ] sup. ras. (pr m uid.) *j*; ܡܢ *f*
53. ܕܢܫܒܩܘܢ ܗܢܘܢ] ܕܫܒܩܘ ܢܡܘܣܟ *a**, sed c pr m | ܕܫܒܩܘܢ] ܕܢܫܒܩܘܢ *ef hj*
57. ܐܢܬ] pr. ܐܠܗܝ *hj*
59. ܐܘܪܚܬܟ] ܐܘܪܚܬܐ ܕܝܠܟ *hj*
63. ܡܫܘܬܦܐ] ܡܫܘܬܦܢܐ *f* | ܕܕܚܠܝܢ ܠܟ] ܠܐܝܠܝܢ ܕܕܚܠܝܢ *hj*
66. ܘܐܝܕܥܬܐ] ܘܝܕܥܬܐ *ef hj*
67. ܕܡܬܡܟܟ *f*] ܡܟܝܠ ܗܘܐ *g h*

CXVIII

68 [illegible]
[illegible]
[illegible]
69 [illegible]
[illegible]
[illegible]
70 [illegible]
[illegible]
71 [illegible]
[illegible]
72 [illegible]
[illegible]
[illegible]
73 [illegible]
[illegible]
74 [illegible]
[illegible]
75 [illegible]
[illegible]
76 [illegible]
[illegible]
77 [illegible]
[illegible]
78 [illegible]
[illegible]
[illegible]
79 [illegible]
[illegible]
80 [illegible]

CXVIII

[illegible]
81 [illegible]
[illegible]
82 [illegible]
[illegible]
83 [illegible]
[illegible]
84 [illegible]
[illegible]
[illegible]
85 [illegible]
[illegible]
86 [illegible]
[illegible]
87 [illegible]
[illegible]
88 [illegible]
[illegible]
89 [illegible]
90 [illegible]
[illegible]
91 [illegible]
[illegible]
92 [illegible]
[illegible]
[illegible]
93 [illegible]
[illegible]

ae(fg) hj

68. [illegible]] [illegible] *f*
71. [illegible]] [illegible] *e*
72. [illegible]] [illegible] *f* | [illegible] > *j*
73. [illegible]] [illegible] *e*, [illegible] *h* (c. duobus punctis ordinatis ad perpendiculum sup. ∘, quorum significatio inc.), [illegible] *j* | [illegible]] [illegible] *hj*[c] pr m uid. ([illegible] > *j**)
74. [illegible]] [illegible] *hj*
81. [illegible]] [illegible] *hj*[c] (uerbum secundum erat [illegible] [sic] *j**, sed correctum est per rasuram)
82. [illegible]] [illegible] *f* | [illegible]] [illegible] *hj* (s. puncto)
83. [illegible]] [illegible] *h* | [illegible]] [illegible] *hj*
85. ab [illegible] ad [illegible] u. 87 sup. ras. (pr m) *a*
86. ab [illegible] ad [illegible] u. 87 sup. ras. (qua manu inc.) *j* | [illegible]] [illegible] *hj* (*j* sup. ras., cf. supra)
87. [illegible]] [illegible] *j* (primae duae litterae sup. ras., cf. u. 86)
89. [illegible]] c. sey. *e*
90. [illegible]] [illegible] *hj*
91. [illegible]] *f*mg* (sed hab. [illegible] pro [illegible]) | [illegible]] [illegible] *hj* | [illegible] > *j**, sed c pr m uid.
92. [illegible]] [illegible] *j*
93. [illegible] > *e*

CXVIII

94 [illegible]

95 [illegible]

96 [illegible]

97 [illegible]

98 [illegible]

99 [illegible]

100 [illegible]

101 [illegible]

102 [illegible]

103 [illegible]

104 [illegible]

CXVIII

105 [illegible]

106 [illegible]

107 [illegible]

108 [illegible]

109 [illegible]

110 [illegible]

111 [illegible]

112 [illegible]

113 [illegible]

114 [illegible]

115 [illegible]

116 [illegible]

117 [illegible]

a(b)e(fg) hj

96. [illegible]] [illegible] *f*

98. [illegible] > *h**, sed c pr m

99. [illegible]] [illegible] *f*mg uid. (postea dicitur haec duo membra non esse in Pesh, sed in textu sunt membra congruentia in lineis Pesh et SyrPs [linea SyrPs partim testata est]; *g*mg eget [illegible] et hab. [illegible] pro [illegible] [uerbum languet in *f*mg]) | [illegible]] [illegible] *f*mg(cf. supra) *hj*

103. [illegible] > *e*

104. [illegible]] [illegible] *e j* | [illegible] 2°] *f*mg†; > *e*

110. [illegible]] c. sey. *e hj* | [illegible]] [illegible] *hj*

111. [illegible]] tr. *e*

113. [illegible] > *bef*

115. [illegible]] *f*mg† (sed hab. [illegible] pro [illegible]: cf. infra; de hac linea, cf. Rahlfs et Pesh) | [illegible]] ras. uid. sup. [illegible] 1° (erant uid. puncta sey.) *a*; c. sey. *ef*mg†(cf. supra) *hj*

116. [illegible]] [illegible] *e*c pr m (*e** non apparet)

CXVIII

118 [illegible]
119 [illegible]
120 [illegible]
121 [illegible]
122 [illegible]
123 [illegible]
124 [illegible]
125 [illegible]
126 [illegible]
127 [illegible]

CXVIII

128 [illegible]
129 [illegible]
130 [illegible]
131 [illegible]
132 [illegible]
133 [illegible]
134 [illegible]
135 [illegible]
136 [illegible]
137 [illegible]

ae(fg) hj

118. ܠܟܠܗܘܢ] ܟܠܗܘܢ *ef hj*
119. [illegible] *j*
120. [illegible] c. sey. *e*
121. [illegible] *e*, [illegible] *h*; [illegible] *f*, [illegible] *g*
123. [illegible] *f* (primo in *g* uerbum secundum erat [illegible] uid., deinde mutatum est pr m)
126. [illegible] *hj*
127. [illegible] *e j*; *f* testatur tantum [illegible] sub ÷ ex [illegible] in linea Pesh | [illegible] *e*
128. [illegible] *f* | [illegible] *e hj* | [illegible] *f*; [illegible] (sic) *g* | [illegible] *h*
129. [illegible] *e hj*; *f* testatur tantum [illegible] sub ÷ ex [illegible] in linea Pesh | [illegible] s. sey. *e hj*
130. [illegible] *e*, [illegible] *f*; [illegible] *hj* | [illegible] *h*, [illegible] *j*
131. [illegible] *h* | [illegible] *hj*
132. [illegible] *hj*(s. puncto)
133. [illegible] *e* | [illegible] *f*] [illegible] *g*
134. [illegible] *e*; *f* testatur tantum [illegible] sub [illegible] ex [illegible] in linea Pesh
136. [illegible] *a*mg*f*mg(s. puncto diacritico) | [illegible] *h* (in *j* uerbum prius est [illegible])
137. [illegible] *hj*

CXVIII

138 [illegible]
[illegible]
139 [illegible]
[illegible]
140 [illegible]
[illegible]
141 [illegible]
[illegible]
142 [illegible]
[illegible]
143 [illegible]
[illegible]
144 [illegible]
[illegible]
145 [illegible]
[illegible]
146 [illegible]
[illegible]
147 [illegible]
[illegible]
148 [illegible]
[illegible]
149 [illegible]
[illegible]
[illegible]
150 [illegible]

CXVIII

[illegible]
[illegible]
151 [illegible]
[illegible]
152 [illegible]
[illegible]
153 [illegible]
[illegible]
154 [illegible]
[illegible]
155 [illegible]
[illegible]
156 [illegible]
[illegible]
157 [illegible]
[illegible]
158 [illegible]
[illegible]
159 [illegible]
[illegible]
160 [illegible]
[illegible]
161 [illegible]
[illegible]

αe(fg) hj

CXVIII 145. [illegible]] [illegible] *a* (cf. u. 149)

138. [illegible]] [illegible] *hj*
139. [illegible]] [illegible] *j* (in *h* uerbum secundum est [illegible])
143. [illegible]] [illegible] *ef* | [illegible] *j* | [illegible] *e*,
144. [illegible]] s. sey. *e* | [illegible] *hj*; [illegible] *e*;
148. [illegible]] [illegible] *hj* c pr m([illegible] > *j**) | [illegible] *e j* | [illegible] *h*; [illegible]] [illegible] *f*
149. [illegible]] [illegible] *f*mg* | [illegible] *h* (in *j* uerbum prius est [illegible]) | [illegible] *f*,
150. [illegible]] [illegible] *hj* ([illegible] bis scr. *j**, sed c pr m uid.) | [illegible] *h* + [illegible]
151. [illegible] 2° > *e*
152. [illegible]] c. sey. *e* | [illegible] *hj* | [illegible] *e*
155. [illegible]] [illegible] *h* (in *j* uerbum prius est [illegible])
156. [illegible]] s. sey. *f hj*
157. [illegible]] c. sey. *e*
158. [illegible]] c. sey. (sic) *h*; [illegible] (sic) *f*
159. [illegible] > *j**, sed c pr m
160. [illegible]] [illegible] *f*

CXVIII

162 [Syriac]

163 [Syriac]

164 [Syriac]

165 [Syriac]

166 [Syriac]

167 [Syriac]

168 [Syriac]

169 [Syriac]

170 [Syriac]

171 [Syriac]

172 [Syriac]

173 [Syriac]

174 [Syriac]

175 [Syriac]

176 [Syriac]

CXIX

[Syriac]

1 [Syriac]

2 [Syriac]

3 [Syriac]

4 [Syriac]

5 [Syriac]

6 [Syriac]

7 [Syriac]

ae(fg) hj

162. [Syriac]] [Syriac] *j*

164. [Syriac]] s. sey. *e h* | [Syriac]] s. sey. *h*

166. [Syriac]] [Syriac] *f*

167. [Syriac]] [Syriac] *f*, [Syriac] *g*, [Syriac] *hj* | [Syriac]] s. sey. *e hj*

168. fin.] + [Syriac] *e*c pr m uid.

169. [Syriac]] [Syriac] *e* | [Syriac]] [Syriac] *hj* | [Syriac] 2° > *e*

170. [Syriac]] [Syriac] *e*

171. [Syriac]] [Syriac] *e*, [Syriac] *f hj*

172. [Syriac]] *j* hab. [Syriac], sed littera quarta uerbi prioris in *h* s. puncto [Syriac] aut sey.

176. [Syriac]] [Syriac] *e hj* | [Syriac] > *j* (sic)

CXIX

Inscr. [Syriac]] c. sey. *ef hj*

1. [Syriac]] [Syriac] *h*, [Syriac] *j* | [Syriac]] [Syriac] ([Syriac] et spatium ante [Syriac] in ras., sed [Syriac] pr m) *e*

5. [Syriac]] sup. ras. (pr m) *a*; [Syriac] *hj* | [Syriac]] c. sey. *ef hj* | [Syriac]] [Syriac] *e**, [Syriac] *e*c pr m

6. [Syriac]] [Syriac] *hj*c pr m([Syriac] > *j**)

7. [Syriac]] [Syriac] *hj*

CXXI

2 ܕܩܝܡܢ ܐܝܬܝܗܝܢ ܗܘܝ ܪ̈ܓܠܝ
ܒܬܪ̈ܥܝܟܝ ܐܘܪܫܠܡ.
3 ܐܘܪܫܠܡ ܕܡܬܒܢܝܐ ܐܝܟ ܡܕܝܢܬܐ.
ܗܝ ܕܡܫܘ̈ܬܦܬܐ ܕܝܠܗ̇ ܐܟܚܕܐ.
4 ܬܡܢ ܓܝܪ ܣܠܩܘ ܫܒ̈ܛܐ:
ܫܒ̈ܛܐ ܕܡܪܝܐ ܣܗܕܘܬܐ
ܠܐܝܣܪܝܠ:
ܠܡܘܕܝܘ ܠܫܡܗ ܕܡܪܝܐ.
5 ܡܛܠ ܕܬܡܢ ܝܬܒܘ ܟܘܪ̈ܣܘܬܐ
ܒܕܝܢܐ.
ܟܘܪ̈ܣܘܬܐ ܥܠ ܒܝܬܐ ܕܕܘܝܕ.
6 ܫܐܠܘ ܠܫܠܡ ܕܒܝܬܐ ܠܐܘܪܫܠܡ.
ܘܫܝܢܘܬܐ ܠܫܠܡ ܕܪ̈ܚܡܝܢ ܠܟܝ.
7 ܢܗܘܐ ܫܠܡ ܫܝܢܐ ܒܚܝܠܟܝ.
ܘܡܫܝܢܘܬܐ ܒܡܓ̈ܕܠܝ ܩܘܪ̈ܛܝܟܝ.
8 ܡܛܠ ܐܚܝ ܘܩܪ̈ܝܒܝ ܕܝܠܝ.
ܡܡܠܠ ܗܘܝܬ ܕܗܘ ܫܝܢܐ ܡܛܠܬܟܝ.
9 ܡܛܠ ܡܪܝܐ ܐܠܗܢ.
ܒܥܝܬ ܠܟܝ ܛ̈ܒܬܐ. ∴

CXX

∴ ܬܫܒܘܚܬܐ ܕܡܣܩܬܐ ∴
ܐܪܝܡܬ ܥܝܢܝ ܠܛܘܪ̈ܐ. 1
ܡܢ ܐܝܟܐ ܢܐܬܐ ܥܘܕܪܢܝ.
ܥܘܕܪܢܝ ܡܢ ܡܪܝܐ. 2
ܗܘ ܕܥܒܕ ܫܡܝܐ ܘܐܪܥܐ.
ܠܐ ܢܬܠ ܠܙܘܥܐ ܪܓܠܝ. 3
ܘܠܐ ܢܢܘܡ ܗܘ ܕܢܛܪ ܠܝ.
ܗܐ ܠܐ ܢܢܘܡ ܘܠܐ ܢܕܡܟ ܗܘ 4
ܕܢܛܪ ܠܐܝܣܪܝܠ.
ܡܪܝܐ ܢܛܪܟ. ܡܪܝܐ ܢܛܠܠ ܥܠ 5
ܐܝܕܟ ܕܝܡܝܢܐ ܕܝܠܟ.
ܒܐܝܡܡܐ ܫܡܫܐ ܠܐ ܢܘܟܝܟ. 6
ܘܠܐ ܣܗܪܐ ܒܠܠܝܐ.
ܡܪܝܐ ܢܛܪܟ ܡܢ ܟܠ ܒܝܫܬܐ. 7
ܢܛܪ ܢܦܫܟ ܡܪܝܐ.
ܡܪܝܐ ܢܛܪ ܡܥܠܟ ܘܡܦܩܟ. 8
ܡܢ ܗܫܐ ܘܥܕܡܐ ܠܥܠܡ +

CXXI

∴ ܬܫܒܘܚܬܐ ܕܡܣܩܬܐ ܕܕܘܝܕ ∴
ܚܕܝܬ ܟܕ ܐܡܪܝܢ ܗܘܘ ܠܝ. 1
ܠܒܝܬܗ ܕܡܪܝܐ ܢܐܙܠ.

ae(fg) hj

CXX

Insecr. ܕܡܣܩܬܐ] s. sey. *e*

1. ܥܝܢܝ] s. sey. *f* | ܠܛܘܪ̈ܐ] s. sey. *h* | ܢܐܬܐ] ܬܐܬܐ *hj*

3. ܢܬܠ] ܢܬܠܠ *hj* | ܢܢܘܡ] ܢܡ (sic) *f*

4. ܠܐܝܣܪܝܠ] ܠܐܝܣܪܝܠ (c. signo contractionis sup. ܣܪ) *h*

5. ܢܛܠܠ] ܢܛܠܠ *e*

7. ܢܛܪ ∩ ܢܛܪ u. 8 *j*

CXXI

Insecr. ܕܕܘܝܕ] ܠܕܘܝܕ *f*

1. ܟܠܐ] ܡܟܠܐ *g* (*f* absc.)

2. ܐܘܪܫܠܡ] ܐܘܪ̄ܫܠܡ *j*

3. ܐܘܪܫܠܡ] ܐܘܪܫܠܡ *j* | ܕܡܬܒܢܝܐ] ܕܡܬܒܢܝܐ *ef j* | ܕܡܫܘ̈ܬܦܬܐ] s. sey. *f*txt; ܡܫܘܬܦܘܬܐ (pro ܡܫܘ̈ܬܦܬܐ) *a*mg *f*mg

4. ܫܒ̈ܛܐ] ܫܒܛܐ *f*, ܫܒ̈ܛܐ *j* | ܕܡܪܝܐ 1°] inter ܕ ܡ ras., frt erat ܠ, sed ܕ pr m *a* | ܠܐܝܣܪܝܠ] ܠܐܝܣܪܝܠ *e*

5. ܝܬܒܘ] ܝܬܒ (sic) *j* | ܒܕܝܢܐ] ܕܕܝܢܐ *hj*

6. ܠܫܠܡ] ܫܠܡ *f* | ܠܐܘܪܫܠܡ] ܠܐܘܪܫܠܡ *j*

7. ܘܡܫܝܢܘܬܐ] ܘ sup. ras. (qua manu inc.) *j*

8. ܕܝ > *j**, sed c pr m

9. ܛ̈ܒܬܐ] ܛܒܬܐ *g* (pars superior primarum duarum litterarum periit *f*)

CXXII

1 [illegible]

[illegible]

2 [illegible]

[illegible]

3 [illegible]

[illegible]

4 [illegible]

[illegible]

CXXIII

1 [illegible]

2 [illegible]

3 [illegible]

4 [illegible]

5 [illegible]

6 [illegible]

7 [illegible]

8 [illegible]

CXXIV

1 [illegible]

2 [illegible]

3 [illegible]

4 [illegible]

5 [illegible]

ae(fg) hj

CXXII

2. [illegible] (*j* perditum)] [illegible] *f* (puncta sey. languent, sed hab. *g*) ǀ [illegible] [illegible] *f* (omnia puncta languent, sed hab. *g*)
3. [illegible] *e* ǀ [illegible] *f*

CXXIII

1. [illegible] *e hj* ǀ [illegible] *j**, sed c pr m uid. ǀ [illegible] > *e**, sed c pr m ǀ [illegible] > *j**, sed c pr m uid.
2. [illegible] *e*, [illegible] *hj* ǀ [illegible] *e hj*
3. [illegible] *f*; [illegible] (sic) *h** (qua manu correctum est inc.) ǀ [illegible] *hj*
4. [illegible] *hj* ǀ [illegible] *e j* ǀ [illegible] + [illegible] *j**(uid.) (= Pesh), sed erasum est
7. [illegible] *j*; [illegible] *f*

CXXIV

2. [illegible] 1° > *hj* ǀ [illegible] *e*, [illegible] *j* ǀ [illegible] *j*; > *e*
3. [illegible] bis scr. (!) *h* ǀ [illegible] et spatium ante hoc uerbum in ras. *j* (frt *j** habebat [illegible] post [illegible] [= Pesh], deinde Ms correctum est per rasuram)
5. [illegible] + [illegible] *e* ǀ [illegible] *e*

CXXV

[illegible]
[illegible] 1
[illegible]
[illegible] 2
[illegible]
[illegible]
[illegible] 3
[illegible]
[illegible]
[illegible] 4
[illegible]
[illegible] 5
[illegible]
[illegible] 6
[illegible]
[illegible]
[illegible]

CXXVI

[illegible]
[illegible] 1
[illegible]
[illegible]
[illegible]
[illegible] 2
[illegible]

CXXVI

[illegible]
[illegible]
[illegible]
3 [illegible]
[illegible]
4 [illegible]
[illegible]
5 [illegible]
[illegible]
[illegible]
[illegible]

CXXVII

[illegible]
1 [illegible]
[illegible]
2 [illegible]
[illegible]
[illegible]
3 [illegible]
[illegible]
[illegible]
[illegible]
4 [illegible]
[illegible]
5 [illegible]

ae(fg) hj

CXXV

1. [illegible]] [illegible] *e**(frt)(sed nunc hab. lemma pr m)*f*([illegible] languet, sed hab. *g*); [illegible] *h*; [illegible] *j*
2. [illegible]] [illegible] *ef j*
4. [illegible]] [illegible] *ef*; s. sey. *hj* | [illegible]] [illegible] (sic) *j*
5. [illegible]] [illegible] *e*, [illegible] *f j*
6. [illegible] 1°] + [illegible] *a**, sed inductum est pr m | [illegible]] [illegible] *e*, [illegible] *f j*

CXXVI

Inscr. [illegible]] [illegible] *hj*
1. [illegible]] [illegible] *ef hj*
2. [illegible]] [illegible] *hj*(s. puncto) | [illegible]] c. sey. *f j**(uid.)(ras. sup. [illegible]: cf. Pesh)
3. [illegible]] c. sey. *e*
4. [illegible]] [illegible] *f*uid. (uerba languent, sed hab. *g*)
5. [illegible] (*j* perditum)] [illegible] *g* (*f* languet, uerbum non apparet) | [illegible]] s. sey. *e*

CXXVII

3. [illegible]] s. sey. *f hj* | [illegible] *g*] > *f** (item uerbum Pesh in linea supra principio omissum est [!]), sed c pr m | [illegible]] s. sey. *e* | [illegible]] s. sey. *f*uid.(macula uid. tangit [illegible], sed *g* certe s. sey.) *hj*

CXXVII

[illegible]
[illegible]
[illegible] 6
[illegible]
[illegible]

CXXVIII

[illegible] 1
[illegible]
[illegible]
[illegible] 2
[illegible]
[illegible] 3
[illegible]
[illegible] 4
[illegible] 5
[illegible]
[illegible] 6
[illegible]
[illegible] 7
[illegible]
[illegible]
[illegible] 8

CXXVIII

[illegible]
[illegible]

CXXIX

[illegible]
1 [illegible]
2 [illegible]
[illegible]
[illegible]
3 [illegible]
[illegible]
[illegible]
4 [illegible]
5 [illegible]
[illegible]
6 [illegible]
[illegible]
[illegible]
[illegible]
7 [illegible]
8 [illegible]
[illegible]
[illegible]

ae(fg) hj

5. [illegible]] [illegible] *hj*; > *e** (l), sed et [illegible] et [illegible] (sic) *e*int. (pr m) | [illegible]] [illegible] *e*, [illegible] *j*

6. [illegible]] [illegible] *e*, [illegible] *h*(c. signis contractionis sup. - 1° et 2°)

CXXVIII

Inscr. [illegible] > *j**, sed c pr m

1. [illegible]] [illegible] *e*, [illegible] *h* (tantum [illegible] apparet in *j*, reliquum abscond.)

3. [illegible]] [illegible] *f*uid. (punctum [illegible] non apparet, sed hab. *g*), [illegible] *h*

4. [illegible]] [illegible] *hj*

5. [illegible]] [illegible] *hj*(s. puncto diacritico in uerbo priore) | [illegible]] [illegible] *hj* | [illegible]] [illegible] *hj*

6. [illegible]] s. sey. *hj* | [illegible]] [illegible] *e hj*, [illegible] *f*

7. [illegible] > *e** (homtel.), sed c pr m

8. [illegible]] [illegible] *hj*

CXXIX

2. [illegible]] [illegible] *hj*(s. puncto diacritico)

3. [illegible]] [illegible] *e**, sed c pr m | [illegible]] s. sey. *hj*

5. [illegible]] [illegible] *j**(uid.), sed c pr m | [illegible]] [illegible] *hj*

6. [illegible] 1°] [illegible] *hj* | [illegible] 2°] non testatur *f* (prbl.) | [illegible] 2° > *e* | [illegible] 2°] [illegible] *hj* | [illegible]] [illegible] *e*, [illegible] *hj*

7. [illegible]] [illegible] *e*; [illegible] *hj*; [illegible] ([illegible] pro [illegible]) *a*mg *f*mg

8. [illegible]] [illegible] *e*, [illegible] *hj*

CXXX

ܬܫܒܘܚܬܐ ܕܡܣܩܬܐ ܕܕܘܝܕ:

ܡܪܝܐ ܠܐ ܐܬܪܘܪܒ ܠܒܝ. 1
ܘܠܐ ܐܬܪܘܡܘ ܥܝܢܝ.
ܘܠܐ ܗܠܟܬ ܒܪܘܪܒܬܐ.
ܘܠܐ ܒܬܕܡܪܬܐ ܕܠܥܠ ܡܢܝ.
ܐܠܐ ܡܬܪܥܐ ܗܘܝܬ ܘܫܬܩܐ ܗܘܬ ܢܦܫܝ. 2
ܐܝܟ ܚܣܝܠܐ ܥܠ ܐܡܗ.
ܐܝܟ ܦܘܪܥܢܐ ܥܠ ܢܦܫܝ.
ܢܣܒܪ ܐܝܣܪܝܠ ܠܡܪܝܐ. 3
ܡܢ ܗܫܐ ܘܥܕܡܐ ܠܥܠܡ:

CXXXI

ܬܫܒܘܚܬܐ ܕܡܣܩܬܐ:
ܐܬܕܟܪ ܡܪܝܐ ܠܕܘܝܕ. 1
ܘܠܟܠܗ ܡܟܝܟܘܬܗ.
ܐܝܟ ܕܝܡܐ ܠܡܪܝܐ ܢܕܪ ܠܐܠܗܐ 2
ܕܝܥܩܘܒ.

3 ܐܢ ܐܥܘܠ ܠܡܫܟܢܐ ܕܒܝܬܝ.
ܐܢ ܐܣܩ ܥܠ ܥܪܣܐ ܕܫܘܝܝ.
4 ܐܢ ܐܬܠ ܫܢܬܐ ܠܥܝܢܝ.
ܘܠܦܪܚܘܬܝ ܢܘܡܬܐ.
ܘܢܝܚܐ ܠܨܕܥܝ.
5 ܥܕܡܐ ܕܐܫܟܚ ܐܬܪܐ ܠܡܪܝܐ.
ܡܫܟܢܐ ܠܐܠܗܐ ܕܝܥܩܘܒ.
6 ܗܐ ܫܡܥܢܝܗ ܒܐܦܪܬܐ.
ܐܫܟܚܢܝܗ ܒܚܩܠܬܐ ܕܥܒܐ.
7 ܢܥܘܠ ܠܡܫܟܢܘܗܝ.
ܢܣܓܘܕ ܒܕܘܟܬܐ ܕܩܡܘ ܪܓܠܘܗܝ.
8 ܩܘܡ ܡܪܝܐ ܠܢܝܚܬܟ.
ܐܢܬ ܘܩܒܘܬܐ ܕܩܘܕܫܟ.
9 ܟܗܢܝܟ ܢܠܒܫܘܢ ܙܕܝܩܘܬܐ.
ܘܚܣܝܐ ܕܝܠܟ ܢܫܒܚܘܢ.

ae(fg) hj

CXXX

Insc. ܕܕܘܝܕ > *f*

1. ܘܠܐ] *f* testatur tantum ܘܠ sub ∘ ex ܘܠܐ in linea Pesh | ܐܬܪܘܡܘ] ܐܬܪܝܡܘ *f hj*

2. ܐܠܐ-ܕܐܝܟ 2°] *f*mg† (pro ܦܘܪܥܢܐ apparet ܦܘܪܥܢܐ s. punctis ܀ 1° et 2°, *g*mg† hab. ܦܘܪܥܢܐ) | ܕܐܝܟ] ܐܝܟ *h*

3. ܐܝܣܪܝܠ] ܐܝܣܪܐܝܠ *e*

CXXXI

Insc. ܬܫܒܘܚܬܐ ܕܡܣܩܬܐ] ܬܫܒܘܚܬܐ ܕܡܣܩܬܐ *e* (adsignatur ϵβρ' *a*mg*f*mg uid.*g*mg: cf. Field) | ܬܫܒܘܚܬܐ] ܕܡܣܩܬܐ *f*; ܬܫܒܘܚܬܐ *hj*

1. ܐܬܕܟܪ] ܐܬܕܟܪ *e*, ܐܬܕܟܪ *j*

2. ܢܕܪ] ܘܢܕܪ *hj*

4. ܠܥܝܢܝ] ܠܥܝܢܝ ܘܠ *hj*

6. ܒܚܩܠܬܐ] ܘܒܚܩܠܬܐ *j**(uid.) (= Pesh), sed ∘ erasum est | ܒܚܩܠܬܐ] ܒܚܩܠܬܐ *hj*

7. ܢܣܓܘܕ ܒܕܘܟܬܐ] ܢܣܓܘܕ ܒܕܘܟܬܐ *j* (in *h* uerbum prius est ܒܕܘܟܬܐ) | ܕܩܡܘ] ܕܩܡܘ *f j*, ܕܩܡܘ (sic) *h*

8. ܘܩܒܘܬܐ] ܘܩܒܘܬܐ *e* | ܕܩܘܕܫܟ] ܕܩܘܕܫܟ *ef j*, ܕܩܘܕܫܟ *h*

9. ܢܫܒܚܘܢ] ܢܫܒܚܘܢ *ef* (s. puncto diacritico)

CXXXI

10 [illegible]
[illegible]
11 [illegible]
[illegible]
[illegible]
[illegible]
12 [illegible]
[illegible]
[illegible]
[illegible]
[illegible]
13 [illegible]
[illegible]
14 [illegible]
[illegible]
[illegible]
15 [illegible]
[illegible]
16 [illegible]
[illegible]
17 [illegible]
18 [illegible]
[illegible]

CXXXII

1 [illegible]
[illegible]
[illegible]
2 [illegible]
[illegible]
[illegible]
[illegible]
3 [illegible]
[illegible]
[illegible]
[illegible]

CXXXIII

1 [illegible]
[illegible]
[illegible]
[illegible]
[illegible]
2 [illegible]
[illegible]
3 [illegible]

ae(fg) hj

11. [illegible]] bis scr. (l) *e*
12. [illegible]] [illegible] *ef j*, [illegible] *h*
13. [illegible]] [illegible] *hj*
16. [illegible]] [illegible] *e*, [illegible] *f j*
17. [illegible]] [illegible] *j*
18. [illegible]] [illegible] *j**, sed correctum est per rasuram

CXXXII

Insc. [illegible] > *ef*
3. [illegible]] [illegible] *e j* | [illegible]] [illegible] (sic) *j* | [illegible]] s. sey. *hj*

CXXXIII

Insc. [illegible]] s. sey. *f*
1. [illegible]] *f*mg† | [illegible]] + [illegible] *hj* ([illegible] > *j** [i. e. habebat [illegible]], sed insertum est pr m)
2. [illegible]] [illegible] sup. ras. pr m (erat uid. [illegible]) *j*

CXXXIII

[illegible]

CXXXIV

1 [illegible]

2 [illegible]

3 [illegible]

4 [illegible]

5 [illegible]

6 [illegible]

7 [illegible]

8 [illegible]

9 [illegible]

10 [illegible]

11 [illegible]

12 [illegible]

13 [illegible]

14 [illegible]

15 [illegible]

16 [illegible]

17 [illegible]

ae(fg) hj

CXXXIV

Inscr. ܗܠܠܘܝܐ] ܘܗܠܠܘܝܐ *e*

1. ܫܒܚܘ] ܫܒܚܘܗܝ *hj*

4. ܐܝܣܪܐܝܠ] ܘܐܝܣܪܐܝܠ *e* | ܢܟܣܐ] ܠܢܟܣܐ *hj*c pr m uid.(ܠ sup. ras.) | ܠܗ 2° *f*] ܕܝܠܗ *g*c(frt habebat lemma, sed qua manu correctum est inc.) *hj*

5. ܝܕܥܬ ܐܢܐ] ܝܕܥܬ *f* | ܡܪܢ: ܘܡܪܢ] ܕܡܢ Pesh hab. ܡܪܢ ܡܢ, sed *f* testatur ܘ sub et ante ܡ ex ܡܪܢ et ܕܡܢ sub ܡܢ in linea Pesh, itaque non testatur uid. ܡܪܢ e SyrPs | ܐܢܐ] bis scr. *hj*

6. ܘܒܝܡܐ *f*] ܘܒܝܡܐ̈ *g* | ܘܒܬܗܘܡܐ] ܘܒܬܗܘܡܐ̈ *f*uid. (*g* hab. punctum superius, sed non apparet in *f* quamquam uerbum languet)

7. ܒܫܡܝܐ] ܠܫܡܝܐ *hj* | ܪܘܚܐ] ܪܘܚܐ̈ *j*

8. ܡܢ ܡܨܪܝܢ] ܗܘ ܕܡܨܪܝܢ *hj* | ܡܨܪܝܢ] ܡܨܪܝܢ *f* | ܠܒܥܝܪܐ] c. sey. *e*

9. ܒܡܨܪܝܢ] ܕܒܡܨܪܝܢ *hj* | ܦܪܥܘܢ] ܦܪܥܘܢ *f*

10. ܡܢ ܡܨܪܝܢ] ܗܘ ܕܡܨܪܝܢ *hj*

11. ܡܠܟܐ 1°] c. sey *j**, sed puncta sey. inducta sunt pr m uid. | ܕܡܠܟܐ] ܕܡܠܟܐ *e*

12. ܘܝܗܒ] ܘܝܗܒ *e hj* | ܝܪܬܘܬܐ 1° > *j* (hpgr. [I]) | ܠܐܝܣܪܐܝܠ] ܠܐܝܣܪܐܝܠ *e*, ܠܐܝܣܪܐܝܠ *hj*

13. ܘܕܪܐ] ܘܠܕܪܐ *hj*

14. ܘܥܒܕܘܗܝ] ܕܥܒܕܘܗܝ ܘܥܒܕܘܗܝ *hj*c pr m uid.(uerbum prius erat ܘܥܒܕܐ)

15. ܕܥܡܡܐ] s. sey. *f* | ܕܐܢܫܐ] s. sey. *f hj*

16. ܐܝܬ 1° et 2° > *j**, sed c pr m uid. | ܢܫܡܥܘܢ] ܢܫܡܥܘܢ *f*

17. ܒܦܘܡܗܘܢ] ܒܦܘܡܗܘܢ *hj*(s. puncto)

CXXXIV

18 ܕܡ̈ܝܢ ܠܗܘܢ ܢܗܘܘܢ ܐܝܟܠܝܢ ܕܥܒܕܝܢ ܠܗܘܢ.
ܘܟܠܗܘܢ ܐܝܠܝܢ ܕܬܟܝܠܝܢ ܥܠܝܗܘܢ.
19 ܒܝܬܐ ܕܐܝܣܪܝܠ ܒܪܟܘ ܠܡܪܝܐ.
ܒܝܬܐ ܕܐܗܪܘܢ ܒܪܟܘ ܠܡܪܝܐ.
20 ܒܝܬܐ ܕܠܘܝ ܒܪܟܘ ܠܡܪܝܐ.
ܕܕܚܠܝܢ ܠܡܪܝܐ ܒܪܟܘܗܝ.
21 ܒܪܝܟ ܗܘ ܡܪܝܐ ܡܢ ܨܗܝܘܢ.
ܗܘ ܕܫܪܐ ܒܐܘܪܫܠܡ.
ܗܠܠܘܝܐ ∴

CXXXV

1 ܐܘܕܘ ܠܡܪܝܐ ܡܛܠ ܕܛܒ ܗܘ.
ܡܛܠ ܕܠܥܠܡ ܛܝܒܘܬܗ.
2 ܐܘܕܘ ܠܐܠܗܐ ܕܐܠܗ̈ܐ.
ܡܛܠ ܕܠܥܠܡ ܛܝܒܘܬܗ.
3 ܐܘܕܘ ܠܡܪܝܐ ܕܡܪ̈ܘܬܐ.
ܡܛܠ ܕܠܥܠܡ ܛܝܒܘܬܗ.
4 ܠܡܢ ܕܥܒܕ ܬܕܡܪ̈ܬܐ ܪ̈ܘܪܒܬܐ
ܒܠܚܘܕܘܗܝ.
ܡܛܠ ܕܠܥܠܡ ܛܝܒܘܬܗ.
5 ܠܡܢ ܕܥܒܕ ܫܡܝܐ ܒܣܘܟܠܬܢܘܬܐ.
ܡܛܠ ܕܠܥܠܡ ܛܝܒܘܬܗ.
6 ܠܡܢ ܕܩܒܥ ܐܪܥܐ ܥܠ ܡ̈ܝܐ.
ܡܛܠ ܕܠܥܠܡ ܛܝܒܘܬܗ.
7 ܠܡܢ ܕܥܒܕ ܢܗܝܪ̈ܐ ܪ̈ܘܪܒܐ.
ܡܛܠ ܕܠܥܠܡ ܛܝܒܘܬܗ.
8 ܫܡܫܐ ܠܫܘܠܛܢܐ ܕܐܝܡܡܐ.
ܡܛܠ ܕܠܥܠܡ ܛܝܒܘܬܗ.
9 ܣܗܪܐ ܘܟܘܟ̈ܒܐ ܠܫܘܠܛܢܐ ܕܠܠܝܐ.
ܡܛܠ ܕܠܥܠܡ ܛܝܒܘܬܗ.
10 ܠܡܢ ܕܡܚܝܗ ܠܡܨܪܝܢ ܥܡ ܒܘܟܪ̈ܝܗܘܢ.
ܡܛܠ ܕܠܥܠܡ ܛܝܒܘܬܗ.

ae(fg) hj

18. ܕܥܒܕܝ] ܕܥܒܕܝܢ *j**(uid.), sed c pr m quamquam ܢ non erasa est
19. ܐܝܣܪܝܠ/ܐܝܣܪܐܝܠ] ܐܝܣܪܐܝܠ *e* | ܒܪܟܘ 1° et 2°] ܒܪܟܘܗܝ *hj*
20. ܒܪܟܘ] ܒܪܟܘܗܝ *hj* | ܕܕܚܠܝܢ] ܕܚ̈ܠܘܗܝ ܕ *hj*c pr m(ܕܕܚ ex uerbo secundo sup. ras. [pr m], erant uid. litterae ܠܡ ex ܠܡܪܝܐ [cf. infra]) | ܕܡܪܝܐ] ܠܡܪܝܐ *hj*
21. ܒܐܘܪܫܠܡ] ܒܐܘܪܫܠܡ *e*, ܒܐܘܪܫܠܡ *j*

CXXXV

Inscr. ܗܠܠܘܝܐ] ܗܠܠܘܝܗ *e*
2. ܠܐܠܗ̈ܐ] ras. sup. ܠ, erant frt puncta sey. *j*
5. ܫܡܝܐ] s. sey. *hj*
6. ܛܝܒܘܬܗ ∩ ܛܝܒܘܬܗ u. 7 *e**, sed c pr m (pro ܢܗܝܪ̈ܐ primo erat ܢܗܝܪܐ [sic], deinde ̈ inserta est pr m inter ܗܝ)

CXXXV

11 ܘܐܦܩ ܠܐܝܣܪܝܠ ܡܢ ܒܝܢܬܗܘܢ.
ܡܛܠ ܕܠܥܠܡ ܛܝܒܘܬܗ.
12 ܒܐܝܕܐ ܚܣܝܢܬܐ ܘܒܕܪܥܐ ܪܡܐ.
ܡܛܠ ܕܠܥܠܡ ܛܝܒܘܬܗ.
13 ܠܗܘ ܕܦܠܓ ܠܝܡܐ ܕܣܘܦܐ
ܠܦܠܓ̈ܘܬܐ. ܡܛܠ ܕܠܥܠܡ ܛܝܒܘܬܗ.
14 ܘܐܥܒܪ ܠܐܝܣܪܝܠ ܒܗ ܒܡܨܥܬܗ.
ܡܛܠ ܕܠܥܠܡ ܛܝܒܘܬܗ.
15 ܘܢܦܨ ܠܦܪܥܘܢ. ܡܛܠ ܕܠܥܠܡ ܛܝܒܘܬܗ.
ܘܠܚܝܠܗ ܒܝܡܐ ܕܣܘܦܐ.
ܡܛܠ ܕܠܥܠܡ ܛܝܒܘܬܗ.
16 ܠܗܘ ܕܐܗܠܟ ܠܥܡܗ ܒܡܕܒܪܐ.
ܡܛܠ ܕܠܥܠܡ ܛܝܒܘܬܗ.
17 ܠܗܘ ܕܡܚܐ ܠܡ̈ܠܟܐ ܪ̈ܘܪܒܐ.
ܡܛܠ ܕܠܥܠܡ ܛܝܒܘܬܗ.
18 ܘܩܛܠ ܡ̈ܠܟܐ ܥ̈ܫܝܢܐ.
ܡܛܠ ܕܠܥܠܡ ܛܝܒܘܬܗ.
19 ܠܣܝܚܘܢ ܡܠܟܐ ܕܐܡܘܪ̈ܝܐ.
ܡܛܠ ܕܠܥܠܡ ܛܝܒܘܬܗ.

20 ܘܠܥܘܓ ܡܠܟܐ ܕܡܬܢ.
ܡܛܠ ܕܠܥܠܡ ܛܝܒܘܬܗ.
21 ܘܝܗܒ ܐܪܥܗܘܢ ܝܪܬܘܬܐ.
ܡܛܠ ܕܠܥܠܡ ܛܝܒܘܬܗ.
22 ܝܪܬܘܬܐ ܠܐܝܣܪܝܠ ܥܒܕܗ ܕܝܠܗ.
ܡܛܠ ܕܠܥܠܡ ܛܝܒܘܬܗ.
23 ܡܛܠ ܕܒܡܘܟܟܢ ܐܬܕܟܪܢ ܡܪܝܐ.
ܡܛܠ ܕܠܥܠܡ ܛܝܒܘܬܗ.
24 ܘܦܪܩܢ ܡܢ ܒܥܠܕܒܒܝܢ.
ܡܛܠ ܕܠܥܠܡ ܛܝܒܘܬܗ.
25 ܗܘ ܕܝܗܒ ܡܐܟܘܠܬܐ ܠܟܠ ܒܣܪ.
ܡܛܠ ܕܠܥܠܡ ܛܝܒܘܬܗ.
26 ܐܘܕܘ ܠܐܠܗܐ ܕܫܡܝܐ.
ܡܛܠ ܕܠܥܠܡ ܛܝܒܘܬܗ.
ܐܘܕܘ ܠܡܪܝܐ ܡܛܠ ܕܛܒ ܗܘ.
ܡܛܠ ܕܠܥܠܡ ܛܝܒܘܬܗ.

CXXXVI ܠܕܘܝܕ ܡܡܠܠܐ ܒܗ ܐܪܡܝܐ. ܕܠܐ
ܢܐܡܪܘܢ ܫܘܒܚܐ ܕܡܪܝܐ ܠܘܬ ܒܒܠܝܐ.
1 ܥܠ ܢܗܪ̈ܘܬܐ ܕܒܒܠ.

ae(fg) hj

11. ܠܐܝܣܪܝܠ] ܠܒܝܬ ܐܝܣܪܝܠ *e*, ܠܒܝܬ ܐܝܣܪܝܠ *h*, [ ]ܠܐܝܣ *j*

12. ܘܒܕܪܥܐ > *j**, sed c pr m uid.

13. ܠܦܠܓܘܬܐ] s. sey. (sic) *h*

14. ab ܘܐܥܒܪ ad ܒܝܡܐ u. 15 sup. ras. (pr m) *a* ‖ ܠܐܝܣܪܝܠ] ܠܒܝܬ ܐܝܣܪܝܠ *e*

15. ܛܝܒܘܬܗ (i. e. ܕܠܥܠܡ ܛܝܒܘܬܗ) 1° ∩ 2° *j** (sequebatur linea ܠܗܘ-ܕܐܗܠܟ ex u. 16), sed c pr m (pro ܘܠܚܝܠܗ hab. ܘܚܝܠܗ) ‖ ܕܠܥܠܡ ܛܝܒܘܬܗ 2° > *e** (l), sed c pr m

16. ܠܥܡܗ] ܠܥܡܗ *f* ‖ ܕܠܥܠܡ > *j** (l), sed c pr m ‖ ab ܕܐܗܠܟ: ad ܘܩܛܠ u. 18 manuscriptum *j* sartum est, sed scriptio est pr m

17. ܡ̈ܠܟܐ] ܡܠܟܐ *hj*

20. ܘܠܥܘܓ] ܘܠܥܘܓ *ef hj* ‖ ܕܡܬܢ] ܕܡܬܢ *e* ‖ ܘܥܘܓ] ܘܥܘܓ

22. ܠܐܝܣܪܝܠ] ܠܒܝܬ ܐܝܣܪܝܠ *e*, ܠܐܝܣܪܝܠ *hj*

23. ܕܒܡܘܟܟܢ] ܕܒܡܘܟܟܢ *j**, sed correctum est per rasuram ‖ ܐܬܕܟܪܢ] ܐܬܕܟܪ *e*, ܐܬܕܟܪ *f hj*

25. init.] pr. ܘܐܘܕܘ ܠܐܠܗܐ *e** (cf. u. 26), sed haec uerba cincta sunt pr m uid. ‖ ܗܘ] ܘܗܘ *j*

26. ܐܘܕܘ-ܛܝܒܘܬܗ 2°] *f* mg† (pro ܕܛܒ hab. ܕܛܒܐ); > *e*

CXXXVI

Inscr. ܕܘܝܕ > *j**, sed c pr m

1. ܕܒܒܠ] ܕܒܒܠ *e j* c pr m uid.

CXXXVI

[illegible]
[illegible]
[illegible] 2
[illegible]
[illegible] 3
[illegible]
[illegible]
[illegible]
[illegible] 4
[illegible]
[illegible] 5
[illegible]
[illegible] 6
[illegible]
[illegible]
[illegible]
[illegible] 7
[illegible]
[illegible]
[illegible]
[illegible] 8
[illegible]
[illegible]
[illegible] 9
[illegible]

CXXXVII

[illegible]
1 [illegible]
[illegible]
[illegible]
2 [illegible]
[illegible]
[illegible]
[illegible]
[illegible]
3 [illegible]
[illegible]
[illegible]
4 [illegible]
[illegible]
[illegible]
5 [illegible]
[illegible]
6 [illegible]
[illegible]
7 [illegible]
[illegible]
[illegible]
8 [illegible]
[illegible]
[illegible]

ae(fg) hj

2. [illegible]] [illegible] *hj*; [illegible] *f* | [illegible]] [illegible] *j* | [illegible]] [illegible] *e*

3. [illegible] 1° > *j* | [illegible]] [illegible] *hj*

5. [illegible]] [illegible] (sic) *hj* | [illegible]] [illegible] *e*, [illegible] *j* | [illegible]] [illegible] *f*

6. [illegible]] [illegible] *hj* | [illegible]] [illegible] *e j* | [illegible]] c. sey. *h*

7. [illegible]] [illegible] *hj* | [illegible]] [illegible] *e*; [illegible] *h*, [illegible] *j* | [illegible]] + [illegible] *hj*

8. [illegible]] [illegible] *j* | [illegible]] + [illegible] *hj* | [illegible]] [illegible] *hj*

CXXXVII

1. [illegible]] *f*mg†; om. hic *e*txt, sed tr. post finem *e*mg | [illegible]] pr. [illegible] *e**, sed partim cinctum est pr m uid.

5. [illegible]] [illegible] *f*; [illegible] *e**, sed inductum est et [illegible] scriptum est infra pr m | [illegible]] [illegible] *e*

7. [illegible]] c. sey. *f* | [illegible]] [illegible] *h*, [illegible] (sic) *j*

8. [illegible]] s. sey. *f*

CXXXVIII

[illegible]
1 [illegible]
2 [illegible]
[illegible]
3 [illegible]
[illegible]
4 [illegible]
[illegible]
5 [illegible]
[illegible]
6 [illegible]
[illegible]
7 [illegible]
[illegible]
8 [illegible]
[illegible]
9 [illegible]
[illegible]
10 [illegible]
[illegible]
11 [illegible]

CXXXVIII

[illegible]
12 [illegible]
[illegible]
[illegible]
13 [illegible]
[illegible]
[illegible]
14 [illegible]
[illegible]
15 [illegible]
[illegible]
[illegible]
16 [illegible]
[illegible]
[illegible]
[illegible]
17 [illegible]
[illegible]
[illegible]
18 [illegible]
[illegible]

αe(fg) hj

CXXXVIII

1. [illegible]] [illegible] *h*, [illegible] *j*
2. [illegible]] [illegible] *e*, [illegible] *h*
3. [illegible]] c. sey. *f* | [illegible]] [illegible] *j* (cf. σ′ in Field) | [illegible]] [illegible] *g* (*f* hab. [illegible]) | [illegible] > *j* | [illegible]] [illegible] *e hj*, [illegible] *f* | [illegible]] [illegible] *j*
4. [illegible]] [illegible] *ef hj* | [illegible]] [illegible] *e hj*
7. [illegible]] [illegible] *hj*
8. [illegible] 2°] [illegible] *hj* | [illegible]] sup. ras. (pr m uid.) *j*
9. [illegible]] s. sey. *f*
10. [illegible]] [illegible] *h*, [illegible] *f j*
11. [illegible]] [illegible] *α*mg*f*
12. [illegible]] [illegible] *f hj*
13. [illegible]] [illegible] *α**(uid.), sed c pr m | [illegible]] [illegible] *e h* | [illegible]] [illegible] *e*, [illegible] *f j*uid.([illegible]), [illegible] *h*
15. [illegible]] c. sey. (sic) *f*
16. [illegible]] [illegible] *ef j*
17. [illegible] *f*] [illegible] *g*, [illegible] *hj*

CXXXVIII

19 [illegible]
[illegible]
20 [illegible]
[illegible]
21 [illegible]
[illegible]
22 [illegible]
[illegible]
[illegible]
23 [illegible]
[illegible]
24 [illegible]
[illegible]
[illegible]

CXXXIX

1 [illegible]
[illegible]
2 [illegible]
[illegible]
3 [illegible]
[illegible]
[illegible]
4 [illegible]
[illegible]
[illegible]
5 [illegible]
[illegible]
[illegible]
[illegible]
6 [illegible]
[illegible]
[illegible]
7 [illegible]
[illegible]
8 [illegible]
[illegible]
[illegible]
9 [illegible]
[illegible]
10 [illegible]
[illegible]
[illegible]

ae(fg) hj

19. [illegible]] s. sey. *hj* | [illegible]] [illegible] *f*, [illegible] *hj*
21. [illegible]] [illegible] *hj*
23. [illegible] > *j* (prbl. [illegible])

CXXXIX

3. [illegible]] [illegible] *e*, [illegible] *f*, [illegible] *hj* uid.([illegible])
4. [illegible]] c. sey. *hj*
5. [illegible] 1°] c. sey. *hj**(frt)(ras. sup. [illegible]) | [illegible] 1° ∩ 2° *j** (sequebantur uid. uerba [illegible] pro [illegible]; de [illegible] 1° cf. supra), sed c pr m | [illegible] 2°] c. sey. *h* | [illegible]] [illegible] *hj*(c. puncto inferiore) | [illegible]] c. sey. *h* | [illegible]] s. sey. *f* | [illegible]] [illegible] *e*, [illegible] *f j* uid.([illegible]), [illegible] *h*
6. [illegible]] primo [illegible] scripta est uid. (cf. Pesh), deinde erasa est et [illegible] scriptum est pr m *j*
8. [illegible]] sup. ras. (pr m) *a* | [illegible] *f*] [illegible] *g* | fin.] + [illegible] *hj*
10. [illegible] > *e* | [illegible]] s. sey. *f*

CXXXIX

11 [illegible]

12 [illegible]

13 [illegible]

CXL

1 [illegible]

2 [illegible]

3 [illegible]

4 [illegible]

CXL

5 [illegible]

6 [illegible]

7 [illegible]

8 [illegible]

9 [illegible]

10 [illegible]

ae(fg) hj

11. [illegible]] [illegible] *e*, [illegible] *j*
12. [illegible]] [illegible] *hj* | [illegible]] c. sey. *a*mg *f* uid. (puncta languent, sed hab. *g*)
13. [illegible]] [illegible] *j*

CXL

Inscr. [illegible]] [illegible] *e*
1. [illegible]] [illegible] *j* | [illegible]] *e* hab. ob. tantum; s. notis *f hj*
2. [illegible]] [illegible] *e* | [illegible]] [illegible] *j**(uid.), sed c pr m uid. | [illegible]] [illegible] *j*
3. [illegible]] [illegible] *hj*
4. [illegible]] [illegible] *f hj*
5. [illegible]] ras. sup. [illegible] *a*; c. sey. *ef* | [illegible]] [illegible] *f* | [illegible]] s. sey. *f*
6. [illegible]] [illegible] *hj* | [illegible]] [illegible] *e hj*
8. [illegible] 1° > *f* (signum significans praetermissionem in linea SyrPs sub [illegible] in linea Pesh, sed [illegible] alterum testatum est post signum in linea SyrPs)
9. [illegible]] [illegible] *hj*
10. [illegible]] c. sey. *e*

CXLI

[illegible]
[illegible]
[illegible] 1
[illegible]
[illegible] 2
[illegible]
[illegible] 3
[illegible]
[illegible]
[illegible]
[illegible] 4
[illegible]
[illegible]
[illegible]
[illegible] 5
[illegible]
[illegible]
[illegible] 6
[illegible]
[illegible]
[illegible]
[illegible] 7
[illegible]
[illegible]
[illegible] CXLII
[illegible]
[illegible] 1

CXLII

[illegible]
[illegible]
2 [illegible]
[illegible]
3 [illegible]
[illegible]
[illegible]
[illegible]
4 [illegible]
[illegible]
5 [illegible]
[illegible]
[illegible]
6 [illegible]
[illegible]
[illegible]
7 [illegible]
[illegible]
[illegible]
8 [illegible]
[illegible]
[illegible]
[illegible]
[illegible]
9 [illegible]
[illegible]
10 [illegible]

a(b)e(fg) hj

CXLI

1. [illegible]] [illegible] *e*
4. [illegible]] [illegible] *a**(uid.), sed c pr m | [illegible] 2°] [illegible] *hj*
5. [illegible] *f*] [illegible] (sic) *g*; [illegible] *hj*
6. [illegible]] [illegible] *a*mg *f*mg (*b* hab. indicem in textu, sed margo absc.)
| [illegible]] [illegible] *hj*
7. [illegible]] [illegible] *f*

CXLII

Insc. [illegible]] [illegible] *ef* | [illegible] > *h**, sed c pr m
3. [illegible] (*b*inc.)] s. sey. *j*
4. [illegible][o]] [illegible] *b* | [illegible] (*b*uid.)] [illegible] (sic) *h*
6. [illegible]] [illegible] *b hj*, [illegible] *e*, [illegible] *f*
8. [illegible]] [illegible] *hj* | [illegible] > *e* (!) | [illegible]] [illegible] *j**(uid.) (cf. Pesh), sed [illegible] correctum est pr m ad [illegible] (sicut hab. *h*)

CXLII

[illegible]
[illegible]
[illegible]
[illegible] 11
[illegible]
[illegible] 12
[illegible]
[illegible]

CXLIII

[illegible]
[illegible] 1
[illegible]
[illegible] 2
[illegible]
[illegible]
[illegible]
[illegible] 3
[illegible]
[illegible]
[illegible] 4
[illegible]
[illegible] 5
[illegible]
[illegible] 6

[illegible]
7 [illegible]
[illegible]
[illegible]
8 [illegible]
[illegible]
9 [illegible]
[illegible]
10 [illegible]
[illegible]
11 [illegible]
[illegible]
[illegible]
[illegible]
12 [illegible]
[illegible]
[illegible]
[illegible]
13 [illegible]
[illegible]
[illegible]
[illegible]

a(b)e(fg) hj

10. [illegible]] [illegible] (c. signo contractionis sup. [illegible]) *h* | [illegible]] sup. ras. praeter [illegible] (pr m) *a* | [illegible]] [illegible] *j**(uid.) (= Pesh), sed c pr m uid.

11. [illegible]] [illegible] *hj*

12. [illegible]] [illegible] *f* | [illegible]] [illegible] *b*; [illegible] *h**, sed c pr m

CXLIII

1. [illegible]] [illegible] *h*(om. punctum [illegible])*j* | [illegible]] [illegible] *hj*

2. [illegible]] [illegible] *f*, [illegible] *g* | [illegible]] [illegible] *hj*

4. [illegible] *f*] [illegible] *e*, [illegible] *g j*, [illegible] *h*

5. [illegible] > *e* | [illegible]] s. sey. *hj* | [illegible]] [illegible] *f*, [illegible] *hj*; [illegible] *b*, [illegible] *e*

6. [illegible]] c. sey. *hj*

7. [illegible] 3°] [illegible] *e j* | [illegible]] [illegible] *j*

9. [illegible]] [illegible] *f j* | [illegible] 1° ∩ 2° *h* | [illegible]] [illegible] *j* | [illegible]] s. sey. *e* | [illegible]] [illegible] *e*, [illegible] *j*

10. [illegible]] [illegible] *f* | [illegible]] [illegible] *j* | [illegible]] [illegible] *f*

11. [illegible] > *e** (l), sed c pr m

12. [illegible]] [illegible] *hj*

13. [illegible]] [illegible] *e*; [illegible] *hj* | [illegible]] s. sey. *j*

CXLIII

14 [illegible]

15 [illegible]

CXLIV

1 [illegible]

2 [illegible]

3 [illegible]

4 [illegible]

5 [illegible]

6 [illegible]

7 [illegible]

8 [illegible]

9 [illegible]

10 [illegible]

11 [illegible]

12 [illegible]

13 [illegible]

14 [illegible]

15 [illegible]

16 [illegible]

17 [illegible]

18 [illegible]

ae(fg) hj

14. [illegible]] [illegible] *f* | [illegible]] [illegible] *ef hj*
15. [illegible]] [illegible] *hj*

CXLIV

Insc. [illegible]] [illegible] > *ef hj*
2. [illegible]] [illegible] *e* | [illegible]] [illegible] *h*
3. [illegible]] [illegible] *hj*
4. [illegible]] [illegible] *h* (in *j* uerbum prius est [illegible])
5. [illegible]] [illegible] *hj*
6. [illegible]] [illegible] *f*
7. [illegible]] [illegible] (sic) *e*
12. [illegible]] [illegible] *hj*c pr m(scriptor coepit scribere [illegible] uid. post [illegible] ita principio omittens [illegible] [homtel.])
13. [illegible]] [illegible] *ef hj* | [illegible] (*e* absc.)] [illegible] *f*
15. [illegible]] [illegible] *f*
18. [illegible]] [illegible] *j**(uid.) (= Pesh), sed c pr m (s. dubio puncta : simul inserta sunt post [illegible] 1°) | [illegible] 2°] [illegible] (sic) *j**, sed c pr m | [illegible]] sup. ras. (frt erat [illegible]), sed pr m uid. *e*

CXLIV

19 ܨܒܝܢܐ ܕܕܚ̈ܠܘܗܝ ܢܥܒܕ·
ܘܠܬܟܫܦܬܗܘܢ ܢܫܡܥ ܘܢܦܪܘܩ ܐܢܘܢ·
20 ܢܛܪ ܡܪܝܐ ܠܟܠܗܘܢ ܐܝܠܝܢ ܕܪܚܡܝܢ ܠܗ·
ܘܠܟܠܗܘܢ ܚ̈ܛܝܐ ܢܘܒܕ·
21 ܬܫܒܘܚܬܗ ܕܡܪܝܐ ܢܡܠܠ ܦܘܡܝ·
ܘܢܒܪܟ ܟܠ ܒܣܪܐ ܠܫܡܗ ܩܕܝܫܐ ܠܥܠܡ·
ܠܥܠܡ ܘܠܥܠܡ ܥܠܡܝܢ ⁘

CXLV

⁘ ܗܠܠܘܝܐ. ܕܚܓܝ ܘܙܟܪܝܐ ⁘
1 ܫܒܚܝ ܢܦܫܝ ܠܡܪܝܐ·
2 ܐܫܒܚ ܠܡܪܝܐ ܒܚܝ̈ܝ·
ܐܙܡܪ ܠܐܠܗܝ ܟܡܐ ܕܐܝܬܝ·
3 ܠܐ ܬܬܬܟܠܘܢ ܥܠ ܪ̈ܘܪܒܢܐ·
ܘܥܠ ܒ̈ܢܝܐ ܕܐܢܫܐ ܕܠܐ
ܐܝܬ ܠܗܘܢ ܦܘܪܩܢܐ·
4 ܬܦܘܩ ܪܘܚܗܘܢ ܘܢܗܦܟܘܢ ܠܥܦܪܗܘܢ·
ܒܗܘ ܝܘܡܐ ܢܐܒܕܘܢ ܟܠܗܘܢ
ܚܘ̈ܫܒܝܗܘܢ·
5 ܛܘܒܘܗܝ ܠܐܝܢܐ ܗܘ ܕܐܠܗܗ
ܕܝܥܩܘܒ ܡܥܕܪܢܐ ܗܘ ܕܝܠܗ·
ܘܣܒܪܗ ܥܠ ܡܪܝܐ ܐܠܗܗ·
6 ܗܘ ܕܥܒܕ ܫܡܝܐ ܘܐܪܥܐ·
ܠܝܡܐ ܘܠܟܠ ܕܒܗܘܢ·
ܗܘ ܕܢܛܪ ܫܪܪܐ ܠܥܠܡ·
7 ܥܒܕ ܕܝܢܐ ܠܕܡܬܥܠܒܝܢ·
ܝܗܒ ܠܚܡܐ ܠܟܦܢܐ·
ܡܪܝܐ ܫܪܐ ܐܣܝ̈ܪܐ·
8 ܡܪܝܐ ܡܚܟܡ ܠܣ̈ܡܝܐ·
ܡܪܝܐ ܙܩܦ ܠܟܦܝܦܐ·
ܡܪܝܐ ܪܚܡ ܠܙܕܝ̈ܩܐ·
9 ܡܪܝܐ ܢܛܪ ܠܬܘܬܒܐ·
ܠܝܬܡܐ ܘܠܐܪܡܠܬܐ ܢܣܥܘܕ·
ܘܐܘܪܚܐ ܕܚ̈ܛܝܐ ܢܘܒܕ·
10 ܢܡܠܘܟ ܡܪܝܐ ܠܥܠܡ·
ܐܠܗܟܝ ܨܗܝܘܢ ܠܕܪ ܕܪܐ ⁘

CXLVI

⁘ ܗܠܠܘܝܐ· ܕܚܓܝ ܘܙܟܪܝܐ ܢܒ̈ܝܐ ⁘
1 ܫܒܚܘ ܠܡܪܝܐ ܡܛܠ ܕܛܒ ܗܘ
ܙܡܪܘܗܝ·
ܠܐܠܗܢ ܕܒܣܝܡܐ ܬܫܒܘܚܬܐ·
2 ܒܢܐ ܠܐܘܪܫܠܡ ܡܪܝܐ·
ܒܕܪ̈ܐ ܕܐܝܣܪܝܠ ܢܟܢܫ·

a(befg) hj

19. ܕܕ̈ܚܠܘܗܝ] ܠܗ ܕܕܚܠܝܢ ܕܐܚܠܝ *hj* | ܢܥܒܕ] ܢܥܒܕ *f* frt (sic *g*), sed init. uerbi languet et frt punctum superius est residuum ex ܕ ante ܥ

20. ܢܛܪ] ܢܗܪ *g* (cf. Pesh; *f* hab. lemma uid. quamquam litterae ܢܛ partim perierunt) | ܕܪܚܡܝܢ] ܕܦܫܚܝܢ *f*

CXLV

Insc. ܗܠܠܘܝܐ] ܗܠܠܘܝܗ *e* | ܘܙܟܪܝܐ] ܕ > *j**, sed c pr m

3. ܬܬܬܟܠܘܢ] ܬܬܐܬܟܠܘܢ *b*, ܬܬܬܟܠܘܢ *e* | ܪܘܪܒܢܐ] c. sey. *a**(sed alterum punctorum ex ̈ erasum est)*ef hj*; ܪܘܪܒܢܐ *b* | ܕܐܢܫܐ] s. sey. *f hj*

4. ܐܦܘܗܝ] ܐܦܘܗܝ *e*

9. ܠܝܬܡܐ ܘܠܐܪܡܠܬܐ] c. sey. *h*

10. ܕܪܐ] ras. ante ܕ, sed ܕ non conectebatur litterae praecedenti *a*; ܘܕܪܐ *bf hj*

CXLVI

1. ܕܛܒ] ܕܛܒܐ *hj*(s. puncto superiore) | ܠܐܠܗܢ] add. (sub ※ *a*mg*b*mg) ܦܐܝܐ *a*mg*b*mg*f*mg uid.(litterae ܐ non apparent, sed hab. *g*mg); ܦܐܝܐ *j*

2. ܠܐܘܪܫܠܡ] ܠܐܘܪܫܠܡ *j* | ܒܕܪ̈ܐ (*f* inc., *g* deest)] c. sey. *hj*

CXLVI

3 [illegible]
[illegible]
4 [illegible]
[illegible]
5 [illegible]
[illegible]
[illegible]
[illegible]
6 [illegible]
[illegible]
7 [illegible]
[illegible]
8 [illegible]
[illegible]
[illegible]
[illegible]
9 [illegible]
[illegible]
10 [illegible]
[illegible]
11 [illegible]
[illegible]

[illegible]
[illegible]

CXLVII

1(12) [illegible]
[illegible]
2(13) [illegible]
[illegible]
3(14) [illegible]
[illegible]
4(15) [illegible]
[illegible]
5(16) [illegible]
[illegible]
6(17) [illegible]
[illegible]
[illegible]
7(18) [illegible]
[illegible]
8(19) [illegible]
[illegible]
9(20) [illegible]
[illegible]

a(befgh1) (h)j

3. [illegible]] [illegible] *a*mg*b*mg*f*mg | [illegible]] [illegible] *f*
4. [illegible]] c. sey. *f* | [illegible]] [illegible] *f*
7. [illegible]] c. sey. *f*uid. (puncta languent, sed hab. *g*)
8. [illegible]] [illegible] *f*, [illegible] *g* | [illegible]] *f*mg* | [illegible]]
[illegible] *h1*
9. [illegible]] s. sey. *eh1* | [illegible]] [illegible] *f* | [illegible]] [illegible] *f**, sed [illegible] uid. inserta est inter [illegible] (qua manu inc.)
10. [illegible]] [illegible] *h1*
11. [illegible]] [illegible] *j*

CXLVII

Insor. [illegible]] [illegible] *e*
1(12). [illegible]] [illegible] *e*, [illegible] *j* | [illegible]] [illegible] *efh1 j*
3(14). [illegible]] [illegible] *j*
4(15). [illegible]] [illegible] *j* | [illegible]] [illegible] *eh1*
5(16). [illegible]] [illegible] *f*
6(17). [illegible]] [illegible] *efh1*; [illegible] *j* (pars superior ex [illegible] sup. ras., sed [illegible] pr m)
7(18). [illegible]] [illegible] *e*, [illegible] *h1* | [illegible] *g*] tr. *f* | [illegible]] [illegible] *h1*, [illegible] *j* | [illegible] > *j**, sed c pr m
8(19). [illegible]] [illegible] *eh1*, [illegible] *f j*
9(20). [illegible]] [illegible] *j*

CXLVIII

[illegible]

[illegible] 1

[illegible]

[illegible] 2

[illegible]

[illegible] 3

[illegible]

[illegible] 4

[illegible]

[illegible] 5

[illegible]

[illegible]

[illegible] 6

[illegible]

[illegible] 7

[illegible]

[illegible] 8

[illegible]

[illegible] 9

[illegible]

[illegible] 10

[illegible]

11 [illegible]

[illegible]

12 [illegible]

[illegible]

13 [illegible]

[illegible]

[illegible]

[illegible]

14 [illegible]

[illegible]

[illegible]

CXLIX

[illegible]

1 [illegible]

[illegible]

2 [illegible]

[illegible]

3 [illegible]

[illegible]

4 [illegible]

[illegible]

a(befg)h_1 j

CXLVIII

Insc. [illegible] 1°] [illegible] *e*; > *f* | [illegible] 2°] [illegible] *e*

1. [illegible]] s. sey. *j*

4. [illegible]] s. sey. *f j* | [illegible]] c. sey. *eh_1* | [illegible]] c. sey. *eh_1*

6. [illegible]] [illegible] *h_1**, sed c pr m

8. [illegible]] [illegible] *efh_1 j* | [illegible]] [illegible] *f*

9. [illegible]] [illegible] *e*; [illegible] *j*

10. [illegible]] s. sey. *fh_1 j*

11. [illegible]] [illegible] *h_1*

12. [illegible]] [illegible] *e*; [illegible] (sic) *j*

13. [illegible]] [illegible] *j**, sed c pr m

14. [illegible]] [illegible] *h_1* | [illegible]] [illegible] *f j*, [illegible] *h_1*

CXLIX

Insc. [illegible] 2°] [illegible] *h_1*

2. [illegible]] [illegible] *h_1* | [illegible]] [illegible] *j* | [illegible]] [illegible] *j*

3. [illegible]] c. sey. *f*

CL

[illegible]
1 [illegible]
[illegible]
2 [illegible]
[illegible]
3 [illegible]
[illegible]
4 [illegible]
[illegible]
5 [illegible]
[illegible]
6 [illegible]

CXLIX

5 [illegible]
[illegible]
6 [illegible]
[illegible]
7 [illegible]
[illegible]
8 [illegible]
[illegible]
[illegible]
9 [illegible]
[illegible]
[illegible]

ab(cefgh1) j

5. [illegible]] [illegible] *j*
6. [illegible]] s. sey. *f*; [illegible] *j* | [illegible]] c. sey. *a*b*h1*; [illegible] *j*
7. [illegible] *f*] s. sey *g* (cf. Pesh); [illegible] *j*
8. [illegible]] [illegible] *f*
9. [illegible]] [illegible] *b*

CL

1. [illegible]] [illegible] *j*
2. [illegible]] [illegible] *j*
3. [illegible]] [illegible] *f* | [illegible]] [illegible] (sic) *j* | [illegible]] [illegible] *b*
4. [illegible]] [illegible] *e*
6. [illegible]] [illegible] *e*

SUBSCRIPTIO

[illegible] *b*

[illegible] (sic) [illegible] *j*

[illegible] *c* (post Canticum 8 [= Dan. 3:52-88]: cf. Wright, *Catalogue*, vol. 1, p. 36)

CLI

ܗܢܐ ܡܙܡܘܪܐ ܕܠܗ ܒܝܕ ܕܘܝܕ.
ܡܬܟܬܒ. ܠܒܪ ܡܢ ܡܢܝܢܐ ܗܘ.
ܠܘ ܗܘ ܒܠܚܘܕ ...
ܟܕ ܐܬܟܬܫ ܥܡ ܓܘܠܝܕ.
1 ܙܥܘܪܐ ܗܘܝܬ ܒܐܚܝ.
ܘܛܠܝܐ ܒܒܝܬ ܐܒܝ.
ܪܥܐ ܗܘܝܬ ܥܢܗ ܕܐܒܝ.
2 ܐܝܕܝ ܥܒܕ ܐܪܓܢܐ.
ܘܨܒܥܬܝ ܬܩܢ ܟܢܪܐ.
3 ܘܡܢܘ ܢܚܘܐ ܠܡܪܝ.
ܗܘ ܡܪܝܐ.
ܗܘ ܐܠܗܐ ܗܘ.
4 ܗܘ ܫܠܚ ܠܡܠܐܟܗ.
ܘܐܘܒܠܢܝ ܡܢ ܒܬܪ ܥܢܐ ܕܐܒܝ.
ܘܡܫܚܢܝ ܒܡܫܚܐ ܕܡܫܝܚܘܬܗ.
5 ܐܚܝ ܫܦܝܪܐ ܘܪܘܪܒܐ.
ܘܠܐ ܐܨܛܒܝ ܒܗܘܢ ܡܪܝܐ.
6 ܢܦܩܬ ܠܐܘܪܥܗ ܕܦܠܫܬܝܐ.
ܘܠܛ ܠܝ ܒܦܬܟܪܘܗܝ.
7 ܐܢܐ ܕܝܢ ܟܕ ܫܡܛܬ ܣܝܦܗ
ܦܣܩܬ ܪܫܗ.
ܘܐܥܒܪܬ ܚܣܕܐ ܡܢ ܒܢܝ
ܐܝܣܪܝܠ ✝

a(befg) j

CLI

Inscr. [illegible] pr. [illegible] *e*; + [illegible] *f* | [illegible] [illegible] pr. [illegible] *a*mg(manu seriore) *j*

1. [illegible] c. sey. *ef*; [illegible] *j*

2. [illegible] *e* | [illegible] *f*; [illegible] *j* | [illegible] *ef*

3. [illegible] *e*

6. [illegible] *j*

III

SYRPSS AND THE QUESTION OF HEXAPLARIC INFLUENCE

Alfred Rahlfs' assertion, mentioned in the introduction to this study, that the SyrPs text tradition of Mss *a*, *b*, and *c* is not inherently hexaplaric, is based on his comparison of that text with fragmentary Greek hexaplaric Psalms Mss 1098 and 2005, with Jerome's Gallican Psalter (the best and only complete hexaplaric Psalms witness), and with Jerome's Psalter quotations in his *Letter to Sunnia and Fretela*. This comparison shows that the text of these SyrPs Mss often differs from that of the witnesses to the Hexapla's fifth column.[1] The remaining members of SyrPs, as well as SyrPs^{a} and SyrPs^{b}, normally agree with *a*, *b*, and *c* at these points of divergence.[2] However, Rahlfs' lists of the marked hexaplaric readings in these three Mss furnish proof that material from Origen's fifth column was incorporated at some point in the text history. The other Mss also have these readings—sometimes with, but mostly without, Aristarchian signs. It should be noted, however, that SyrPss attests some, but not all, asterisked and obelized readings. A comparison of SyrPss with the Gallican Psalter can provide an indication of the extent to which the former has been subjected to hexaplaric influence. Rahlfs, in his comparison, deals primarily with marked readings. However, even within these limitations, his analysis is incomplete because he includes only a fraction of those found in the Gallican Psalter.[3] Yet a comprehensive investigation must also include unmarked corrections to the Hebrew since many Aristarchian signs have been lost in the course of transmission. Such an investigation is undertaken in this chapter.

The extant Greek witnesses to the hexaplaric Psalter (Mss 1098 and 2005) unfortunately lack the Aristarchian signs usually associated with Origen's recension. However, the Gallican Psalter, Jerome's revision of the Old Latin Psalter on the basis of the

Hexapla's fifth column,[4] has a good number of them. Jerome's *Letter to Sunnia and Fretela*, Augustine's *Enarrationes in Psalmos*, the writings of Origen and Eusebius, and some SyrPss Mss attest these symbols in fewer numbers.[5] The problem with the Gallican Psalter is that the signs found in its Mss are sometimes not original, particularly in the later Mss. Information regarding one way in which secondary signs came to be introduced is given by a ninth century deacon of Lyon, named Florus, who tells the Abbot, Hyldradus, in a letter that he has compared the Gallican Psalter with Jerome's Hebrew Psalter

> ut ex utrisque, quid in nostris minus quidve maius haberetur codicibus, curiosius investigarem, et quid in Septuaginta ex Hebraeo sub asterisco ※ additum, quid praenotatum obelo ÷ plus in his quam in Hebraeorum voluminibus haberetur, solerti indigatione colligerem.[6]

Since Jerome's Hebrew Psalter seemed corrupt, Florus also compared the Hebrew itself and consulted the *Letter to Sunnia and Fretela* as well, "et his omnibus Psalterium vestrum, prout potui, correxi, asteriscos ※ et obelos ÷ suis locis restitui, erasi vitia, recta quaeque et probata subieci."[7] It appears as though other less astute Middle Age scholars added signs to the Gallican text since, especially in the later Mss, a good many signs contradict Greek and Hebrew evidence.[8] The testimony of earlier Mss like the eighth century Vatic. Regin. 11 (Ga)—Rahlfs' source for the Gallican Psalter in *Psalmi cum Odis*—is more reliable, although Rahlfs points out that even Ga's signs are not always original.[9]

In the lists of this chapter, the SyrPss witnesses which are cited constitute all extant Mss of our edition. When no SyrPss Mss are mentioned, it may be assumed that extant witnesses either attest the lemma reading or are inconclusive, because of the constraints of Syriac, as to which reading they support. It should also be mentioned that, in our analysis, whenever Greek readings are cited, those of the lemma are recorded with accents and breathing marks, whereas divergences from the lemma appear without them (except when identical forms need to be distinguished).

A. ASTERISKED PASSAGES

The following is a list of the forty readings in the Psalter for which an asterisk is extant in Ga:[10]

7:7(6)[3] init. B′ La^{G}] pr. και R′Aug Ga(sub ※) *L′ ab hj* A′ = MT

7:10(9) ἐτάζων *scrutans* La^{R}Aug Uulg, ܒܨܐ *a*^{txt}, ܕܒܨܐ *hj*] pr. ※ *et* Ga = MT; *et scruta* La^{G}; ܘܒܨܐ *a*^{mg}*f*^{mg} (*f*^{txt} non exstat)

7:15(14) συνέλαβεν] pr. ※ *et* Ga(non Uulg) = MT

8:4(3) οὐρανούς = *a*] add. ※ *tuos* GaHi: ex θ′ teste Hi = MT; ουρανον *f hj*

15:3 ἐθαυμάστωσεν] -σας *acf hj*, + ο κυριος *L*$^{a′}$(non Z); add. ※ *mihi* Ga(non Uulg): cf. MT (ואדירי) et α′θ′ (cf. Field)

16:9 fin.] add. ※ *super me* Ga(non Uulg) cf. MT (בנפש יקיפו עלי pro την ψυχην μου περιεσχον)

17:14(13) fin.] add. ※ χαλαζα και ανθρακες πυρος GaHi = MT: teste Hi ex εβρ′ θ′; haec locutio perperam sub ast. in u. 13(12) *abc* sed s. ast. *e hj*

23:2 init.] pr. ※ *quia* Ga = MT

31:4 ταλαιπωρίαν] add. ※ μου GaHi (teste Hi ex εβρ′ θ′) et s. ast. *abce*(*f* testatur tantum ταλ.) *hj* et Aug. enarr. II (in enarr. I plerique codices hab. *aerumnam* tantum), cf. MT (לשדי) et Pesh (ܚܫܢܝ)

31:5 ἐγνώρισα *cognoui* La^{R}Aug] εγνωρ. σοι ThtP *abcef hj* {184} 1219 = MT Pesh, *cognitum* ※ *tibi* : *feci* Ga, *tibi cogn. feci* La^{G}

34:20 ἐπ' ὀργήν (B 2110 -γη)] + γης ελαλουν (184) 1098 ThtTh *abcef*pars *hj*, add. ※ *terrae loquentes* Ga, cf. MT (ועל רגעי־ארץ דברי מרמות) et Pesh (ܘܥܠ ܡܟܝܟܐ ܕܐܪܥܐ ܢܡܠܠ) pro και επ οργην δολους

41:3(2) τὸν θεόν B'' 2013'-2050-2110 R'' *abce hj* He* Orig.] + τον ισχυρον Ga (sub ※) *L'* A'' = MT

41:8(7) ἄβυσσον] pr. ※ *ad* Ga(non Uulg) et s. ast. *abcef hj* = MT, cf. Pesh (ܠܬܗܘܡܐ); αβυσσος 2110

41:12(11) ὅτι] add. ※ ετι *adhuc* GaHi *ac* (s. ast. *hj*, etiam *e*uid. quamquam puncta occulta ante et post uerbum) = MT Pesh: item in 42:5, non in 41:6(5) (sed Uulg add. *adhuc* etiam in 41:6(5); *adhuc* add. etiam Aug, si editioni fides est, in 41:12(11), non in 41:6(5), 42:5; ετι antiquis temporibus post οτι excidisse uid.

41:12(11) ὁ θεός B'' Sa-2110uid. AugP] pr. και 2013(om. ο) R'' (etiam AugP) GaHi *L' ace hj* A'' = MT Pesh (GaHi *ac* sub ※ [※ܘܐܠܗܝ *ac*] sed s. ast. *e hj*, teste Hi ex εβρ' θ'): cf. u. 6 et 42:5

42:5 ὅτι] add. ※ ετι GaHi *ac* (s. ast. *e hj*) = MT Pesh: cf. 41:12(11)

42:5 ὁ θεός B'' Sa Aug] κ̂ς θ̂ς 2110; pr. και rel. (etiam Th) = MT Pesh (Ga sub ※, *ace hj* s. ast.): cf. 41:12(11)

44:13(12) θυγατέρες B' 2013'-2110 R'Aug ThtHeThCh *acef hj* A'] θυγατηρ S Ga(Gac pr. *et* = MT sub ast., θυγατερες Τυρου εν δωροις sub ast. *a h* sed s. ast. *cef*pars *j*) *L* = MT Pesh; και θυγατερες LaG Uulg

48:10(9) ζήσεται] add. ※ ετι Ga(※ ex ÷ correctum) *ace h*, s. ast. 2110uid. *f j* = MT, cf. Pesh (ܠܥܠܡ)

48:18(17) συγκαταβήσεται αὐτῷ] σ. μετ αυτου R = *simul descendet cum eo* La; add. ※ *pone* Ga(non Uulg), i. e. οπισω = אחר,

cf. *L*^{pau} *acef hj* in fine u. οπισω αυτου = אחריו (et ܒܬܪܗ Pesh) addentes

55:13(12) αἱ εὐχαί B″ 2013′-2110 *L*$^{b(sil)}$THe$^{c(uid.)}$] αι > R *L*$^{a\prime}$ 55, add. ※ *tua* GaAug (MT hab. נדריך) sed non SyrPss (*abcef hj* hab. αινεσεως σου pro αιν. σοι et tr. post ευχαι)

64:1(inscr.) ᾠδή B′ La^{R}Aug Ga(sub ※) *L*^{a}Tht^{P} *hj* 2110$^{uid.}$ = MT] ωδης Sa R *L*^{b}He *ef* sed sub ※ *ac*, > S La^{G} *L*^{pau}TTht^{P} 55

67:13(12) τοῦ ἀγαπητοῦ 2° B′(Bo tr. τοῦ ἀγ. post οἴκου) Ga(sub ※) *abcf hj* 55, cf. MT (ידדון)] > S Sa-2110 R$^{s\prime\prime}$ *L′ e* 1219, cf. Aug: "repetitionem [uerborum του αγ.] non omnes codices habent, et eam diligentiores [i. e. Psalt. Gall.] stella apposita praenotant, quae signa uocantur asterisci, quibus agnosci uolunt ea non esse in interpretatione Septuaginta, sed esse in Hebraeo, quae talibus insigniuntur notis"

88:3(2) fin. = *ab hj*] add. (sub ※ Ga) *in eis* Ga *e* = MT

88:19(18) ἀντίλημψις] add. ※ *nostra* Ga = MT

88:48(47) πάντας = *j* MT Pesh] om. Bo *L*^{pau} et complures Latini; om. etiam *abe* (*f* non testatur παντας) *h*, sed add. *abef h omnium* post τους υιους; pr. ※ Ga

89:17 fin. B′ R″ 55] add. stichum και το εργον των χειρων ημων κατευθυνον S GaAug^{uar} *L′* (non SyrPss sed *abef* hab. in u. 17^{2} το εργον pro τα εργα [*hj* hab. τα εργα]) A′ = MT Pesh: haec sub ast. hab. Ga, cf. Aug: "cui uersui diligentes et docti praenotant stellam, quos asteriscos uocant, quibus significant ea, quae in Hebraeo uel aliis interpretibus graecis reperiuntur, in LXX uero interpretatione non sunt;" add. duo stichos *si conuertimini in fide, toto tempore quo in dispersione estis sine malo eritis* Sa

91:10(9)[1] S R′ Ga(sub ※) *L′ abe hj* 1219′ = MT Pesh] > B′ Sa-2110 La^{G}Aug A

92:3 fin. B″ Sa-2110 R″] add. stichum αρουσιν οι ποταμοι επιτριψεις αυτων Ga(sub ※; Uulg *eleuauerunt* pro *eleuabunt*) *L′ abef*^{pars} *hj* (sub ※ *ab* quamquam *a* s. metob.) A″ = MT, cf. Pesh (ܐܬܬܪܝܡܘ ܢܗܪ̈ܘܬܐ ܒܪ̈ܘܡܬܐ)

94:9 ἐδοκίμασαν B″ Sa R″] + με Ga(sub ※) *L′ aef hj* A″ = MT; εν δοκιμασια 2110: cf. Heb. 3:9

103:25 εὐρύχωρος] add. ※ χερσιν GaHi = MT: teste Hi ex εβρ′ θ′

105:38 θυγατέρων] add. (sub ※ GaAug) αυτων GaAug *ae hj* = MT Pesh

115:4(116:13) fin. S′ Sa-1093-2110 R″ L^{pau}T′He A′ Orig. Cyp.] + u. 5(14) τας ευχας μου τω κυριω αποδωσω εναντιον παντος του λαου αυτου Ga(sub ※; Ga[non Uulg] om. αυτου) *L*Ch *e* (*a hj* om. εναντ.-αυτου) 1219 = MT Pesh (praeter Pesh non testatur αυτου), cf. u. 9(18)

115:8(116:17) fin. S′ Sa-2110 R″ 55] add. stichum και εν ονοματι κυριου επικαλεσομαι Ga(sub ※) *L′* A′, add. και το ονομα κυριου επ. ⟨204⟩ *aef*^{pars} *hj* (cf. u. 4[13]), MT hab. ובשׁם יהוה אקרא et Pesh hab. ܘܒܫܡܗ ܕܡܪܝܐ ܐܩܪܐ

117:5 fin.] add. ※ κυριος Ga = MT

117:10,11,12 ἠμυνάμην] pr. ※ οτι GaHi = MT

127:2 φάγεσαι] pr. ※ οτι Ga = MT

146:1 ἡδυνθείη = ܢܐܐ $a^{txt}b^{txt}f^{txt}$ uid.(uerbum languet sed hab. g^{txt}) *h*, *iucunda sit* uel *sit iuc*. La] add. ※ *decoraque* Ga, item (sub ※ $a^{mg}b^{mg}$) πρεπει (ܦܐܐ) $a^{mg}b^{mg}f^{mg}$ uid.-(litterae ܐ non apparent, sed hab. g^{mg}): = MT, cf. Pesh (ܘܠܗ ܗܘ ܐܐ); πρεπει (ܦܐܐ) *j*

Two further readings which are obelized in the Gallican Psalter should, if they have any sign, have an asterisk:

17:13(12) νεφέλαι] + αυτου (156) La^{R}Aug Ga(non Uulg) *abce hj* = MT Pesh (in Ga sub ÷ pro ※)

24:7 σύ U'-2110 *L' acef hj* 1219' = MT] hab. Ga sub ÷ (pro ※?); *deus* Aug; > B″ R″ A: exciditne post μου?

In addition, there is one reading which, though attested by Ga and the vast majority of witnesses, is asterisked only in *b*:

73:15^{2} = MT Pesh (quamquam Pesh hab. ܚܝܠܬܢܐ pro איתן/'Ηθάμ)] > B' La^{G} 2110$^{uid.}$, hab. *b* sub ※ sed s. ast. in *aef*^{pars} *hj*

The Gallican Psalter attests all forty-three readings listed above. Only the last three are not asterisked in Ga. The reading which Ga does not mark at all (73:15) constitutes original LXX and cannot, therefore, be used as a hexaplaric indicator in the Gallican Psalter. It may, however, have been lacking in Origen's Greek *Vorlage* (perhaps because of parablepsis) since it does not occur in B' La^{G} 2110$^{uid.}$ and is asterisked in *b*. For that reason, it is included in the present analysis of asterisked additions.

Ten of the readings asterisked in Ga are also attested with asterisk in the *Letter to Sunnia and Fretela*: 8:4(3), 17:14(13), 31:4, 41:12(11) 1° and 2°, 42:5 1°, 103:25, 117:10, 11, 12. Two other readings are mentioned by Augustine in his *Enarrationes in Psalmos* as having asterisks:[11] 67:13(12), 89:17.

In SyrPss, twenty-six of the forty-three readings are attested.[12] Seven of the forty-three are correctly asterisked in some SyrPss Mss:

41:12(11) 1° *ac*

42:5 1° *ac*

48:10(9) *ace h*

64:1(inscr.) *ac*

73:15 *b*

92:3 *ab* (*a* without metobelus)

146:1 *a*mg*b*mg

One additional reading is asterisked in two SyrPss Mss, but incorrectly because of the constraints of Syriac. In 41:12(11) 2°, και ὁ θεός μου, rather than just και, is *sub asterisco* in *ac* because that Greek phrase is represented by just one word in those texts.

Another eighteen of the forty-three readings are not asterisked in any SyrPss Mss: 7:7(6), 10(9), 17:13(12), 24:7, 31:4, 5, 34:20, 41:8(7), 42:5 2°, 48:18(17), 67:13(12), 88:3(2),[13] 48(47), 91:10(9), 94:9, 105:38, 115:4(116:13)-5(14), 8(17). Of the eighteen, four constitute original LXX:[14] 24:7, 67:13(12), 88:48(47), 91:10(9). These four are of no value in determining hexaplaric influence on SyrPss.

A factor which must not be overlooked in the consideration of the remaining fourteen plusses which are not asterisked in SyrPss is that those which also correspond to Peshitta readings may, in fact, derive from the Peshitta. It would seem logical to assume that, generally speaking, the closer the correspondence, the greater the likelihood of Peshitta influence. Of these fourteen, ten correspond to Peshitta readings which are longer than the LXX. Four of the ten are textually identical, or nearly so, and may therefore be the result of Peshitta influence. In the following list (and subsequent ones like it), the plus is parenthesized in the accompanying Greek text:

17:13(12) αἱ νεφέλαι (αυτου)
ܥܢܢܘܗܝ *abce* Pesh, c. uar. *hj*

42:5 2° (και) ὁ θεός μου
ܘܐܠܗܝ *abe* Pesh, c. uar. *hj*

105:38 καὶ θυγατέρων (αυτων)
ܘܒܢܬܗܘܢ *ae* Pesh, c. uar. *hj*

115:4(116:13) (5[14]) (τας ευχας μου τω κυριω αποδωσω εναντιον παντος του λαου αυτου)
ܢܕܪܝ ܠܡܪܝܐ ܐܦܪܘܥ *a*, c. uar. *hj*; ܢܕܪܝ ܠܡܪܝܐ [ܐ]ܦܪܘܥ. ܩܕܡ ܟܠܗ ܥܡܗ ܕܝܠܗ *e*, ܕܝܠܗ > Pesh [15]

In the remaining six instances, Peshitta influence seems less likely:

31:4 εἰς ταλαιπωρίαν (μου)
ܠܒܘܫܝܐ ܕܝܠܝ *abcef*^{pars} *hj*
ܒܫܢܝ Pesh

31:5 ἐγνώρισα (σοι)
ܝܕܥܬ ܠܟ *abcef hj*
ܐܘܕܥܬܟ Pesh

34:20 ὀργὴν (γης ελαλουν)
ܪܘܓܙܐ ܕܐܪܥܐ ܡܡܠܠܝܢ ܗܘܘ *abcef*^{pars} *hj*
ܡܟܝܟܐ ܕܐܪܥܐ Pesh

41:8(7) (προς?) ἄβυσσον
ܠܘܬ ܬܗܘܡܐ *abcef hj*
ܠܬܗܘܡܐ Pesh

48:18(17) συγκαταβήσεται αὐτῷ ἡ δόξα αὐτοῦ (οπισω αυτου)
ܢܚܬ ܥܡܗ ܫܘܒܚܗ ܒܬܪܗ *acef*, c. uar. *hj*
ܢܚܬ ܒܬܪܗ ܫܘܒܚܗ Pesh

115:8(116:17) (και το ονομα κυριου επικαλεσομαι)
ܘܠܫܡܗ ܕܡܪܝܐ ܐܩܪܐ *aef*^{pars}, c. uar. *hj*
ܘܒܫܡܗ ܕܡܪܝܐ ܐܩܪܐ Pesh

Another important observation *vis-à-vis* the preceding fourteen plusses not asterisked in SyrPss is that, according to Rahlfs' apparatus, six of them are also attested in Mss of the *L* family: 7:7(6), 42:5 2°, 48:18(17), 94:9, 115:4(116:13)-5(14), 8(17). Furthermore, in the H-P apparatus which Rahlfs digests in his own edition and which is his source for texts he designates *L*, minimal support (one Ms each time) is listed in three additional cases:[16] 17:13(12), 31:5, 34:20. Thus, *L* too is a witness to hexaplaric readings. It is also evident that, while SyrPss and *L* may be related, it is not uncommon to see them diverge.[17]

One of the fourteen plusses just discussed deserves special comment. The longer reading in 88:3(2) is, apart from Ga, attested only by *e*. The Greek column of *e* (*e𝒮*) does not attest it, but the Hebrew column (*e^h^*), like MT, does. This polyglot Ms appears to have been compiled by one individual who gives evidence of having consulted the Hebrew while producing his Syriac column.[18] Thus, he may have introduced the plus himself after having checked *e^h^*. The possibility of hexaplaric influence on *e* in this context is, therefore, diminished.

Seventeen of the forty-three marked plusses under consideration are not found in SyrPss. In two of the seventeen cases, however, some SyrPss Mss have (misplaced) asterisks:

17:14(13) χαλαζα και ανθρακες πυρος is missing in SyrPss, but the identical phrase in verse 13(12) is asterisked in *abc*;

44:13(12) *et* of Ga^c^ is lacking in SyrPss, but the phrase θυγατέρες Τύρου ἐν δώροις is asterisked in *a h*.

The remaining fifteen instances in which SyrPss does not attest the marked plusses are the following: 7:15(14), 8:4(3), 15:3, 16:9, 23:2, 41:3(2), 55:13(12), 88:19(18), 89:17, 103:25, 117:5, 10, 11, 12, 127:2.

B. NON-ASTERISKED PLUSSES EQUALLING THE MT

An examination of hexaplaric plusses which equal the MT cannot be limited to passages which are asterisked in the text tradition, since the Aristarchian signs were frequently omitted by later copyists, most of whom were unaware of their significance. That these non-asterisked plusses represent originally asterisked additions to the Old Greek seems likely. However, though Rahlfs' *Psalmi cum Odis* is the best critical edition available, one dare not assume that in every single instance his text represents the original LXX. Consequently, each longer reading equalling the MT in the apparatus has been scrutinized to ensure that it does not, in fact, constitute the Old Greek.

There are twenty instances in which SyrPss agrees with Ga in the recording of a non-asterisked addition to the original LXX in conformity with the MT:[19]

16:14 κατάλοιπα = *e*] + αυτων Ga ThtP^{p} *acf*$^{\text{uid.}}$ *hj* = MT

21:17(16) πόδας B′ R′ et Aug. enarr. I et Tert. et Cyp.^{p} *hj*] + μου U La^{G} Ga *L′ ae* A′ et Aug. enarr. II et Cyp.^{p} = MT Pesh

41:6(5) ψυχή 2013-2110$^{\text{uid.}}$ Orig.] pr. η B, *anima* La^{G}; η ψ. μου rel. (etiam *abce hj*) = MT Pesh

41:9(8) ᾠδή Rahlfs = שִׁירָה] ωδη αυτου Ga *L*^{d}′Th *abcef hj* A″ (του periit in 1219) = MT (שִׁירֹה), cf. Pesh (ܬܫܒܘܚܬܗ); ωδη αυτω *L*^{a}S^{c}; δηλωσει B″ 2013′-2110$^{\text{uid.}}$ R, *declarabit* La(sic Aug, sed La^{RG} *-auit*).

41:12(11) ψυχή B^{c} 2013-2110$^{\text{uid.}}$] pr. η B*′, *anima* La^{G}, ...χη s. μου 1219; η ψ. μου rel. (etiam *abce hj*) = MT Pesh

42:5 ψυχή B′ 2013-2110, *anima* La^{G}] η ψ. μου rel. (etiam *ace hj*) = MT Pesh

54:9(8) καί] + απο Ga(non Uulg) *L′ abcef hj* 1219′: cf. MT (מסער) et u. 4(3)

54:11(10) ἀνομία] pr. και Ga(non Uulg) *L′ abcef hj* 55 = MT

54:18(17) ἀπαγγελῶ B′(S -γελλω) 2013 1220 La^{G}] και απαγγ. R′Aug Ga *L′ abcef hj* 55 = MT, cf. Pesh (ܘܐܡܪ)

55:10(9) init.] pr. τοτε Ga ‹39 156› *abcef hj* S^{c} = MT Pesh

83:11(10) θεοῦ B″ Sa-1093-2110uid. 2149 LaG ThtP] + μου Ga *L*ThtP *aef hj* A′ = MT; κυριου R′Aug

87:11(10) fin.] + διαψαλμα Ga (112 190mg 266 269) *abef hj* = MT

90:15 ἐξελοῦμαι B′ R′ 55 2110] + αυτον LaGAug Ga *L′ abef hj* A′ 2020 = MT Pesh

94:9 ἐπείρασαν B″ Sa-2110uid. LaG A′] + με R′Aug Ga *L′ ae hj* 1219 = MT Pesh: cf. Heb. 3:9

97:8 fin. B″ Sa-2110 R″] + *in*(Uulg *a*) *conspectu domini* Ga = MT Pesh, + απο προσωπου κυριου οτι ερχεται Aug *L′ aef*pars *hj* A″(55 προ pro απο: cf. 95:13) et alii Latini = 95:13[1]

104:28 καί 2° B′ Sa R″ 55] οτι *L* A et Psalt. Rom.; και ου S GaAuguar (142 156 190txt) Tht *abef hj* (*a*txt*b*txt*ef*txt οὐ, *a*mg*b*mg*f*mg *hj* οὗ) 2110 = MT [20]

106:27 ἐσαλεύθησαν S* *L*ThtP-2040 A″] pr. και R″ Ga (99 156 210 269) ThtPHeSc *aef hj* 2029 = MT Pesh

108:11[2] init. S R″ 55 2110] pr. και GaAug *L′ aef hj* A′ = MT Pesh

121:1(inscr.) BoP Sa R′Aug Uulg *L′* A″] + τω δαυιδ SBoP LaG Ga *f* = MT: cf. 123:1(inscr.); + του δαυιδ *ae hj* [21]

145:5 βοηθός B′ LaR A] + αυτου R′Aug Ga *L′ abe*uid.*f hj* 1219s′ = MT Pesh: cf. 143:12

Thirteen of the preceding twenty readings correspond to Peshitta readings which are longer than the Old Greek. In six of the thirteen, the textual similarity between SyrPss and Pesh is such that Peshitta influence on SyrPss is a possibility:

21:17(16) καὶ πόδας (μου)
ܘܪ̈ܓܠܝ *ae* Pesh

41:6(5) ψυχή (μου)

ܢܦܫܝ *abce* Pesh, c. uar. *hj*

41:12(11) ψυχή (μου)

ܢܦܫܝ *abce* Pesh, c. uar. *hj*

42:5 ψυχή (μου)

ܢܦܫܝ *ace* Pesh, c. uar. *hj*

55:10(9) (τοτε) ἐπιστρέψουσιν

ܗܝܕܝܢ ܢܗܦܟܘܢ *abcef hj* Pesh

94:9 οὗ ἐπείρασαν (με)

ܐܝܟܐ ܕܢܣܘܢܝ *ae*, c. uar. *hj* [ܐܝܟܢܐ pro ܐܝܟܐ]; ܐܝܟܐ > Pesh

Peshitta influence on SyrPss in the remaining seven instances is less likely:

41:9(8) ᾠδή (αυτου)

ܬܫܒܘܚܬܐ ܕܝܠܗ *abcef hj*

ܬܫܒܘܚܬܗ Pesh

54:18(17) διηγήσομαι· (και) ἀπαγγελῶ

ܐܫܬܥܐ ܘܐܚܘܐ *abcef hj*

ܐܪܢܐ ܘܐܢܗܡ Pesh

90:15 ἐξελοῦμαι (αυτον) καὶ δοξάσω αὐτόν

ܐܦܪܩܝܘܗܝ ܘܐܫܒܚܝܘܗܝ *abef hj*

ܐܚܠܨܝܘܗܝ ܘܐܝܩܪܝܘܗܝ Pesh

97:8(-9) (απο προσωπου κυριου οτι ερχεται)

ܡܢ ܩܕܡ ܦܪܨܘܦܗ ܕܡܪܝܐ ܕܐܬܐ *aef*pars, c. uar. *hj*

ܩܕܡ ܡܪܝܐ Pesh

106:27 ἐταράχθησαν (και) ἐσαλεύθησαν

ܐܬܕܠܚܘ ܘܙܥܘ *aef hj*

ܙܥܘ ܘܬܘ Pesh

108:11[2] αὐτῷ, (και) διαρπασάτωσαν

ܠܗ. ܘܢܚܛܦܘܢ *a h*, c. uar. *ef j* [ܘܢܬܚܛܦܘܢ pro ܘܢܚܛܦܘܢ]

ܠܗܘܢ. ܘܢܒܙܘܢ Pesh

145:5 βοηθὸς (αυτου)

ܡܥܕܪܢܐ ܗܘ ܕܝܠܗ *abe*uid.[partim abscond.]*f hj*

ܡܥܕܪܢܗ Pesh

According to Rahlfs' apparatus, Mss of the *L* family attest fourteen of the twenty non-asterisked plusses on which SyrPss and Ga agree: 21:17(16), 41:6(5), 9(8), 12(11), 42:5, 54:9(8), 11(10), 18(17), 83:11(10), 90:15, 94:9, 97:8, 108:11, 145:5. In four of the remaining six instances, the H-P apparatus lists Ms support from a few witnesses (two to four in each case) which Rahlfs does not mention: 55:10(9), 87:11(10), 104:28, 106:27. These observations further illustrate the degree to which the *L* family has been subjected to hexaplaric influence.

Besides the non-asterisked plusses shared with Ga, there are twenty-eight in SyrPss which equal the MT but are not found in Ga:[22]

7:12(11) μὴ (= אַל) ὀργὴν ἐπάγων] pr. και *L' af hj*: cf. MT (וְאֵל זֹעֵם), *numquid irascitur* La^{G}(*-cetur*) Ga

21:2(1) ὁ θεός 1° = *hj*] + μου *ae* = MT Pesh

25:10^{2} init.] pr. και R' *abcef hj* = MT Pesh

26:5 σκηνῇ B' La^{G} Ga 2021 2110 = בְּסֻכָּה] + αυτου Bo U' R'Aug Uulg *L' abcef hj* A' 2030 2150: cf. MT (בְּסֻכֹּה), Pesh (ܡܛܠܬܗ)

31:9 ἡμίονος] pr. ως U *abce hj* (non 1098-Ga) = MT Pesh

36:14 ἐνέτειναν] -νον 2013(non 2046), pr. *et* La^{G} *ace hj* = MT Pesh

40:13(12) ἀκακίαν B' La^{R} Ga *L*Tht^{P} A''] + μου Bo 2013'-2050-2110$^{uid.}$ R'Aug *L*^{pau}Tht^{P} *acef hj* = MT Pesh

40:13(12) ἀντελάβου (αντι- [sic] R)] + μου R {188} *acef hj* = MT Pesh; La^{G} hab. pro u. 13(12)^{1} *propter innocentiam autem meam suscepisti me*: item alii Latini

41:6 ὁ θεός B'' 2013'-2110 GaHiAug 55] pr. και R'' Uulg *L' abce hj* Su A = Pesh: cf. MT (פניו אלהי) et u. 12(11) et

42:5

54:11(10) καὶ ἀδικία] + εν μεσω αυτης Sa *abe hj*: cf. MT (הוות בקרבה pro και αδικια εν μεσω αυτης), + εν μεσω της γης *c f*mg†

59:2(inscr.) τὴν φάραγγα B″ R′ Ga *L*d(sil)He *abf hj* 55 2010(-γαν) 2110uid.] τον εδωμ εν τη φαραγγι Sa LaRAug Uulg *L*d′ *e* = MT

61:4(3) φονεύετε πάντες B′ R 1219 2110] *interficite*(LaR *-ciente*) *omnes* LaRAug, *et interficere uniuersos* LaG, *interficitis uniuersos* Ga et Psalt. Rom.; + υμεις Uulg (*interficitis uniuersi uos*) *L′ abcdef hj* 55 = MT

67:9(8) τοῦ θεοῦ 2° = *abcf hj*] + θεου *e* (cf. σ′: Field) = MT Pesh

70:7 βοηθός B″-2042 La Ga] + μου Sa-2110 R *L′ abcef hjk* 1102 55 = MT Pesh

70:8 αἰνέσεως] + σου LaG (144 156 173 188) *abce hjk* et alii Latini = MT Pesh

71:19 γένοιτο 2° = *abcef*] pr. και *hj*, cf. MT (ואמן) et Pesh (ܘܐܡܝܢ)

72:2 οἱ πόδες = *hj*] + μου *abce* = MT Pesh

76:9(8)2 init.] pr. συνετελεσεν ρημα *L′*Su *abe hj* 1219′ (non GaHi) = גמר אמר, cf. Pesh (ܐܘ ܡܫܠܡ ܡܠܬܗ)

82:10(9) καί] + ως *ae hj* = Pesh: cf. MT (כסיסרא)

82:12(11) καί 2°] + ως *ae hj* = MT Pesh

88:53(52) γένοιτο 2° = *abef*] pr. και *hj*, cf. MT (ואמן) et Pesh (ܘܐܡܝܢ); > 1219 2039

105:1(inscr.) ἀλληλούϊα] + αλληλουια Aug *abef hj*: in MT הללו יה et in fine Ps. praec. (non Pesh) et in initio huius Ps. adest; cf. Aug: "quidam dicunt unum *halleluia* pertinere ad finem

Psalmi superioris, alterum ad huius principium"

106:3 init. S R" Ga A'] pr. και Uulg *L' ae hj* 1219 = MT Pesh

124:5 ἀπάξει = *af hj*] + αυτους *e* = MT Pesh

147:8(19) δικαιώματα] + αυτου *aefh1 j* = MT Pesh

148:1(inscr.) ἀλληλούϊα = *f*] + αλληλουια Tht *aeh1 j* (Uulg {262} add. αλληλουια ad Ps. 147 fin.: Uulg item 148 fin., 149 fin., 150 fin.: = MT [non Pesh]; cf. uerba Augustini ad 105:1[inscr.] commemorata)

149:1(inscr.) ἀλληλούϊα] + αλληλουια ThtP *afh1*(και αλληλουια) *j* et Psalt. Rom. (Uulg add. αλληλουια ad Ps. 148 fin. = MT [non Pesh]): cf. 148:1(inscr.)

150:1(inscr.) ἀλληλούϊα] > *L*pau; + αλληλουια {268} Tht *abf j* (Uulg add. αλληλουια ad Ps. 149 fin. = MT [non Pesh]): cf. 148:1(inscr.)

In twelve of the preceding twenty-eight instances, there is enough similarity between SyrPss and Pesh to suggest the possibility of Peshitta influence:

21:2(1) ὁ θεός (μου)
ܐܠܗܝ *ae* Pesh

25:10[2] (και) ἡ δεξιὰ αὐτῶν
ܘܝܡܝܢܐ ܕܝܠܗܘܢ *abcef hj*
ܘܝܡܝܢܗܘܢ Pesh

31:9 καὶ (ως) ἡμίονος
ܘܐܝܟ ܟܘܕܢܐ *abce hj* Pesh

36:14 (και) ἐνέτειναν
ܘܡܬܚܘ *ace hj* Pesh

41:6 (και) ὁ θεός μου
ܘܐܠܗܝ *abce* Pesh, c. uar. *hj*

67:9(8) ἀπὸ προσώπου τοῦ θεοῦ, (θεου) Ἰσραήλ [cf. σ': Field]

ܡܢ ܩܕܡ ܦܪܨܘܦܐ ܕܐܠܗܐ ܐܠܗܗ ܕܐܝܣܪܝܠ *e*

ܡܢ ܩܕܡ ܐܠܗܐ ܐܠܗܗ ܕܐܝܣܪܝܠ Pesh [23]

70:8 αἰνέσεως (σου)

ܬܫܒܘܚܬܟ *abce* Pesh, c. uar. *hjk*

72:2 οἱ πόδες (μου)

ܪ̈ܓܠܝ *abce* Pesh

82:10(9) καὶ (ως) τῷ Σισαρά

ܘܐܝܟ ܕܠܣܝܣܪܐ *a hj* Pesh, c. uar. *e*

82:12(11) καὶ (ως) Ζέβεε

ܘܐܝܟ ܙܒܝ *ae hj* Pesh

106:3 (και) ἐκ τῶν χωρῶν συνήγαγεν αὐτούς

ܘܡܢ ܐܬܪ̈ܘܬܐ ܟܢܫ ܐܢܘܢ *ae hj*

ܘܡܢ ܟܠܗܝܢ ܐܪ̈ܥܬܐ ܟܢܫ ܐܢܘܢ Pesh

124:5 ἀπάξει (αυτους) κύριος

ܢܘܒܠ ܐܢܘܢ ܡܪܝܐ *e*

ܢܕܒܪ ܐܢܘܢ ܡܪܝܐ Pesh [24]

In eight additional cases, Peshitta readings which are longer than the Old Greek are less likely to have influenced SyrPss:

26:5 ἐν σκηνῇ (αυτου)

ܒܡܫܟܢܐ ܕܝܠܗ *abcef hj*

ܒܡܫܟܢܗ Pesh

40:13(12) 1° διὰ τὴν ἀκακίαν (μου)

ܡܛܠ ܬܡܝܡܘܬܝ *acef*, c. uar. *hj*

ܒܬܡܝܡܘܬܝ Pesh

40:13(12) 2° ἀντελάβου (μου)

ܣܥܕܬܢܝ *acef hj*

ܣܡܟܬܢܝ Pesh

70:7 βοηθός (μου)

ܡܥܕܪܢܐ ܕܝܠܝ *abcef hjk*

ܐܘܟܠܝܢ Pesh

71:19 γένοιτο (και) γένοιτο

ܢܗܘܐ ܘܢܗܘܐ *j*, c. uar. *h* [ܘܢܗܘܐ bis]

ܐܡܝܢ ܘܐܡܝܢ Pesh

76:9(8)[2] (συνετελεσεν ρημα)

ܫܡܠܝ ܡܠܬܐ *abe hj*

ܐܘ ܡܥܠܡ ܡܠܬܗ Pesh

88:53(52) γένοιτο (και) γένοιτο

ܢܗܘܐ ܘܢܗܘܐ *hj*

ܐܡܝܢ ܘܐܡܝܢ Pesh

147:8(19) δικαιώματα (αυτου) καὶ κρίματα αὐτοῦ

ܙܕܩܘܗܝ ܘܕܝܢܘܗܝ *aefh1*, c. uar. *j*

ܢܡܘܣܘܗܝ ܘܦܘܩܕܢܘܗܝ Pesh

Nine of the twenty-eight non-asterisked plusses in SyrPss not found in Ga are, according to Rahlfs' apparatus, also attested by Mss of the *L* family: 7:12(11), 26:5, 40:13(12) 1°, 41:6, 59:2(inscr.), 61:4(3), 70:7, 76:9(8), 106:3. Another four are attested by Mss listed in the H-P apparatus but not included by Rahlfs. All are supported by one Ms each, except the second reading listed below which is attested by four: 40:13(12) 2°, 70:8, 148:1(inscr.),[25] 150:1(inscr.). Corrections to the Hebrew attested by *L* but not by Ga may, firstly, be indicative of direct hexaplaric influence, secondly, be the result of Lucian's consultation of the Hebrew, the Hexapla, or one or more of the post-LXX translations (if, indeed, the *L* text of the Psalter does contain the Lucianic recension), or, thirdly, be due to post-Lucianic hebraizing activity. However, if these corrections do signify direct hexaplaric influence, then *L* would in such instances reflect a better hexaplaric tradition than Ga. If they were introduced by Lucian, then there is evidence for his having been engaged in hebraizing activity in the Psalter. Significantly, one of the characteristics which Rahlfs isolates in the Lucianic text of Kingdoms is revision towards the Hebrew.[26]

Having listed the passages which contain SyrPss plusses equalling the MT but not Ga, we now record the thirteen Ga plusses which correspond to the MT but are not attested in SyrPss, or for which the SyrPss evidence is inconclusive:

3:9(8) fin.] + διαψαλμα Ga = MT

10:2(3) βέλη = *ac hj*, *sagittas* La] + *suas* GaAug = MT; βελος *ƒ*uid.*g*

30:22(21) αὐτοῦ] + επ εμε U'; + εμοι 1098-Ga *L*^{pau}R^{c} = לי

67:25(24) βασιλέως] + μου S^{c} GaHi = MT

68:18(17) init.] pr. και B^{s} Ga = MT (B* om. u. 18[17]^{1})

72:28 τῷ κυρίῳ] *deo* La^{R}Aug; + *deo* Ga: cf. MT (באדני יהוה); + *deo salutis meae* La^{G} (tr. *in domino deo salutis meae* post *spem meam*)

78:12 init.] pr. *et* Ga = MT

88:31(30) τοῖς] pr. εν R'' Ga(non 1098) et Cyp.P = MT [27]

93:23^{2} fin.] + αφανιει αυτους Ga = MT

103:28 τὴν χεῖρα *manum* La^{G}] + *tuam* La^{R}Aug Ga = MT; σου / την χειρα tr. 2110 *aeƒ hj*

114:3^{2} init.] pr. *et* UulgGa^{c} = MT

115:7(116:16) ἐγώ 1°] pr. *quia* Ga = MT

123:1(inscr.) ἀναβαθμῶν] + τω δαυειδ S Ga(non Uulg) = MT: cf. 121:1(inscr.)

A statistical summary of the evidence presented in our analysis of the plusses which equal the MT is found in the following table:

	Ga	SyrPss
Marked Plusses	42	10
Unmarked Plusses	34	66
Gross Total	76	76
Net Total	75	50

Some explanatory comments regarding this table should be made. Firstly, the totals in the SyrPss column represent the plusses equalling the MT which are attested by our Syriac witnesses, whether by one or by all extant Mss. Secondly, among the total number of marked plusses found in Ga, there are two which it mistakenly obelizes. Likewise, two of the asterisks attested by SyrPss do not accompany the relevant additions. Indeed, these plusses are lacking in all SyrPss witnesses, and consequently, in the Mss which are marked, the asterisks are misplaced. Thirdly, whereas the gross total in either column is simply the sum of the marked and unmarked plusses, the net total represents an attempt to gauge, by means of a comparison with Ga, the potential extent of hexaplaric influence on SyrPss. To facilitate this, readings which cannot be used as hexaplaric indicators in Ga or SyrPss are subtracted from the respective gross totals. Specifically, these include asterisked readings (though attested without asterisk in Ga or SyrPss) which nonetheless constitute original LXX, but which significant textual witnesses omit, and unmarked plusses in SyrPss which reflect possible Peshitta influence. Thus, the gross total of Ga is reduced by one (73:15), while that of SyrPss is diminished by twenty-six (four original readings and twenty-two possible Peshitta readings). It will be noted that these deletions reduce not only the gross totals, but also the unmarked plusses by the same numbers, leaving revised totals of thirty-three and forty. The revised number of unmarked plusses in SyrPss might be further diminished if it could be demonstrated conclusively that those additions which *L* also attests (especially those which Ga does not) were introduced by Lucian himself. However, since all such readings may ultimately go back to the Hexapla, it would be best to let the numbers stand as they are. In conclusion, a comparison of the respective net totals of Ga and SyrPss confirms that Ga is the better hexaplaric witness.

C. OBELIZED PASSAGES

Having considered both asterisked and non-asterisked plusses in SyrPss and Ga, we now to turn to an analysis of obelized passages.

There is SyrPss attestation of obelized readings in eleven passages in the Psalter (words without accents or breathing marks are not part of the lemma):[28]

9:6(5) τοῦ αἰῶνος *ab* (ob. abscond., hab. metob. *b*)

9:37(36) καὶ εἰς τὸν αἰῶνα τοῦ αἰῶνος *ac* (om. metob. *c*)

30:24(23) ὅτι ἀληθείας ἐκζητεῖ κύριος *abc*
ὅτι *e*

37:1(inscr.) του (pro περὶ) σαββάτου *ae*

43:24(23) καὶ μὴ ἀπώσῃ ημας εἰς τέλος *ac*

47:1(inscr.) δευτέρᾳ σαββάτου *ace*

48:12(11) καὶ οἱ τάφοι αὐτῶν οἰκίαι αὐτῶν εἰς τὸν αἰῶνα *a*; *c* hab. ob., om. metob.

67:3(2) οὕτως ἀπόλοιντο οἱ ἁμαρτωλοὶ ἀπὸ προσώπου τοῦ θεοῦ *abc* (*c* hab. metob., om. ob.)
οὕτως, προσώπου *e*

110:1(inscr.) της επιστροφης αγγαιου και ζαχαριου *a*
εκ της επιγραφης αγγαιου και ζαχαριου *e*

111:1(inscr.) της επιστροφης αγγαιου και ζαχαριου *a*

140:1 τῆς δεήσεώς μου *a*; *e* hab. ob. tantum (÷ܕܒܥܘܬܝ)

A comparison of the preceding cases with the MT reveals that, besides the *e* reading in 30:24(23) and the first *e* reading in 67:3(2), the following five are correctly obelized:

9:6(5) τοῦ αἰῶνος] ÷ Ga *ab* (÷ abscond. *b*, s. ob. *f hj*), > MT

37:1(inscr.) περὶ σαββάτου] του σ. R" L^{pau}He, των σαββατων *acef hj* (*ae* sub ÷), περι του σαββατου L^{b}ThtP A; > L^{pau}ThtP = MT

47:1(inscr.) δευτέρᾳ (-ρας L^{pau} 55) σαββάτου (-των 2013'-2110)] ÷ Ga *ace* (s. ob. *hj*), > L^{pau}ThtPCh = MT; ܒܫܒܐ ܚܕ ܚܠܦ (pro ܕܬܪܝܢ ܒܫܒܐ) f^{29} (s. ob.): cf. 23:1(inscr.)

110:1(inscr.) ἀλληλούϊα = MT] + της επιστροφης αγγαιου και ζαχαριου Ga(non Uulg) *a*(sub ÷)*f hj*, + εκ της επιγραφης αγγαιου και ζαχαριου *e*(sub ÷): cf. 111:1(inscr.)

111:1(inscr.) ἀλληλούϊα S' Sa-2110 $L^{a'}$ A" = MT] + της επιστροφης αγγαιου και ζαχαριου R" Ga L^{pau} *a*(sub ÷)*f hj*; add. uel pr. της (uel εκ της) επιγραφης αγγαιου και ζαχαριου L^{b} *e*(εκ της etc.); + αγγαιου και ζαχαριου L^{pau}; + ζαχαριου T

In the other six instances, apart from the two *e* readings mentioned above, the SyrPss Mss with Aristarchian signs incorporate too much under the obelus. In the following list, only the material that should be obelized is included:

9:37(36) τοῦ αἰῶνος] ÷ Ga *ac* (s. ob. *hj*), > MT

30:24(23) ὅτι] ÷ Ga *abce* (s. ob. *f hj*), om. S = MT, hab. etiam 1098

43:24(23) καί] ÷ Ga *ac* (s. ob. *e hj*), > MT

48:12(11) καί 1°] ÷ Ga *ac* (s. ob. *ef hj*), > MT

67:3(2) οὕτως] ÷ *abce* (s. ob. *f hj*), > MT

140:1 τῆς δεήσεως] ÷ *ae* (s. ob. *f hj*), > Sa Ga = MT [30]

Ga corroborates the obelus in six of the eleven preceding verses: 9:6(5), 37(36), 30:24(23), 43:24(23), 47:1(inscr.), 48:12(11). In all but one of the remaining five passages, Ga has the reading without obelus. Only in 140:1 does Ga omit the obelized material. Yet, because all other extant LXX witnesses except Sa attest the reading, it seems likely that Origen had it in his Greek *Vorlage* and obelized it, but that sometime in Ga's text history it was deleted. The attestation of the obelus by SyrPss in these five passages (37:1[inscr.], 67:3[2], 110:1[inscr.], 111:1[inscr.], 140:1) appears to represent a better hexaplaric tradition than that of Ga, although the placement of the metobelus in *abc* at 67:3(2) and in *a* at 140:1 is faulty.

While SyrPss attests obeli in five cases where Ga does not, there are eighty-four instances in which the reverse is true. Here is a list of those readings:[31]

1:4 οὐχ οὕτως 2°] ÷ Ga (cf. Field), > *O* teste Hi ed. Morin = MT

1:4 ἀπὸ προσώπου τῆς γῆς] ÷ Ga, > *O* teste He ed. Morin = MT

2:11 αὐτῷ] ÷ Ga, > Cyp. = MT

2:12 κύριος] ÷ Ga, > La^{G} = MT

2:12 δικαίας = *ab*$^{\text{uid.}}$*f j*] ÷ Ga, > MT; *iustitiae eius* Sa, δικαιοσυνης (ܙܕܝܩܘܬܐ) *h*

3:3(2) αὐτοῦ] ÷ Ga, > MT

3:4(3) εἶ] ÷ Ga, > MT

3:8(7) σύ] ÷ Ga, > MT

5:7(6) πάντας] ÷ Ga, > La(non Aug) = MT

6:11(10) σφόδρα ult.] ÷ Ga, > MT

7:12(11) καὶ μακρόθυμος] ÷ Ga, > MT

9:6(5) καί 1°] ÷ Ga, > MT

10:3(4) δέ] ÷ Ga, > MT

10:4(5) εἰς τὸν πένητα] ÷ Ga, > MT; εις την οικουμενην U'; pro εις τον πενητα αποβλεπουσιν hab. 1221-2018 ThtCh *acf hj* επιβλεπουσιν την οικουμενην

10:7(8) καί] ÷ Ga, > 1221 = MT

12:6⁴] ÷ Ga, > MT

13:1 οὐκ ἔστιν ἕως ἑνός B''-2019 U'-1221 R'' A'] ÷ Ga, > *L' ac j* 55 = MT Pesh: cf. u. 3 et 52:4(3)

13:2 ἤ] ÷ Ga, > 2019 = MT; και U-1221; aut και aut nihil hab. Sa

13:3³⁻¹⁰ B''-2019 U'-1221 R'' *ac j* 1219] ÷ Ga, > *L'* A' = MT: ex Rom. 3:13-18

13:5 οὗ οὐκ ἦν φόβος] ÷ Ga, > MT

15:3 αὐτοῦ 1°] ÷ Ga, > (65 201 283) *ac hj* = MT Pesh; *eius* post *sunt* tr. La (*qui in terra sunt eius*, sed GaAug *qui sunt in terra eius*)

17:7(6) ἁγίου] ÷ Ga, > La^G = MT

17:8(7) αὐτοῖς] ÷ Ga, > MT

17:12(11) καί] ÷ Ga, > MT

17:21(20) καί 1°] ÷ Ga, > MT

17:21(20) καί 2°] ÷ Ga, > MT

18:6(5) αὐτοῦ ult. B'' U'-2110 A''] ÷ GaHi, > R'' Uulg *L'*Su *ac hj* Cyp. = MT

20:9(8) πάντας] ÷ Ga, > MT

20:12(11) στῆσαι B'' Sa La Ga *ae* He] ÷ Ga, > MT; στηναι R *L' hj* A'' 2110; ܠܡܩܡܘܗ (pro ܠܡܩܡܘ in *ae*) *f*

21:2(1) πρόσχες μου] ÷ Ga, > MT

21:25(24) μου] ÷ Ga, > MT

21:29(28) αὐτός] ÷ Ga, > MT

21:32(31) ὁ κύριος] ÷ Ga, > La^{G} = MT

22:2 ἐκεῖ] ÷ Ga, > MT

22:5 καί] ÷ Ga, > MT

23:1(inscr.) τῆς μιᾶς (τῶν) σαββάτων = *ace hj*] ÷ Ga, > S *O*(teste Tht) *L*^{pau} 2110 = MT; ܚܕ ܒܫܒܐ *f* (cf. Rahlfs)

23:1 πάντες] ÷ Ga, > MT

24:3 οἱ ult. B*″ U'-2110 La *L'*Su *acef hj* 1219' = MT] pr. παντες B^{c} R GaHi(ambis testibus sub ÷)Aug A

24:4 καί] ÷ Ga, > MT

25:12 σε κύριε = *a*^{c} pr m(σε > *a**)*bce*] σε sub ÷ Ga; *dominum* La^{G}, τον κυριον (188) *hj* = MT Pesh

27:3 μὴ συναπολέσῃς με] ÷ Ga, > MT

30:20(19) κύριε] ÷ Ga, > S Sa$^{B(uid.)}$ La^{G} 1098 = MT

31:4 ἐμπαγῆναι B'Bo^{d} La Uulg 2110(om. μ)] εμ > A; + μοι Bo^{d} R Ga(sub ÷) *L' abcef hj* A': cf. MT (בְּחָרְבֹנָי pro εν τω εμπ.) et θ' (εν ερημια μου: Field), + με ως U'

32:10^{3}] ÷ Ga(metob. post και), > S et Orig. = MT

33:7(6) αὐτοῦ 1°] ÷ Ga, > MT; αυτων S: ex u. 18(17); *auton* R, i. e. αυτον (uid.), = *eum* La Ga

33:10(9) οἱ S U'-2038$^{uid.}$ La^{R} Cyp. = MT] pr. παντες B' R'Aug Ga(sub ÷) *L' abef*^{mg†} *hj* A'

36:29 αἰῶνος] ÷ Ga, > MT

37:17(16) οἱ ἐχθροί μου] ÷ Ga, > S = MT

37:19(18) καί] ÷ Ga, > MT

38:12(11) ταράσσεται B' 2013'-2110 R″ ThtHeTh$^{uid.}$ *acef hj* 1219'] ÷ GaHi, > S *L*Su A = MT

43:21(20) εἰ 2°] ÷ Ga, > MT

44:18(17) τοῦ αἰῶνος = *ace hj*] ÷ Ga, > MT; των αιωνων *f*

47:12(11) κύριε] ÷ Ga, > S = MT

48:21(20) τοῖς ἀνοήτοις] ÷ Ga, > 2110 = MT

50:3(1) μέγα] ÷ Ga, > MT

50:3(1) καί] ÷ Ga, > MT

52:3(2) ἤ] ÷ Ga, > 2110 = MT; και 2013; aut και aut nihil hab. Sa

52:5(4) πάντες] ÷ Ga, > MT

54:17(16) δέ S' 2013' 1220 R' *L*pau *abce hj*] ÷ Ga, > B LaGAug *L'* 55 = MT

59:9(7) ἐστίν 2° (non 1°)] ÷ Ga, > MT

64:2(1) ἐν ἱερουσαλήμ Bo Sa-1093 R" *L' acef hj* 1219'] ÷ Ga, > B' 2110 = MT

65:1(inscr.) ἀναστάσεως] ÷ Ga, > S *O*(teste Tht) = MT: additamentum christianum docens hunc Ps. iam II. uel I. saec.

65:3[1] fin. = MT] add. ÷ *domine* Ga

67:34(33) ψάλατε τῷ θεῷ B' Sa 1220 La Su] ÷ GaHi, > S Rs *L' abce hj* 55 2110(om. ψαλατε τω θεω τω) = MT Pesh

69:4(3) μοι] ÷ Ga, > 2110 = MT

72:13 καὶ εἶπα] ÷ Ga, > MT

72:28[4]] ÷ Ga et *O* teste Euseb. (cf. Field), > MT

73:6 αὐτήν] ÷ Ga, > MT

83:4(3) ἑαυτῷ] ÷ Ga, > MT

83:11(10) μᾶλλον] ÷ Ga, > MT (מִדּוּר pro μαλλον η οικειν)

83:12(11) ἀγαπᾷ] ÷ Ga, > MT

84:9(8) ἐν ἐμοί] ÷ Ga(hab. ÷ per errorem post εν εμοι), > ⟨210⟩ *ae hj* 55 = MT Pesh

85:1 καί 1°] ÷ Ga, > MT

90:13 καί 2°] ÷ Ga, > MT

91:8(7) τοῦ αἰῶνος] ÷ Ga, > MT

101:26(25) σύ, κύριε, τὴν γῆν ἐθεμελίωσας = *abdef*] συ > La^{R}; συ κυριε sub ÷ Ga, συ κυριε > S *hj* = MT Pesh; tr. συ ante εθεμ. 2110$^{uid.}$; την γην συ κυριε εθεμ. B, την γην συ εθεμ. κυριε La^{G}Aug

103:10 ὕδατα] ÷ Ga, > La^{G} 2110 = MT

106:29 καὶ ἐπέταξεν τῇ καταιγίδι καὶ ἔστη εἰς αὔραν La *L' aef hj* A″ 2029] επαταξεν pro επετ. Bo Sa *L*^{b}; επετιμησεν pro επετ. R *L*^{pau}S^{c}Su; post καταιγ. add. αυτης Su; και εστησεν καταιγιδα αυτης S: cf. *a*^{mg}*f*^{mg} "εβρ' εστησεν καταιγιδα αυτης"; *et statuit procellam* ÷ *eius* [‹] *in auram* GaHi: cf. MT (יָקֵם סְעָרָה לִדְמָמָה), Pesh (ܐܩܝܡ ܥܠܥܠܐ ܘܫܠܝܐ)

107:2(1) ἑτοίμη ἡ καρδία μου 2°] ÷ Ga, > 2110 = MT

110:10 τοῦ αἰῶνος] ÷ Ga, > 2110 = MT

133:1^{4} = *hj*^{c} pr m(θεοῦ > *j**)] ÷ Ga, > *O* teste Hi ed. Morin = MT; ημων > *aef*^{mg†}

134:17$^{2-5}$ Bo Sa-2017 R″ A′(1219 om. u. 17^{5})] ÷ Ga, > S Uulg *L' ae hj* 55 Cyp. = MT Pesh: ex 113:14-15(115:6-7)

140:5 δέ] ÷ Ga, > S La^{G} = MT

144:13a$^{1.2}$(13)] ÷ Ga(hab. ÷ ante u. 13a^{2} tantum), > MT: cf. Field; πασιν antecedit τοις λογοις in R Ga *L' ae*$^{uid.}$*f hj* 1219^{s}' (sed non in B″ Sa La A)

Three additional readings in Ga are marked with an asterisk instead of an obelus:

17:25(24) καί 1° = MT] ÷ Ga, sed ÷ ante καὶ 2° (> MT) transponendum uid., ubi in ms. ※ est

117:28 εἶ σύ 2° = *aef*^{pars} *hj*^{c} pr ^{m}(εἶ > *j** [I])] hab. Ga sub ※ (pro ÷), > La^{R} 2110$^{uid.}$ = MT

132:3 καί S' 2017 R" Ga(pr. ※ : pro ÷ ?) A] > Sa Aug *L' aef hj* 55 = MT

Most readings in the two preceding lists are attested (though without obelus) in extant SyrPss Mss. However, in twelve instances, all or some Mss, as indicated here, omit them: 13:1, 15:3, 18:6(5), 24:3, 25:12 [*a** *hj*; *a*^{c} pr ^{m}*bce* have the longer reading], 65:3, 67:34(33), 84:9(8), 101:26(25) [*hj*; *abdef* have the longer reading], 106:29, 132:3, 134:17. Rahlfs recognizes four of the twelve shorter readings as original LXX (24:3, 65:3, 106:29, 134:17). It seems as though the one in 13:1 could also be original.[32] Despite the impressive textual support for the phrase, οὐκ ἔστιν ἕως ἑνός (B"-2019 U'-1221 R" A' Ga[sub ÷]), it appears to be an *ex par.* addition from verse 3 and 52:4(3), in the same way as the identical phrase in 52:2(1) of 2013'-2110 R" is.

In five of the seven remaining passages, the SyrPss omissions correspond to Peshitta readings which are shorter than the LXX. Three of the five may be due to Peshitta influence. In the following list (and subsequent ones like it), the minus is parenthesized in the accompanying Greek text:

25:12 εὐλογήσω (σε), κύριε
ܐܒܪܟ ܠܡܪܝܐ *hj* Pesh [33]

67:34(33) τῷ κυρίῳ. διάψαλμα. (ψάλατε τῷ θεῷ) τῷ ἐπιβεβηκότι
ܠܡܪܝܐ: ܠܗܘ ܕܪܟܒ *abce hj*; ܠܗܘ > Pesh [34]

84:9(8) τί λαλήσει (ἐν ἐμοὶ) κύριος
ܡܢܐ ܡܡܠܠ ܡܪܝܐ *ae hj* Pesh

Peshitta influence is less likely in the other two passages:

15:3 τοῖς ἁγίοις τοῖς ἐν τῇ γῇ (αὐτοῦ) ἐθαυμάστωσεν

ܠܩܕܝ̈ܫܐ ܕܒܐܪܥܐ ܐܕܡܪ *ac*, c. uar. *hj*

ܐܦ ܠܩܕܝ̈ܫܐ ܕܒܐܪܥܐ ܘܡܥܫܢܐ Pesh

101:26(25) κατ' ἀρχὰς (σύ, κύριε,) τὴν γῆν ἐθεμελίωσας

ܡܢ ܪܘܫܐ ܠܐܪܥܐ ܫܬܐܣܬ *hj*

ܡܢ ܠܘܩܕܡܝܢ ܐܪܥܐ ܫܬܐܣܬ Pesh

According to Rahlfs' apparatus, three of the preceding seven shorter readings are attested by Mss of the *L* family: 18:6(5), 67:34(33), 132:3. In the H-P apparatus, three other shorter readings have Ms support which Rahlfs does not mention: the one in 15:3 is attested by three texts, those in 25:12 and 84:9(8) by one each.

D. MINUSES EQUALLING THE MT

The logical counterpart to non-asterisked plusses which equal the MT is minuses which equal the MT. Admittedly, Origen did not delete Greek readings which were longer than his Hebrew text, but obelized them. Nevertheless, where hexaplaric witnesses exhibit a text in which the Old Greek has been shortened in conformity with the Hebrew, there is the distinct possibility that later copyists deleted originally obelized passages. As always, care must be exercised with regard to Rahlfs' Greek edition which does not always have the original LXX for the lemma. Indeed, in the following twelve passages where SyrPss and/or Ga attest a reading which is both shorter than Rahlfs' text and equals the MT, the shorter reading appears to constitute the Old Greek:

24:14[2] B USa(Sa^{B} ex corr.)-2110 R'Aug A'] > S Sa^{B*} La^{G} Ga *L' ace hj* 1219 = MT

This stich, which Rahlfs himself brackets in his edition signifying that it is not to be considered original LXX, seems to be a Greek doublet on the first stich, with καὶ τὸ ὄνομα κυρίου substituting for κραταίωμα κύριος.[35]

55:5(4) ὅλην τὴν ἡμέραν B' 2013' R" 55 (ex uu. 2[1], 3[2], 6[5])] > S GaAug *L' abce hj* 1219 = MT

Despite some weighty textual support for the longer reading, a good case can be made for the originality of the shorter one. As Rahlfs himself indicates, ὅλην τὴν ἡμέραν occurs three additional times within the space of verses 2(1)-6(5), all three times equalling the MT. In verse 5(4), however, this phrase is without an MT equivalent. Furthermore, with the addition of ὅλην τὴν ἡμέραν to the preceding phrase, τοὺς λόγους μου, an identical chiastic parallel is formed with the first part of stich 1 in verse 6(5). Therefore, it seems likely that ὅλην τὴν ἡμέραν in verse 5(4) is a post-translation, *ex par.* addition influenced particularly by verse 6(5), though also by verses 2(1) and 3(2).

64:1(inscr.) ἱερεμίου-fin. sic uel sim. hab. Bo Sa La Ga *L*] > B' R *O*(teste Tht) L^{b}THe *acef hj* 1219' = MT, reprobat Tht

There are a number of factors which indicate the secondary nature of this portion of the title to Ps. 64.[36] First of all, in the Psalms, ὅτε occurs only in the titles which the MT does not attest, in whole (92, 95, 96) or in part (64, 142). However, whenever the Hebrew has a titular equivalent, ב plus the bound infinitive is rendered by either ὁπότε with a finite verb (3, 33, 55, 58, 59) or ἐν followed by an articular infinitive (50, 51, 53, 56, 62, 141), but never by a ὅτε construction (there is no occurrence of either ὁπότε or ὅτε in the Psalms apart from the titles). It is probable, therefore, that ὅτε clauses in the titles were added after the Psalms had been translated into Greek. Secondly, nowhere else in Psalms does παροικία convey the sense of גולה. Finally, there are a large number of textual witnesses which omit the longer reading.

74:3(2) πάντα B' Sa^{B} R" *L'*Su 55 $2149^{uid.}$] > S Sa^{L}-2110 GaHi *abe hj* = MT

The phrase, διηγεῖσθαι πάντα τὰ θαυμάσια, occurs in Ps. 9:2(1), 25:7, and 104:2 where, in each case, the MT has כל. However, in 144:5, the LXX records the (transposed) phrase minus πάντα, in conformity with the Hebrew. In all four instances, the Greek reading is uncontested. It seems, therefore, that πάντα in 74:3(2) is an *ex par.* or/and *ad sensum* variant.[37]

77:6 αὐτά > S La^G^Aug Ga 2054 2149 = MT

The shorter reading is undoubtedly original not only because αὐτά has the feel of an *ad sensum* addition, but also because of the likelihood of *ex par.* influence from stich 4 of verse 5.[38]

79:1(inscr.) ὑπὲρ τοῦ ἀσσυρίου > S Ga *L*pau *aef hj* 2110 2149 = MT: cf. 75:1(inscr.)

Despite the numerous textual witnesses which support the longer reading, there are a number of factors which suggest that the omission of the phrase in question may constitute the original text, although the possibility of MT influence remains a live option.[39] In the first place, additions were made to some Psalter titles after the Greek Psalms were translated (see the discussion on 64:1[inscr.] above). That this lament should secondarily become associated with the Assyrian invasion is quite understandable, though it is always possible that the Psalm was composed about that time. Secondly, the quality of Greek witnesses—particularly S, 2110, and 2149—which attest the shorter reading is rather impressive, though S and 2110 do contain some hebraizing corrections. After a careful weighing of the evidence, it seems prudent to take the shorter reading as original, keeping in mind that the possibility of Hebrew influence cannot be lightly dismissed.

85:10 ὁ μέγας B' Sa-2110 R" 55 2016] > S Ga *L' abe hj* A 2149 = MT

The reading, ὁ μέγας, can, with a reasonable degree of confidence, be regarded as a later addition.[40] First of all, μέγας is commonly used in the Psalter as a divine epithet (cf. 46:3[2], 47:2[1], 3[2], 76:14[13], 88:8[7], 94:3, 95:4, 98:2, 134:5, 144:3, 146:5 as well as 20:6[5],

75:2[1], 98:3, 137:5). Secondly, the phrase, ὅτι μέγας εἶ σύ, occurs in the first stich of 85:10. Thus, ὁ μέγας in 85:10² appears to have been introduced secondarily because of the Psalter's not infrequent use of this divine epithet and/or the influence of μέγας in 85:10¹.

87:3(2) κύριε B' Sa R" A] post κλινον tr. *abef hj* 2149; > S GaAug *L'* 1219' 2110 = MT

The fairly weighty textual support for κύριε makes it easy to see why Rahlfs regards it as original. If κύριε is Old Greek, it must presuppose a Hebrew *Vorlage* different from the MT, since the translator is unlikely to have added it without textual basis. However, in view of the diversity of witnesses which do not attest κύριε, the lack of unanimity among witnesses which do attest it as to its location in the stich, and the possibility of its being added secondarily under the influence of verse 2(1), the originality of κύριε seems less defensible than that of the shorter reading.[41]

118:18 σου 1° S' *L*pauT A Orig.] > Sa R" Ga *L' ae hj* 55 = MT

Apart from the sheer number of textual witnesses which do not attest the longer reading, there are several other factors which suggest that the shorter reading is to be preferred. First of all, of the thirty-two occurrences of θαυμάσια in the Psalter, eight appear without a pronominal modifier: 71:18, 76:15(14), 77:12, 85:10, 87:11(10), 130:1, 135:4, 138:14. Only in 87:11(10) is the absence of a pronoun contested, and there by Bo and Sa which add *tua* without support from the Hebrew but possibly under the influence of verse 13(12) (cf. below). Of the remaining twenty-four, twelve are modified by σου: 9:2(1), 25:7, 39:6(5), 70:17, 74:3(2), 76:12(11), 87:13(12), 88:6(5), 105:7, 118:18, 27, 144:5.[42] Only in 118:18 is σου contested. Secondly, with the similarity of structure in verses 17 and 18 of Ps. 118, the addition of σου to θαυμάσια may also have been partially influenced by (τοὺς λόγους) σου in verse 17², and not just by the frequency of the θαυμάσιά σου combination in the Psalter. Thirdly, there may even have been some influence from (ἐκ τοῦ νόμου) σου in verse 18[2] to produce this addition.

118:103 καὶ κηρίον S' R" *abf hj* He 1219' Tert. (cf. 18:11[10])] > Sa GaAug^uar *L' e* A = MT

There is some good textual support for the longer reading, and thus Hebrew influence is a possible explanation for the shorter one. However, because of the rather close parallel in 18:11(10) where καὶ κηρίον corresponds to the MT (γλυκύτερα ὑπὲρ μέλι καὶ κηρίον as compared to ὡς γλυκέα...ὑπὲρ μέλι καὶ κηρίον in 118:103), and because the great majority of textual witnesses in 118:103 support the shorter reading in agreement with the Hebrew, it seems much more likely that καὶ κηρίον in the latter passage is an *ex par.* addition.

118:139 τοῦ οἴκου σου S' Sa R"Aug^uar A^c': cf. 68:10(9), Jn. 2:17] σου Aug^uar *L' aef hj* A*'; μου GaAug = MT

That the GaAug reading is due to Hebrew influence is certain. The question here is whether Rahlfs' lemma or the σου variant constitutes the Old Greek. A strong case can be made for the originality of the latter. In the first place, Rahlfs' lemma, (ἐξέτηξέν με ὁ ζῆλος) τοῦ οἴκου σου, can readily be explained in terms of influence from 68:10(9), (ὁ ζῆλος) τοῦ οἴκου σου (κατέφαγέν με), a phrase which is cited in Jn. 2:17 in connection with Jesus' cleansing of the temple.[43] Secondly, the great majority of textual witnesses (including A* plus the earlier of the other two members of that group, 1219) attest σου. It seems likely, then, that τοῦ οἴκου is an *ex par.* insertion.

135:7 μόνῳ (cf. u. 4) > Sa(non 2017) GaHi *ae hj* 1219 = MT

Admittedly, μόνῳ has strong textual support, whereas its omission might be the result of hexaplaric influence. However, there is a close parallel to stich 1 (τῷ ποιήσαντι φῶτα μεγάλα μόνῳ) in verse 4[1] (τῷ ποιοῦντι θαυμάσια μεγάλα μόνῳ) where μόνῳ has an equivalent in the MT.[44] It seems, therefore, that μόνῳ in verse 7 is an *ex par.* addition.

Apart from the preceding twelve cases in which SyrPss and/or Ga attest the Old Greek, there are quite a number of other instances in which one or both depart from the original LXX in support of a shorter reading which equals the MT. In forty-one cases, some or all extant SyrPss Mss and Ga agree on the shorter reading.[45]

9:35(34) οὖν B″ 1221 A′] > Sa R″ Ga *L′ ac hj* = MT Pesh

11:4(3) καί > Ga(non Uulg)Aug *L′ acf hj* = MT

29:1(inscr.) εἰς τὸ τέλος B USa^L 1220 R″ *L*^d(sil)He 55] post οικου tr. *L*^b′, > S′ Sa^B-2110 1098-Ga *L*^bT *abcef hj* A = MT

30:23(22) ἄρα B″ U′ R 55] > La 1098-Ga *L′ abce hj* A′ = MT Pesh

34:12 καί > Ga (188) *abcef hj* = MT

37:21(20)³ Bo 2013′-2110 R′Aug ThtTh *acg*^mg†(pars deest; *f*^mg† omnia desunt) *hj* (με > Tht^P *acg*^mg†(uid.) *hj*) 1219′ (55 pr. et add. ※)] > B′ La^G Ga *L e* A = MT Pesh

38:10(9) εἶ ὁ ποιήσας B′ R′Aug(sed R *i o epyesas*)] εποιησας 2013-2110^uid. La^G Ga *L′ ace hj* A′ = MT Pesh

38:10(9) με B″ 2013′-2110 R″ A] > Ga *L′ ace hj* 55 = MT Pesh

41:10(9) μου ult. B″ 2013′ R′ A] > La^GAug Ga *L′ abce hj* 55 2110 = MT

42:2 μου ult. B″ 2013′-2110^uid. R′ A] > La^GAug Ga *L′ ace hj* 55 = MT

48:10 ὅτι B″ 2013′ 1220 R″ 1098 A^c′] > Ga *L′ ace hj* A* 2110 = MT; και Pesh

49:1 καί ult. B′ 2013-2110 *ace*^c pr m *hj* A′] > 2018 R″ Ga *L′ e** Cyp. = MT

59:14(12) δέ B′ 55] > R″ Ga *L′ abdef*^mg† *hj* 1219 2110 = MT: cf. 107:14(13) [46]

68:30(29) καί 2° B″ La^G^Aug] > R^s′ Ga *L′ abcef hj* 55 2110 = MT Pesh

68:30(29) τοῦ προσώπου B″ Sa-2110 1220 La^G^Aug ThtP *abcf hj* 1219′] > R^s′ Ga *L*ThtP *e* = MT Pesh

71:3 σου B′ Sa-2110 R″Aug^uar^] > S GaAug *L′ abce hj* 55 = MT; cf. u. 2

71:6 καί 1° B′ R″ 1219′ 2110] > Ga *L′ ace hj* = MT Pesh

71:12 χειρός B″ Sa R′ He* 1219′] > La^G^Aug Ga *L′ ace hj* Tert. 2110 = MT Pesh

73:23 πρὸς σέ B″ Sa-2110 RAug 55 2149] ante δια παντος tr. La^R^ *ab hj* (*f* testatur προς σε sed non δια παντος) He 1219, > La^G^ GaHi *L′ e* = MT Pesh

77:57 καί 3° B″ Sa *L′* 2149] > R″ Ga T (55 156 222* 262) *abe hj* 55 2110 = MT Pesh

82:8(7) καί 3° B′-2049 R″ A′ 2110 2149] > Ga *L′ aef hj* 1219 = MT [47]

83:6(5) κύριε > Ga *L′ ae* = MT Pesh

87:6(5) ἐρριμμένοι B″ Sa^LBc^] ρερειμεναι 55, post καθευδοντες tr. R″; > Sa^B*^ GaAug *L′ abe hj* A′ 2110 2149 = MT Pesh

90:15 καί 2° B′ La^G^Aug A 2110] > R′ Ga *L′ abef hj* 1219′ 2020 = MT Pesh

93:8 δή *nunc* La] > Ga (284*) *abe hj* = MT Pesh

93:19 κύριε B″ Sa R″] > Ga *L′ abe hj* A″ 2110 = MT Pesh

105:16 καί 2° B′ R″] > GaAug *L′ aef hj* A′ 2110 = MT

113:11(115:3) ἐν τῷ οὐρανῷ ἄνω | ἐν τοῖς οὐρανοῖς S′ La^G^Aug] εν τω ουρανω ανω | εν τω ουρανω R′ *a j* (*a j* om. ανω: aut prbl. aut hpgr.) et alii Latini, εν το[ις ου]ρανοις ανω 2110; εν τοις ουρανοις Sa, εν τω ουρανω Ga *L′ e*(*f* testatur tantum εν τω ουρανω) *h* A′ = MT Pesh [48]

113:11(115:3) καὶ ἐν τῇ γῇ = *aef j*] > GaHi *h* 2110 = MT Pesh

114:8 καί > La^{G}Aug Ga (223) *aef hj* 1219 = MT

118:7 κύριε S' R'' A'] > Sa-2110 Ga *L' ae hj* 1219 = MT Pesh

118:93 κύριε S' Sa R'' *af hj* 1219'] > GaAug *L' e* A = MT Pesh

118:119 διὰ παντός S' Sa-2009 R'' Aug^{uar} He 1219' (cf. u. 117)] > GaAug *L' ae hj* A = MT [49]

118:168 κύριε = *e*^{c} pr m uid.] > S Ga *ae* hj* = MT Pesh

135:16$^{3.4}$ Bo Sa-2017 R'': cf. Deut. 8:15] > S GaAug *L' ae hj* A'' = MT Pesh [50]

138:3 σύ S R *L' aef h* A'] > B' Sa La Ga *j* = MT Pesh

139:9(8) με 1° B'' R'Aug Uulg *L'* A''] > Sa La^{G} Ga *L*^{pau}THe *ae hj* = MT Pesh

139:14(13) καί > Ga(non Uulg)HiAug *aef hj* A = MT

141:8(7) κύριε B'' Sa La^{G} He A] > R'Aug Ga *L' abe hj* 55 = MT Pesh

142:5 καί B' R' A'] > La^{G}Aug Ga *L' abef hj* 55 = MT

146:2 καί B' R'' A] > Ga *L' ab hj* 1219^{s}' = MT

Of the preceding forty-one shorter readings equalling the MT which Ga and SyrPss share, twenty-six correspond to shorter Peshitta readings. In at least ten of these twenty-six cases, the SyrPss readings may be due to Peshitta influence:

38:10(9) 1°, 2° ὅτι σὺ (εἶ) ὁ ποιήσας (με)
ܡܛܠ ܕܐܢܬ ܥܒܕܬ *ace hj* Pesh

68:30(29) 1°, 2° (καὶ) ἡ σωτηρία (τοῦ προσώπου) σου
ܦܘܪܩܢܐ ܕܦܪܨܘܦܟ *abcf*, c. uar. *hj*
ܦܘܪܩܢܐ ܕܝܠܟ *e*
ܦܘܪܩܢܟ Pesh [51]

71:6 (καὶ) καταβήσεται ὡς ὑετός

ܢܚܘܬ ܐܝܟ ܡܛܪܐ *ace hj* Pesh

77:57 καθὼς (καὶ) οἱ πατέρες αὐτῶν

ܐܝܟ ܐܒܗܝܗܘܢ *abe* Pesh, c. uar. *hj*

93:8 σύνετε (δή), ἄφρονες

ܐܣܬܟܠܘ. ܫܛܝܐ *abe hj* Pesh

118:7 ἐξομολογήσομαί σοι, (κύριε), ἐν εὐθύτητι καρδίας

ܐܘܕܐ ܠܟ ܒܬܪܝܨܘܬܐ ܕܠܒܐ *ae hj*

ܐܘܕܐ ܠܟ ܒܬܪܝܨܘܬܗ ܕܠܒܝ Pesh

118:168 αἱ ὁδοί μου ἐναντίον σου, (κύριε)

ܐܘܪܚܬܝ ܠܘܩܒܠܟ *ae** Pesh, c. uar. *hj*

135:16[3.4] ὅτι εἰς τὸν αἰῶνα τὸ ἔλεος αὐτοῦ·

(τῷ ἐξαγαγόντι ὕδωρ ἐκ πέτρας ἀκροτόμου,

ὅτι εἰς τὸν αἰῶνα τὸ ἔλεος αὐτοῦ·)

ܡܛܠ ܕܠܥܠܡ ܛܝܒܘܬܗ *ae*, c. uar, *hj*; ܡܛܠ > Pesh [52]

In the remaining sixteen passages in which Pesh has a shorter reading than the LXX, it appears less likely that SyrPss has been influenced by the Peshitta:

9:35(34) εἰς χεῖράς σου· σοὶ (οὖν) ἐγκαταλέλειπται

ܒܐܝܕܝܟ ܕܠܟ: ܠܟ ܫܒܝܩ *ac*, c. uar. *hj*

ܒܐܝܕܝܟ. ܠܟ ܫܒܝܩ Pesh

30:23(22) ἀπέρριμμαι (ἄρα) ἀπὸ προσώπου τῶν ὀφθαλμῶν σου

ܐܬܚܪܒܬ ܐܢܐ ܡܢ ܩܕܡ ܦܪܨܘܦܐ ܕܥܝܢܝܟ *abce*, c. uar. *hj*

ܕܐܬܚܪܒܬ ܡܢ ܩܕܡ ܥܝܢܝܟ Pesh

37:21(20)[3] δικαιοσύνην, (καὶ ἀπέρριψάν με τὸν ἀγαπητὸν ὡσεὶ νεκρὸν ἐβδελυγμένον)

ܙܕܝܩܘܬܐ *e*

ܛܝܒܘܬܐ Pesh [53]

48:10 (ὅτι) οὐκ ὄψεται

ܠܐ ܢܚܙܐ *ace hj*

ܘܠܐ ܐܢܫܐ Pesh

71:12 ἐκ (χειρὸς) δυνάστου

ܡܢ ܚܣܝܢܐ ace hj

ܡܢ ܡܢ ܕܚܣܝܢ ܡܢܗ Pesh

73:23 ἀνέβη διὰ παντὸς (πρὸς σέ)

ܣܠܩ ܒܟܠܙܒܢ e

ܕܣܠܩ ܒܟܠܙܒܢ Pesh [54]

83:6(5) οὗ ἔστιν ἡ ἀντίλημψις αὐτοῦ παρὰ σοῦ, (κύριε)

ܗܘ ܕܐܝܬܘܗܝ ܡܥܕܪܢܘܬܗ ܠܘܬܟ ae

ܕܐܝܬ ܗܘ ܡܥܕܪܢܘܬܗ Pesh

87:6(5) ὡσεὶ τραυματίαι (ἐρριμμένοι) καθεύδοντες

ܐܝܟ ܡܚ̈ܝܠܐ ܕܕܡܟܝܢ abe hj

ܐܝܟ ܩܛ̈ܝܠܐ ܕܕܡܟܝܢ Pesh

90:15 (καὶ) ἐξελοῦμαι

ܐܦܨܝܘܗܝ abef hj

ܐܚܠܨܝܘܗܝ Pesh

93:19 (κύριε), κατὰ τὸ πλῆθος

ܐܝܟ ܣܘܓܐܘܬܐ abe hj

ܒܣܘܓܐܐ Pesh

113:11(115:3) 1° e,[55] 1° et 2° *h*

ὁ δὲ θεὸς ἡμῶν ἐν τῷ οὐρανῷ (ἄνω· ἐν τοῖς οὐρανοῖς) (καὶ ἐν τῇ γῇ) πάντα, ὅσα ἠθέλησεν

ܐܠܗܢ ܕܝܢ ܕܒܫ̈ܡܝܐ. ܒܫܡܝܐ ܘܒܐܪܥܐ. ܟܠܗܘܢ ܐܝܠܝܢ ܕܨܒܐ e; ܘܒܐܪܥܐ > *h*

ܐܠܗܢ ܒܫܡܝܐ ܗܘ. ܘܟܠ ܕܨܒܐ Pesh

118:93 ὅτι ἐν αὐτοῖς ἔζησάς με, (κύριε)

ܡܛܠ ܕܒܗܘܢ ܐܚܝܬܢܝ. e

ܡܛܠ ܕܒܗܘܢ ܐܢܬ ܚܝܬܢܝ. Pesh [56]

138:3 τὴν τρίβον μου καὶ τὴν σχοῖνόν μου (σὺ) ἐξιχνίασας

ܠܫܒܝܠܝ ܕܝܠܝ ܘܡܫܟܢܝ ܕܝܠܝ ܒܥܩܒܬ j

ܐܘܪܚܝ ܘܡܫܒ̈ܝܠܝ ܝܕܥ ܐܢܬ Pesh [57]

139:9(8) μὴ παραδῷς (με), κύριε
ܠܐ ܬܫܠܡܢܝ ܡܪܝܐ *ae hj*
ܠܐ ܬܫܒܘܩ ܡܪܝܐ Pesh

141:8(7) τοῦ ἐξομολογήσασθαι τῷ ὀνόματί σου, (κύριε)
ܠܡܘܕܝܘ ܠܫܡܟ ܕܡܪܝܐ *abe hj*
ܕܐܘܕܐ ܠܫܡܟ Pesh

According to Rahlfs' apparatus, all but eight of the preceding forty-one shorter readings which SyrPss Mss and Ga share are also attested in texts of the *L* family. Those eight exceptions are: 34:12, 77:57, 93:8, 113:11(115:3) 2°, 114:8, 118:168, 138:3, 139:14(13). In H-P, four of the eight have textual support which Rahlfs does not mention: by four Mss——77:57; by one Ms each——34:12, 93:8, 114:8.

Apart from the shorter readings equalling the MT which SyrPss Mss and Ga share, there are another twenty-two instances in which a SyrPss shorter reading equals the Hebrew but not Ga:[58]

2:2 διάψαλμα B' Sa *O*(teste Euseb., cf. Field)-Ga {21} *hj*] post u. 2^2 tr. La^R; > R^{s}' *ab* $2150^{uid.}$ = MT Pesh, in libris Hebraeorum non continebatur teste Hilar.

5:5(4) οὐδέ B" Ga A'] ου R" *L' af hj* = MT

17:31(30) ὁ θεός μου = *abe hj*] μου > {270} *c* = Pesh, cf. MT (האל)

25:12 γάρ B" U'-$2110^{uid.}$ 1220 La^G Ga A'] > R'Aug Uulg *L' abce hj* 2021 = MT

49:7 σοι 1° *tibi* GaAug] > R" Uulg {188} *ace hj* = MT; cf. 80:9(8)

57:9(8) καί > *abce hj* 2110 = MT

57:12(11) εἰ > R' $L^{pau}$$Tht^{P}$ *abce hj* = MT Pesh

67:14(13) διάψαλμα = *abe hj*] > *c* = MT Pesh

77:12 ἅ *quae* La^{R}Aug Ga] οσα R He; > La^{G} Uulg {282} *abe hj* = MT

77:57 καί 4° B′ La Ga 2149] > R UulgAug *L′ abef hj* 55 2110 = MT

77:60 αὐτοῦ B″ Sa La Ga He* 55 2149] > R *L′*-1046 *abe hj* 2110 = MT Pesh

79:18(17) καί = *ae k*] > *hj* = MT

87:17(16) καί > *L′ abef hj* A*′ 2110 = MT

88:11(10) καί B′ R″ Ga Tht^{P}He 1219′] > Uulg *L*Tht^{P} *abef hj* A = MT Pesh

89:9 καί = *e*^{c}] > *abe* hj* S^{c} 2110 = MT

93:12 σύ B″ R′Aug GaHi 55 2110(tr. post παιδεύσῃς)] > Sa$^{uid.}$ La^{G} *O*(teste Hi) *L′*Su *abe hj* A′ = MT

104:39 αὐτοῖς 2°] αυτους *L*^{b}′S^{c}R^{c} 55; > S T *abe hj* 2110 = MT Pesh

113:20(115:12) ἐμνήσθη ἡμῶν καί S R″ Ga 55 2110$^{uid.}$] μνησθεις ημων *L′ aef hj* A′ 2029, cf. MT (זכרנו יברך pro εμνησθη ημων και ευλογησεν ημας)

115:1(inscr.) [116:10] ἀλληλούϊα = *ae hj*] > {208} *f* = MT Pesh

121:6 δή > *ae hj* = MT Pesh

135:26$^{3.4}$ Bo Sa(om. 3)-2009$^{uid.}$-2017 La^{G}Aug Ga *af*^{mg†} *hj* (*af*^{mg†} *hj* hab. οτι αγαθος pro *τῶν κυρίων*: ex u. 1)] > S R′ *L′ e* A″ = MT Pesh

137:1^{2} (cf. u. 4^{2})] > La^{G} Tht^{P} A {210} *e*^{txt}(*e*^{mg} tr. post u. 1^{3} = *L*Tht^{P}Ch *e*𝔤 55) = MT Pesh; παντα antecedit τα ρηματα in Bo^{P} *L*Ch *ae*^{mg}(cf. supra)*f*^{mg†} *hj* 1219′ et Psalt. Rom.: cf. u. 4^{2} (sed non in SBo^{P} Sa-2017 R′Aug Ga T)

Of the preceding twenty-two readings, eleven correspond to shorter Pesh readings. The possibility of Peshitta influence on

SyrPss must, therefore, be considered. At least seven of the eleven may reflect such influence:

2:2 κατὰ τοῦ κυρίου καὶ κατὰ τοῦ χριστοῦ αὐτοῦ (διάψαλμα)
ܥܠ ܡܪܝܐ ܘܥܠ ܡܫܝܚܐ ܕܝܠܗ *ab*
ܥܠ ܡܪܝܐ ܘܥܠ ܡܫܝܚܗ Pesh

17:31(30) ὁ θεός (μου)
ܐܠܗܐ *c* Pesh

77:60 σκήνωμα (αὐτοῦ), οὗ κατεσκήνωσεν
ܡܫܟܢܐ ܗܘ ܕܫܪܐ *abe hj*; ܗܘ > Pesh

104:39 καὶ πῦρ τοῦ φωτίσαι (αὐτοῖς) τὴν νύκτα
ܘܢܘܪܐ ܠܡܢܗܪܘ ܒܠܠܝܐ *abe hj* Pesh

115:1(inscr.) [116:10] (ἀλληλούϊα)
nihil *f* Pesh [59]

135:26[3.4] ἐξομολογεῖσθε τῷ θεῷ τοῦ οὐρανοῦ,
ὅτι εἰς τὸν αἰῶνα τὸ ἔλεος αὐτοῦ·
(ἐξομολογεῖσθε τῷ κυρίῳ τῶν κυρίων,
ὅτι εἰς τὸν αἰῶνα τὸ ἔλεος αὐτοῦ.)
ܐܘܕܘ ܠܐܠܗܐ ܕܫܡܝܐ: ܡܛܠ ܕܠܥܠܡ ܛܝܒܘܬܗ *e*
ܐܘܕܘ ܠܐܠܗܐ ܕܒܫܡܝܐ ܕܠܥܠܡ ܛܝܒܘܬܗ Pesh [60]

137:1[2] ἐν ὅλῃ καρδίᾳ μου,
(ὅτι ἤκουσας τὰ ῥήματα τοῦ στόματός μου),
καὶ ἐναντίον ἀγγέλων ψαλῶ σοι. προσκυνήσω
ܒܟܠܗ ܠܒܝ: ܘܩܕܡ (ܐܠܗ̈ܐ) ܡܠܐܟ̈ܐ ܐܙܡܪ ܠܟ. ܐܣܓܘܕ *e*txt
ܡܢ ܟܠܗ ܠܒܝ. ܘܩܕܡ ܡܠܐܟ̈ܐ ܐܙܡܪ ܠܟ. ܐܣܓܘܕ Pesh [61]

In the four remaining cases, it seems less likely that SyrPss has been influenced by the Peshitta:

57:12(11) καὶ ἐρεῖ ἄνθρωπος (Εἰ) ἄρα ἔστιν καρπός
ܘܢܐܡܪ ܒܪܢܫܐ ܟܝ ܐܝܬ ܦܐܪܐ *abce hj*
ܢܐܡܪ ܒܪܢܫܐ ܐܝܬ ܟܝ ܦܐܪ̈ܐ Pesh

67:14(13) ἐν χλωρότητι χρυσίου. (διάψαλμα)

ܒܡܘܪܩܘܬܐ (sic) ܕܕܗܒܐ c

ܒܕܗܒܐ ܚܣܝܐ Pesh

88:11(10) ὡς τραυματίαν ὑπερήφανον (καὶ) ἐν τῷ βραχίονι τῆς δυνάμεώς σου

ܐܝܟ ܕܠܡܬܡܚܝܢܐ· ܠܡܫܬܥܠܐ. ܒܕܪܥܐ ܕܚܝܠܟ *abe*, c. uar. *f hj*

ܠܡܬܘܪܢܐ ܐܝܟ ܕܠܩܛܝܠܐ. ܒܕܪܥܟ ܚܣܝܢܐ Pesh

121:6 ἐρωτήσατε (δὴ) τὰ εἰς εἰρήνην τὴν 'Ιερουσαλήμ

ܫܐܠܘ ܠܘܬܗܝܢ ܕܫܠܡܐ ܠܐܘܪܫܠܡ *ae h*, c. uar. *j*

ܫܐܠܘ ܫܠܡܗ ܕܐܘܪܫܠܡ Pesh

According to Rahlfs' apparatus, of the twenty-two shorter readings of SyrPss which equal the MT but not Ga, ten are also attested by Mss of the *L* family: 5:5(4), 25:12, 57:12(11), 77:57, 60, 87:17(16), 88:11(10), 93:12, 113:20(115:12), 135:26. In H-P, there is considerable *e silentio* support for the shorter reading in two additional instances which Rahlfs does not mention (both times it is the lemma in H-P): 2:2, 67:14(13). Minimal attestation (one Ms each) occurs in another five cases: 17:31(30), 49:7, 77:12, 115:1(inscr.)[116:10], 137:1.

In comparison to SyrPss with twenty-two minuses equalling the MT which Ga does not attest, Ga has a total of ninety-seven omissions equalling the Hebrew which do not occur in SyrPss or for which the Syriac evidence is inconclusive:

2:10 πάντες > La^{G} Ga Cyp. = MT

4:5(4) καί 2° R" *ab hj* Cyp. = Pesh] > B" Sa GaAug *L'* A': = MT, sed MT hab. ו in seq. [62]

7:6(5) ἄρα *ergo* La^{R}Aug] > La^{G} Ga = MT

9:36(35) δι' αὐτήν B" Sa-1221 R ThtCh *acf hj* A', *propter illud* La^{R}Aug] > La^{G} Ga *L* = MT

11:3(2) ἐν ult. > 1221-2018 La Ga = MT

15:10 οὐδέ] ου Ga(non Uulg) = MT

17:7(6) καί 1° > U Ga = MT

17:8(7) ὁ θεός > Ga = MT

17:40(39) πάντες > S La^G^Aug GaHi(1098 deest) = MT

19:10(9) σου B″ Sa-2110 *acef hj*] > R″ Ga *L*′ A″ = MT

24:21 κύριε > S La^G^ GaHi 2110 = MT

26:5 μου B″ R′Aug *L*′ *abcef hj* A″ 2021^uid.^ 2030 2150^uid.^] > U′-2110 La^G^ Ga = MT

26:6 καὶ νῦν ἰδού *et nunc ecce* La^R^ et Aug. enarr. I] *nunc autem* La^G^; *et nunc* GaHi et Aug. enarr. II = MT

29:8(7) δέ > R′Aug Ga(non 1098) = MT

30:1(inscr.) ἐκστάσεως > S La^G^ 1098-Ga(non Uulg) *L*^pau^ = MT

30:2(1) καὶ ἐξελοῦ με > S La^G^ Ga(non 1098) = MT

33:18(17) αὐτῶν 1°] αυτους R = *eos* La Uulg; > Ga = MT

34:13 καί 1° > 1221 Ga = MT

34:18 κύριε B′ Sa-2110^uid.^ R″ ThtHeTh *abcef hj* 1219′] > S 1098-Ga *L* A = MT

34:23 κύριε > S^c^ 1098^txt^Ga^c^Uulg = MT

37:19(18) ἐγώ Bo 2013′-2110 R′Aug(La^G^ deest) *L*′ *acef hj* A] > B′ Ga He 55 = MT

39:17(16) κύριε > Ga = MT

42:2 καί > S La^G^ Ga(non Uulg) 55 = MT: cf. 41:10(9)

43:1(inscr.) ψαλμός] > S La^R^Aug Ga *L*^d^′He 1219 = MT; tr. ante εις το τελος 2110

43:9(8) ἐν 2° > Ga(non Uulg) 55 = MT

43:27(26) κύριε] post βοηθησον ημιν tr. 2013′; > Ga^c^Hi(non Ga*Uulg) 2110^uid.^ = MT

44:5(4) καί 2° > Ga*Uulg: cf. MT (צלח pro και κατευοδου)

44:6(5) δυνατέ > GaHi = MT

45:10(9) καί ult. > Ga(non Uulg) = MT

53:6(4) καί > Ga(non Uulg) = MT

54:10(9) καί 1° > 2013 Ga = MT

57:11(10) ἀσεβῶν B Sa R″ *f hj* (-βους *abce*: ad u. 11(10)[2] adapt.)] > S' GaAug *L'* 55 2110 = MT

58:10(9) εἶ > S GaHi = MT

64:3(2) μου > S R Ga(non Uulg) 55 2110 = MT

65:15 καί > Sa GaHi 2110 = MT

65:19 μου 1°] > GaHi = MT; tr. post ο θεος 2110

67:19-20(18-19) κύριος ὁ θεὸς εὐλογητός, εὐλογητὸς κύριος] + *deus* Aug; *dominus deus benedictus est* La[G]: sim. Sa (2110 hab. ο κ̂ς̂ ο θ̂ς̂ ευλογητος ει κ̂ς̂); *dominum* (ad. u. 19[18][3] tractum), *deus benedictus dominus* GaHi, *dominum deum, benedictus dominus* Uulg: cf. MT (יה אלהים: ברוך אדני)

68:20(19) γάρ > S Ga = MT

68:27(26) αὐτοί > Ga = MT

71:19 καὶ εἰς τὸν αἰῶνα τοῦ αἰῶνος > GaHi = MT

72:17 καί > Ga(non Uulg)Hi 2110[uid.] = MT

72:20 σου > Ga(non Uulg) = MT

73:3 σου ult. > Ga 2110 = MT

73:8 δεῦτε καί = *ab hjk*] > Ga = MT; δευτε > *e* = Pesh; και > B[c]S R″ *f*(frt hpgr., i. e. ܢܒܛܠ ܐܠ pro ܘܢܒܛܠ ܐܠ) 2110

73:13 σύ 2° > La[G]Aug GaHi = MT

79:8(7) κύριε > Sa-2110 Ga = MT; κ̂ε̂ 2149 [63]

79:8(7) διάψαλμα > S Ga 2110 = MT

79:16(15) ἀνθρώπου > Ga(non Uulg) 1102 2004 = MT

80:1(inscr.) ψαλμός > $\mathcal{L}^{pau}$Tht^{P} Ga 2110 = MT

86:4 καί 2° > R′ Ga = MT

88:7(6) καὶ τίς B″ Sa-2110 $a^{txt}b^{txt}ef^{txt}$ *hj* He* 1219′ et Aug. IV 939 E] η τις R″ Tht^{P} $a^{mg}b^{mg}$ (f^{mg} perperam hab. ܐ. ܘܡܢܘ [= α′ και τις] pro ܐܘ ܡܢܘ [= η τις]) et Aug. IV 939 F (bis). 940 A; > Ga $\mathcal{L}$Tht^{P} A = MT

89:10 ἐφ' ἡμᾶς > GaHi = MT

94:6 αὐτῷ > Ga 55 = MT

96:10 κύριος] αυτος Sa; > La^{G} Ga(non Uulg) 2110 = MT

97:1 κύριος > Ga = MT

97:3 τῷ ἰακώβ > S GaHi = MT

102:11 κύριος > Sa^{B}-2110 La^{G} Ga = MT

102:20 πάντες > Ga(non Uulg) = MT

103:28 δέ > La^{G} Ga $\mathcal{L}^{a}$(non THe) = MT

104:33 πᾶν > S GaHi 2110 = MT

105:32 αὐτόν > S Ga(non Uulg) = MT

108:21 ἔλεος 1° S' Sa-2110 R′Aug^{uar} He* A$^{c″}$] το ελεος σου La^{G} $aef^{uid.}g$ *hj*: cf. u. 21^{2}; > GaAug $\mathcal{L}$′ A* = MT

108:27 καί 2° > La^{G} Ga(non Uulg) 2110 = MT

109:2 καί > GaHi = MT

110:1 μου > Ga^{c}(non Uulg)Hi = MT

113:4 καί > Ga(non Uulg) = MT

113:6 ὅτι > S Ga $\mathcal{L}^{pau}$ = MT

117:2 οἶκος > La^{G} Ga 2110 = MT

117:3 ὅτι ἀγαθός > Sa Ga = MT

117:4 πάντες > Bo Ga 2110$^{uid.}$ = MT

117:4 ὅτι ἀγαθός > Sa GaAug A'(non 1219) 2110 = MT

117:12 κηρίον > La^{G} Ga = MT

118:24 ἐστίν > Ga(non Uulg) = MT

118:47 σφόδρα (sic etiam Aug^{uar})] > GaHiAug = MT

118:68 κύριε > Sa GaAug^{uar} = MT

118:69 μου] σου S*, > S^{c} La^{G} GaHi(non Uulg) = MT

118:84 μοι > R'' Ga = MT

118:85 κύριε > Sa Ga = MT

118:97 κύριε > Ga(non Uulg) = MT

118:145 μου 1° > S Ga^{c}(non Ga*Uulg) = MT

118:174 ἐστίν > Ga(non Uulg) = MT

119:2 καί > Ga^{c}Hi(non Ga*Uulg) = MT

121:7 γενέσθω δή] γ. δε A: cf. u. 8; γενηθητω R, *fiat* La Ga: cf. MT (יהי) et u. 8

132:1 ἀλλ' ἤ] > La Ga Tert. Cyp. = MT; αλλ > S 2017

135:23 ὁ κύριος > La^{G}Aug Ga = MT

137:3 ταχύ > La^{G} Ga = MT

137:3 ἐν δυνάμει *in uirtute* Bo R' A] + πολλη S Sa-2017; *uirtute* GaAug(Uulg *-tem*) = עז; δυναμει σου *L'* 1219', εν δυναμει σου He, *in uirtute tua* La^{G}: εν/*in* inc. in *aef hj* [64]

138:2 σύ 2° > Sa La Ga = MT

138:13 κύριε B R'' T A] post συ tr. S *aef hj* 1219 et Psalt. Rom.; > *L'* Ga 55 = MT

139:6(5) τοῖς ποσίν μου > GaHi = MT

142:8 κύριε] post ηλπισα tr. La^G et alii Latini, > Ga = MT

142:9 ὅτι B'' Sa R'Aug *abef hj* He A'] > La^G Ga *L'* 55 = MT

144:1 μου 2° > Ga = MT

145:3 καί B' R'Aug *abe hj* He A] *neque* La^G, > Ga *L'* 1219^s' = MT

147:1(inscr.) ἀγγαίου καὶ ζαχαρίου > La^G Ga *L*^pau' = MT (MT hunc Ps. cum praec. connectens nullam hab. inscriptionem)

148:1(inscr.) ἀγγαίου καὶ ζαχαρίου > La^G Ga *L*^b' = MT

149:5 καί > GaAug = MT

The following table summarizes the evidence presented in our analysis of obelized readings and minuses equalling the MT:

	Ga	SyrPss
Obelized Readings	93	11
Minuses = MT	139	75
Gross Total	232	86
Net Total	232	61

Some explanatory remarks about this table are in order. Firstly, the totals in the SyrPss column represent the obelized readings (apart from those found only in *e*, whose compiler introduced many of the signs himself) and the minuses equalling the MT which any or all SyrPss Mss attest. Secondly, among the total number of obelized readings attested by Ga, three are incorrectly marked with an asterisk instead of an obelus. Thirdly, the twenty-five cases deleted from the gross total of SyrPss to produce the net total consist of five passages in which our Syriac witnesses, conforming not only to the MT but also to the original LXX, lack a reading which is obelized in Ga, and twenty passages in which the minus equalling the MT in SyrPss may be the result of Peshitta influence. These readings cannot be used as indicators of hexaplaric activity in SyrPss. In conclusion, Ga, with a significantly greater net total than that of SyrPss, proves once again to be the better witness to Origen's text.

E. TRANSPOSITIONS EQUALLING THE MT

Besides obelizing readings in his Greek text which he did not find in the Hebrew, and adding asterisked readings where his Greek text was shorter than the Hebrew, Origen apparently from time to time also changed the Greek word order in conformity with the Hebrew. These transpositions, which he unfortunately did not mark, were undoubtedly occasioned by the fact that each column of the Hexapla could accomodate no more than a few words per line. When Greek word order differed significantly from that of the Hebrew, rearrangement of the Greek was necessary in order to avoid sequencing problems. Evidence of such transpositions towards the MT is to be found in the Psalter. There is, however, one instance in which Rahlfs' lemma appears to be the transposition of the original reading which is recorded in the apparatus:

> 70:18 πάσῃ / τῇ γενεᾷ B′, *omni / generationi* La^{G}] tr. La^{R}Aug Ga *L′ abce*(*f* non testatur τη γενεα, παση > *hj*) 1219$^{uid.}$ 2110, *natiuitati uniuersae* Tert.: cf. MT (לדור לכל); π. γενεα γενεα R, τη > 55

Although both R and 55 differ somewhat from the lemma, they do support the word order attested by B′ and La^{G}. However, the alleged transposition enjoys the support of many more witnesses. Furthermore, the placement of πᾶς after the substantive it modifies in conformity with the MT is a phenomenon which occurs in four other passages of the Psalter (8:8[7], 66:4[3], 6[5], 86:7). Since πᾶς much more frequently precedes a substantive, it would seem to be easier to explain Rahlfs' lemma as a modification of the supposed transposition than vice versa. This is all the more true when one notes that in the two other cases in the Psalter besides 70:18 which involve πᾶσα and γενεά (44:18[17], 144:13), πᾶσα precedes γενεά. Thus Rahlfs' lemma reading in 70:18 may not simply be an *ad sensum* modification, but it could also be the result of *ex par.* influence.

When one examines word order in SyrPss, a distinction must be made between that which happens to conform to the MT because of the constraints of Syriac, and that which reflects a transposition already present in the Greek parent. There are fourteen instances of the latter variety of word order change in SyrPss which are also attested in Ga:[65]

9:37(36) βασιλεύσει κύριος B R′ ThtCh *acf* A'] tr. S 1221 La^G^Aug Ga Z *hj*, βασιλευσει κυριος uel κυριος βασιλευσει Bo Sa; κυριος βασιλευς *L* = MT Pesh [66]

27:3 συνελκύσῃς (+ με U) μετὰ ἁμαρτωλῶν τὴν ψυχήν μου B' Sa-2110 R′Aug He* A] σ. με μετα αμ. S La^G^ Ga *L′* *abcef*^pars^(non testatur μετα) *hj* 1219' = MT, cf. Pesh (ܐܘܒܕܢܝ ܥܡ ܚܛ̈ܝܐ) [67]

47:1(inscr.) ψαλμὸς ᾠδῆς B' R″ Uulg *L*^a′^ 55 2110] ψαλμος 2013-Sa^B^; ωδη ψαλμου S Sa^L^(-μος pro -μου?) Ga *L*^pau^T *ac*(*c* hab. -μων pro -μου)*ef hj* = MT; *laus cantici* (i. e. αινος ωδης) Aug

70:1 ὁ θεός, ἐπὶ σοὶ ἤλπισα B] pr. ο θεος Sa, pr. κυριε La^G^, + κυριε Bo 2110; επι σοι ηλπ. κυριε R′Aug; επι σοι κυριε ηλπ. S Ga *L′ abce hj* 1219' = MT Pesh: cf. 30:2(1) [68]

70:17 ἐδίδαξάς με / ὁ θεός B″ R′] tr. La^G^Aug GaHi 2110(Sa?) = MT, cf. Pesh (ܐܠܗܐ ܐܠܦܬܢܝ); ο θ. μου α εδιδ. με *L′*(μου etiam Su) *abcef hj*, α εδιδ. με ο θ. 55 [69]

73:1 ἀπώσω / ὁ θεός] tr. GaHi *L′*(non Su) *abef hj* 1219 = MT

88:24(23) τοὺς ἐχθροὺς αὐτοῦ / ἀπὸ προσώπου αὐτοῦ B R″ A′(A μου pro αὐτοῦ 1°)] tr. S Ga *L′ abe*(*f* testatur nec τους εχθρους αυτου nec ܡܢ ex ܡܢ ܩܕܡ pro απο) *hj* 1219 =

MT Pesh

96:5 ἐτάκησαν / ὡσεὶ κηρός B R A'] tr. S *L' ae*(*f* non testatur ετακησαν ωσει) *hj* 1219 2110 = MT Pesh; *fluxerunt sicut cera* La^{R}Aug, *sicut cera fluxerunt* Ga, *sicut cera liquefacti sunt* Tert., *liquefacti sunt sicut cera et fluxerunt* La^{G} [70]

101:2(1) εἰσάκουσον κύριε B R"] tr. S Ga *L' ab*$^{uid.}$(εισακουσον [ܫܡܥ] absc.)*e hj* A' 2110 = MT Pesh

101:3(2) τὸ οὖς σου / πρός με B R"(La^{G} add. *domine* post *me*) 55 2110] tr. S Ga *L' ade*(*f* non testatur το ους σου) *hj* A' = MT Pesh

116:2 τὸ ἔλεος αὐτοῦ / ἐφ' ἡμᾶς S *L'* 1219] tr. R" Ga (156 289) *aef*(*f* testatur επ αυτον pro εφ ημας) *hj* A' 2110 = MT Pesh

138:19 ἁμαρτωλούς (La^{G} *peccatorem*) / ὁ θεός] tr. La Ga (156 277) *ae hj* = MT Pesh

142:12 ἐγώ B' La^{R}Aug] > R, ante ειμι tr. La^{G}; ante δουλος tr. Ga *L' abe hj* A" = MT Pesh [71]

145:8^{1}/8^{2} B" Sa R"(La^{G} tr. u. 8^{1} ante u. 7^{3}) A] tr. Ga *L' abf*^{pars}(testatur nec κυριος u. 8^{2} nec κυριος ανορθοι u. 8^{1}) *hj* 1219^{s}' = MT Pesh

Twelve of the preceding fourteen word order changes in SyrPss and Ga correspond to Peshitta readings which follow Hebrew sequence rather than that of the LXX. In three of these twelve, Peshitta influence on SyrPss is possible:[72]

70:1 ὁ θεός, ἐπὶ σοὶ ἤλπισα
ܒܟ ܡܪܝܐ ܣܒܪܬ *abce hj* Pesh

101:2(1) εἰσάκουσον κύριε
ܡܪܝܐ ܫܡܥ *ab*$^{uid.}$*e hj* Pesh

138:19 ἐὰν ἀποκτείνῃς ἁμαρτωλούς, ὁ θεός

ܐܢ ܬܩܛܘܠ ܐܠܗܐ ܚܛܝ̈ܐ *ae hj*

ܐܢ ܬܩܛܘܠ ܐܠܗܐ ܠܚܛܝ̈ܐ Pesh

In the remaining nine readings, Peshitta influence is less likely:

9:37(36) βασιλεύσει κύριος

ܡܪܝܐ ܢܡܠܟ *hj*

ܡܪܝܐ ܡܠܟܐ ܗܘ Pesh

27:3 συνελκύσῃς μετὰ ἁμαρτωλῶν τὴν ψυχήν μου

ܠܬܓܪܘܪܝܢ ܢܦܫܝ ܥܡ ܚܛܝ̈ܐ *abcef*pars *hj*

ܠܐ ܬܡܢܝܢܝ ܥܡ ܪ̈ܫܝܥܐ Pesh

70:17 ἐδίδαξάς με, ὁ θεός, ἐκ

ܐܠܗܝ ܐܠܦܬܢܝ ܕܐܠܦܬܢܝ ܡܢ *abcef*, c. uar. *hj*

ܐܠܗܐ ܡܠܦܬܢܝ ܕܡܢ Pesh

88:24(23) τοὺς ἐχθροὺς αὐτοῦ ἀπὸ προσώπου αὐτοῦ

ܡܢ ܩܕܡ ܦܪܨܘܦܗ ܠܒܥܠܕܒ̈ܒܘܗܝ *abef*pars, c. uar. *hj*

ܡܢ ܩܕܡܘܗܝ ܠܒܥܠܕܒ̈ܒܘܗܝ Pesh

96:5 ἐτάκησαν ὡσεὶ κηρός

ܐܝܟ ܩܘܪܬܐ ܐܬܦܫܪܘ *af*pars *hj*, c. uar. *e*

ܐܝܟ ܫܥܘܬܐ ܐܬܦܫܪܘ Pesh

101:3(2) κλῖνον τὸ οὖς σου πρός με

ܪܟܢ ܠܘܬܝ ܐܕܢܟ *adef*pars, c. uar. *hj*

ܐܠܐ ܐܪܟܢ ܠܝ ܐܕܢܟ Pesh

116:2 τὸ ἔλεος αὐτοῦ ἐφ' ἡμᾶς

ܥܠܝܢ ܪ̈ܚܡܘܗܝ *ae*, c. uar. *f hj*

ܥܠܝܢ ܛܝܒܘܬܗ Pesh

142:12 ὅτι δοῦλός σού εἰμι ἐγώ

ܡܛܠ ܕܐܢܐ ܥܒܕܐ ܕܝܠܟ ܐܢܐ *abef*pars *hj*

ܡܛܠ ܕܐܢܐ ܐܢܐ ܥܒܕܟ Pesh

145:8 κύριος ἀνορθοῖ κατερραγμένους, κύριος σοφοῖ τυφλούς

ܡܪܝܐ ܡܬܪܨ ܠܟܦܝܦܐ. ܡܪܝܐ ܡܚܟܡ ܠܣܡܝ̈ܐ *abf*pars *hj*

ܡܪܝܐ. ܦܠܛ ܠܥܒܕܟ ܡܪܝܐ. ܐܘܪ ܡܫܝܚܐ Pesh

Rahlfs records in his apparatus that Mss of the *L* family attest all but two of the preceding fourteen transpositions. In H-P, even that pair (116:2, 138:19) receives textual support from two Mss each.

Apart from transpositions equalling the MT which both SyrPss and Ga support, there are an additional four which SyrPss, but not Ga, attests:[73]

18:14(13) μου κατακυριεύσουσιν = *hj*] tr. *ac* = MT Pesh

49:12 σοι εἴπω] tr. *ace hj* = MT Pesh

68:13(12) κατ' ἐμοῦ / ἠδολέσχουν] tr. *abcef h*(καθ ημων pro κατ εμου)*j* = MT Pesh

90:6 διαπορευομένου / ἐν σκότει B′ R″ Ga A′ 2043 2048] tr. *L′ abef hj* 1219 2020 2110 = MT

Three of these four transpositions correspond to Peshitta readings which also follow Hebrew, rather than Greek, word order. In two of the three, Peshitta influence on SyrPss is possible:

18:14(13) μου κατακυριεύσουσιν
ܢܫܠܛܘܢ ܒܝ *ac* Pesh

49:12 οὐ μή σοι εἴπω
ܠܐ ܐܡܪ ܠܟ *ace hj* Pesh

In the remaining instance, Peshitta influence is unlikely:

68:13(12) κατ' ἐμοῦ ἠδολέσχουν
ܡܦܩܩܝܢ ܗܘܘ ܥܠܝ *abcef*, c. uar. *hj*
ܘܪܢܘ ܒܝ Pesh

Only one of the four transpositions (90:6) is attested by *L*.

Whereas SyrPss has four transpositions equalling the Hebrew which are not found in Ga, Ga has thirteen which SyrPss does not attest, or for which it is inconclusive or neutral:[74]

30:15(14) σὺ εἶ ὁ θεός μου] *deus meus es tu* Ga = MT

31:7 μου εἶ καταφυγή *mihi es refugium* La] ει κ. μου 1098, *es ref. meum* Ga: cf. MT (אתה סתר לי pro συ μου ει καταφυγη)

41:10(9) μου ἐπελάθου] tr. Ga = MT

59:2(inscr.) τὴν μεσοποταμίαν συρίας *mesopotamiam syriae* UulgAug] τ. μ. συριαν R He, *m. syriam* La^R; *syriae* > La^G; *syram m.* Ga = MT

60:8(7) αὐτοῦ τίς ἐκζητήσει S R *L' abcdef*^pars(non testatur τίς) *hj* 1219' 2110, *eius quis requiret* Uulg] *quis* > La^R; *quis req. eius* Ga, *qui* (sic) *req. eum* La^G: cf. MT (מן ינצרהו); + αυτων (sic) B, *eius quis req. ei* Aug

68:5(4) οἱ ἐχθροί μου / οἱ ἐκδιώκοντές με] tr. La^G Ga = MT

68:30(29) εἰμι ἐγώ] tr. GaAug 55; *ego sum* ante πτωχος tr. Ga = MT (sed ו 1° deest etiam in Ga)

72:26 καρδία...σάρξ] tr. GaHi = MT

85:4 ἦρα / τὴν ψυχήν μου] tr. La^G Ga 2110(hab. ηραν pro ηρα) = MT

93:22 μοι κύριος] tr. Ga(non Uulg) = MT

105:9 τῇ ἐρυθρᾷ / θαλάσσῃ *rubrum mare* La] tr. GaAug 2110(add. τη ante θαλασσῃ): cf. MT (בים־סוף)

118:149 κύριε] post σου 1° tr. Ga = MT, et hic et ibi hab. La^G, et hic et ante u. 149^2 hab. *ae*(*f* testatur κυριε ante u. 149^2 tantum) *hj* (R" Uulg hab. και ante u. 149^2)

123:2 ἀνθρώπους / ἐφ' ἡμᾶς] tr. Ga(non Uulg) = MT

We now summarize the evidence recorded in the preceding analysis of transpositions equalling the MT:

	Ga	SyrPss
Transpositions	27	18
Net Total	27	13

It should be noted that the SyrPss totals in this table represent the transpositions attested by any or all Mss of our edition. Furthermore, the five cases deleted from the initial SyrPss total to produce the net total are readings which reflect possible Peshitta influence. Thus they cannot be used as hexaplaric indicators in SyrPss. Finally, a comparison of the net totals of this table leads to the same conclusion that was articulated in each of the two earlier preliminary summaries, namely, that Ga is a more faithful witness to the hexaplaric text than SyrPss.

F. SUMMARY AND CONCLUSIONS

The following table combines the evidence of all three preliminary summaries in this chapter. The sum total of each column is produced by adding up the respective net totals:

	Ga	SyrPss
Marked Plusses	42	10
Unmarked Plusses	34	66
Gross Total	76	76
Net Total	75	50
Obelized Readings	93	11
Minuses = MT	139	75
Gross Total	232	86
Net Total	232	61
Transpositions	27	18
Net Total	27	13
Sum Total	334	124

This combined table provides an indication of the potential extent of hexaplaric influence on SyrPss. Admittedly, the possibility of interference from both the Peshitta and the Greek *L* tradition clouds the issue to some extent. In this connection, it should be noted that the SyrPss totals are somewhat conservative due to the fact that potential hexaplaric readings which are also possible Peshitta readings are eliminated from contention. Nevertheless, the overall picture which emerges is that SyrPss has been subjected to only a fraction of the hebraizing activity that is manifest in Ga. The actual number of hexaplaric readings in SyrPss is, however, greater than Rahlfs allows for, since he deals primarily with the relatively few asterisked and obelized passages in our Syriac Psalter, but does not carry out a systematic analysis of unmarked hexaplaric materials. Nonetheless, he is correct in his assertion that Ga is a much better witness to Origen's recension. His grouping of SyrPss with *L* is, therefore, understandable. Yet, as this study has shown, the amount of hebraizing activity which is attested in that vast textual family is rather significant. The question as to whether or not some of that activity is attributable to Lucian is one which will hopefully be answered as textual study in this area progresses.

Within the context of the readings listed in this chapter, it might be useful to tally the number of times which SyrPs^{a} and SyrPs^{b} diverge from SyrPs with shorter, longer, or transposed readings, and to note how many of these divergences constitute agreements with, and how many are departures from, the MT.[75] Cases in which one or more SyrPs Mss also attest these divergences are excluded. Usually the extant SyrPs^{a} or SyrPs^{b} witnesses agree on a departure from SyrPs. However, even divergent readings which do not receive the unanimous support of extant group members are included in these totals. Thus, two SyrPs^{a} divergences correspond to the Hebrew (9:37[36], 25:12) whereas four do not (2:2, 18:14[13], 21:2[1], 21:17[16]). However, the possibility of Peshitta influence must be considered in at least two instances (18:14[13], 25:12). In another one (9:37[36]), SyrPs^{a} and the Peshitta agree on word order which equals the MT but differ as to actual wording. Six SyrPs^{b} divergences correspond to the Hebrew (71:19, 79:18[17], 88:53[52], 101:26[25],

113:11[115:3] 2°, 138:3) while only one does not (72:2). In just two of these seven cases (72:2, 79:18[17]) do SyrPs[b] and the Peshitta disagree as to the actual additions or omissions involved. However, contextual differences in all seven readings make the primacy of Peshitta influence less likely than in cases where the degree of contextual similarity is high. The fact that the SyrPss tradition is one in which hexaplaric influence was often only a margin away must not be overlooked. That this influence did at times extend to the text even in SyrPs[b] Mss which attest few marginal hexaplaric readings, can, for example, be seen in 138:3. There part of the verse in *j* is the same as a reading which, in *af*, occurs in the margin and is attributed to Symmachus. However, in conclusion, when one takes into account all the Syriac readings examined in this chapter, it is clear that SyrPs, SyrPs[a], and SyrPs[b] are not appreciably different from one another in the amount of hexaplaric evidence which they attest.

IV

SYRPSS AND THE BYZANTINE TEXT

The preceding chapter has shown that SyrPss, while giving evidence of more hexaplaric influence than Rahlfs allows for, is not a primary witness to Origen's recension. It is likewise evident from an examination of the apparatus of *Psalmi cum Odis* that SyrPss is not affiliated with Rahlfs' so-called older textual groups, i. e. the Lower-Egyptian (LE), the Upper-Egyptian (UE), and the Western (We), but that it aligns itself with that vast aggregate of "younger" witnesses, the Byzantine (*L*) family.[1] This is illustrated in the following table which compares the number of times which SyrPss, in two randomly selected Psalms (54 and 93), diverges from the LXX to equal *L*, LE, UE, or We:[2]

	Gross Total	Net Total
SyrPss = *L*	16	8
SyrPss = LE	2	1
SyrPss = UE	7	3
SyrPss = We	6	0

It should be noted that gross totals include agreements between SyrPss and the designated group as well as any or all of the other three groups, while net totals represent agreements between SyrPss and the designated group only.

Although Rahlfs' assignment of SyrPss to the *L* family of Mss is undoubtedly correct, this association does little to elucidate the textual character of SyrPss. As already mentioned, *L* embraces the great majority of Greek Psalter Mss (nearly 1000 in all) which Rahlfs fails to break down properly into textual groups; of these Mss he employs only about 100 in his edition. It is evident, therefore, that before one can begin to move in the direction of greater precision with respect to the textual affiliation of SyrPss, an attempt must be made to divide this large textual mass into more workable units. The purpose of this chapter, then, is two-fold:

1/ to carry out a delineation of textual groups within Rahlfs' *L* family;

2/ to examine the relationships between these groups and SyrPs, SyrPs[a], and SyrPs[b].

The delineation of *L* groups is the concern of The Byzantine Psalter Project, with which the present writer was involved as a Research Assistant from 1980 to 1986. At the time of this writing, the project is still ongoing, with final results not yet having been written up. Nevertheless, nearly 400 Mss have already been analyzed. Since it appears as though no more than 450 Mss will be made available to the project, this would seem to constitute a sufficient data base for the grouping of Byzantine Psalter Mss.

The methodology of The Byzantine Psalter Project is that of the Claremont Profile Method developed by Frederik Wisse[3] and Paul R. McReynolds[4] in the course of their work with the International Greek New Testament Project. The collation base is the text of Rahlfs' *Psalmi cum Odis*. Test readings were selected from four blocks of text: I/ Pss. 9–11; II/ Pss. 64–66; III/ Pss. 101–102; IV/ Pss. 143–147.[5] It will be noted that these blocks fall within Books 1, 2, 4, and 5 of the Psalter, respectively. With such a broad-based sampling, any change of textual affiliation in a given Ms should be detected.

A total of 299 test readings were selected in the four Psalter blocks: I/ 74; II/ 82; III/ 59; IV/ 84. These readings were chosen from the H-P apparatus which is digested in Rahlfs' *Psalmi cum Odis*. In the selection process, care was taken to represent the various textual groups in the Greek Psalter, not just the *L* family. Each test reading received a number. The process of collation involved the comparing of a given Ms with Rahlfs' lemma at each of the test readings. The appropriate numerical designation was recorded every time a Ms contained the selected variant, as opposed to either the lemma *or* something other than the lemma or the selected variant. The number of instances in which the absence of the numerical designation did *not* correspond to the lemma was found to be statistically negligible. Therefore, to all intents and purposes, such an absence at a given test reading meant that the Ms in question had the lemma. Whenever a Ms was found to be wanting with respect to a test reading, the numerical designation was bracketed in order to distinguish such a lacuna from the lemma reading. Mss with two or more scribal hands in evidence, including those with non-original corrections, were treated as multiple Mss. Thus, for each hand besides the original one, an upper case letter of the alphabet was added to the Ms number (e. g. 177, 177A).

Once the collation process had been completed, the data for each Ms was recorded on computer disk. It was then decided that a Block Clustering Algorithm was the most appropriate type of analysis available for the grouping of these Mss. Not only would such a program group the Mss, but it would also indicate the variables (i. e. the test readings) on which these clusters were based.[6] The inclusion of Mss with a high number of lacunae would have caused the program to produce many meaningless clusters. Consequently, after careful testing to determine the optimum cutoff point, the data base was revised to include only Mss with twelve or fewer lacunae per block. This reduced the number of Mss being analyzed to 318. Thereafter, the running of the program led to the delineation of forty groups within the *L* family. The overall profile of each of these groups proved to be quite similar, as might be expected given the fact that they are all part of the same general family. This means that usually only a fraction of the total number of test readings was crucial to the delineation of a given group. It was observed that Ms clusters were produced not only on the basis of readings unique to each cluster, but also on the basis of unique combinations of readings, some of which were significant for the formation of two or more clusters. The process of defining the various $\mathcal{L}$ groups included the incorporation of those Mss which exhibited partial affiliation with the core members. These secondary members were ones which showed textual agreement in at least two consecutive blocks. In the following list of the respective group witnesses, such Mss are enclosed in parentheses. Mss for which there was evidence in all four blocks are underlined. It must be stressed that these groups are based on limited probes of the Psalter text, and that their ultimate validation will need to be based on more extensive collations.

$\mathcal{L}^{1}$ 152, 1145, 1198, (1123)

$\mathcal{L}^{2}$ 142, 1068

$\mathcal{L}^{3}$ 1128, 1641, 1682, (197)

$\mathcal{L}^{4}$ 1034, 1895

$\mathcal{L}^{5}$ 1157, 1555

$\mathcal{L}^{6}$ 1162, 1823

$\mathcal{L}^{7}$ 80, 1680, (1017)

$\mathcal{L}^{8}$ 187, 1533

$\mathcal{L}^{9}$ 1070, 1159, 1787, (1166, 1167)

$\mathcal{L}^{10}$ 1446, 1917, (190)

$\mathcal{L}^{11}$ 1156, 1186, 1187, 1191

$\mathcal{L}^{12}$ 1086, 1450, 1652, (1003, 1020, 1242)

$\mathcal{L}^{13}$ 165, 1820, (1067, 1204)

$\mathcal{L}^{14}$ 277, 1814, 1899

$\mathcal{L}^{15}$ 179, 212, 1146, (1171, 1227)

$\mathcal{L}^{16}$ *e9*, 1819

$\mathcal{L}^{17}$ 1224, 1891

$\mathcal{L}^{18}$ 203, 1139, (1013, 1047)

$\mathcal{L}^{19}$ 140, 177A

$\mathcal{L}^{20}$ 167, 1665, (1748)

$\mathcal{L}^{21}$ 1089, 1798

$\mathcal{L}^{22}$ 1154, 1650

$\mathcal{L}^{23}$ 1030, 1213

$\mathcal{L}^{24}$ 141, 1614, 1711

$\mathcal{L}^{25}$ 180, 1161

$\mathcal{L}^{26}$ 102, 162, (1445, 1871)

$\mathcal{L}^{27}$ 1087, 1199

$\mathcal{L}^{28}$ 113, 205, (1007, 1818)

$\mathcal{L}^{29}$ 1065, 1158, 1543, (1228)

$\mathcal{L}^{30}$ 275, 613, 1828

$\mathcal{L}^{31}$ 166, 271, 1456, 1677, (193, 291, 1079, 1202)

$\mathcal{L}^{32}$ 213, 1023, 1811, (1005, 1055, 1134, 1195)

$\mathcal{L}^{33}$ 145, 199, 267, 1029, 1144, 1433, 1679, 1816, (1035, 1485, 1817)

$\mathcal{L}^{34}$ 1027, 1176, 1182, 1732, 1760

$\mathcal{L}^{35}$ 182, 1728, (194)

$\mathcal{L}^{36}$ 169, 1904, (1097)

$\mathcal{L}^{37}$ 629, 1137, 1192, (283, 1180)

$\mathcal{L}^{38}$ 292, 1138, 1149, 1177, 1424, (163, 164, 191, 1181, 1655)

$\mathcal{L}^{39}$ 1432, 1719, 1890

$\mathcal{L}^{40}$ 1720, 1756

Apart from the 149 Mss of the preceding $\mathcal{L}$ groups, there are some 169 Mss for which no significant pattern of affiliation could be delineated: 43, 65, 69, 81, 100, 111, 112, 140, 143, 146, 156, 168, 170,

174, 175, 176, 178, 189, 192, 195, 196, 200, 201, 202, 211, 214, 215, 216, 217, 219, 225, 226, 227, 265, 266, 268, 273, 278, 279, 280, 281, 285, 287, 290, 1004, 1006, 1008, 1009, 1010, 1011, 1012, 1015, 1018, 1019, 1028, 1033, 1036, 1037, 1044, 1048, 1050, 1051, 1053, 1056, 1058, 1060, 1061, 1062, 1066, 1069, 1072A, 1073, 1074, 1075, 1076, 1083, 1088, 1091, 1095, 1096A, 1099, 1112, 1115, 1116, 1117, 1118, 1127, 1132, 1133, 1143, 1147, 1155, 1160, 1174, 1179, 1189, 1190, 1196, 1197, 1200, 1201, 1203, 1207, 1211, 1214, 1215, 1218, 1226, 1406, 1409, 1415, 1429, 1430, 1435, 1457, 1459, 1486, 1514, 1530, 1551, 1553, 1570, 1579, 1581, 1599, 1609, 1621, 1623, 1630, 1653, 1661, 1664, 1671, 1675, 1681, 1695, 1697, 1702A, 1704, 1706, 1712, 1735, 1745, 1747, 1757, 1758, 1759, 1761, 1762, 1770, 1777, 1786, 1802, 1803, 1822, 1824, 1825, 1826, 1827, 1830, 1831, 1867, 1869, 1882, 1898, 1905, 1911, 1915, 1916.

The basis for comparison between SyrPss and each *L* group was the set of readings specified in the cluster analysis as being significant for the delineation of the group. This sort of comparison was not without its problems, however, since the test readings of The Byzantine Psalter Project were not selected with the Syriac in mind. Consequently, in most blocks of each *L* group, there were determining readings for which it was impossible to ascertain whether the Syriac reflected the lemma or the variant: e. g. 101:2(1) lemma = ἐλθάτω, variant = ελθετω, SyrPss = ܬܐܬܐ. Such readings had to be eliminated from consideration. In the few cases when SyrPs witnesses were divided in their attestation of the lemma and the variant, preference was given to the reading supported by the lemma of our diplomatic edition. As far as Mss *hj* are concerned, only once, in block II (located in their SyrPs^b section), did they not agree on a crucial test reading. In that block, the percentages of agreement between both *h* and *j*, on the one hand, and the relevant *L* groups, on the other, were averaged to produce a figure for the SyrPs^b text tradition as a whole.

The following table contains the percentages of agreement between SyrPs and the relevant determining readings of all four blocks of each *L* group, along with the average percentage for the whole group. The number of relevant readings for each block is recorded in parentheses with the block percentage. Whenever a Ms is not extant in a given block or there are no block determining readings which are relevant to the Syriac, a dash (—) is substituted for the percentage value, and that block is not included in calculation of the percentage of agreement for the group. Great caution must be exercised in the evaluation of these percentages since, in most blocks, there are unfortunately rather few readings to be compared. As mentioned earlier, this is due to the fact that the cluster analysis usually formed groups on the basis of only a handful of crucial readings—sometimes as few as one or two per block. Thus, the Syriac's attestation, or lack thereof, of these few key readings can mean, alternately, total agreement or disagreement in a given block.

	I	II	III	IV	AV.
$\mathcal{L}^{1}$	—	80.0 (5)	100.0 (1)	50.0 (2)	76.7
$\mathcal{L}^{2}$	—	50.0 (2)	100.0 (1)	0.0 (1)	50.0
$\mathcal{L}^{3}$	81.3 (48)	0.0 (4)	100.0 (1)	0.0 (1)	45.3
$\mathcal{L}^{4}$	81.3 (48)	87.3 (71)	100.0 (1)	—	89.5
$\mathcal{L}^{5}$	—	0.0 (2)	100.0 (1)	85.2 (54)	61.7
$\mathcal{L}^{6}$	81.3 (48)	50.0 (2)	100.0 (1)	85.2 (54)	79.1
$\mathcal{L}^{7}$	—	0.0 (2)	50.0 (2)	100.0 (1)	50.0
$\mathcal{L}^{8}$	81.3 (48)	0.0 (1)	100.0 (1)	33.3 (3)	53.7
$\mathcal{L}^{9}$	50.0 (2)	0.0 (2)	50.0 (2)	85.2 (54)	46.3
$\mathcal{L}^{10}$	50.0 (2)	87.3 (71)	50.0 (2)	85.2 (54)	68.1
$\mathcal{L}^{11}$	50.0 (6)	33.3 (3)	50.0 (2)	33.3 (3)	41.7
$\mathcal{L}^{12}$	0.0 (1)	50.0 (2)	50.0 (2)	25.0 (4)	31.3
$\mathcal{L}^{13}$	—	0.0 (2)	0.0 (1)	85.2 (54)	28.4
$\mathcal{L}^{14}$	81.3 (48)	0.0 (2)	0.0 (1)	0.0 (2)	20.3
$\mathcal{L}^{15}$	50.0 (2)	0.0 (2)	0.0 (1)	—	16.7
$\mathcal{L}^{16}$	—	0.0 (3)	—	0.0 (2)	0.0
$\mathcal{L}^{17}$	—	87.3 (71)	—	100.0 (2)	93.7
$\mathcal{L}^{18}$	—	0.0 (1)	100.0 (1)	—	50.0

$\mathcal{L}^{19}$	0.0 (1)	87.3 (71)	—	33.3 (3)	40.2
$\mathcal{L}^{20}$	81.3 (48)	0.0 (2)	—	0.0 (1)	27.1
$\mathcal{L}^{21}$	—	0.0 (3)	100.0 (1)	—	50.0
$\mathcal{L}^{22}$	—	0.0 (1)	—	85.2 (54)	42.6
$\mathcal{L}^{23}$	50.0 (2)	87.3 (71)	—	85.2 (54)	74.2
$\mathcal{L}^{24}$	—	0.0 (2)	—	85.2 (54)	42.6
$\mathcal{L}^{25}$	—	87.3 (71)	—	100.0 (1)	93.7
$\mathcal{L}^{26}$	100.0 (1)	0.0 (2)	—	85.2 (54)	61.7
$\mathcal{L}^{27}$	50.0 (2)	50.0 (2)	—	33.3 (3)	44.4
$\mathcal{L}^{28}$	81.3 (48)	0.0 (2)	87.1 (31)	0.0 (2)	42.1
$\mathcal{L}^{29}$	100.0 (1)	0.0 (2)	87.1 (31)	0.0 (2)	46.8
$\mathcal{L}^{30}$	—	0.0 (2)	87.1 (31)	85.2 (54)	57.4
$\mathcal{L}^{31}$	81.3 (48)	0.0 (2)	87.1 (31)	85.2 (54)	63.4
$\mathcal{L}^{32}$	81.3 (48)	0.0 (2)	87.1 (31)	85.2 (54)	63.4
$\mathcal{L}^{33}$	—	0.0 (3)	87.1 (31)	85.2 (54)	57.4
$\mathcal{L}^{34}$	—	0.0 (3)	87.1 (31)	0.0 (1)	29.0
$\mathcal{L}^{35}$	—	0.0 (2)	87.1 (31)	0.0 (2)	29.0
$\mathcal{L}^{36}$	—	0.0 (2)	87.1 (31)	0.0 (1)	29.0
$\mathcal{L}^{37}$	50.0 (2)	50.0 (2)	87.1 (31)	0.0 (2)	46.8
$\mathcal{L}^{38}$	—	50.0 (2)	87.1 (31)	33.3 (3)	56.8
$\mathcal{L}^{39}$	50.0 (2)	0.0 (2)	87.1 (31)	100.0 (1)	59.3
$\mathcal{L}^{40}$	100.0 (1)	—	87.1 (31)	25.0 (4)	70.7

The next table contains percentages of agreement between SyrPs[a] and the $\mathcal{L}$ groups. The fluctuation in the percentage values of this table is even more jarring than that which occurs in the preceding one because, with SyrPs[a] being extant in only the first of the four blocks, there is no opportunity for the modulating effect of the averaging procedure. Furthermore, since, as in other blocks, there is overlapping among groups with respect to the use of some of the same determining readings, it is often impossible to ascertain the comparative degree of SyrPs[a]'s affiliation with competing groups.

$\mathcal{L}^{1}$	—	$\mathcal{L}^{3}$	81.3 (48)
$\mathcal{L}^{2}$	—	$\mathcal{L}^{4}$	81.3 (48)

L^{5}	—
L^{6}	81.3 (48)
L^{7}	—
L^{8}	81.3 (48)
L^{9}	50.0 (2)
L^{10}	50.0 (2)
L^{11}	33.3 (6)
L^{12}	0.0 (1)
L^{13}	—
L^{14}	81.3 (48)
L^{15}	50.0 (2)
L^{16}	—
L^{17}	—
L^{18}	—
L^{19}	0.0 (1)
L^{20}	81.3 (48)
L^{21}	—
L^{22}	—
L^{23}	50.0 (2)
L^{24}	—
L^{25}	—
L^{26}	100.0 (1)
L^{27}	50.0 (2)
L^{28}	81.3 (48)
L^{29}	100.0 (1)
L^{30}	—
L^{31}	81.3 (48)
L^{32}	81.3 (48)
L^{33}	—
L^{34}	—
L^{35}	—
L^{36}	—
L^{37}	50.0 (2)
L^{38}	—
L^{39}	50.0 (2)
L^{40}	100.0 (1)

The table below contains percentages of agreement between SyrPs^{b} and the L groups. Since SyrPs^{b} is extant in blocks II, III, and IV, the average values in the final column are, generally speaking, more realistic indicators of group affiliation than those in the single column of the preceding SyrPs^{a} table. However, the same impediments to a definitive statement concerning SyrPs' group affiliation obtain here.

	II	III	IV	AV.
L^{1}	80.0 (5)	100.0 (1)	50.0 (2)	76.7
L^{2}	50.0 (2)	100.0 (1)	0.0 (1)	50.0
L^{3}	0.0 (4)	100.0 (1)	0.0 (1)	33.3
L^{4}	88.0 (71)	100.0 (1)	—	94.0
L^{5}	25.0 (2)	100.0 (1)	86.8 (53)	70.6
L^{6}	50.0 (2)	100.0 (1)	86.8 (53)	78.9
L^{7}	0.0 (2)	50.0 (2)	0.0 (1)	16.7

L^{8}	0.0 (1)	100.0 (1)	33.3 (3)	44.4
L^{9}	0.0 (2)	50.0 (2)	86.8 (53)	45.6
L^{10}	88.0 (71)	50.0 (2)	86.8 (53)	74.9
L^{11}	33.3 (3)	50.0 (2)	33.3 (3)	38.9
L^{12}	0.0 (2)	50.0 (2)	25.0 (4)	25.0
L^{13}	0.0 (2)	0.0 (1)	86.8 (53)	28.9
L^{14}	0.0 (2)	0.0 (1)	0.0 (2)	0.0
L^{15}	0.0 (2)	0.0 (1)	—	0.0
L^{16}	0.0 (3)	—	0.0 (2)	0.0
L^{17}	88.0 (71)	—	100.0 (2)	94.0
L^{18}	0.0 (1)	100.0 (1)	—	50.0
L^{19}	88.0 (71)	—	33.3 (3)	60.7
L^{20}	0.0 (2)	—	0.0 (1)	0.0
L^{21}	0.0 (3)	100.0 (1)	—	50.0
L^{22}	0.0 (1)	—	86.8 (53)	43.4
L^{23}	88.0 (71)	—	86.8 (53)	87.4
L^{24}	0.0 (2)	—	86.8 (53)	43.4
L^{25}	88.0 (71)	—	100.0 (1)	94.0
L^{26}	0.0 (2)	—	86.8 (53)	43.4
L^{27}	0.0 (2)	—	33.3 (3)	16.7
L^{28}	0.0 (2)	83.9 (31)	0.0 (2)	28.0
L^{29}	25.0 (2)	83.9 (31)	0.0 (2)	36.3
L^{30}	0.0 (2)	83.9 (31)	86.8 (53)	56.9
L^{31}	0.0 (2)	83.9 (31)	86.8 (53)	56.9
L^{32}	0.0 (2)	83.9 (31)	86.8 (53)	56.9
L^{33}	0.0 (3)	83.9 (31)	86.8 (53)	56.9
L^{34}	0.0 (3)	83.9 (31)	0.0 (1)	28.0
L^{35}	0.0 (2)	83.9 (31)	0.0 (2)	28.0
L^{36}	0.0 (2)	83.9 (31)	0.0 (1)	28.0
L^{37}	50.0 (2)	83.9 (31)	0.0 (2)	44.6
L^{38}	0.0 (2)	83.9 (31)	33.3 (3)	39.1
L^{39}	0.0 (2)	83.9 (31)	0.0 (1)	28.0
L^{40}	—	83.9 (31)	25.0 (4)	54.5

The following table contains the average percentages of agreement for the text traditions represented in our edition, except in the case of SyrPs[a] which is extant in just the first block and whose values therefore relate to only that segment of the analysis. The groups are arranged in the order of greatest to least agreement with respect to SyrPs.

	SyrPs	SyrPs[a]	SyrPs[b]
$\mathcal{L}^{17}$	93.7	—	94.0
$\mathcal{L}^{25}$	93.7	—	94.0
$\mathcal{L}^{4}$	89.5	81.3	94.0
$\mathcal{L}^{6}$	79.1	81.3	78.9
$\mathcal{L}^{1}$	76.7	—	76.7
$\mathcal{L}^{23}$	74.2	50.0	87.4
$\mathcal{L}^{40}$	70.7	100.0	54.5
$\mathcal{L}^{10}$	68.1	50.0	74.9
$\mathcal{L}^{31}$	63.4	81.3	56.9
$\mathcal{L}^{32}$	63.4	81.3	56.9
$\mathcal{L}^{5}$	61.7	—	70.6
$\mathcal{L}^{26}$	61.7	100.0	43.4
$\mathcal{L}^{39}$	59.3	50.0	28.0
$\mathcal{L}^{30}$	57.4	—	56.9
$\mathcal{L}^{33}$	57.4	—	56.9
$\mathcal{L}^{38}$	56.8	—	39.1
$\mathcal{L}^{8}$	53.7	81.3	44.4
$\mathcal{L}^{2}$	50.0	—	50.0
$\mathcal{L}^{7}$	50.0	—	16.7
$\mathcal{L}^{18}$	50.0	—	50.0
$\mathcal{L}^{21}$	50.0	—	50.0
$\mathcal{L}^{29}$	46.8	100.0	36.3
$\mathcal{L}^{37}$	46.8	50.0	44.6
$\mathcal{L}^{9}$	46.3	50.0	45.6
$\mathcal{L}^{3}$	45.3	81.3	33.3
$\mathcal{L}^{27}$	44.4	50.0	16.7

$\mathcal{L}^{22}$	42.6	—	43.4
$\mathcal{L}^{24}$	42.6	—	43.4
$\mathcal{L}^{28}$	42.1	81.3	28.0
$\mathcal{L}^{11}$	41.7	33.3	38.9
$\mathcal{L}^{19}$	40.2	0.0	60.7
$\mathcal{L}^{12}$	31.3	0.0	25.0
$\mathcal{L}^{34}$	29.0	—	28.0
$\mathcal{L}^{35}$	29.0	—	28.0
$\mathcal{L}^{36}$	29.0	—	28.0
$\mathcal{L}^{13}$	28.4	—	28.9
$\mathcal{L}^{20}$	27.1	81.3	0.0
$\mathcal{L}^{14}$	20.3	81.3	0.0
$\mathcal{L}^{15}$	16.7	50.0	0.0
$\mathcal{L}^{16}$	0.0	—	0.0

The high degree of fluctuation in the percentages of the preceding tables is, as mentioned earlier, due to the frequent scarcity of group determining readings which are relevant to the Syriac. However, in contrast to this fluctuation, there is the stability of the percentages of agreement between SyrPss and the 204 (of the original 299) relevant test readings from all four blocks which the majority of $\mathcal{L}$ witnesses support (I/ 48; II/ 71; III/ 31; IV/ 54).

	I	II	III	IV	AV.
SyrPs	81.3	87.3	87.1	85.2	85.2
SyrPs^{a}	81.3	—	—	—	81.3
SyrPs^{b}	—	88.0	83.9	86.8	86.2

These figures confirm the relationship between SyrPss and the $\mathcal{L}$ family as a whole. Whether or not the percentage of agreement between SyrPss and each of the forty $\mathcal{L}$ groups is, in every instance, a reliable indicator of the degree of their affiliation is something which can only be determined through more extensive collations.

V

THE TEXTUAL HISTORY OF SYRPSS

A. INTRODUCTION

In chapter three of the present study, it was demonstrated by means of a thoroughgoing comparison with Ga that SyrPss, though exhibiting evidence of some hexaplaric influence, is not inherently hexaplaric. This is rather surprising in view of the fact that the SyrPss Psalter is commonly associated with Paul, the Jacobite bishop of Tella in Mesopotamia, who produced the Syriac version of the Old Testament known as the Syrohexapla. This seventh century version is generally regarded as one of the chief witnesses to the Greek fifth column of Origen's Hexapla. The Syrohexapla's proximity, textually speaking, to the Hexapla is due to the fact that it constitutes a translation of that fifth column which, in turn, is a revision towards the Hebrew of the Greek text current in Origen's day. The anomaly of SyrPss' non-hexaplaric character naturally raises the question as to why Paul—if, in fact, he is responsible for SyrPss—would, in the Psalter, depart from the pattern established elsewhere in the Old Testament. In the present chapter, this text-historical problem is addressed.

The SyrPss Psalter (which, as will presently be demonstrated, actually embraces three text traditions) displays a certain kinship with the Syrohexapla in other books. For example, in the matter of physical layout, some SyrPss Mss feature the sort of marginal apparatus containing primarily hexaplaric readings that is generally found in Paul of Tella's version.[1] Furthermore, there are distinctive agreements with respect to translation technique between SyrPss and the Syrohexapla.[2]

A number of sources attribute the Syriac translation of the LXX to Paul. These include a Catena Patrum in Ms Br. Mus. Add.

12,168,[3] the IV Kingdoms colophon in Ms Par. syr. 27,[4] and, as well, the literary references of Mōšē bar Kēphā (circa 815-903 A. D.)[5] and Barhebraeus (1226-86 A. D.).[6] The evidence of these and other sources is that Paul carried out this translation project during the second decade of the seventh century in the Antonian monastery at the Enaton of Alexandria (a relay post nine miles from the city) after having fled his homeland in the face of the Persian invasion led by Khosrau II.[7] However, as already indicated, the problem with linking Paul with SyrPss—or with one of SyrPs, SyrPs[a], or SyrPs[b]—is that it/they, unlike the Syrohexapla in other books, is/are not innately hexaplaric. The most that can be said is that the SyrPss Mss give evidence of hexaplaric influence, though some—perhaps much—of it may well have been indirect. Furthermore, the fact that there are three text traditions makes it likely that more than one individual worked at producing a graecized Syriac Psalter. Although the sources are unanimous in ascribing the Syrohexapla to Paul, there is no source which explicitly attributes the Psalter to him. In view of the above, it would seem prudent, before conceding responsibility for SyrPss to Paul, to search additional sources for someone other than him who might be associated with a Syriac translation of the Old Testament, and particularly with the Psalter—especially someone who might have used a *Vorlage* which was not inherently hexaplaric.

One individual whose name is associated with a Syriac translation from the Greek is the sixth century Nestorian, Mār 'Ābā, who is said to have translated the Old Testament.[8] Since, however, textual evidence for this alleged version is lacking,[9] nothing can be said about the type of Greek *Vorlage* he may have employed.[10] There is, however, both textual and literary evidence for the version ascribed to Philoxenus, the renowned Monophysite bishop of Mabbūg in the ecclesiastical province of Euphratesia, who lived circa 440-523 A. D. The earliest literary reference to this version is dated to the mid-sixth century and comes from the Mesopotamian monk, Mōšē of Aghel. In an introduction to his Syriac translation of Cyril of Alexandria's *Glaphyra*,[11] Mōšē refers to the New Testament and the Psalter of the Philoxenian version, which, he says, was prepared for Philoxenus by a certain chorepiscopus (rural bishop) named Polycarp.[12] Though Polycarp may, indeed, have done the actual work, it is, nonetheless, Philoxenus' name which is normally linked with this version. Such is the case in a report by the thirteenth century monk, Eli of Qartamin, who claims that the Philoxenian version embraced both the Old and the New Testaments.[13] Thomas of Harkel,[14] the creator of the seventh century Harklean New Testament which was prepared in the Antonian monastery near Alexandria at the same time Paul was working there on the Syrohexapla, is another source of information about the Philoxenian version. In various colophons of the Harklean New Testament, Thomas makes it known that his text constitutes a revision of the version which was made "in the days of...Philoxenus."[15] This assertion is echoed by Barhebraeus.[16]

The wide-ranging literary evidence for the Philoxenian version indicates that its existence cannot be questioned. What has long been debated, however, is its scope. In the New Testament, controversy has surrounded both the so-called Pococke Epistles (that is, the version of the Four Minor Catholic Epistles—II Peter, II and III John, and Jude—first published by Edward Pococke in 1630)[17] and the Crawford Apocalypse (contained in Ms Crawford Syr. 2).[18] The problem is that although these books (which were not included in the Peshitta canon) are ascribed to Philoxenus, he does not cite them in his own writings. Nevertheless, these books share distinctive linguistic characteristics with Biblical quotations in, for example, Philoxenus' commentary on the Gospel of John.[19] In this commentary, he makes use of a text which is distinct from both the Old Syriac and the Peshitta, and which undoubtedly comes from the version bearing his name. Thus, the case for the Philoxenian character of the Pococke Epistles and the Crawford Apocalypse rests on objective textual evidence.[20]

Another focal point in the debate regarding the scope of the Philoxenian version has been Mōšē of Aghel's reference to a Philoxenian Psalter. A translation reflecting the word order of the relevant portion of his statement reveals why the possibility of a gloss has been entertained in some quarters:[21]

> When one encounters the version of the New (Testament) which made, and of David, Polycarp...for...'Aksenāyā (Philoxenus) of Mabbūg in Syriac, one is amazed at the differences which exist in the Syriac translation from the Greek language.[22]

Yet the dismissal of this Psalter reference without a careful analysis of the textual evidence seems rather arbitrary. The same can be said for Joseph Lebon's contention that the Philoxenian version did not include the Old Testament.[23]

There is not only literary, but also textual, evidence that the Philoxenian version extended to the Old Testament. In the Ambrosian Ms of the Syrohexapla published by Ceriani, there is a scholion consisting of a variant reading to Is. 9:6(5)^{b}–7(6)a$^{\alpha}$ which is attributed to the version of Philoxenus, bishop of Mabbūg.[24] The major difference between the scholion's reading and that of the Syrohexapla is the scholion's twelve word addition following ܡܠܐܟܐ ܕܬܪܥܝܬܐ ܪܒܬܐ ≈ Μεγάλης βουλῆς ἄγγελος in verse 6(5). The addition is clearly the scholion's primary *raison d'être*. Hexaplaric support for this interpolation is limited to V from the *O* group, to the *oII* group, and to the Palestinian Syriac (Syp), but it is solidly attested in non-hexaplaric (particularly *L*) Mss.

Another fragmentary Isaiah text,[25] unfortunately not preserved in chapter 9, is extant in 28:3-17, 42:17-49:18, and 66:11-23. Joseph Ziegler designates it Syl, for "syrolukianisch," in the Göttingen LXX edition, and this is indicative of its non-hexaplaric textual character.[26] Despite the fact that Syl is anonymous, a good case can be made for its inclusion in the Philoxenian corpus. In the first place, there is clearly a kinship between Syl and some of Philoxenus' Isaiah quotations in his own writings. Philoxenus' citation of Is. 45:9 in his commentary on the Gospel of John, for example, is identical (except for two slight discrepancies) to the Syl rendering of that verse, even where this means divergence from the Peshitta (of which the Philoxenian version is a revision) and distinctive translation of the Greek.[27] The affinity between Syl and these Isaiah quotations is observable also in general linguistic characteristics even when the texts do not overlap. Not surprisingly, these same characteristics link the Isaianic and other Philoxenian quotations to the Pococke Epistles and the Crawford Apocalypse.[28]

The question which naturally arises at this juncture is: If Syl is Philoxenian, why is it that, of the Old Testament books, only the Psalter is associated by Mōšē of Aghel with Philoxenus' version? In reply, it should be pointed out that the wording of Mōšē's statement in no way precludes the possibility that the Philoxenian Old Testament was more extensive.[29] Mōšē mentions the Psalter in connection with the New Testament. It is not uncommon, in either Greek or Syriac Mss, to find the book of Psalms in a substantially New Testament codex.[30] With this in mind, it would seem logical to suggest that Mōšē's statement reflects, not the extent of the Philoxenian version, but the fact that the Psalter was grouped with the New Testament in the current Philoxenian text, perhaps because these books were translated before the rest of the Old Testament.[31]

The association of a given text with the Philoxenian version should be based on both literary and textual evidence. The literary evidence for a Philoxenian Psalter is found in Mōšē of Aghel's introduction to his Syriac translation of Cyril's *Glaphyra*. What remains now is to determine whether or not there are stylistic and translational agreements between one or more of the three SyrPss text traditions and the *Philoxeniana*. As the following analysis will show, such textual evidence does indeed exist. The investigation begins with SyrPs.[32]

B. TEXTUAL CHARACTERISTICS OF SYRPS

One stylistic feature which has long been recognized as a characteristic of the Philoxenian version is what Arthur Vööbus terms "the ostentatious predilection for the use of the interrogative pronoun," ܐܝܠܝܢ.[33] This pronoun is often used in the rendering of the Greek plural articulated participle: e. g. Is. 44:9 οἱ πλάσσοντες = ܐܝܠܝܢ ܕܓܒܠܝܢ (Syl). In Syl of Isaiah, ܐܝܠܝܢ translates the article of the plural articulated participle twenty-one times,[34] while the only other equivalent used—the demonstrative pronoun, ܗܠܝܢ—translates it just once.[35] Both the Pococke Epistles and the Crawford Apocalypse share with Syl a fondness for the interrogative pronoun.[36] Like the *Philoxeniana*, SyrPs favours ܐܝܠܝܢ. In the first fifty Psalms, for example, the article of the participle is rendered by the interrogative fifty-six times,[37] by ܗܢܘܢ twenty-two times,[38] and by ܗܠܝܢ once.[39] In Pss. 90-110, ܐܝܠܝܢ is used fourteen times,[40] ܗܢܘܢ four times,[41] but ܗܠܝܢ not at all.

A second point of agreement between SyrPs and the *Philoxeniana* is a preference for the pronominal suffix attached directly to the substantive, as opposed to the use of the independent possessive pronoun which is customary in the Syrohexapla (Syh) and the Harklean New Testament: e. g. Is. 43:3 ὁ θεός σου = ܐܠܗܟ (Syl), ܐܠܗܐ ܕܝܠܟ (Syh). In Syl of Isaiah, the ܕܝܠ form occurs only four times,[42] in contrast to 205 occurrences of the directly attached pronominal suffix.[43] The same preference is exhibited in the Pococke Epistles and the Crawford Apocalypse.[44] SyrPs likewise has an overall predilection for the attached suffix. Although the ܕܝܠ form is favoured by a count of 310 to 132 (70.1% to 29.9%) in the first twenty-four Psalms, there is a dramatic switch towards the attached suffix in Ps. 25, and it remains predominant in the rest of the Psalter:[45]

e. g. Pss. 25-50: 331 to 240 (58% to 42%)
Pss. 60-70: 168 to 64 (72.4% to 27.6%)
Pss. 90-110: 358 to 91 (79.7% to 20.3%)
Pss. 140-151: 148 to 37 (80% to 20%)

The similarities between SyrPs and the *Philoxeniana* are not restricted to stylistic features, but also involve translation equivalents. One such equivalency is θέλω = ܨܒܐ, which stands in contrast to the more usual θέλω = ܪܓܐ. In Syl of Isaiah, ܨܒܐ translates θέλω the only time it occurs (28:4). This rendering is also seen in Pococke III Jn. 13 and Crawford Apoc. 11:5.[46] In SyrPs, ܨܒܐ is the equivalent on six occasions.[47] Interestingly, Syh of Isaiah, which R. G. Jenkins has suggested is a revision of Syl,[48] shows ܨܒܐ in three of the places where the LXX of Isaiah has θέλω.[49]

Another point of agreement between SyrPs and the Philoxenian version is the translation of the adjective, τίμιος. Syl of Isaiah has no occasion to render it, but in the Pococke Epistles and the Crawford Apocalypse, the equivalent is the Pe'al participial adjective, ܝܩܝܪ, in six instances,[50] and the adjectival ܝܩܪ root once.[51] Of the three times τίμιος appears in the Psalter, it is translated twice by ܝܩܝܪ,[52] and on one occasion, indistinguishable in significance from the other two, by the ܝܩܪ root.[53]

Finally, in the only place where διδαχή appears in the LXX—Ps. 59:1(inscr.)—SyrPs shows agreement with the New Testament *Philoxeniana* in the choice of ܝܘܠܦܢܐ as equivalent. This equivalency occurs five times in the Pococke Epistles and the Crawford Apocalypse,[54] while διδαχή = ܡܠܦܢܘܬܐ occurs just once.[55]

In addition to the preceding agreements between SyrPs and the *Philoxeniana*, there are those which also find strong support in the Syrohexapla and the Harklean New Testament. These agreements include characteristics whose appearance is not made inevitable by the constraints of Syriac. Such characteristics involve both stylistic features (e. g. relating to the use of particles, pronouns, and the copula)[56] and translation equivalencies (e. g. ἀλήθεια = ܫܪܪܐ).[57]

Not only does SyrPs contain characteristics which are common to the Philoxenian, Syrohexaplaric, and Harklean versions, but it also exhibits those which are both Syrohexaplaric/Harklean and non-Philoxenian. Six representative examples are:

1/ ܗܘ ܠܗ, ܗܘܢ ܠܗܘܢ and similar combinations for the Greek third person reflexive pronoun, ἑαυτοῦ etc. (Philoxenian: ܢܦܫܐ with appropriate suffix);[58]

2/ the uncontracted negative, ܠܐ ܐܝܬ, with or without accompanying suffix (Philoxenian: the contracted form, ܠܝܬ etc.);[59]

3/ the ܛܘܒܬܢܐ root for μακάριος (Philoxenian: ܛܘܒܘܗܝ etc.);[60]

4/ the composite term, ܠܐ ܢܡܘܣܝܘܬܐ, for ἀνομία (Philoxenian: ܥܘܠܐ);[61]

5/ the εἰρήνη = ܫܝܢܐ equivalency (Philoxenian: εἰρήνη = ܫܠܡܐ);[62]

6/ the θηρίον = ܚܝܘܬ ܒܪܐ equivalency (Philoxenian: θηρίον = ܚܝܘܬܐ);[63]

The inference to which the preceding evidence points is that SyrPs is not simply Philoxenian, but that it constitutes a revision of the Philoxenian Psalter, no longer extant in its unrevised state. Furthermore, the features of this revision are those which characterize the Syrohexapla and the Harklean version. In that light, one cannot be certain as to who is responsible for the characteristics in SyrPs which are prominent in all three versions. Yet the conclusion that SyrPs is based on the Philoxenian Psalter seems inescapable. This is due, not only to the fact that it has agreements with the *Philoxeniana*, but also to the fact that it is distinct in terms of various criteria from other Syriac versions. Disagreements between SyrPs and the Peshitta include those which are the result of SyrPs' close conformity to the Greek (such as additions, deletions, word order), stylistic divergences, and the use of different synonyms.[64] SyrPs, with its innately non-hexaplaric text, stands apart from the Syrohexapla as well. It also distinguishes itself from both the Syrohexapla and the Harklean New Testament in some features which it shares with the *Philoxeniana*. The following examples are illustrative:

1/ SyrPs and the *Philoxeniana* prefer ܐܝܠܝܢ as the rendering of the article of the Greek plural articulated participle, but the Syrohexapla and the Harklean version prefer the demonstrative pronouns, ܗܢܘܢ and ܗܠܝܢ;[65]

2/ the directly attached pronominal suffix is predominant in SyrPs and the Philoxenian version, while the independent possessive pronoun (the ܕܝܠ form) is favoured in the Syrohexapla and the Harklean New Testament;[66]

3/ the somewhat unusual θέλω = ܨܒܐ equivalency of SyrPs, the *Philoxeniana*, and the Syrohexapla of Isaiah, stands in contrast to the θέλω = ܪܓܐ equivalency which is normal in the Syrohexapla and the Harklean version;[67]

4/ SyrPs and the Philoxenian version use the Pe'al participial adjective, ܝܩܝܪ, and occasionally the adjective, ܛܒ, to render τίμιος, whereas the Syrohexapla and the Harklean New Testament usually employ ܡܝܩܪ, the Pa'el participial adjective.[68]

SyrPs agrees with the *Philoxeniana* against the Harklean version on the use of ܝܘܠܦܢܐ as the equivalent for διδαχή in Ps. 59:1(inscr.)——its only occurrence in the LXX. The Harklean version is characterized by the διδαχή = ܡܠܦܢܘܬܐ equivalency.[69] SyrPs also stands apart from the version of the anonymous Isaiah fragments preserved in Ms Br. Mus. Add. 14,441——a version which undoubtedly represents the recension of the Monophysite bishop, Jacob of Edessa (circa 640–708 A. D.).[70] A comparison of the Isaiah fragments published by Ceriani (28:1–21, 45:7–16, 46:2–49:25)[71] with SyrPs reveals that distinguishing features involve both style (e. g. relating to the use of pronouns and ܠܝܬ or ܐܝܬ ܠܐ)[72] and the choice of synonyms

(e. g. as equivalents for ἀλήθεια and εἰρήνη).[73]

Having established that SyrPs must be based on the Philoxenian Psalter, one needs to address the question as to who is responsible for giving SyrPs its present character. When one takes into consideration its fidelity to the Greek and its textual features, the most plausible candidates are Paul of Tella and Thomas of Harkel. On the face of it, there is little to choose between them. First of all, as has already been mentioned, SyrPs shares physiognomic similarities with the Syrohexapla and the Harklean version. Secondly, the Isaiah scholion in the Ambrosian Ms and the colophons of the Harklean New Testament indicate that both Paul and Thomas made use of the Philoxenian text in the preparation of their respective versions. Thirdly, there is literary evidence indicating that Thomas may have assisted Paul in the translation of at least IV Kingdoms,[74] and similar testimony to suggest that Paul translated the *Pericope de Adultera* in Jn. 7:53-8:11.[75] If Thomas and Paul did work in both Testaments, then either one of them could be responsible for giving SyrPs its present shape.

While it is true that a case can be made for either Paul or Thomas as the preparer of SyrPs, its extensive marginal apparatus of hexaplaric readings—contained primarily in Mss *abcf* (and, of course, *g*, the copy of *f*)—may tip the scales in favour of Paul. Admittedly, Thomas recorded variant readings in the margins of his New Testament version as well. Furthermore, if he did work with Paul on IV Kingdoms, he would have had firsthand experience with hexaplaric notes. Yet, it was under Paul's direction that the hexaplaric apparatus was supplied—in IV Kingdoms and elsewhere in the Syrohexapla—so the presence of such an apparatus in SyrPs is evidence of his probable involvement with the Psalter. It is clear, however, that Paul's work on the Psalter was not limited to the adding of marginal notes to the Philoxenian text. He also carried out a partial textual revision which produced some physiognomic changes and, apparently, some hexaplaric alterations, but which left the inherently non-hexaplaric character of the base text still discernible.[76]

C. TEXTUAL CHARACTERISTICS OF SYRPS^{a} AND SYRPS^{b}

The foregoing reconstruction accounts for most of the Mss collated for this Psalter edition. However, the text found in the initial sections of Mss *hj* (substantially 1:5–27:6 in *h* and 1:1–27:6 in *j*)[77] stands apart from the revision of the Philoxenian Psalter attested by the majority text (SyrPs). Evidently the initial portions of Mss *hj* attest to another revision of the Philoxenian Psalter (SyrPs^{a})—a revision which, like SyrPs, is not primarily hexaplaric, but which is characterized by even closer conformity to the Greek than SyrPs.[78] SyrPs^{a} further distinguishes itself from SyrPs in places where the latter displays features which have been shown above to be typical of the Philoxenian version. In such cases, SyrPs^{a} usually has readings which are characteristic of Paul of Tella and Thomas of Harkel.[79]

1/ Where SyrPs translates the article of a Greek plural articulated participle with ܐܝܠܝܢ ܕ, SyrPs^{a} normally has ܗ̇ܢܘܢ.[80]

2/ SyrPs^{a} is almost totally consistent in the use of the ܕܝܠ form.[81] This distinguishes it from SyrPs even in Pss. 1–24 where the latter prefers the ܕܝܠ form, but, as has been shown above, not as consistently.

3/ SyrPs' use of ܝܩܝܪ or ܝܩܪ to render τίμιος is in contrast with the consistent employment of ܡܝܩܪ in SyrPs^{a}.[82]

Other examples which illustrate both the distinction between SyrPs^{a} and SyrPs, and the comparability of SyrPs^{a} to the versions of Paul and Thomas are:

1/ SyrPs^{a}'s translation of μακάριος with ܛܘܒܢܐ, the characteristic Syrohexaplaric/Harklean equivalent, where SyrPs has the μακάριος = ܛܘܒܘܗܝ equivalency;[83]

2/ the employment of composite terms by SyrPs^a to render Greek compound words in passages where SyrPs does not have composite terms.[84]

SyrPs^a also contains the features which SyrPs has been shown above to share with the Syrohexapla and the Harklean version.[85]

As already intimated, Ps. 27:7–146:8 in *h*,[86] and Ps. 27:7–fin. in *j*, contain a noticeably different text from that found in the initial sections of this Ms pair, though neither Ms shows a change of scribal hand in 27:7. Ms *k* has a similar text where extant (70:7–16, 73:4–14, 77:28–38, 79:9[8]–18[17]) to that contained in Ps. 27:7 ff. of *hj*.[87] The text tradition attested by these three Mss (SyrPs^b) is considerably more closely related to SyrPs than SyrPs^a is. Thus, features which SyrPs shares with the *Philoxeniana* and which are atypical of the Syrohexapla and the Harklean version, occur in SyrPs^b as well (i. e. the preference for ܐܝܠܝܢ as the equivalent for the article of the Greek plural articulated participle,[88] and the θέλω = ܨܒܐ and διδαχή = ܡܠܘܦܢܐ equivalencies[89]). However, some characteristics of SyrPs^a are also found in SyrPs^b (e. g. the strong preference for the ܕܝܠ form, the frequent avoidance of the proleptic suffix in genitival constructions,[90] and the τίμιος = ܝܩܝܪ equivalency[91]). Hence, SyrPs^b, which stands between SyrPs and SyrPs^a in the matter of textual relations, may constitute a light reworking of the SyrPs text based on SyrPs^a, which, for its part, presumably included the whole Psalter originally.

A possible explanation for the lack of textual homogeneity in Mss *hj* is that an ancestor of theirs, which had lost Ps. 1:1–27:6, was furnished with the corresponding portion of the SyrPs^a text. Whether the individual who filled this lacuna in the earlier Ms was also the creator of SyrPs^b is impossible to determine. The probability of that scenario would certainly be enhanced if it could be shown that the eighth century *k*, which predates Mss *hj* by four to five centuries, also contained the SyrPs^a text in Ps. 1:1–27:6. What is apparent, however, is that the SyrPs^{b} text tradition can be dated to at least the eighth century.

The question as to who is responsible for SyrPs^{a}—the text which often differs from SyrPs with readings characteristic of the Syrohexapla and the Harklean version—has yet to be addressed. Since Paul of Tella is already associated, in the present reconstruction, with SyrPs, the possibility that Thomas of Harkel prepared SyrPs^{a} must be entertained.[92] Yet this raises another query, namely: Why would Paul and Thomas each produce a version of the Psalter based on the Philoxenian text, seeing that they were contemporaries who laboured in the same monastery? That Paul, whose primary focus was the Old Testament, would produce a Psalter, working from the version attributed to the venerated Philoxenus, is understandable. However, the rationale for a Harklean Psalter is not as obvious. Nevertheless, it should be remembered that Thomas' New Testament version is a revision of the Philoxenian New Testament. Furthermore, as mentioned earlier, there is evidence to indicate that the Psalter may have been grouped with the New Testament in the current Philoxenian text. In that light, it is not illogical to suggest that Thomas too carried out a revision of the Philoxenian Psalter—a revision of which the initial sections of Mss *hj* are the surviving remnants.

In response to the suggestion that SyrPs^{a} represents a Harklean revision of the Philoxenian Psalter, the objection might be raised that the Harklean New Testament quotations of the Psalter do not always agree with SyrPs^{a}, even where the LXX and the Greek text underlying Thomas' New Testament version are identical. Yet Thomas may, at times, have found it expedient, for one reason or another, to render given passages differently in separate contexts.[93] On other occasions, such differences could have been the result of variations, either in the parent Philoxenian version (the unrevised Psalter of which is no longer extant) or in the Peshitta.[94] It should also be pointed out that SyrPs^{a} has some features which are not typical of the Harklean New Testament.[95] However, according to Harklean New Testament colophons (Corpus Paulinum, Apocalypse),[96] Thomas did have co-workers who assisted him in the preparation of at least parts of his version. It may be that the input of another set of assistants for the Psalter led to its somewhat distinctive textual flavour.

D. SUMMARY

To sum up, literary evidence attests to the existence of a Philoxenian Psalter. Careful textual analysis yields significant agreements in terms of translation technique between SyrPs and SyrPs^{b}, on the one hand, and what remains of the Philoxenian version in both the Old and New Testaments, on the other. Yet SyrPs and SyrPs^{b}, along with SyrPs^{a}, exhibit non-Philoxenian features which are, however, characteristic of the Syrohexaplaric and Harklean versions. SyrPs and SyrPs^{a} are apparently revisions of the Philoxenian Psalter, the original form of which has not survived. In this chapter, a case has been made for associating Paul of Tella with SyrPs, and Thomas of Harkel with SyrPs^{a}. SyrPs^{b} which, though closely related to SyrPs, also contains some features typical of SyrPs^{a}, can perhaps be attributed to some unknown individual who lightly reworked a SyrPs text on the basis of the SyrPs^{a} revision.

Finally, in view of the fact that Syl of Isaiah reflects the *L* text, and that—at least as far as the Gospels are concerned—both the Harklean version and Philoxenus' citations from his own version show the influence of the Koine text associated with Lucian,[97] it is interesting to note that Rahlfs, in his edition of the Greek Psalter, groups SyrPss with *L*.[98] Unfortunately, however, he fails to define in systematic fashion what is actually Lucianic in the Psalter. Yet if Rahlfs should prove to be correct in his assertion that SyrPss is basically Lucianic, this would only serve to corroborate the present writer's thesis that the Philoxenian Psalter lies behind the subsequent Syriac text traditions represented in this edition.

APPENDIX

One of the striking features of SyrPss is that several of its Mss (especially *a*, *b*, *c*, *f*, and *g*, the copy of *f*) contain an extensive marginal apparatus of primarily hexaplaric readings from Aquila, Symmachus, Theodotion, Quinta, and Sexta.[1] The apparatus is a valuable source of textual material from these translations which Origen included in the Hexapla. As suggested in chapter five, the incorporation of the apparatus into this Syriac Psalter version was probably the work of Paul of Tella, who regularly included hexaplaric readings in the margins of the Syrohexapla. His source(s) for such readings is/are a matter of conjecture. The most probable scenario, however, is that the Greek text(s) which he used for his Old Testament version already contained them, and that all he had to do was translate them.[2] These hexaplaric readings may well have been derived from catena Mss, whose citations from the Church Fathers often contain such readings embedded in their homiletical remarks.[3]

A comprehensive analysis of the marginal hexaplaric apparatus of SyrPss is outside the scope of the present study, whose focus is the *text* of that Psalter. However, most of these readings have already been published by Field, who has recorded those in *a*, along with variants from fragmentary Mss *b* and *c*. Thus, the bulk of SyrPss marginal evidence is readily available to scholars. Besides these three Mss, only *f* and its copy, *g*, attest large numbers of hexaplaric readings. Yet the great majority of them are, with some minor variations, the same as those in *abc*.[4] This homogeneity further confirms the likelihood that the marginal apparatus in our Syriac Mss is attributable to one individual—namely, Paul of Tella.

This appendix contains corrections of, and supplements to, Field's evidence. The present writer has compared *abc* against Field's entries, checking for errors or omissions in his recording of the Syriac evidence. In addition, the other SyrPss Mss have been examined for significant variants (i. e. superior readings to *abc* or such as would likely reflect differences in the underlying Greek) and new readings. The following lists of significant Syriac variants and new readings are accompanied by their Greek counterparts. Syriac readings with known Greek equivalents are recorded in the normal Greek font, whereas retroversions into Greek which are not attested in extant Greek sources appear in italicized script. We begin, however, with a list of corrections of Field *vis-à-vis* the recording of evidence from *abc*.[5]

A. CORRECTION OF RECORDED SYRIAC READINGS

Of the following six corrections, only the first requires a corresponding modification of Field's Greek entry. In each case, Field's reading appears before the square bracket, while the correct one follows it:

15:4 p. 107, n. 9
ܐܚܪ̈ܢܐ] ܐܚܪܢܐ
ἄλλοι] *ἄλλον* (cf. α', n. 7)
אַחֵר MT
μετὰ ταῦτα LXX

58:12(11) p. 187, n. 12
ܐܪܘ] ܐܪܘܠ

67:32(31) p. 204, n. 69
ܐܬܝܐ] ܐܬ̈ܝܐ

72:21 p. 215, n. 36
ܟܠܐ] ܟܠܗܝ

87:5(4) p. 239, n. 4
ܢܫܐ] ܢܫܠ

103:26 p. 261, n. 29
.ܐ.] ascriptio non testata *a* [Note: The only Ms which
has the marginal reading, ܟܘܬܝ, is *a*. However, contrary

to what Field records, it displays an unattested reading, though he is probably correct in ascribing it to Aquila (cf. Field at 73:14).][6]

B. THE INCLUSION OF OMISSIONS

In this category, we include readings found in *a* and/or *b* and/or *c* which Field does not record. Where there are page and note numbers, Field has a partial reading (in such cases, retroverted material which has no equivalent in Field is set off by « »).[7] Where there are no such numbers, Field has no reading at all:

8:1(inscr.) p. 96, n. 3
לדוד MT
τῷ Δαυίδ LXX
ܠܕܘܝܕ .ܐ. *a**(uid.)*f* = α′ τῷ Δαυίδ (ܕܕܘܝܕ *a*[c] pr m = *τοῦ* Δαυίδ)[8]

17:23(22) p. 111, n. 37
וחקתיו MT
καὶ τὰ δικαιώματα αὐτοῦ LXX
ܘܚܬܝܬܘܬܐ ܕܝܠܗ .ܐ. *b**(uid.)*c* = α′ «*καὶ*» *ἀκριβασμοὺς αὐτοῦ* (ο 1° [= *καί*] > *ab*[c]*f*)[9]

23:6 סלה MT
διάψαλμα LXX
ܠܥܠܡ .ܐ. *acf* = α′ *ἀεί*[10]

35:1(inscr.) p. 142, n. 1
למנצח לעבד־יהוה לדוד MT
εἰς τὸ τέλος· τῷ δούλῳ κυρίου τῷ Δαυίδ LXX
ܠܡܢܨܚ ܕܡܪܝܐ ܠܥܒܕܗ ܕܡܪܝܐ ܠܕܘܝܕ .ܐ. *abc* = α′ τῷ νικοποιῷ *τῷ δούλῳ κυρίου τῷ Δαυίδ* [Note: The α′ column of Ms 1098 reads: τῷ ν̣ικ̣οποιῷ τοῦ δούλου יהוה τοῦ δαυε̣ίδ.][11]

35:8(7) p. 142, n. 14
חסדך אלהים MT

τὸ ἔλεός σου, ὁ θεός LXX
ܐ.ܣ.ܗ. ܚܣܕܟ ܐܠܗܐ *abcf* = α'σ'ε' *τὸ ἔλεός σου «θεέ»*

36:4 על־יהוה MT
τοῦ κυρίου LXX
ܣ. ܠܡܪܝܐ *f* = σ' *τῷ κυρίῳ* (s. ascriptione *abc*; in textu R ∠pau)[12]

40:14(13) p. 154, n. 27
אמן ואמן MT
γένοιτο, γένοιτο LXX
ܐ.ܣ. ܐܡܝܢ ܘܐܡܝܢ *cf* ≈ σ' ἀμὴν «*καὶ*» ἀμήν (ܘ [= *καί*] > *a*)
[Note: It appears that ascriptions have been interchanged in our Syriac Mss. This reading seems to be the σ' reading, while ܡܗܝܡܢܐܝܬ ܘܡܗܝܡܢܐܝܬ = πεπιστωμένως καὶ πεπιστωμένως most likely comes from α' (and ε'?): cf. Field re: 71:19.]

47:9(8) סלה MT
διάψαλμα LXX
ܐ.ܗ. ܒܘܣܡܬܐ *acf* = α'ε' *cantilena* (cf. Field, p. 149, n. 37)

59:6(4) סלה MT
διάψαλμα LXX
ܐ. ܐܡܝܢܐܝܬ *a* (s. ascriptione *b*) = α' *ἀεί* (cf. 23:6 supra)

61:1(inscr.) p. 191, n. 1
לדוד MT
τῷ Δαυίδ LXX
ܐ. ܠܕܘܝܕ *cf* = α' *τῷ* Δαυίδ (ܕܕܘܝܕ *ab* = τοῦ Δαυίδ)

61:9(8) p. 192, n. 18
מחסה MT
βοηθός LXX
ܣ. ܠܐ ܕܚܠܬܐ *cf* = σ' *ἀφοβία* [cf. Field re: Ps. 60:4(3) σ'] (ܠܐ ܕܚܠ̈ܬܐ *ab* = *ἀφοβίαι*)

93:18 p. 252, n. 13

יסעדני MT

βοηθεῖ μοι LXX

[ܣ]ܣܡܟܬ݁ .ܡ. *b*, ܣܡܟܢܝ .ܡ. *f* = σ' *sustinuit me* [Note: The subject of the verb is ܛܝܒܘܬܟ = τὸ ἔλεός σου. The difference between *b* and *f* in regard to the number of the verb is not, therefore, that significant. A possible equivalent for ܣܡܟ is στηρίζω (cf. Field and SyrPss[txt] re: 103:15, and SyrPss[txt] re: 50:14[12]). The Syriac reflects either an aorist or a perfect indicative: *ἐστήριξέ/ἐστήρικταί με*.] (ܫܒܩܢܝ *a* = *dimisit me*)

C. VARIANTS FROM NEW SOURCES

This list contains variants to entries in Field from *fg* (as always, *g* is mentioned only when it differs from *f* or when *f* is defective):

7:5(4) p. 94, n. 4

צוררי MT

ἀπὸ τῶν ἐχθρῶν μου LXX

ܠ ܗܢܘܢ ܕܐܠܨܝܢ [ܠ]ܗܘܢ .ܐ. *f* = α' *τοὺς θλίβοντάς με*[13] (ܠܗܘܢ ܠ ܕܡܥܩܝܢ *ab* = *τοὺς ἐνδεσμοῦντάς με*)[14]

9:7(6) p. 98, n. 10

תמו חרבות MT

ἐξέλιπον αἱ ῥομφαῖαι LXX

ܫܠܡܬ ܚܘܪܒܐ .ܣ.ܘ. *f* = ϝ'σ' *consumpta sunt* ἐρείπια (ܫܠܡܘ ܚܘܪܒܐ *ab* [Note: This could be a case of a singular verb with a neuter plural subject: cf. Field.])

9:23(22) p. 99, n. 41

This reading is ascribed to α'σ'θ' in *a*, but only to α'σ' in *f*.

18:1(insc.) p. 113, n. 1

לדוד MT

τῷ Δαυίδ LXX

ܠܕܘܝܕ s. ascriptione *f* = [α': cf. Field] τῷ Δαυίδ (ܕܕܘܝܕ ܐܣ. *ac* = α'σ' τοῦ Δαυίδ: cf. Field re: σ')

21:1(inscr.) p. 117, n. 1

לדוד MT

τῷ Δαυίδ LXX

ܠܕܘܝܕ .ܐ. *f*uid.*g* = α' τῷ Δαυίδ (ܕܕܘܝܕ *a* = *τοῦ* Δαυίδ)

38:8(7) p. 149, n. 23

תוחלתי MT

καὶ ἡ ὑπόστασίς μου LXX

ܣܘܟܝܐ ܕܝܠܝ .ܣ. *f* = σ' ἡ ἀναμονή μου (pr. ܘ [= *καί*] *ac*)

40:1(inscr.) p. 152, n. 1

לדוד MT

τῷ Δαυίδ LXX

ܠܕܘܝܕ .ܐ. *f* = α' τῷ Δαυίδ (ܕܕܘܝܕ *abc* = *τοῦ* Δαυίδ)

49:5 p. 172, n. 12

אספו MT

συναγάγετε LXX

ܟܢܫܘ .ܐ. *f* = α' συλλέξατε (ܟܢܘܫ *ac* = *σύλλεξον*)

54:16(15) p. 180, n. 29

במגורם MT

ἐν ταῖς παροικίαις αὐτῶν LXX

ܒܟܘܢܫܐ ܕܝܠܗܘܢ .ܣ. *f* = σ' ἐν συστροφῇ αὐτῶν (ܒܟܘܢܫܝܐ ܕܝܠܗܘܢ *abc* = ἐν *συστροφαῖς* αὐτῶν)

56:1(inscr.) p. 183, n. 1

בברחו MT

ἐν τῷ αὐτὸν ἀποδιδράσκειν LXX

ܐܡܬܝ ܕܥܪܩ ܗܘܐ .ܣ. *f* = σ' *ἡνίκα ἀπεδίδρασκεν* (ܐܡܬܝ ܕܥܪܩ *ab* [*c* hab. ܕܚܪܩ pro ܕܥܪܩ] = *ἡνίκα ἀπέδρα*)

60:1(inscr.) p. 190, n. 1

עַל־נְגִינַת MT (sed cf. *BHS*)

ἐν ὕμνοις LXX

.ܣ. ܒܝܕ ܟܢܪܐ *f* = σ′ *διὰ ψαλτηρίου* (ܒܝܕ ܟܢ̈ܪܐ *ab* = *διὰ ψαλτηρίων*)[15]

63:1(inscr.) pp. 193–4, n. 1

לדוד MT

τῷ Δαυίδ LXX

.ܐ. ܠܕܘܝܕ *f* = α′ *τῷ Δαυίδ* (ܕܕܘܝܕ *abc* = *τοῦ Δαυίδ*)

63:10(9) p. 195, n. 26

פעל MT

τὰ ἔργα LXX

.ܣ. ܣܘܥܪܢܘܬܐ *f* = σ′ *τὴν πρᾶξιν* (ܣܘܥܪ̈ܢܘܬܐ *ac* = *τὰς πράξεις*)[16]

67:32(31) p. 204, n. 69

ידיו MT

χεῖρα αὐτῆς LXX

.ܣ. ܐܝܕܐ *f* = σ′ χεῖρα (ܐܝ̈ܕܐ *abc* = *χεῖρας*)

68:3(2) p. 205, n. 3

טבעתי MT

ἐνεπάγην LXX

.ܣ. ܥܡܕܬ *f* = σ′ ἐβαπτίσθην (ܥܡܪܬ *ab* = *habitaui*; ܥܨܪܬ *c*^c pr m = *pressi/perseueraui*, sed pro ܨ fuerat ܡ uel ܟ)[17]

71:5 p. 211, n. 4

The reading which is unattested in *abc* is attributed to σ′ in *f*. [Note: *f* has ܠ instead of ܡܢ, but this does not reflect a different Greek *Vorlage* since φοβέομαι plus accusative is translated by both ܕܚܠ ܡܢ (e. g. 66:8[7] text) and ܕܚܠ ܠ (e. g. 30:20[19] text) in SyrPss.]

71:10 p. 211, n. 15

In *ac*, this σ′ reading is indexed to ܢܩܪܒܘܢ ܡܘܗ̈ܒܬܐ 1° in the text (i. e. מנחה ישיבו ≈ δῶρα προσοίσουσιν), but in *f*, as in Field, it is associated with ܩܘܪܒܢܐ ܢܩܪܒܘܢ 2° (i. e. אשכר יקריבו ≈ δῶρα προσάξουσιν).

72:21 p. 215, n. 37
יתחמץ MT
ἐξεκαύθη LXX
ܣ. ܡܬܟܪܝܢ ܗܘܐ *f* = σ' συνεστέλλετο[18] (ܡܬܡܚܠ ܗܘܐ *ab* = *infirmabatur*)

73:1(inscr.) p. 216, n. 1
מַשְׂכִּיל MT
συνέσεως LXX
ܐ. ܝܕܘܥܬܢܐ *f* = α' *ἐπιστήμων*[19] (ܕܝܕܘܥܬܢܘܬܐ *ab* = *ἐπιστημοσύνης*)

77:1(inscr.) p. 224, n. 1
מַשְׂכִּיל MT
συνέσεως LXX
ܐ. ܝܕܘܥܬܢܘܬܐ *f* = α' *ἐπιστημοσύνη* (ܕܝܕܘܥܬܢܘܬܐ *a* = *ἐπιστημοσύνης*)[20]

77:35 p. 226, n. 34
In *f*, the reading, ܡܢܘ ܩܪܝܒܐ ܕܝܠܗܘܢ (= *ἀγχιστεὺς αὐτῶν*), corresponds to ܦܪܘܩܗܘܢ ܐܝܬܘܗܝ (i. e. גאלם ≈ λυτρωτὴς αὐτῶν ἐστιν) as Field indicates it should, not to ܡܥܕܪܢܐ ܕܝܠܗܘܢ ܐܝܬܘܗܝ (i. e. צורם ≈ βοηθὸς αὐτῶν ἐστιν) as in *a*. However, *f*, like *a*, persists in attributing it to σ', though it would seem to be an α' reading.[21]

82:18(17) p. 235, n. 18
ויחפרו MT
καὶ ἐντραπήτωσαν LXX
ܣ. ܘܢܬܚܦܪܘܢ *f* = σ' *καὶ κατορυγήσονται* (ܘ [= *καί*] > *a*)[22]

83:1(inscr.) p. 235, n. 1
לבני־ MT

τοῖς υἱοῖς LXX

ܠܒܢܝܐ [sey. et ascriptio perierunt aut omissi sunt] *f* = [α′] *τοῖς υἱοῖς* (ܕܒܢ̈ܝܐ .ܐ. *α* = α′ *τῶν υἱῶν*)

84:4(3) p. 236, n. 3

עברתך MT

τὴν ὀργήν σου LXX

ܡܗܝܡܢܘܬܟ <ܠܐ> [ascriptio periit aut omissa est] *f* = [α′] *<ἀν>υπερθεσίαν σου*[23] (ܡܗܝܡܢܘܬܟ ܠܐ .ܐ. *α* = α′ *incredibilitatem tuam*)

88:20(19) p. 243, n. 27

The ܚܝܠܐ reading, which appears without attestation in the margins of *ab*, is ascribed to α′σ′ in *f*. However, note the Eusebian σ′ reading in Field (the ascription in *f* could be a carry over from the α′σ′ reading earlier in the same verse). In *e hj*, ܚܝܠܐ is the textual reading, whereas ܡܪܝܡ is found in the texts of *abf*.

88:48(47) pp. 244–5, n. 56

זכר־אני מה־חלד MT

μνήσθητι τίς μου ἡ ὑπόστασις LXX

.ܣ. ܐܬܕܟܪ ܡܢܐ ܐܢܐ ܡܢ ܒܪ ܝܘܡܐ ܐܝܬܝ *f* = σ′ μνημόνευσον τί εἰμι ἡμερόβιος ὤν[24] (ܡܢ] + .ܚܝ [= *ζῶν*] *ab*)

105:7 p. 262, n. 5

חסדיך MT

τοῦ ἐλέους σου LXX

ܕܛܝܒܘܬܟ .ܐ. *f* = α′ *τῶν χαρίτων σου*[25] (ܛܝܒܘܬܟ *ab*uid. [Note: Field retroverts this as *χάριτός σου*, which is clearly what the context calls for, although, strictly speaking, the Syriac equals *χάρις σου*.])

106:4 p. 263, n. 2

בישימון MT

ἐν ἀνύδρῳ LXX

.ܣ.ܐ. ܒܠܐ ܡܬܥܡܪܢܘܬܐ *f* = α′σ′ *ἐν τῇ ἀοικήτῳ*[26] (ܒܠܐ

ܡܠܐܟܒܪܝܢܘܬܐ *a* = *ἐν ἀβάτῳ*)[27]

118:10 p. 271, n. 8

Ms *a* shows a dittograph here (ܡܘܒܠ ܠܐ | ܠܐ), but *f* has the correct reading (ܡܘܒܠ ܠܐ: cf. Field).

118:17 p. 271, n. 10

גמל על־עבדך MT

ἀνταπόδος τῷ δούλῳ σου LXX

ܣ. ܥܒܕ ܛܒ ܠܥܒܕܟ *f* [de ܥܒܕ, punctum ܕ periit aut omissum est in *f*, ܕ > *g*] = σ′ *εὐεργέτησον τὸν δοῦλόν σου*[28] (ܛܒ] + ܠܝ [= *με*] *a*)

118:51 p. 273, n. 39

This reading is attributed to α′ in *a*, but to σ′ in *f*.

123:4 p. 282, n. 4

נחלה MT

χείμαρρον LXX

ܣ. ܐܝܟ ܪܓܠܬܐ *f* = σ′ *ὡς χείμαρρος* (ܐܝܟ ܪ̈ܓܠܬܐ *a* = *ὡς χείμαρροι*)[29]

140:4 p. 297, n. 8

במנעמיהם MT

μετὰ τῶν ἐκλεκτῶν αὐτῶν LXX

ܣ. ܒܣܝ̈ܡܬܗܘܢ *f* = σ′ τὰ ἡδέα αὐτῶν (ܒܣܝܡܬܗܘܢ *a* = *τὸ ἡδὺ αὐτῶν*)

143:2 p. 300, n. 2

This reading is attributed to α′ in *ab*, but to α′σ′ in *f*.[30]

D. NEW SYRIAC READINGS

This list contains hexaplaric readings from the margins of Syriac Mss other than *abc*. Field records at least partial Greek counterparts to each of them, but he obviously does not include the Syriac readings. Retroversions are supplied wherever Greek textual evidence is lacking:

41:12(11) p. 156, n. 37

MT מה־תשתוחחי נפשי ומה־תהמי עלי הוחילי לאלהים כי־עוד אודנו
ἵνα τί περίλυπος εἶ, ψυχή, καὶ ἵνα τί συνταράσσεις με;
ἔλπισον ἐπὶ τὸν θεόν, ὅτι ἐξομολογήσομαι αὐτῷ LXX
ܐ. ܠܡܢܐ ܡܬܟܦܦܬܝ ܢܦܫܝ ܘܡܣܠܬܝ (sic) ܥܠܝ. ܣܟܝ ܠܐܠܗܐ
ܡܛܠ ܕܐܘܕܐ ܕܐܘܕܐ (sic) ܠܗ *f* ≈ α′ τί κατακύπτεις, *ψυχή μου, καὶ <τί> ὀχλάζεις ἐπ' ἐμέ; καραδόκησον τὸν θεόν, ὅτι <ἔτι> ἐξομολογήσομαι αὐτῷ*

Several comments should be made with respect to this reading. At the outset, there are some textual matters that need dealing with. In the Syriac text, ܘܡܣܠܬܝ (= *et contemnis*) is apparently the result of metathesis. It should undoubtedly read ܘܡܣܬܠܝ as in the α′ reading of verse 6(5) of this same Psalm (cf. Field). Likewise the dittograph, ܕܐܘܕܐ ܕܐܘܕܐ (*g* has ܕܐܘܕܐܘܕܐ), should be corrected to ܕܐܘܕܐ. The Syriac text is shorter than that of the MT, lacking equivalents for מה 2° and עוד (cf. verse 6[5]). However, the presence of both Hebrew words is uncontested in *BHS*. Thus, given Aquila's slavishly literal method of translation, one presumes that his version had corresponding equivalents—i. e. the two words in angular brackets in the retroverted section.

The parallel α′ reading of verse 6(5), part of which is attested only in Syriac and which Field therefore retroverts into Greek, is helpful in the retranslation of the reading in verse 12(11). Field's choice of *ὀχλάζεις* as the equivalent for תהמי is undoubtedly correct.[31] However, it appears as though improvements can be made on the *ἀνάμεινον-αὐτῷ* section. Here Field adopts, except for one word, a reading attributed to α′ which he finds in Flaminius Nobilius' annotations to the Latin version of the Sixtine edition of the LXX.[32] This reading is almost identical to the corresponding σ′ reading attested by Eusebius and SyrPss. Indeed, one suspects that if, in fact, it is an α′ reading, it has been subjected to scribal modification under the influence of σ′. In the first place, nowhere else in the extant Aquilanic corpus does ἀναμένω appear as the equivalent for the Hiph'il of יחל. However, καραδοκέω is the root used in Ps. 129:6 (Field and Reider: verse 5).[33] Secondly, the preferred equivalent for the Hiph'il of ידה in the Psalter of α′ is ἐξομολογέομαι: Ps. 27:7, 29:5(4), 10(9), 13(12), 31:5, 34:18, 44:18(17), 78:13, 91:2(1), 98:3.[34] Only in Prov. 28:13 is ὁμολογέω, the equivalent which Field adopts in Ps. 41:6(5), thus employed.[35]

79:12(11) p. 232, n. 16

תשלח קצירה עד־ים MT

ἐξέτεινεν τὰ κλήματα αὐτῆς ἕως θαλάσσης LXX

ܠܝܡܐ ܥܕܡܐ (uid.) ܢܣܪܗ ܢܫܕܪ ℓ. *f* ≈ α′ ἀποστελεῖ θερισμὸν αὐτῆς *ἕως θαλάσσης*

There is no ܢܣܪܐ listing in *A Compendious Syriac Dictionary*, although perhaps a nominal derivative of ܢܨܪ (= "to shoot, sprout, bud") like ܢܨܪܐ (= "shooting, budding, sprouting") is intended here.[36] Such a term would correspond to קציר root II (= "bough[s], branch[es]") in *BDB*. Yet θερισμός, which is attested in Field's witnesses as the equivalent for קציר in this passage, reflects קציר root I (= "harvesting, harvest"). In that light, one wonders whether ܢܣܪܗ (or what looks like it) is not a corruption of ܚܨܕܗ (= "its reaping/ harvest"), which would correspond exactly to θερισμὸν αὐτῆς.

105:33 p. 263, n. 18

ויבשׁא MT

καὶ διέστειλεν LXX

ܘܦܠܓ ≮ *j* = α′ καὶ διέκρινεν

E. CONCLUSION

This portion of the current study has been concerned with the presentation of those marginal hexaplaric readings in SyrPss which are not already recorded in Field. It should be pointed out that a number of the supplementary and variant readings in lists

B and C are lexically identical, or nearly so, to SyrPss^{txt} and/or the Peshitta. In such cases, influence from those sources is a possibility. Thus, special attention should be given to the following readings in list B: 8:1(inscr.), 35:1(inscr.), 35:8(7), 40:14(13), 61:1(inscr.). The same is true of these entries in list C: 18:1(inscr.), 21:1(inscr.),[37] 40:1(inscr.), 49:5,[38] 56:1(inscr.), 63:1(inscr.), 67:32(31), 83:1(inscr.), 105:7.

Although *Origenis Hexaplorum quae supersunt* is still the standard work on the Hexapla, the discovery of new sources of non-LXX readings since the time of its publication (1875) has meant that Field's work has had to be updated periodically. This portion of the present study is intended as a supplement to Field's "Psalmi" segment.

NOTES

INTRODUCTION

[1]The Peshitta Psalter also gives evidence of some LXX influence (see the apparatus in *BHS*). See also M. P. Weitzman, "The Origin of the Peshitta Psalter," *Interpreting the Hebrew Bible: Essays in Honour of E. I. J. Rosenthal*, J. A. Emerton and S. C. Reif, eds. (Cambridge: University Press, 1982), pp. 283–4.

[2]My designation for the Psalter of this Ms is *a*. Besides the Psalter, this Ms contains the Syrohexapla of Job, Proverbs, Ecclesiastes, Song of Songs, Wisdom of Solomon, Sirach, the Minor Prophets, Jeremiah, Baruch, Lamentations, the Epistle of Jeremiah, Daniel, Susanna, Bel and the Dragon, Ezekiel, and Isaiah.

[3]*Septuaginta*, vol. 10: *Psalmi cum Odis* (Göttingen: Vandenhoeck & Ruprecht, 1931), pp. 18–19.

[4]C. Bugati's unfinished edition of the Ambrosian Psalter was brought to press, "though apparently not very carefully," by P. Cighera as *Psalmi secundum editionem LXX interpretum...ex codice Syro-Estranghelo Bibliothecae Ambrosianae* (Milan: n. p., 1820) (see W. Baars, *New Syro-Hexaplaric Texts* [Leiden: E. J. Brill, 1968], p. 6). It was rendered obsolete by A. Ceriani's facsimile edition of the whole Ms: *Codex Syro-Hexaplaris Ambrosianus photolithographice editus*, Monumenta sacra et profana, vol. 7 (Milan: Typis et impensis Bibliothecae Ambrosianae, 1874). Ceriani's edition is the one used in this study. The fragmentary Ms *k* (see note 6) was published by N. Pigulewskaya in "Греко-сиро-арабская рукописб IX B.," Палестинский Сборник I (63) (1954), pp. 59–90.

[5]My designations for these Mss appear in parentheses: Br. Mus., Add. 14,434, f. 1–79 (*b*); Br. Mus., Add. 14,434, f. 80–128 (*c*); Br. Mus., Add. 17,257, f. 84–94 (*d*); Paris, Nat. Libr., Syr. 9 (*j*).

[6]The continuous Mss are: Moscow, Publičnaja Biblioteka S.S.S.R. im. V. I. Lenina, Gr. 432 (*k*); Baghdad, Libr. of the Chald. Patr., 1112 (*h* and h_1); Cambridge, Univ. Libr., Orient. 929 (*e*). For the edition offered in this study, I have also collated two non-continuous texts: Baghdad, Libr. of the Chald. Patr., 211 (*f*); Vat. Libr., Borg. sir. 113, f. 1–135 (*g*)—*g* is a copy of *f*. Two other Mss mentioned by A. Vööbus (*Discoveries of Very Important Manuscript Sources for the Syro-Hexapla*, Papers of the Estonian Theological Society in Exile 20 [Stockholm: ETSE, 1970], pp. 32–3, 37–40) are not available to me: Diyarbakir Mār Ja'qōb 1/13 (which contains a Psalter commentary) and Mār Mattai 153 (a Peshitta Psalter with a catena commentary and an apparatus consisting of "Hexaplaric readings" and readings

of "the Syro-Hexaplaric text" in the margin [Vööbus, *ibid.*, p. 38]).

[7]SyrPs = *a*, *b*, *c*, *d*, *e*, *f*, *g*, h_1; $SyrPs^a$ = the initial sections of *h* (1:5–27:6 where extant) and *j* (1:1–27:6); $SyrPs^b$ = 27:7–146:8 where extant in *h*, 27:7–151:7 in *j*, and *k*.

[8]The texts of Aquila, Symmachus, and Theodotion were found in columns three, four, and six, respectively, of the Hexapla.

[9]*S.-St.* 2, pp. 124–8.

[10]*Psalmi cum Odis*, pp. 18–19.

[11]*S.-St.* 2, pp. 122–4; *Psalmi cum Odis*, pp. 52, 66–7.

[12]Rahlfs, *Psalmi cum Odis*, p. 61; See Rahlfs, *Verzeichnis der griechischen Handschriften des Alten Testaments*, Mitteilungen des Septuaginta-Unternehmens 2 (Berlin: Weidmannsche Buchhandlung, 1914).

[13]Rahlfs, *Psalmi cum Odis*, pp. 60–2.

[14]This is an outgrowth of my participation as a Research Assistant in The Byzantine Psalter Project directed by Professor Albert Pietersma of the University of Toronto.

[15]Namely, Mss *a*, *b*, *c*, *f*, and *g*, the copy of *f*. Occasional marginal hexaplaric readings occur in Mss *e*, h_1, and *j*.

[16]2 vols. (Oxford: Clarendon Press, 1875); "Psalmi," vol. 2.

CHAPTER I

[1]See Baars, *New Syro-Hexaplaric Texts*, pp. 2–7.

[2]As indicated in a note of a later hand on folio 193b of the Ms.

[3]*Codex Syro-Hexaplaris Ambrosianus photolithographice editus*, Monumenta sacra et profana, vol. 7 (Milan: Typis et impensis Bibliothecae Ambrosianae, 1874). Ceriani also recorded variants from Mss *b* (= B), *c* (= C), *d* (= E), and *j* (= D) in his accompanying "Notae," pp. 10–37.

[4]Although 16:5 [illegible] is partially cut off, and 17:7(6) [illegible] is totally missing. Where the verse numbering of Rahlfs' Greek edition and Ceriani's Syriac edition differs, Rahlfs' numbering appears first and Ceriani's follows in parentheses.

[5]Antwerp: Ex officina Christophori Plantini, 1572. This is the Syriac lexicon contained in volumes 7 or 8 of the so-called Antwerp Polyglot or Biblia Regia (1569 [rē verā:] 1571-3) (see Baars, *New Syro-Hexaplaric Texts*, p. 3, n. 1).

[6]This was first published in the Amsterdam edition of the Critici Sacri (1698 ff.) (see Baars, *ibid.*, p. 3, n. 2).

[7]*Josuae imperatoris historia illustrata atque explicata* (Antwerp: n. p., 1574). Biblical quotations and notes from Masius' *Syrorum Peculium* and his Deuteronomy and Joshua studies have been collected in P. de Lagarde's *Bibliothecae Syriacae...quae ad philologiam sacram pertinent* (Göttingen: Prostant in aedibus Dieterichianis Luederi Horstmann, 1892), pp. 19-32[i], 121-60.

[8]See Baars, *New Syro-Hexaplaric Texts*, p. 4; Lagarde, *Bibliothecae Syriacae*, p. 32[h].

[9]S. Jellicoe, *The Septuagint and Modern Study* (Oxford: Oxford University Press, 1968; Ann Arbor: Eisenbrauns, 1978 [Repr.]), p. 125.

[10]One folio before the current folio 1 is missing, although Ceriani has been able to supplement part of what was lost from *b*, folios 1a-2a in the "Notae" accompanying his photolithographic edition of *a* (pp. 3-4). See also Baars, *New Syro-Hexaplaric Texts*, p. 5, n. 2 regarding additional source material for this introduction.

[11]Field also records variants from *b* and *c*. For corrections of, and supplements to, Field, see the appendix which follows this study.

[12]See W. Wright, *Catalogue of Syriac Manuscripts in the British Museum*, 3 vols. (London: British Museum, 1870-2), vol. 1, pp. 35-6 and vol. 3, p. xiii; Baars, *New Syro-Hexaplaric Texts*, p. 10.

[13]Wright, *Catalogue*, vol. 1, p. 36.

[14]Wright, *Catalogue*, vol. 1, pp. 36-7 and vol. 3, p. xiii; Baars, *New Syro-Hexaplaric Texts*, pp. 10, 15-16.

[15]E. g. verse 55: ܟܠܗ ܡܙܡܘܪܐ ܕܡܘܫܐ ܘܡܠܟܘܬܐ ܕܡܠܟ. Note that verses 54 and 55 are transposed in this Ms.

[16]Folio 128b.

[17]Wright, *Catalogue*, vol. 1, p. 37 and vol. 3, pp. xiii-xv; Baars, *New Syro-Hexaplaric Texts*, p. 10.

[18]Typically it has just ܡܙܡܘܪܐ with the Psalm number, and the number of ܦ̈ܬܓܡܐ or στίχοι.

[19]A. Scher, "Notice sur les manuscrits syriaques conservés dans la Bibliothèque du patriarcat chaldéen de Mossoul," *Revue des bibliothèques* 17 (1907), p. 229. See also The Peshitta Institute, ed., *List of Old Testament Peshitta Manuscripts*, Preliminary Issue (Leiden: E. J. Brill, 1961), p. 31; Baars, *New Syro-Hexaplaric Texts*, pp. 12-13, 16, 29; Vööbus, *Discoveries*, pp. 27-31.

[20]Folio 158a.

[21]Given the siglum 12t3 in *List*, p. 31.

[22]The interlinear method is explained on folio 8b prior to the beginning of the Psalter text.

[23]The same applies to *g*, the copy of *f*. See the description of *g* below.

[24]Psalm 151, however, has no such appended remarks.

[25]*A Compendious Syriac Dictionary*, s. v. "ܬܐܘܠܘܓܘܣ;" *The Oxford Dictionary of the Christian Church*, 2nd ed., s. v. "Gregory of Nazianzus, St."

[26]This actually includes both the Song of Moses (verses 1-19) and the Song of Miriam (verses 20-1), the latter being largely a repetition of the words of Moses' song in verse 1.

[27]*Oxford Dictionary*, s. v. "Nicaea, First Council of (325)," "Nicene Creed, The."

[28]*List*, p. 41; Baars, *New Syro-Hexaplaric Texts*, pp. 13, 16; A. Scher, "Notice sur les manuscrits syriaques du Musée Borgia aujourd'hui à la Bibliothèque vaticane," *Journal asiatique*, 10th series, vol. 13 (1909), pp. 272-3; Vööbus, *Discoveries*, p. 31.

[29]Given the siglum 19<12t6 in *List*, p. 41.

[30]The local photographer in either Mosul or Baghdad whom the Peshitta Institute of Leiden contracted to make microfilm copies of both *f* and h/h_1 (a description of the latter appears below) did not do first rate work.

[31]E. G. Browne, *A Supplementary Hand-List of the Muḥammadan Manuscripts...Preserved in the Libraries of the University and Colleges of Cambridge* (Cambridge: University Press, 1922), p. 195; Baars, *New Syro-Hexaplaric Texts*, pp. 13, 16; S. Brock, "A Fourteenth-Century Polyglot Psalter," *Studies in Philology in Honour of Ronald James Williams*, G. E. Kadish and G. E. Freeman, eds. (Toronto: SSEA Publications, 1982), pp. 1-15.

[32]Brock ("Polyglot Psalter," p. 7) suggests that *e* may have originated in the Syrian monastery of the Nitrian Desert (Desert of Sketis) in Egypt, Dair as-Suryan, which produced Mss *abcd*. He notes that a comment in the margin of *a* on the term ܡܘܢܝܘܣ = μονιός in Ps. 79:14(13) (MT 80:14) is reproduced in *e*, and postulates that the compiler of *e* could have used *a* as one of his sources. However, it should be pointed out that this comment is also found in *f*, which was written in Maragāh, and in its copy, *g*, which was written in Barṭellī.

[33]In marginal notes to the Syriac column, the Hebrew text is sometimes quoted in Hebrew characters and/or transliteration (e. g. folio 109a on 89[90]:2-3 and the אֵל/אֱל problem). Transliterated Hebrew is quite common in interlinear glosses in the Syriac column. Brock remarks that "in all probability we have the autograph of the compiler of this remarkable work of scholarship." ("Polyglot Psalter," p. 4).

[34]E. g. folio 155a; i. e. the Syrian Orthodox (see Brock, *ibid.*, p. 4).

[35]See Brock, *ibid.*, pp. 2-3.

[36]Even *Kᵉthîbh-Qᵉrê* readings are indicated (e. g. 66:7, 74:11, 102:24; see *BHS* for the readings in question). I have compared e^h with *BHS* in a number of probes and found that, apart from some orthographic differences (such as *plēnē* spelling), it has only occasional variants: e. g. 41:5 רפאה נפשי] רפה את נפשי e^h. (References are listed according to Hebrew numeration).

[37]The glosses are in small Nestorian script. The divine names are commonly transliterated (e. g. יהוה, אדני, אלהים, אל) although they are by no means the only Hebrew words so rendered.

[38]E. g. Psalm 118(119).

[39]See note 33; see also Brock, "Polyglot Psalter," pp. 6-9, 11.

[40]A. Scher, "Notice sur les manuscrits syriaques et arabes conservés à l'archevêché chaldéen de Diarbékir," *Journal asiatique*, 10th series, vol. 10 (1907), p. 332. See also Baars, *New Syro-Hexaplaric Texts*, pp. 12, 16; Vööbus, *Discoveries*, pp. 31-2.

[41]According to Baars, *New Syro-Hexaplaric Texts*, p. 12. Vööbus, *Discoveries*, p. 31, n. 2 claims there are 141 folios, but then says the end of the codex is folio 143a (p. 31, n. 7). However, in the microfilm copy which I received from the Peshitta Institute, folios 129b ff. are missing.

[42]Note that 83:6(5)-9(8) is omitted (parablepsis on ܕܡܣܩܬܐ [*pro* ܕܡܣܩܬܗ]).

[43]H. Zotenberg, *Manuscrits orientaux. Catalogues des manuscrits syriaques et sabéens (mandaïtes) de la Bibliothèque nationale* (Paris: Imprimerie nationale, 1874) pp. 2-3; *List*, p. 36; Baars, *New Syro-Hexaplaric Texts*, pp. 10-11.

[44]Ms *j* even has the same omission in 83:6(5)-9(8) [cf. note 42].

[45]Given the siglum 13a1 in *List*, p. 36.

[46]Rahlfs, *Verzeichnis*, p. 141. See also Baars, *New Syro-Hexaplaric Texts*, p. 12.

[47]Given the number 1102 in Rahlfs, *Verzeichnis*, p. 141.

[48]"Греко-сиро-арабская рукописб IX В.," Палестинский Сборник I (63) (1954), pp. 59-90. Mistakes in the transcription of the Syriac (other than those involving only diacritical points and punctuation) include the following (transcription appears first, actual reading follows):

70:12 ܐܘܪ̈ܚܟ] ܐܘܪܚܟ (cf. Pesh)
70:15 ܣܦܪܘܬܐ] ܣܦܕܘܬܐ
73:8 ܥܐܕ̈ܐ] ܥܕܘܬܐ
73:9 ܢܒܝܐ] ܢܒܐ
73:11 ܥܘܒܐ ܕܝܠܟ ܠܓܡܪ.] ܥܘܒܐ ܕܝܠܟ ܠܓܡܪ
73:13 ܒܥܘܙܐ] ܥܘܙܐ
77:28 ܡܫܪܝܬܗ] ܘܡܫܪܝܬܗ
77:30 ܒܦܘܡܐ ܕܝܠܗܘܢ] ܒܦܘܡܐ ܕܝܠܗܘܢ
77:31 ܒܦ̈ܛܝܡܐ] ܒܫܡܝܢܐ
77:31 ܕܐܝܣܪܐܝܠ] ܕܐܝܣܪܐܠ
77:32 ܒܟܠܗܝܢ] ܒܟܘܠܗܝܢ
77:33 ܝܘܡ̈ܬܐ ܕܝܠܗܘܢ.] ܝܘܡܬܐ ܕܝܠܗܘܢ.
77:33 ܘܫܢ̈ܝܐ ܕܝܠܗܘܢ.] ܘܫܢܝܐ ܕܝܠܗܘܢ
77:34 ܒܥܝܢ ܗܘܘ] ܒܥܝܢ ܗܘܐ
77:35 ܦܪܘܩܐ ܕܝܠܗܘܢ ܐܝܬܘܗܝ̱.] ܦܪܘܩܐ ܕܝܠܗܘܢ ܐܝܬܘܗܝ.
79:10(9) ܫܪ̈ܫܝܗ] ܫܪܫܝܗ

The following transcription errors *vis-à-vis* the Greek column should be corrected:

73:8 Εἶπας] Εἶπαν
77:28 αὐτῶν 1°] ἀυτῶν (sic)
77:28 των σκηνομάτῶν] τῶν σκηνωμάτων
77:28 αὐτῶν 2°] ἀυτῶν (sic)
77:31 Κκὶ] Καὶ
77:34 ἀπέκτεινεν] ἀπέκτεννεν
79:9(8) καταφύτευσας] κατεφύτευσας
79:10(9) καταφύτευσας] κατεφύτευσας

79:16(15) ἑαυτῷ· (ἑ languet)] ἑαυτῷ·

[49]See Rahlfs, *Psalmi cum Odis*, p. 70. The following is a collation list which incorporates the evidence of the Greek text of *k* (1102). It will be noted that this list also includes evidence from Mss 2110 and 2149. For the present study, I have collated the preceding three witnesses, as well as 2150, in order to supplement Rahlfs' edition. Ms 2110 has been published by R. Kasser and M. Testuz, *Papyrus Bodmer XXIV* (Cologny-Geneva: Bibliotheca Bodmeriana, 1967), while 2149 and 2150 have been published by A. Pietersma, *Two Manuscripts of the Greek Psalter*, Analecta Biblica 77 (Rome: Biblical Institute Press, 1978). With regard to the Syriac evidence, notice that SyrPs and SyrPs^a/SyrPs^b witnesses are grouped separately:

70:7 βοηθός B″-2042 La Ga] + μου Sa-2110 R *L′ abcef hjk* 1102 55 = MT

70:9 ἀπορρίψῃς] αποριψης 1102 2110

70:9 γήρους B R *L*^b(sil)He*S^c 1219′] γηρως S *L*^a′ 1102 2110

70:9 ἐγκαταλίπῃς] εγκαταλειπης 1102

70:11 ἐγκατέλιπεν] εγκατελειπεν 1102

70:12 ὁ θεός 1° B′ La^G(uid.) GaHi = MT] + μου Bo Sa-2110 R′ *L′*Su *abcef hjk* 1102 1219′; *domine deus meus* Aug

70:13 ἐκλιπέτωσαν] εκλειπετωσαν 1102

70:13 περιβαλέσθωσαν] περιβαλλεσθωσαν 1102

70:15 ἐξαγγελεῖ B R(-λλ-) 1219′ 2110(-λλ-)] αν- S *L′* 1102

73:5 εἴσοδον B′ Sa R″ 55 2149: sim. MT] εξοδον *L′ abe hjk* (-ους pro -ον *f*) 1102, *egressum* Aug, *exitu* Ga; οδον S 2110

73:8 κατακαύσωμεν Grabe et teste H-P codex 39 nunc perditus (cf. MT)] καταπαυσ. mss. (etiam 1102)

73:12 αἰῶνος *saeculum* Ga et Cyp.] -νων *L*^bThtP 1102 2110^uid., -*la* La Uulg

77:28 ἐπέπεσον B R *L*^b(sil)He*S^c 2110] επεσον S 2149(επησων); επεπεσαν 1046 55; επεπεσεν *L*^aThtP 1102 1219, επεσεν *L*^pauThtP

77:29 ἐφάγοσαν B 2149(ηφαγωσαν)] -γον rel. (etiam 1102)

77:30 τῆς βρώσεως αὐτῶν B″ R Ga *ae* 2149 = MT] αυτων > Sa-2110 La *L′ hjk* 1102 1219′

77:31 ἐν τοῖς πίοσιν *O* et θ′ε′ teste Hi = MT] *pingues* GaHiAug^uar; *plurimos* La, τοις πλ(ε)ιο/ωσιν (55 195) 2149, εν (τ.) πλ(ε)ιο/ωσι(ν) rel. (etiam 1102) = *in plurimis* Aug

77:33 ἐξέλιπον] εξελειπον 1102

77:36 ἠπάτησαν Grabe = MT] ηγαπησαν mss. (etiam 1102) (La^G *dixerunt* pro *dilexerunt*)

79:10(9) ἐπλήσθη ἡ γῆ B" Sa-2110 R' He*(uid.) 55] επληρωσε(ν) την γην GaAug *L' ae hjk* 1102 1219 2004 2149; *replesti* (= MT) *terminos terrae* La^G

79:12(11) ποταμοῦ B" Sa-2110 La Ga T *aef hjk* 2004 2149 = MT] -μων R *L'* 1102 A"

79:14(13) σῦς B'] υς R *L'* 1102 A" 2004 2149; ους 2110

79:15(14) ἐπίβλεψον B' R" Ga 55 2004 2149 = MT] pr. και *L' ae hjk* 1102 A' 2110uid.

79:16(15) ἀνθρώπου > Ga(non Uulg) 1102 2004 = MT

79:16(15) σεαυτῷ] εαυτω 1102 2149

CHAPTER III

[1]Rahlfs, *S.-St.* 2, pp. 109-24; cf. *Psalmi cum Odis*, pp. 52-60.

[2]However, this chapter does document some divergences with respect to hexaplaric readings among SyrPs, SyrPs[a], and SyrPs[b].

[3]*S.-St.* 2, pp. 81-2, 124-41; *Psalmi cum Odis*, pp. 46, 59-60.

[4]Jerome does speak of the Gallican Psalter as a translation of the Hexapla (J.-P. Migne, ed., "Epistola...ad Sunniam et Fretelam," *Sancti Eusebii Hieronymi...Opera omnia*, Patrologiae cursus completus...Ser. latina 22 [Petit-Montrouge: Ex typis Migne, 1845], col. 838). Yet he also admits to retaining some Old Latin readings. Note, for example, the following comment made in the course of his discussion of a reading in Ps. 21:24(23):

> Nos emendantes olim Psalterium, ubicumque sensus idem est, veterum Interpretum consuetudinem mutare noluimus, ne nimia novitate lectoris studium terreremus (*ibid.*, col. 843).

Apparently Jerome began with an existing Latin text which he altered on the basis of the Hexapla (see Rahlfs, *Psalmi cum Odis*, pp. 54-5).

It should be noted that the Vulgate Psalter is, in fact, the Gallican Psalter. The Psalter of the Vulgate edition which Rahlfs used, the so-called "Clementine edition" (*Biblia sacra vulgatae editionis Sixti Quinti Pont. Max. iussu recognita atque edita* [Rome: Typographia Apostolica Vaticano, 1592]; see Rahlfs, *Psalmi cum Odis*, p. 19), does not contain Aristarchian signs (Rahlfs, *S.-St.* 2, p. 128). However, the Psalter of the current Vulgate edition (*Biblia sacra iuxta latinam vulgatam versionem*, vol. 10: *Liber Psalmorum* [Rome: Typis Polyglottis Vaticanis, 1953]) does have them. Yet the primary source for signs included in the text of this latter edition is Codex Vatic. Regin. 11 (*ibid.*, pp. VIII, XIV), the same Ms which Rahlfs collated (including the signs) as his primary Gallican Psalter witness. Rahlfs' collations are the source for Gallican Psalter evidence in the present study.

[5]I disregard signs which occur outside the Origenic tradition: e. g. obeli in 2013 (49:6), He (94:4; cf. also 79:19^{1}); asterisks, though with a significance other than that in the Hexapla, in 55 (37:21^{3}); (see Rahlfs, *Psalmi cum Odis*, pp. 32, 59–60).

[6]A. Mai, ed., *Scriptorum veterum nova collectio*, 10 vols. (Rome: Apud Burliaeum, 1825–38), vol. 3, pt. 2, pp. 251–5; see Rahlfs, *S.-St.* 2, p. 133.

[7]See note 6.

[8]See Rahlfs, *S.-St.* 2, pp. 128–33.

[9]*Psalmi cum Odis*, pp. 17, 59. Rahlfs excises "nur die sicher falschen Zeichen" though he does acknowledge that others are probably secondary (p. 59). In the latter category I would include the following:

Asterisks:

22:6 καὶ τὸ κατοικεῖν με *et ut inhabitem* La Ga, cf. MT (ושבתי)] δια τ. κ. μ. U'-2110; *et* sub ※ Ga, *et* > Aug

65:7 τοῦ αἰῶνος, cf. MT (עולם)] *in aeternum* La Ga(sub ※)

69:2(1) fin. B Sa-2110 La^{G}Aug] add. stichum κυριε εις το βοηθησαι μοι σπευσον S'(S θελησον pro σπευσον) R' Ga(sub ※) *L' abcef*^{pars} *hj* 1219': cf. MT Pesh et 39:14(13) [Note: The added stich more exactly translates stich 2 of the MT, and may thus be regarded as a doublet. The Hebrew does not, however, have a third stich as the asterisk suggests.]

87:1(inscr.) αιμαν = MT] pr. ※ Ga (sic); αιθαμ *L*^{a} *a*^{txt}*b*^{txt}*f* *hj* (non TTht *a*^{mg}*b*^{mg}*e*) A 2149(εθαμ): ex 88:1(inscr.); *b* hab. [illegible] inter textum et marginem in manu seriore

96:5 ἀπὸ προσώπου κυρίου 1° = *af*^{pars} *hj* MT] ※ Ga (sic), > *L*^{pau} *e*

Obeli:

9:6(5) καί 2° = MT] ÷ Ga (÷ per errorem)

27:5 αὐτούς ult. = MT] ÷ Ga (sic)

118:120 γάρ, cf. MT (hab. ו)] ÷ Ga; *autem* La^{R}

Dubious or erroneous signs in other sources which attest hexaplaric material include:

Asterisks:

19:4(3) διάψαλμα = MT] sub ※ *c* (sed s. metob.; s. notis *af hj*)

105:7 ἐν τῇ ἐρυθρᾷ θαλάσσῃ *in rubro mari* Aug^{uar}, cf. MT (בים־סוף)] *in rubrum mare* La; *in mare* (Aug *-ri*) *mare rubrum* GaAug, cf. Aug: "duobus uerbis ultimis, quod dictum est *mare rubrum*, stella [= asteriscus] fuerat praenotata, qua significantur quae in Hebraeo sunt et in interpretatione LXX non sunt" [Note: Despite Augustine's testimony, the originality of the asterisk is suspect simply because the MT and the LXX already correspond (and undoubtedly did so in Origen's Greek *Vorlage*) when the whole of stich 3 is compared: וימרו על־ים בים־סוף ≈ καὶ παρεπίκραναν ἀναβαίνοντες (= עֹלִים, cf. *BHS*) ἐν τῇ ἐρυθρᾷ θαλάσσῃ. The longer GaAug reading (*et irritauerunt ascendentes in mare* [Aug *-ri*], *mare rubrum*) may be the result of an incorporation of both MT and LXX interpretations of the letters עלים; it does not, however, stem from a longer Hebrew reading.]

Obelus:

61:9(8) διάψαλμα post u. 9(8)^{2} tr. et u. 9(8)^{3} cum u. 10(9)^{1} iungit Sa; διαψ. > La^{G}; pro διαψ. hab. GaHi *in aeternum* (hinc codices latinizantes 27 156 188 [cf. 47:10(9)] εις τον αιωνα) = סלה (cf. Targ. לעלמין), sed in epist. ad Sunniam et Fretelam adnotatur *in aeternum* in LXX non adesse, ad quod Hi mire respondet: "ergo *in aeternum* obelus est"

None of the readings listed in the present note are included in the analysis of hexaplaric influence on SyrPss in this chapter.

[10]The Greek edition used is Rahlfs' *Psalmi cum Odis*, the Hebrew edition is *BHS*, and the Peshitta edition is *The Old Testament in Syriac*, pt. 2, fasc. 3: *The Book of Psalms* edited by the Peshitta Institute (Leiden: E. J. Brill, 1980). Rahlfs' text is supplemented with collations from Greek Mss 1102, 2110, 2149, and 2150 (see notes 48 and 49 of chapter one). For other witnesses apart from SyrPss, I have consulted Rahlfs' apparatus. As already indicated, Rahlfs' source for the Gallican Psalter (Ga) is the eighth century Ms Vatic. Regin. 11.

Some of the asterisked readings (64:1[inscr.], 67:13[12], 88:48[47], 91:10[9]) and one mistakenly obelized reading (24:7) constitute original LXX. However, judging from the sources which omit them, these readings may well have been lacking in Origen's Greek *Vorlage*.

[11]Augustine also asserts that the GaAug reading of *mare rubrum* in 105:7 is asterisked, but see note 9.

[12]Some of these twenty-six plusses are not, however, attested in some SyrPss Mss:

7:10(9) *et* > *a*^{txt} *hj*

67:13(12) τοῦ ἀγαπητοῦ 2° > *e*

88:3(2) *in eis* > *ab hj*

88:48(47) πάντας > *abe h* [Note: *abef h* add *omnium* after τοὺς υἱούς.]

115:4(116:13) (5[14]) εναντιον παντος του λαου αυτου > *a hj* [Note: These Mss do, however, attest τας ευχας μου τω κυριω αποδωσω, the first part of the addition.]

146:1 πρεπει > $a^{txt}b^{txt}$ *h* [Note: In *j*, πρεπει is attested instead of ἡδυνθείη in the text, and there is no addition in either text or margin.]

[13]Ms *e* spuriously marks this addition ÷ܘܩܕܡ.

[14]Nevertheless, judging from the witnesses which omit them, these readings may well have been lacking in Origen's Greek *Vorlage*.

[15]It should be mentioned that e^g, like the *L* family of which it is a part, has this addition (as does e^h: note that this Hebrew text has כל for the MT's -לכל). In the Syriac column of *e*, the *L* tradition is most likely being followed here, though neither the Peshitta nor the Hebrew will have been without influence.

[16]Rahlfs does not record H-P "*L*" variants with support from fewer than two Mss (*Psalmi cum Odis*, pp. 6, 62).

[17]See Rahlfs, *Psalmi cum Odis*, pp. 66-7.

[18]See Brock, "Polyglot Psalter," pp. 3-4.

[19]Cases in which Uulg agrees with SyrPss against Ga on non-asterisked additions are not included here, but are grouped with those involving non-asterisked additions found in SyrPss but not Ga. It cannot automatically be assumed that these readings of Uulg which happen to agree with the MT were included by Jerome in the Gallican Psalter. They may well have been introduced subsequent to the eighth century, the date of the Ga Ms which Rahlfs uses (see *Psalmi cum Odis*, p. 57). Thus, wherever SyrPss and Ga are compared in this chapter, Uulg readings which agree with SyrPss against Ga are included in lists of SyrPss readings not attested by Ga.

Note that *hj* do not attest the addition of μου in 21:17(16). In 97:8, aef^{pars} *hj* have a longer addition than that of Ga. Those extra words (ὅτι ἔρχεται) undoubtedly reflect the influence of the parallel in 95:13.

[20]The variety of readings in this passage is indicative of the problems in determining what is original LXX. The most difficult reading is και οὐ (και οὖ [ܘܐܝܟܐ] is an exegetical modification which can only have stemmed from the Greek), since the context of verse 28 (the sending of the plague of darkness) suggests that the subject of the plural verb, παρεπίκραναν, is the enemies of Israel (verse 24), i. e. the Egyptians. If the Egyptians did *not* rebel against the Lord's words, there would appear to be no justification for the

sending of the other plagues described in verses 29 ff. Of the witnesses which are known to have και ου (Rahlfs gives no evidence for the badly mutilated Ms 1219 at this point), three *contra* the MT attest the singular verb, παρεπικρανεν (S Ga 2110). The singular verb solves nothing, however, since its subject would presumably be the land of Ham (verse 27) which is paralleled with Egypt in verse 24. In any case, παρεπίκραναν is clearly original. One is tempted to take και ου as the reading which originally preceded this verb despite the fact that the relatively few witnesses which support it are either hexaplaric or else subject to hexaplaric or other hebraizing influence. It is contextually much easier to envisage the secondary omission of ου than its addition. However, since only these kinds of witnesses support this longer reading, one is forced to conclude that Origen introduced ου *sub asterisco* and that later copyists omitted the Aristarchian signs but retained the reading. Whether ου in 2110 is due to hexaplaric influence or is an independent addition is a moot question, since the possibilities of a pre- or post-Origenian date for this Ms are still being debated (see A. Pietersma, "The Edited Text of *P. Bodmer XXIV*," *Bulletin of the American Society of Papyrologists* 17 [1980], pp. 67-8).

What is not hexaplaric in 2110 (or at least does not agree with either the MT or α′ σ′ θ′ ε′ ϛ′: see Field) though it is also attested by Ga and S (as well as 1219) is the already-discussed singular verb, παρεπικρανεν, which follows ου. This rather early modification must have been triggered by the presence of two other third singular aorists in verse 28 (ἐξαπέστειλεν and ἐσκότασεν). However, the verb variant sheds no light on the question as to whether or not hexaplaric influence precipitated the addition of ου in 2110, since each of these two variants had an ultimately different origin (i. e. ου stems from the Hebrew whereas the singular verb does not).

As for the οτι variant of *L*, A, and Psalt. Rom., it would appear to be an *ad sensum* modification of the lemma.

[21]A. Pietersma suggests that τω δαυιδ should be regarded as original LXX ("David in the Greek Psalms," *VT* 30 [1980], p. 225). In arguing for the secondary omission of τω δαυιδ, he observes that the evidence both for and against the addition is relatively evenly divided and states that "none of the other 'Songs of Ascent' (cxix-cxxxiii) is connected with David" (p. 217, n. 11). However, τῷ δαυίδ does occur in the titles of Psalms 130 and 132 in agreement with the MT, and while both times it is contested, it appears to be original in both contexts. Since the evidence against τω δαυιδ in 121:1(inscr.) is perhaps qualitatively, but certainly quantitatively, better than that for it, and in view of the fact that two other Songs of Ascent are associated with David in the LXX Psalter, one would hesitate to rule out the possibility that here, as in Psalm 123, the Davidic connection is a hexaplaric addition and not original.

[22]Some of these twenty-eight plusses are not, however, attested in some SyrPss Mss:

21:2(1) μου > *hj*

59:2(insc.) τὴν φάραγγα pro τον εδωμ εν τη φαραγγι in *abf hj*

67:9(8) θεου > *abcf hj*

71:19 και > *abcef*

72:2 μου > *hj*

88:53(52) και > *abef*

124:5 αυτους > *af hj*

148:1(inscr.) αλληλουια > *f*

[23]This addition is not attested in *e*^{g}, but it does equal *e*^{h} (and the MT). Thus, it is also possible that the addition was introduced by the *e* scribe because of Hebrew influence.

[24]See note 23.

[25]Ms 262, like Uulg, adds αλληλουια to Ps. 147 fin.

[26]"Lucians Rezension der Königsbücher," *S.-St.* 3, pp. 171-4.

[27]Mss *abef hj* all have the ܒ preposition, but the underlying Greek could have been either the lemma or the variant.

[28]I exclude, of course, the obeli of *e*, except where such coincide with obeli in other SyrPss Mss. Ms *e* usually obelizes each word of a longer reading rather than marking the onset of such a reading with an obelus and the conclusion with a metobelus. The only readings among those which other SyrPss Mss obelize, in which *e* exhibits the obelus-metobelus pattern, are 37:1(inscr.) and 110:1(inscr.). Although *e* does employ the obelus-metobelus pattern elsewhere, this configuration is no more reliable an indicator of original hexaplaric markings than is the single obelus: e. g. 41:9(8) παρ' ἐμοί = MT Pesh] ÷ܠܘܬܝ ⸆ܠܘܬܝ *e*, ܠܘܬܝ .ܠܘܬܝ *abcf hj* [Note: Here the obelization in *e* can only signify a longer reading in SyrPss, since both the MT and the LXX (as well as *e*^{h} and *e*^{g}) agree on attesting just one παρ' ἐμοί.]

Hereafter, I consistently use ÷ for the obelus, though SyrPss Mss use both ÷ and ⸚ .

[29]Curiously, Barhebraeus attributes this reading to Symmachus (P. de Lagarde, כתבא דמזמורא מן כתבא דאוצר ארזא, *Praetermissorum libri duo* [Göttingen: Sumptibus editoris in officina academica Dieterichiana, 1879], p. 156). The only σ′ source referred to in Field is SyrPss, and *a*^{mg}*c*^{mg}*f*^{mg} do not include these words in the σ′ reading they attest. See Field on 23:1(inscr.).

[30]In *aef*, the first person suffix is attached directly to the noun (ܕܚܘܠܝ). Thus, it is because of the constraints of Syriac that at least *a* includes too much under the obelus.

[31]I do not here include readings whose obeli are apparently secondary: see note 9 for 9:6(5) καί 2°, 27:5 αὐτούς ult., and 118:120 γάρ. Two passages in which the obelus was written instead of the asterisk (17:13[12] αυτου [post νεφέλαι] and 24:7 σύ) have been discussed earlier in this chapter. A list of readings in which the asterisk has displaced the obelus follows the present list. Readings which clearly do not constitute original LXX (cf. 13:3$^{3-10}$, 65:1[inscr.], and 134:17$^{2-5}$) appear nonetheless to have been part of Origen's Greek *Vorlage* which, when his Hebrew text was shorter, he dutifully obelized.

There are a handful of obeli attested in hexaplaric witnesses when neither Ga nor SyrPss does so:

28:1 ἐνέγκατε 1°-θεοῦ] ÷ Orig. (cf. Field; obelus deest in Ga; ενεγκατε 1°-θεου et ενεγκατε 2°-κριων eadem uerba הבו ליהוה בני אלים reddunt), Hi in "Psalt. iuxta Hebraeos" deleuit; 1098 hab. in textu ενεγκατε τω יהוה υιους κριων et add. post יהוה in marg. υιοι θ̂ῦ ενεγκατε τω κ̂ῶ (eodem teste uerterunt α'σ' ενεγκατε τω יהוה υιους κριων, θ' ενεγκατε τω יהוה υιους ισχυρων)

44:10(9) περιβεβλημένη πεποικιλμένη] ÷ Euseb. (cf. Field), > Cyp.$^{uid.}$ = MT

66:2(1) ἡμᾶς ult. B' Sa-2110 Aug = MT] + και ελεησαι ημας Bo R$^{s''}$ Ga *L' abcef hj* 55: ex Num. 6:25, teste Euseb. obelo notatum (cf. Field)

131:4^{3}] ÷ *O* (sic εν τω οκτασελιδω, stichus deerat εν τω τετρασελιδω, cf. Field), > MT

[32]A case could be made for the originality of the shorter reading in 18:6(5) as well, since αὐτοῦ ult. could be a secondary addition inspired by the parallel αὐτοῦ in the first stich and, indeed, by a total of four others in verses 5(4) and 7(6). However, the strength of the support for αὐτοῦ ult. in verse 6(5) (B'' U'-2110 A'' GaHi[sub ÷]) coupled with the fact that the translator is not averse to making *ad sensum* modifications (e. g. verse 5[4] ἐν τῷ ἡλίῳ ἔθετο τὸ σκήνωμα αὐτοῦ pro לשמש שם-אהל בהם) seems to enhance the likelihood of the longer reading being original.

Similarly, in 67:34(33), it is possible that ψάλατε τῷ θεῷ constitutes a post-translation insertion inspired by the imperative clauses in the preceding verse (ᾄσατε τῷ θεῷ, ψάλατε τῷ κυρίῳ), and that the shorter reading is original. However, once again the support for the longer reading is rather strong (B' Sa 1220 La Su GaHi[sub ÷]). Furthermore, the extended parameters of the 2110 omission (ψάλατε τῷ θεῷ τῷ) makes one suspect that the *Vorlage* of 2110, like its congener, Sa, had the longer reading, but that the eye of the scribe making the hebraizing correction skipped from θεῷ to τῷ 2°. Hexaplaric influence could easily explain the omission of ψάλατε τῷ θεῷ in S R^{s} *L' abce hj* 55. Whether the translator had a *Vorlage* which differed from the MT, or whether the longer reading constitutes his *ad sensum* addition, is a moot question. Given the fact that he does make such modifications from time to time, the latter possibility cannot be ruled out.

[33]The *a* scribe apparently wrote أضنو originally but then corrected it himself to أضنوم and continued with صنا (see Ceriani, "Notae," *Codex Syro-Hexaplaris*, p. 16).

[34]Note that neither SyrPss nor the Peshitta has an equivalent for διάψαλμα.

[35]Rahlfs, *Psalmi cum Odis*, p. 8; *S.-St.* 2, p. 229.

[36]See Pietersma, "David," p. 221.

[37]Pietersma, *Two Manuscripts*, p. 45.

[38]*Ibid.*, pp. 46–7.

[39]*Ibid.*, p. 52.

[40]*Ibid.*, p. 50.

[41]Pietersma argues (*Two Manuscripts*, p. 54) that although the textual evidence, apart from 2110 and 2149, is quite evenly divided, the weight of these two early papyri tips the scales in favour of the originality of the shorter reading. Despite the fact that 2149, like SyrPss, has κύριε but places it after κλῖνον rather than at the end of the verse, Pietersma groups SyrPss with the witnesses which attest κύριε but 2149 with those that omit it. For the sake of consistency, 2149 should be included with the former group. This realignment of that early witness would not, however, appear to negate the likelihood of the originality of the shorter reading.

[42]In the twelve remaining instances, the modifier is always αὐτοῦ: 77:4, 11, 32, 95:3, 104:2, 5, 106:8, 15, 21, 24, 31, 110:4. Only in 77:11 is the modifier contested, and there only by La[R] which omits it *contra* the MT.

[43]In Jn. 2:17, as in B′ of Ps. 68:10(9), the form of the verb is καταφάγεται rather than κατέφαγεν.

[44]Cf. 71:18 ὁ ποιῶν θαυμάσια μόνος where μόνος = MT, and 76:15(14) ὁ ποιῶν θαυμάσια where, *contra* the MT, μονος is added to θαυμάσια in Sa R″ L[pau]′S[c] *a*(non *e*) *hj* 1219, and precedes ὁ in He*(uid.) 55. The addition of μονος in 76:15(14) is most likely due to *ex par.* influence from 71:18.

[45]Some of these forty-one minuses are not attested in some SyrPss Mss:

37:21(20)[3] *acg*[mg†](*f*[mg†] non apparet) *hj*

49:1 *ace*[c] pr m *hj*

73:23 *abf hj*

113:11(115:3) 1° *a j*

113:11(115:3) 2° *aef j*

118:93 *af hj*

118:168 *e*c pr m uid.

138:3 *aef h*

[46]Not only does the MT not support δέ here, but it is not found in either the Hebrew or the Greek of the parallel in 107:14(13) (except for Ms 55—B is not extant). Yet this is the type of particle which the Greek translator was not averse to inserting in the interests of style and clarity. Thus, the many textual witnesses which omit δέ in 59:14(12) apparently reflect the influence of both the Hebrew here and of the parallel in Ps. 107 (the scribe of Ms 55 seems, in Ps. 107, to have added δε under the influence of 59:14[12]).

[47]L. Perkins ("The So-Called 'L' Text of Psalms 72-82," *Bulletin of the International Organization for Septuagint and Cognate Studies* 11 [1978], pp. 54-5) suggests that the shorter reading constitutes original LXX. However, the array of witnesses for the longer reading is, as he himself admits, formidable. His appeal to verse 7(6) where, in a similar list of nations, stich 2 is not introduced by και in agreement with the MT, does not appear to be of sufficient weight to overturn that body of evidence. Moreover, the avoidance of και in verse 7(6) may possibly be a reflection of the fact that the two nations in the first stich are more or less parallel to those in the second (i. e. the tents of the Idumeans and the Ishmaelites, Moab and the Hagarites), whereas the introduction of καί in verse 8(7) may be intended to signal the distinctiveness of the nations in the two stichs (i. e. Gebal, Ammon, and Amalek versus "other tribes" [Philistines] and the inhabitants of Tyre). Furthermore, the Greek translator does introduce conjunctions and other particles in the interests of promoting clarity. Perkins' argument that Lucian (whose recension is ostensibly to be found in the *L* text, and who is supposed to have produced a smooth and unambiguous text) would not have removed the καί in question in verse 8(7) presupposes that *L* in the Psalter = Lucian—something that has not yet been established and which Perkins himself admits may not be true (*ibid.*, pp. 60-1). Moreover, *L* displays clear evidence of hexaplaric influence, a fact which has already been demonstrated in this chapter.

[48]It would seem to be easier to explain the listed variants as modifications of the lemma text than vice versa. This is certainly true of the reading attested by R' *a j* et alii Latini, which is essentially the lemma except that τοῖς οὐρανοῖς has been made singular to conform with τῇ γῇ (the omission of ἄνω in *a j* may be explained either by parablepsis on the part of the Syriac translator or by haplography in his Greek exemplar, i. e. οὐρανῷ ἄνω).

The reading of 2110 is interesting in that, although it is shorter, it retains first τοῖς οὐρανοῖς of the second stich and then (*contra* the MT) ἄνω of the first. Therefore, it too appears to be based on the longer reading which seems to have been abbreviated, presumably due to Hebrew influence.

Nothing of the second stich is represented in the MT. Yet it is clear that at least the phrase καὶ ἐν τῇ γῇ constitutes original LXX, with only 2110, GaHi, and *h* having omitted it in conformity with the Hebrew. It is possible that ἐν τοῖς οὐρανοῖς is a secondary addition, since the "heaven and earth" pairing is a common enough one in the Psalms (and, indeed, throughout the Bible). Furthermore, besides this passage, there are seven others in the Psalter where the οὐρανοί...γῆ sequence is attested: 56:6(5), 12(11), 68:35(34), 88:12(11), 95:11, 107:6(5), 135:5-6. However, there are fifteen instances of the οὐρανός...γῆ sequence: 49:4, 72:9, 25, 78:2, 101:20(19), 102:11, 112:6, 113:23(115:15), 24(16), 120:2, 123:8, 133:3, 134:6, 145:6, 146:8 (γῆ...οὐρανοί is attested three times: 8:2[1], 67:9[8], 101:26[25]; γῆ...οὐρανός is attested twice: 84:12[11], 148:13). Thus, one might expect the first half of 113:11(115:3)[2] to be singular rather than plural if it were a secondary addition. This expectation is heightened when one notes that in the other two Psalter passages where both elements in the sequence are preceded by ἐν (112:6, 134:6), both elements are uncontestedly singular. The reading in 134:6 is particularly significant because it closely parallels the passage under consideration (cf. also 72:25 where the sequence is ἐν τῷ οὐρανῷ...ἐπὶ τῆς γῆς).

That the *Vorlage* of the Greek translator in 113:11(115:3) was longer than the MT, at least with respect to καὶ ἐν τῇ γῇ, should be self-evident. A good case can also be made for a Hebrew antecedent to ἐν τοῖς οὐρανοῖς—a conclusion with which Rahlfs would obviously concur. All shorter readings are therefore attributable to Hebrew influence.

49Although one might argue that διὰ παντός is an *ex par.* addition influenced by verse 117, the differences in the contexts of these two verses make such a connection somewhat tenuous. The evidence for the longer reading is quite good, so the safest option would seem to be to posit a *Vorlage* which contained תמיד (perhaps through dittography of עדתיך as the *BHS* editors suggest, though the suggestion does tend to stretch one's credulity) and to regard the shorter reading as a correction to the MT.

50Although the attestation for the longer reading seems rather sparse whereas the witnesses for the shorter one are numerous, the longer reading would seem to be original. Rahlfs notes a parallel in Deut. 8:15, but differences in both wording and context appear to preclude the possibility of a secondary importation from Deuteronomy. Furthermore, an examination of the textual support for the longer reading in this verse shows that that support is more substantial than it may seem at first, since all extant members of Rahlfs' so-called older textual groups (Lower-Egyptian, Upper-

Egyptian, and Western) except S support it (not extant are B from the Lower-Egyptian and U-2013-2110 from the Upper-Egyptian). S, like the other witnesses supporting the omission, not infrequently contains hexaplaric readings (see Rahlfs, *Psalmi cum Odis*, p. 26). One concludes, therefore, that the Greek translator's *Vorlage* contained a longer text than the MT at this point, a text which was perhaps inspired by Deut. 8:15.

[51] With regard to the omission of τοῦ προσώπου in *e*, it should be noted that, while Peshitta influence is possible, e^g, like *L*, also omits these words—a shorter reading which is corroborated by e^h. Thus, the minus in *e* might be the result of Greek or/and Hebrew influence.

[52] There is, of course, also the possibility of omission due to parablepsis.

[53] Neither e^g (= *L*) nor e^h has verse 21(20)^3. The omission in *e* could, therefore, be due to Greek or/and Hebrew influence.

[54] Note that the other Syriac Mss translate αναβαιη προς σε δια παντος. Thus, the omission in *e* is from the middle, not the end, of the phrase. Neither e^g (= *L*) nor e^h attests πρὸς σέ. Once again, the *e* reading could reflect Greek or/and Hebrew influence.

[55] Ms *e* follows e^g and *L* in attesting καὶ ἐν τῇ γῇ but not ἄνω· ἐν τοῖς οὐρανοῖς. Like the MT, e^h attests neither phrase. Ms *h*, too, omits both.

[56] Neither e^g (= *L*) nor e^h supports the reading of κύριε. The omission in *e* could, therefore, be due to Greek or/and Hebrew influence.

[57] Ms *j* has the reading which in $a^{mg}f^{mg}$ is attributed to σ′, and which Field quite plausibly retroverts as τὴν πορείαν μου καὶ τὴν κοίμησίν μου ἐξιχνίασας.

[58] Some of these twenty-two omissions are not, however, attested in some SyrPss Mss:

2:2	*hj*
17:31(30)	*abe hj*
67:14(13)	*abe hj*
79:18(17)	*ae k*
89:9	e^c
115:1(inscr.)[116:10]	*ae hj*
135:26$^{3.4}$	*a*$f^{mg\dagger}$ *hj*
137:1^2	*a*$e^{mg}f^{mg\dagger}$ *hj*

[59] Ms *f*, essentially a Peshitta Ms, has a non-continuous interlinear SyrPs text, except in the Psalm titles which are not

interlinear and are normally complete. In this passage where the Peshitta, like the MT, does not begin a new Psalm, there is no title. Furthermore, the SyrPs text is not attested in the immediate context of this passage. However, since *f* normally attests titles, one assumes that the reason for this omission is Peshitta influence.

Incidentally, there is an index mark at this point in the text which corresponds to the number 115 in the margin. A note there also states, "Here the Greek numbering agrees with the Peshitta" (ܗܪܟܐ ܡܢܝܢܐ ܝܘܢܝܐ ܫܘܐ ܥܡ ܦܫܝܛܬܐ). This agreement comes about because *f* joins Hebrew Pss. 114 and 115 under the number 114 (the Greek combines the same two under the number 113, though Sa-2110 and Aug divide the Psalm after verse 11 rather than verse 8), and then numbers Hebrew 116 as 115 (the Greek divides this Psalm into 114 [verses 1-9] and 115 [verses 10-19]).

[60]This omission in *e* may also be due to parablepsis, or to influence from *e*^{g} (= *L*) and *e*^{h} which omit stichs 3 and 4.

[61]Like the MT, *e*^{h}(uid.) has no equivalent for stich 2 (there are lacunae in *e*^{h}, but not of sufficient size to allow for stich 2). However, *e*^{g}, like *L* et al., transposes stichs 2 and 3, and *e*^{mg} agrees with this arrangement of verse 1 (in contrast to *f*^{mg†} which does not transpose the stichs). Note that *e*^{txt} creates a doublet on ἀγγέλων with ܡܠܐܟܐ ܐܠܗܐ. In the margin, the source for ܐܠܗܐ is identified as the Hebrew which reads אלהים (much of the word in *e*^{h} is lost in a lacuna). It is certain, therefore, that the *e* compiler consulted the Hebrew at this point. However, no mention is made of the word which corresponds to ἀγγέλων in the Peshitta, i. e. ܡܠܟܐ (only three Peshitta Mss in the Leiden edition have ܡܠܐܟܐ). Thus, while there is a fairly high degree of textual similarity between *e*^{txt} and the Peshitta, the possibility of direct Hebrew influence should not be ruled out.

[62]The textual support for the shorter reading is certainly impressive, and one might well argue that καί is a stylistic addition. However, as Rahlfs indicates, the MT has the conjunction later in stich 3 preceding the final verb (ודמו = κατανύγητε). In view of the fact that the translator at times makes *ad sensum* modifications, it seems just as plausible to suggest that, rather than completely removing the conjunction, he has simply moved it, thus balancing the structure of stichs 2 and 3. Significantly, the Peshitta Psalter, which seems partly dependent on the LXX Psalter, has the conjunction in the same place (see Weitzman, "Peshitta Psalter," p. 284, n. 39). The omission of καί by the majority of LXX witnesses seems, therefore, to have been done in conformity with the Hebrew, although none of these witnesses have then inserted καί before κατανύγητε to agree with the MT.

[63]The 2149 reading could easily be a corruption of the lemma, since κ̂ς̂, the standard abbreviation for κυριος, is very similar to κ̂ε̂, which the scribe writes for κύριε in 78:5, for example. The

nominative form in 79:8(7) could also be a mistake influenced by ο θ̂ς̂ (= ὁ θεός) which follows it (the scribe also writes κ̂ς̂ ο θ̂ς̂ for κύριε ὁ θεός in verse 5[4]).

Although one might argue that κύριε in verse 8(7) is an *ex par.* addition influenced by the identical phrase, κύριε ὁ θεὸς τῶν δυνάμεων, in verses 5(4) and 20(19), the fact that the phrase minus κυριε occurs in verse 15(14) indicates that the translator did not automatically include the Greek equivalent for the divine name whether or not it was found in his *Vorlage*. Thus, it appears that the omission of κύριε in verse 8(7) is a correction to the Hebrew, and that the longer reading attested by the great majority of textual witnesses is original.

[64]The Syriac Mss all attest δυνάμει σου, exhibiting the ܒ preposition in the process. This is the same preposition that is used in translating both ἐν...ἡμέρᾳ and ἐν ψυχῇ μου in this verse, so Rahlfs' grouping of the Syriac witnesses with *L* as opposed to He and La^G seems presumptuous. Admittedly, the Syriac's underlying Greek *could* have lacked the preposition, but that is far from certain.

[65]In 9:37(36), *acf* do not attest the transposition.

[66]It seems easier to explain the listed variants as modifications of the lemma than to regard the lemma as a variation of one of the other readings. Thus, Rahlfs is probably correct in his choice of βασιλεύσει κύριος as original. The underlying Hebrew is apparently יִמְלֹךְ יְהוָה (cf. 145[146]:10) rather than יְהוָה מֶלֶךְ of the MT. Only *L* literally equals the Hebrew, but since Ga is among the witnesses which transpose the lemma, it appears likely that that transposition also reflects the influence of the MT.

[67]Strictly speaking, the variant reading involves the omission of τὴν ψυχήν μου and the addition of με to συνελκύσῃς. However, since the lemma and the variant are semantically equivalent, the variant is grouped with transpositions equalling the Hebrew rather than with omissions and additions, respectively.

[68]Despite the fact that ἐπὶ σοὶ κυριε ἤλπισα is attested by the great majority of witnesses, κυριε is undoubtedly secondary—influenced not only by the Hebrew but also by the parallel in 30:2(1). Support for Rahlfs' lemma is not as sparse as it may at first seem, since the readings of Sa, La^G, and Bo 2110 appear to be modifications of it. The R'Aug reading, on the other hand, is seemingly a variation of the majority reading.

[69]The lemma reading, though once again attested by few witnesses, is undoubtedly original. The simple transposition of the lemma by La^{G}Aug GaHi 2110(Sa?) is a correction to the Hebrew. The reading of *L* et al. seems to be an exegetical expansion of that transposition, whereas 55 combines the word order of the lemma with the relative pronoun of the expanded transposition.

[70]Although there are some differences (primarily with respect to translation equivalents), in the matter of word order La[R]Aug and La[G] should be grouped with lemma witnesses, and Ga and Tert. with those supporting the transposition. The transposed reading is likely a correction to the Hebrew.

[71]Once again, sparse attestation for the lemma opens up the possibility of its being secondary. In Rahlfs' text, ἐγώ is preceded by εἰμί. This is a common enough sequence in the Psalter, occurring in a total of ten passages (including this one) in Rahlfs' edition. In seven instances, it corresponds to אני: 24:16 [tr. R'], 68:30(29) [tr. GaAug 55], 85:1, 87:16(15), 118:94, 125 [tr. Aug *aef hj* 1219], 142:12 [tr. La[G] Ga *L' abe hj* A"]. The remaining three times it is equivalent to אנכי: 49:7, 118:141 [tr. R'Aug *L' aef hj* A'], 140:10 [tr. R"]. In contrast to this, Rahlfs' text has ἐγώ εἰμι nine times. Six times this pronoun-verb sequence renders אנכי: 21:7(6), 38:13(12) [tr. S La[G]], 45:11(10), 80:11(10), 108:22 [tr. R *L' aef hj* A' 2110 et complures Latini], 118:19 [tr. La[G]]. On three other occasions it translates אני: 34:3 [tr. R *L'* A'], 39:18(17), 118:63. Whether or not Rahlfs is correct as to what sequence is original in every instance, the fact that there are uncontested occurrences of both Greek pairings for both Hebrew pronouns suggests that the translator used them interchangeably. He seems, however, to have preferred εἰμὶ ἐγώ for אני, and ἐγώ εἰμι for אנכי.

The εἰμὶ ἐγώ = אני equivalency of the lemma in 142:12 fits the preceding pattern, although the placement of the verb-pronoun pair does not agree with the MT. A similar discrepancy occurs in the lemma of 68:30(29). There, however, Ga transposes both verb and pronoun (though inverting the sequence to pronoun-verb) to the appropriate spot *vis-à-vis* the Hebrew. In 142:12, Ga et al. transpose just the pronoun, although little or nothing would change semantically if the verb were also moved. Thus, with the lemma word order in 142:12 being apparently original, the transposition of ἐγώ by Ga et al. must constitute a correction to the MT. The La[G] reading undoubtedly represents a stylistic modification unrelated to the MT.

[72]The context of some readings is expanded beyond that which pertains to the transposition in order to facilitate comparison between the Peshitta and SyrPss.

[73]Note that the transposition in 18:14(13) is not attested by *hj*. The fact that these Mss follow the Greek word order here despite the rather awkward Syriac which this produces justifies the inclusion of the *ac* transposition in the present discussion. The one in 49:12 is of a similar ilk and thus merits inclusion by analogy, though no Syriac witness follows the Greek word order here.

[74]SyrPss is inconclusive in 31:7, 41:10(9), and 105:9. In 118:149, *ae hj*, like La[G], are neutral *vis-à-vis* the transposition (the evidence of *f* is only partial, and therefore inconclusive).

[75]For the sake of convenience, the designations SyrPs, SyrPs[a], and SyrPs[b] are used even when not all group members are extant.

CHAPTER IV

[1]Rahlfs also groups A, 1219, and 55 together (Mss which often agree with *L*), although he notes that "diese Gruppe noch weniger fest geschlossen ist als andere Gruppen" (*Psalmi cum Odis*, p. 70).

[2]Note that divergences from the LXX by any or all SyrPss Mss are included in this table. Furthermore, attestation of such divergences by half or more extant members of *L* (i. e. the approximately 100 witnesses represented in Rahlfs' edition), LE, UE, or We is regarded as constituting group support.

[3]See F. Wisse, *The Profile Method for the Classification and Evaluation of Manuscript Evidence as Applied to the Continuous Greek Text of the Gospel of Luke*, Studies and Documents 44 (Grand Rapids: Eerdmans, 1982).

[4]See P. R. McReynolds, "The Claremont Profile Method and the Grouping of Byzantine New Testament Manuscripts" (Ph. D. Dissertation, Claremont Graduate School, 1968).

[5]This selection process was carried out by the initiator and director of The Byzantine Psalter Project, Professor Albert Pietersma of the University of Toronto.

[6]The Byzantine Psalter Project is indebted to Mr. Mark Dornfeld, a Ph. D. student at the University of Toronto's Department of Near Eastern Studies, for setting up the computer program to facilitate the profiling of these Mss.

CHAPTER V

[1]See Field.

[2]Examples are given in the analysis which follows.

[3]Folio 161b. See Wright, *Catalogue*, vol. 2, p. 907 (cf. p. 906).

[4]Folio 90a. See Lagarde, *Bibliothecae Syriacae*, p. 256; H. Middeldorpf, ed., *Codex Syriaco-Hexaplaris* (Berlin: Enslin, 1835), p. 66.

[5]In his commentary on the Hexaemeron, cited by J. P. P. Martin (*Introduction à la critique textuelle du Nouveau Testament*, 5 vols. [Paris: Maisonneuve frères et C. Leclerc, 1884-5], vol. 1, p. 101) from Ms Par. syr. 241.

[6]In the *prooemium* to his *Auṣar Rāzē* (*Horreum Mysteriorum*) (M. Sprengling and W. C. Graham, eds., *Barhebraeus' Scholia on the Old Testament*, The University of Chicago Oriental Institute Publications 13 [Chicago: The University of Chicago Press, 1931], pp. 4-5).

[7]Ms Br. Mus. Add. 14,437, folio 122a. See also A. Vööbus, *The Hexapla and the Syro-Hexapla*, Papers of the Estonian Theological Society in Exile 22 (Stockholm: ETSE, 1971), pp. 35-40; G. Zuntz, *The Ancestry of the Harklean New Testament*, The British Academy Supplemental Papers 7 (London: Oxford University Press, 1945), pp. 7-12; M. L. Margolis and A. Marx, *A History of the Jewish People* (New York: Atheneum, 1972), p. 247. Khosrau's forces reached Jerusalem in 614 A. D.

[8]This is the testimony of 'Abdīšō' (Ebedjesu) (J. S. Assemanus, *Bibliotheca Orientalis Clementino-Vaticana*, 3 vols. [Rome: Typis sacrae congregationis de propaganda fide, 1719-28], vol. 3, pt. 1, p. 75).

[9]*A Dictionary of Christian Biography*, s. v. "Thomas (8) Edessenus," by J. Gwynn; Vööbus, *History of the School of Nisibis*, CSCO, Subsidia 26 (Louvain: Secrétariat du CorpusSCO, 1965), pp. 167-8; Vööbus, *The Hexapla*, p. 48.

[10]Assemanus' contention that Simeon "Abbas monasterii Licinii" translated the Greek Psalter into Syriac (*Bibliotheca Orientalis*, vol. 1, p. 612; vol. 2, p. 83) is based on a mistaken reading of the correspondence between Simeon and a certain monk named Barlāhā. What Simeon actually translated was a ܟܬܒܐ "writing, treatise" having to do with the Psalms, which was penned by the fourth century patriarch of Alexandria, Athanasius. The ܟܬܒܐ appears to have been Athanasius' *Letter to Marcellinus* (cf. I. Guidi, "Mosè di Aghel e Simeone Abbate," *Rendiconti della R. Accademia dei Lincei* 4/2 [1886], pp. 547-54).

[11]A Syriac translation of part of the *Glaphyra*, apparently the one made by Mōšē, is preserved in Ms Br. Mus. Add. 14,555. Other fragments are preserved in Cod. Vat. Sir. 107, folios 67a-71b, and Cod. Vat. Sir. 96, folio 164b. These Vatican fragments are published by Guidi, *ibid.*, pp. 404-16, 546-7.

[12]Mōšē's introduction to his translation of the *Glaphyra* comes in his *Letter to Paphnutius*, of which the following is an excerpt (Guidi, "Mosè...e Simeone," p. 404):

ܟܕ ܡܬܦܓܥ ܐܢܫ ܒܡܦܩܢܘܬܐ ܕܚܕܬܐ ܘܕܕܘܝܕ: ܗܝ ܕܦܘܠܘܩܪܦܘܣ ܢܝܚ ܢܦܫܐ ܟܘܪ ܐܦܝܣܩܘܦܐ:
ܥܒܕ ܠܡܒܪܟܐ ܕܒܛܘܒܐ ܡܗܝܡܢܐ ܘܡܠܦܢܐ ܐܟܣܢܝܐ ܕܡܒܘܓ ܣܘܪܝܐܝܬ. ܡܬܕܡܪ
ܒܡܫܘܚܬܐ ܕܐܝܬ ܒܡܦܩܢܘܬܐ ܕܣܘܪܝܝܐ ܡܢ ܟܠܗ ܫܘܝܐ.

> When one encounters the version of the New (Testament) and of David which the chorepiscopus, Polycarp, whose soul is at rest, made in Syriac for 'Aksenāyā of Mabbūg, of blessed memory, the faithful and learned one, one

is amazed at the differences which exist in the Syriac translation from the Greek language.

Beginning with J. Lebon (*Le monophysisme sévérien* [Louvain: J. van Linthout, 1909], p. 145), the consensus of scholarly opinion has been that Philoxenus did not know Greek (e. g. Vööbus, "New Data for the Solution of the Problem concerning the Philoxenian Version," *Spiritus et Veritas*, Festschrift K. Kundzinš, Auseklis, ed. [Eutin: Andr. Ozolins Buchdruckerei, 1953], p. 184; A. de Halleux, *Philoxène de Mabbog: sa vie, ses écrits, sa théologie* [Louvain: Imprimerie orientaliste, 1963], p. 22) despite the fact that he was educated at the Edessene "School of the Persians" where Greek was taught and Greek works were translated into Syriac (see Simeon of Beth-Aršam's *Letter on Nestorianism* in Assemanus, *Bibliotheca Orientalis*, vol. 1, pp. 351-3; see also Vööbus, *School of Nisibis*, pp. 13-24 and D. J. Fox, *The "Matthew-Luke Commentary" of Philoxenus*, SBL Dissertation Series 43 [Missoula: Scholars Press, 1979], pp. 8-10).

[13]De Halleux, *Élī de Qartamīn, Mēmrā sur S. Mār Philoxène de Mabbog*, CSCO, Syr. 101 (Louvain: Secrétariat du CorpusSCO, 1963), p. 5, vv. 130-4. This is corroborated in a document entitled (in translation), "Victory of Mar Akhsnaya, who is Philoxenus, bishop of the town of Mabbūg" (A. Mingana, "New Documents on Philoxenus of Hierapolis, and on the Philoxenian Version of the Bible," *The Expositor*, 8th series, vol. 19 [1920], pp. 150-3).

[14]Apparently Heracleia in Cyrrhestice (*A Dictionary of Christian Biography*, s. v. "Thomas (17) Harklensis," by J. Gwynn; B. M. Metzger, *The Early Versions of the New Testament* [Oxford: Clarendon Press, 1977], pp. 68-9).

[15]Gospels colophon: J. White, ed., *Sacrorum Evangeliorum versio syriaca Philoxeniana* (Oxford: Clarendon Press, 1778), pp. 561-2. [Note: White's edition of the Harklean version (which he calls the Philoxenian) is used in this study for all New Testament books except the Apocalypse (see below) which the edition does not include.]

Acts and Catholic Epistles colophon: J. White, ed., *Actuum Apostolorum et Epistolarum tam Catholicarum quam Paulinarum, versio syriaca Philoxeniana*, vol. 1 (Oxford: Clarendon Press, 1799), pp. 274-5.

Corpus Paulinum colophon: W. Wright and S. A. Cook, *A Catalogue of the Syriac Manuscripts Preserved in the Library of the University of Cambridge*, vol. 1 (Cambridge: University Press, 1901), p. 11.

Apocalypse colophon: A. Vööbus, *The Apocalypse in the Harklean Version*, CSCO, Subsidia 56 (Louvain: Secrétariat du CorpusSCO, 1978), pp. 35*, 52-62. [Note: This facsimile edition of Ms Mardin Orth. 35 is the Apocalypse text used in the present study.]

[16]In the *procemium* to his *Auṣar Rāzē* (*Horreum Mysteriorum*) (Sprengling and Graham, eds., *Barhebraeus' Scholia*, p. 4).

[17]*Epistolae Quatuor, Petri secunda, Johannis secunda et tertia, et Judae, fratris Jacobi una* (Lugduni Batavorum: Ex officina Bonaventurae & Abrahami Elzeviri, 1630). A revised edition of the Four Minor Catholic Epistles in the Philoxenian version was published by J. Gwynn in *Remnants of the Later Syriac Versions of the Bible*, pt. 1 (London: Williams and Norgate, 1909). This revised edition is the one used in the present study, though, for the sake of convenience, the epistles are referred to collectively as the Pococke Epistles.

[18]Published by Gwynn in *The Apocalypse of St. John in a Syriac Version Hitherto Unknown* (Dublin: Hodges, Figgis, and Co. Ltd., 1897). Lebon is very skeptical of the association of the Pococke Epistles and the Crawford Apocalypse with the Philoxenian version ("La version philoxénienne de la Bible," *Revue d'histoire ecclésiastique* 12 [1911; repr. 1967], pp. 415-16, 424-36; cf. de Halleux, *Vie*, p. 118 and Fox, *The "Matthew-Luke Commentary"*, pp. 22-3).

[19]Preserved in Ms Br. Mus. Add. 14,534 and published by de Halleux, *Philoxène de Mabbog: Commentaire du prologue johannique (Ms. Br. Mus. Add. 14,534)*, CSCO, Syr. 165 (Louvain: Secrétariat du CorpusSCO, 1977); see also A. Vööbus, *Early Versions of the New Testament*, Papers of the Estonian Theological Society in Exile 6 (Stockholm: ETSE, 1954), pp. 110-18. Some characteristics result from the effort of the translator to stay close to his Greek *Vorlage*, others are inner-Syriac. Examples of Philoxenian characteristics appear later in the chapter.

[20]This is recognized by most modern scholars, as is indicated by the fact that in *The Greek New Testament* (edited by K. Aland et al.), these books are designated syr^{ph}, which represents Syriac-Philoxenian (3rd ed. [corrected] [Stuttgart: United Bible Societies, 1983], pp. xxxv, lvii).

[21]Lebon, "La version philoxénienne," pp. 413-15; L. Delekat, "Die syrolukianische Übersetzung des Buches Jesaja und das Postulat einer alttestamentlichen Vetus Syra," *ZAW* N. F. 28 (1957), p. 23, n. 11.

[22]See note 12 for the Syriac text.

[23]"La version philoxénienne," p. 435.

[24]Folio 176r. The statement of attribution is:

ܡܢ ܡܫܠܡܢܘܬܐ ܐܚܪܬܐ ܗܝ ܕܐܬܦܫܩܬ ܠܣܘܪܝܐ: ܒܝܘܨܦܢܘܬܐ ܕܩܕܝܫܐ ܦܝܠܘܟܣܝܢܘܣ
ܐܦܝܣܩܘܦܐ ܕܡܒܘܓ܀

> From another tradition which was translated into Syriac by the care of the holy Philoxenus, bishop of Mabbūg.

A comparison of the scholion reading (Sch) with the corresponding portion of the Syrohexaplaric text (Syh) is instructive:

Verse 6(5) ܘܐܬܩܪܝ ܫܡܗ ܕܝܠܗ: ܡܠܐܟܐ ܕܡܠܟܬܐ ܪܒܬܐ. Sch, item praeter ÷ܡܠܐܟܐ↘ Syh
ܕܘܡܪܐ. ܡܠܟܐ. ܐܠܗܐ ܓܢܒܪܐ. ܫܠܝܛ ܥܠ ܟܠ. Sch, nihil Syh
ܪܫܐ ܕܫܠܡܐ. ܐܒܐ ܕܥܠܡܐ ܕܥܬܝܕ. Sch, nihil Syh
ܐܝܬܐ ܓܝܪ ܫܠܡܐ ܥܠ ܪܫܢܐ: ܫܠܡܐ ܘܚܘܠܡܢܐ ܠܗ. Sch, ܫܠܡܐ 2° > Syh

Verse 7(6) ܪܒ ܫܘܠܛܢܐ ܕܝܠܗ. ܘܠܫܠܡܗ ܠܐ ܐܝܬ ܣܘܟܐ܀ Sch
ܪܒܐ ܪܫܢܘܬܐ ܕܝܠܗ. ܘܕܫܠܡܐ ܕܝܠܗ ܠܐ ܐܝܬ ܣܘܟܐ Syh

The corresponding Greek texts for Sch and Syh are:

Verse 6(5) Καὶ καλεῖται τὸ ὄνομα αὐτοῦ, μεγάλης βουλῆς ἄγγελος, Gk-Sch, item praeter ÷ἄγγελος: Gk-Syh
θαυμαστός, σύμβουλος, θεὸς ἰσχυρός, ἐξουσιαστής, Gk-Sch, nihil Gk-Syh
ἄρχων εἰρήνης, πατὴρ τοῦ μέλλοντος αἰῶνος· Gk-Sch, nihil Gk-Syh
ἄξω γὰρ εἰρήνην ἐπὶ τοὺς ἄρχοντας, εἰρήνην καὶ ὑγίειαν αὐτῷ. Gk-Sch, εἰρήνην 2° > Gk-Syh

Verse 7(6) μεγάλη ἡ ἐξουσία αὐτοῦ, καὶ τῇ εἰρήνῃ αὐτοῦ οὐκ ἔστιν ὅριον. Gk-Sch
μεγάλη ἡ ἀρχὴ αὐτοῦ, καὶ τῆς εἰρήνης αὐτοῦ οὐκ ἔστιν ὅριον. Gk-Syh

(Gk-Sch from Field; Gk-Syh from J. Ziegler, ed., *Septuaginta: Vetus Testamentum Graecum*, vol. 14: *Isaias* [Göttingen: Vandenhoeck & Ruprecht, 1967]. Ziegler's edition is, of course, the one used in this study for the LXX of Isaiah.)

[25]Ms Br. Mus. Add. 17,106. It has been published with an introduction, notes, and a Greek translation by Ceriani (*Esaiae fragmenta syriaca versionis anonymae et recensionis Jacobi Edesseni*, Monumenta sacra et profana, vol. 5, fasc. 1 [Milan: Typis et impensis Bibliothecae Ambrosianae, 1868], pp. 1–40).

[26]There are, however, five asterisked readings (42:19, 45:9, 47:1 49:1, 8) and one obelized reading (28:13) in Syl. For a discussion on Aristarchian signs in the Lucianic recension of Isaiah, see Ziegler, *Isaias*, pp. 90–1.

[27]The following layout facilitates comparison of the pertinent versions of this verse (in the Greek lines, only words of Ziegler's lemma text receive accents and breathing marks):

ܘܝ ܠܕܕܐܢ ܥܡ ܥܒܘܕܗ. ܚܨܦܐ ܡܢ ܥܦܪܐ ܕܐܪܥܐ. Pesh
nihil LXX
ουαι ο κρινομενος μετα του πλασαντος αυτον *L*
ܘܝ ܠܕܕܐܢ ܥܡ ܥܒܘܕܗ: Phil
item Syl

ܕܠܡܐ ܐܡܪ ܛܝܢܐ ܠܦܚܪܐ Pesh
μὴ ἐρεῖ ὁ πηλὸς τῷ κεραμεῖ LXX *L*
ܕܠܡܐ ܐܡܪ ܛܝܢܐ ܠܦܚܪܗ Phil

item praeter ܠܦܘܠܚܢܐ Syl

ܡܢܐ ܥܒܕ ܐܢܬ: Pesh
Tί ποιεῖς, ὅτι οὐκ ἐργάζῃ LXX
item praeter τι pro ὅτι *L*
ܕܡܢܐ ܥܒܕ ܐܢܬ: ܐܘ ܠܡܢܐ ܠܐ ܦܠܚ ܐܢܬ: Phil
item praeter ܡܢܐ pro ܕܡܢܐ Syl

ܘܠܐ ܗܘܬ ܥܒܕܐ ܕܐܝܕܝܟ: Pesh
οὐδὲ ἔχεις χεῖρας; LXX
και το εργον ουκ ἔχεις (+ εις *II*-233 403′ Syl Tht.) χεῖρας *L*
ܘܠܐ ܐܝܬ ܥܒܕܐ ܠܐܝܕܝܟ. Phil
item Syl

nihil Pesh
nihil LXX
μη αποκριθησεται το πλασμα προς τον πλασαντα αυτο *L*
ܕܠܡܐ ܡܦܢܐ ܓܒܝܠܬܐ ܠܘܬ ܓܒܘܠܗ: Phil
item Syl

(Pesh = Peshitta: S. Lee, ed., *Vetus Testamentum Syriace* [London: The Biblical Society, 1823]; Phil = Philoxenus: de Halleux, ed., *Prologue johannique*, p. 90, ll. 26-9. See also R. G. Jenkins, "Some Quotations from Isaiah in the Philoxenian Version," *Abr-Nahrain* 20 [1981-2], pp. 21-4.)

Both discrepancies between Phil and Syl merely involve affixable particles, and the text is perfectly intelligible with or without either or both of them.

The Philoxenian version will have been a revision of the Peshitta in those books which were part of the Peshitta canon. Those which were not (II Peter, II and III John, Jude, and the Apocalypse) will have been translated afresh.

[28]Philoxenian characteristics are specified below.

[29]See Ceriani, *Esaiae fragmenta*, p. 5.

[30]Examples of Greek Mss of this sort are: 69, 283, 1011, 1024, 1025, 1031, 1063, 1087, 1109, 1226 (see Rahlfs, *Verzeichnis*, pp. 394-6). An example of such a Syriac Ms is the Gospels and Psalter text described by Gwynn in *Remnants*, pt. 1, pp. xviii-xix.

[31]Gwynn claims that in the portion of Mōšē's Syriac translation of Cyril's *Glaphyra* which is preserved in Ms Br. Mus. Add. 14,555, four of its Isaiah citations which fall within the extant sections of Syl (28:14, 43:10, 45:21-2, 49:9) "agree almost verbatim" with Syl's rendering of those passages. He suggests that this is due to Mōšē's quoting from the Philoxenian version (*A Dictionary of Christian Biography*, s. v. "Polycarpus (5)." [Note: Gwynn mistakenly writes 38:14 for the first of the four references, though Syl is not extant in chapter 38. Undoubtedly 28:14 is meant; cf. Delekat, "Die syrolukianische Übersetzung," p. 23, n. 10]). Unfortunately, Ms Br. Mus. Add. 14,555 is not available to me for confirmation of Gwynn's

findings. However, I have been able to compare two Isaiah quotations (43:18–19, 45:18) in one of the Vatican fragments of Mōšē's translation (Cod. Vat. Sir. 107 in Guidi, "Mosè...e Simeone," pp. 406, 408) with their Syl counterparts and have found some significant differences:

43:18–19[a] Pesh ܠܐ ܬܬܕܟܪܘܢ ܩܕܡܝܬܐ. ܘܕܡܢ ܥܠܡܐ. ܠܐ ܬܣܬܟܠܘܢ.
Glaph ܠܐ ܬܬܕܟܪܘܢ ܡܩܕܡܝܬܐ. ܘܕܡܢ ܒܪܫܝܬ ܠܐ ܬܬܒܩܘܢ.
Syl ܠܐ ܬܬܥܗܕܘܢ ܡܩܕܡܝܬܐ. ܘܕܡܢ ܥܠܡܐ ܠܐ ܬܬܒܩܘܢ.

Pesh ܗܐ· ܥܒܕ ܐܢܐ ܚܕܬܐ. ܘܗܫܐ· ܬܬܠܕ. ܘܬܕܥܘܢܗ.
Glaph ܗܐ ܐܢܐ ܥܒܕ ܐܢܐ ܚܕܬܬܐ. ܘܗܠܝܢ ܕܗܫܐ ܕܢܚܢ. ܘܬܕܥܘܢ ܐܢܝܢ܀
Syl ܗܐ ܗܢܐ ܐܢܐ ܥܒܕ ܐܢܐ ܚܕܬܬܐ ܐܝܠܝܢ ܕܗܫܐ ܕܢܚܢ. ܘܬܕܥܘܢ ܐܢܝܢ.

45:18[aγ] Pesh ܠܐ ܗܘܐ ܣܪܝܩܐܝܬ ܒܪܝܗ̇. ܐܠܐ ܕܢܬܒ ܒܗ̇ ܒܪܝܬܗ.
Glaph ܠܐ ܣܪܝܩܐܝܬ ܒܪܝܗ̇. (ܐܝܟܢܐ ܗܘ ܕܠܐܪܥܐ:) ܐܠܐ ܕܬܬܝܬܒ.
Syl ܠܐ ܗܘܐ ܣܪܝܩܐܝܬ ܒܪܝܗ̇. ܐܠܐ ܕܬܬܥܡܪ ܥܒܕܗ̇.

On the basis of Mōšē's *Letter to Paphnutius* (Guidi, *ibid.*, p. 404), it would seem as though the reason for these discrepancies is that Mōšē and his assistants translated Biblical citations in the *Glaphyra* afresh, as they did the rest of Cyril's treatise. Mōšē mentioned the Philoxenian version, not for the purpose of acknowledging a source from which he excerpted the Biblical text, but to point to a version which, like his own, differed from the current Syriac text because it was a translation from the Greek (see Lebon, "La version philoxénienne," p. 424).

32 For the sake of convenience, the designations SyrPs, SyrPs[a], and SyrPs[b] are used even when not all members of those groups are extant.

I have checked Psalter quotations in Philoxenian writings which postdate the Philoxenian version (circa 505–8 A. D.; see de Halleux, *Vie*, pp. 122–5 and Jenkins, "Quotations from Isaiah," p. 24) and have found that they do not correspond to SyrPss (A. Vaschalde, ed., *Philoxeni Mabbugensis: Tractatus tres de Trinitate et Incarnatione*, CSCO, Syr. 9 [Paris: E typographeo reipublicae, 1907]; de Halleux, ed., *Prologue johannique*; J. W. Watt, ed., *Philoxenus of Mabbug: Fragments of the Commentary on Matthew and Luke*, CSCO, Syr. 171 [Louvain: Secrétariat du CorpusSCO, 1978]). Instead they follow the Peshitta, though there are some variants, mostly of an inner-Syriac nature. A *Tractatus tres* rendering (p. 24) of Ps. 109(110):3, however, reflects the LXX:

MT מִשְׁחָר לְךָ טַל יַלְדֻתֶיךָ
Pesh ܡܢ ܩܕܡ ܠܟ ܛܠܝܐ ܐܝܠܕܬܟ
LXX πρὸ ἑωσφόρου ἐξεγέννησά σε
Phil ܡܢ ܩܕܡ ܟܘܟܒ ܢܘܗܪܐ ܐܝܠܕܬܟ
aef pars *hj* ܩܕܡ ܟܘܟܒ ܢܓܗܐ ܝܠܕܬܟ

The fact that Philoxenus does not quote from SyrPss does not preclude the possibility that it is to be associated with the Philoxenian version. In the first place, if Mōšē of Aghel is correct, it was not Philoxenus, but the chorepiscopus, Polycarp, who did the actual work of preparing the version. Secondly, Philoxenus would have been well into his sixties by the time Polycarp completed his task. Having for many years used the Peshitta, the aging bishop would naturally have been disposed to cite from the text with which he was most familiar, even after the translation with which his name became associated was brought to him. That inclination would have been particularly strong for him when quoting from the Psalter because of its liturgical nature. It seems, then, that apart from occasional instances of inner-Syriac alteration, something other than the current Syrian text appeared in Philoxenus' writings only when he deliberately consulted Polycarp's text, or, if Philoxenus knew Greek, when he translated a given passage himself (could this be the reason for the difference between Phil [*Tractatus tres*] and SyrPss in Ps. 109[110]:3?).

[33]Vööbus, *Early Versions*, p. 115. See also Gwynn, *The Apocalypse of St. John*, p. xxviii. In the Philoxenian version, ܐܝܠܝܢ is pressed into service in contexts involving Greek relative pronouns and plural articulated participles.

[34]28:9 *bis*, 17, 42:19, 25, 44:3, 7, 9 *ter*, 10, 45:16, 20 *bis*, 24(25), 46:6, 8, 12, 48:1, 66:14, 17. The parenthesized number is the one which Ceriani assigns the verse in Syl as compared to the number of the Göttingen LXX.

[35]45:11.

[36]The only pronoun used to render the article of the plural articulated participle in the Pococke Epistles is ܐܝܠܝܢ: II Pet. 1:1, 2:10, 18 *bis*; II Jn. 1, 7; III Jn. 10; Jude 4, 5, 6, 12, 17, 18, 19. In the Crawford Apocalypse, the same preference is exhibited, though the picture is slightly more complex. In the first place, the first eight verses of chapter one are not Philoxenian but Harklean, as a comparison with that younger version shows. At some point in the Crawford Apocalypse's text history, those verses must have been lacking—a deficiency which some copyist remedied from a Harklean text. In that eight verse section, the ܗܢܘܢ demonstrative is used at both occurrences of a plural articulated participle (1:3 *bis*). Elsewhere, ܐܝܠܝܢ is the favoured pronoun. Thus, from 1:9 through to the end of the book, it is used in this fashion twenty-six times: 2:2, 9, 22, 3:9, 6:11, 7:14, 9:15, 11:1, 11, 18, 12:12, 13:8, 14:11, 12, 13, 16:2, 14, 18:19, 19:18, 20 *bis*, 20:12, 21:9, 27, 22:9, 19. In comparison, ܗܠܝܢ occurs three times (12:17, 19:10, 20:4), ܗܢܘܢ twice (15:6, 18:9), and ܗܢܘܢ ܐܝܠܝܢ once (13:8).

[37]2:12, 3:8(7), 5:12(11) *bis*, 8:9(8), 9:11(10) *bis*, 13:4, 16:7 *bis*, 9, 17:31(30), 21:8(7), 27(26), 30(29), 23:1, 24:3 *bis*, 10, 14, 30:7(6), 16(15), 19(18), 20(19) *bis*, 24(23), 25(24), 32:18, 33:10(9), 11(10), 22(21), 23(22), 34:1 *bis*, 3, 4 *bis*, 10, 19, 26 *bis*, 27 *bis*, 36:9, 22, 37:13(12) *bis*, 20(19), 39:15(14) *bis*, 16(15), 17(16) *bis*, 43:6(5), 48:7(6), 49:22. The parenthesized numbers are those in Ceriani's Ambrosian edition (*a*) which differ from the numbers of Rahlfs' LXX edition, *Psalmi cum Odis*.

[38] 2:10, 5:6(5), 6:9(8), 7:2(1), 5(4), 11:5(4), 13:4, 17:40(39), 49(48), 21:26(25), 22:5, 27:3, 29:4(3), 30:12(11), 31:7, 9, 32:8, 14, 37:21(20), 43:8(7), 44:1(inscr.), 49:5.

[39] 34:19.

[40] 91:12(11), 96:7 *bis*, 10, 97:7, 98:6, 102:18, 105:3, 106:2, 108:20 *bis*, 28, 29, 110:10.

[41] 101:21(20), 105:46, 106:34, 108:31.

[42] In 43:1 and 44:21 for ἐμός, and in 43:21 and 45:1 for μοῦ.

[43] Excluding those joined to the copula, ܐܝܬ, and those of the proleptic variety.

[44] The Pococke Epistles show the attached suffix eighty-four times and the ܕܝܠ form twenty-one times. In the first eight (Harklean) verses of the Crawford Apocalypse, only the ܕܝܠ form is used (seven times). Elsewhere, the attached suffix is preferred. For example, from 1:9 through to the end of chapter 10, it is employed 129 times, but the ܕܝܠ form only five times.

[45] The implications of this switch are discussed below (see note 66).

[46] θέλω is also translated by ܨܒܐ on four occasions in the extant Philoxenian New Testament books: II Pet. 3:5; Apoc. 2:21, 11:5, 6. There is no apparent reason for this difference other than the desire for variation in usage.

[47] 17:20(19), 21:9(8), 33:13(12), 34:27 *bis*, 39:15(14). Rahlfs does, in 77:10 of his edition, have another instance of the θέλω root (i. e. ἤθελον) where SyrPs has the ܨܒܐ root. But it is likely that the reading which he lists as the variant, η/εβουληθησαν, is original here, not least because of the added support of the subsequently discovered ancient papyri, Mss 2110 and 2149 (see A. Pietersma, "Proto-Lucian and the Greek Psalter," *VT*, 28 [1978], pp. 71–2). In any case, both θέλω (see above) and βούλομαι (69:3[2]) are translated by ܨܒܐ in the Psalter, so the presence of the ܨܒܐ root in 77:10 decides nothing with respect to the Greek *Vorlage*.

θέλω is also translated by ܨܒܐ on thirteen occasions in the Psalms: 5:5(4), 36:23, 39:7(6), 40:12(11), 50:18(16), 67:31(30), 72:25, 108:17, 111:1, 113:11(115:3), 118:35, 134:6, 146:10.

[48] "Quotations from Isaiah," p. 34, n. 22.

[49] 5:24, 28:4, 66:3. ܨܒܐ is the equivalent in six instances: 1:19, 20, 9:5(4), 28:12, 55:11, 56:4.

[50] II Pet. 1:4; Apoc. 18:12 *bis*, 16, 21:11, 19.

[51] Apoc. 17:4.

[52] 20:4(3), 115:6(116:15).

[53] 18:11(10).

[54] II Jn. 9 *bis*, 10; Apoc. 2:15, 24.

[55] Apoc. 2:14.

[56] These characteristics are seen clearly against the backdrop of the Peshitta and the Greek. Stylistic features are illustrated in the following representative examples:

1/ Note particularly the Syriac counterparts to ὅτι and the copula verb:

Is. 45:14

ܕܒܟܝ ܗܘ ܐܠܗܐ Pesh
ὅτι ἐν σοὶ ὁ θεός ἐστι LXX
ܡܛܠ ܕܒܟܝ ܐܝܬܘܗܝ ܐܠܗܐ Syl
ܡܛܠ ܕܒܟ ܐܠܗܐ ܐܝܬܘܗܝ Syh

Ps. 24(25):6

ܐܬܕܟܪ ܡܪܝܐ ܪ̈ܚܡܝܟ ܕܡܢ ܥܠܡ ܘܛܝܒܘܬܟ Pesh
μνήσθητι τῶν οἰκτιρμῶν σου, κύριε, καὶ τὰ ἐλέη σου, ὅτι ἀπὸ τοῦ αἰῶνός εἰσιν LXX
ܐܬܕܟܪ ܚܢܢܟ ܡܪܝܐ: ܘܪ̈ܚܡܝܟ. ܡܛܠ ܕܡܢ ܥܠܡ ܐܝܬܝܗܘܢ SyrPs (*acef* pars[c. uar. *g* pars]); c. uar. SyrPs[a] (*hj*)

2/ Contrast the Syriac counterparts to the Greek relative pronoun:

Is. 48:12

ܘܐܝܣܪܝܠ ܕܩܪܝܬ Pesh
καὶ Ἰσραὴλ ὃν ἐγὼ καλῶ LXX
ܘܐܝܣܪܝܠ ܗܘ ܕܩܪܝܬ Syl
ܘܐܝܣܪܝܠ ܗܘ ܕܐܢܐ ܩܪܐ ܐܢܐ Syh

Ps. 1:3

ܕܦܐܪܘܗܝ ܝܗܒ Pesh
ὃ τὸν καρπὸν αὐτοῦ δώσει LXX
ܗܘ ܕܦܐܪܗ ܒܙܒܢܗ ܝܗܒ SyrPs (*af*); item SyrPs[a] (*j*)

3/ Compare the conjunctive particles:

Is. 49:14

ܘܐܡܪܬ ܨܗܝܘܢ Pesh
Εἶπε δὲ Σιών LXX
ܐܡܪܐ ܕܝܢ ܨܗܝܘܢ Syl
item Syh

Ps. 5:8(7)

ܘܐܢܐ Pesh
ἐγὼ δέ LXX
ܐܢܐ ܕܝܢ SyrPs (*af*); item SyrPs[a] (*hj*)

For similar New Testament comparisons involving quotations from Philoxenus' Gospel of John commentary, the Harklean version, and the Peshitta, see Vööbus, "New Data," pp. 180-4 and Vööbus, *Early Versions*, pp. 110-18.

[57]In Syl of Isaiah, ܫܪܪܐ translates ἀλήθεια in both places where its Greek *Vorlage* would have had it (45:19, 48:1). The same is true of all relevant passages in Syh of Isaiah (10:20, 11:5, 16:5, 26:2, 3, 10, 37:18, 38:3, 42:3, 45:19, 48:1, 59:14, 15) as well as those in the surviving Philoxenian New Testament books and their Harklean counterparts (II Pet. 1:12, 2:2; II Jn. 1 *bis*, 2, 3, 4; III Jn. 1, 3 *bis*, 4, 8, 12; [Note that the relevant phrase in II Jn. 2 does not occur in White's Harklean text though he does record it as being "in margine MSti."]).

The ἀλήθεια = ܫܪܪܐ equivalency occurs fifty-seven times in SyrPs: 5:10(9), 14:2, 24:5, 10, 25:3, 29:10(9), 30:6(5), 24(23), 35:6(5), 39:11(10) *bis*, 12(11), 42:3, 44:5(4), 50:8(6), 53:7(5), 56:4(3), 11(10), 60:8(7), 68:14, 70:22, 83:12(11), 84:11(10), 12(11), 85:11, 87:12(11), 88:2(1), 6(5), 9(8), 15(14), 25(24), 34(33), 50(49), 90:4, 91:3(2), 95:13, 97:3, 99:5, 107:5(4), 110:7, 8, 113:9(115:1), 116:2, 118:30, 43, 75, 86, 90, 138, 142, 151, 160, 131:11, 137:2, 142:1, 144:18, 145:6. Only twice is ἀλήθεια translated by something else: ܫܪܝܪܬܐ (for Greek plural) 11:2(1); ܗܝܡܢܘܬܐ (= Peshitta) 88:3(2). In the Peshitta Psalter, ܗܝܡܢܘܬܐ occurs in twenty-seven of the preceding cases (Peshitta verse numbering is followed here for Peshitta Psalter references): 12:2, 26:3, 30:10, 36:6, 40:11 *bis*, 12, 43:3, 57:11, 85:12, 88:12, 89:2, 3, 6, 9, 25, 34, 50, 92:3, 96:13, 98:3, 100:5, 108:5, 119:30, 75, 90, 138. In another twenty-three instances, ܩܘܫܬܐ is the term used: 15:2, 25:5, 10, 31:6, 45:5, 51:8, 54:7, 57:4, 61:8, 71:22, 85:11, 86:11, 89:15, 91:4, 111:7, 8, 115:1, 119:43, 151, 160, 138:2, 145:18, 146:6. Only two of the remaining passages have ܫܪܪܐ: 119:142, 132:11.

Of the thirteen passages listed above in connection with Syh of Isaiah, seven have ܩܘܫܬܐ (10:20, 16:5, 38:3, 42:3, 48:1, 59:14, 15) and two have ܗܝܡܢܘܬܐ (11:5, 26:2) in the Peshitta, while only one (26:3[2]) has ܫܪܪܐ.

[58]SyrPs translates the third person reflexive with ܗܘ ܠܗ etc. eight times: 21:19(18), 26:12, 35:2(1), 43:11(10), 65:7, 72:27, 82:13(12), 104:22. This corresponds to normal usage in both the Syrohexapla and the Harklean New Testament. The ܢܦܫܗ rendering is typical of Syl of Isaiah (44:14, 45:25, 49:27) and the surviving Philoxenian New Testament books (II Pet. 2:1; II Jn. 8; Jude 12, 21; Apoc. 2:2, 9, 20, 3:9, 6:15, 19:7). It is interesting to note that, although Syh of Isaiah (like the rest of the Syrohexapla) translates the reflexive with a combination rendering characteristic of the Syrohexapla and the Harklean version, it also uses ܢܦܫܗ twice (5:21 *bis*). This may be another indication of the fact that Syh is a revision of Syl.

[59]This negative, whether contracted or uncontracted, translates both οὐκ εἰμί etc. and οὐκ ἔχω etc. The focus here is on cases involving οὐκ ἔστιν. SyrPs uses the uncontracted form to translate that Greek combination thirty-six times: 3:3(2), 5:10(9), 6:6(5), 9:25(24),

13:1 *bis*, 3 *ter*, 18:7(6), 21:12(11), 31:2, 33:10(9), 35:2(1), 37:4(3) *bis*, 8(7), 11(10), 39:6(5), 13(12), 52:2(1) *bis*, 4(3) *bis*, 68:3(2), 70:11, 73:9, 85:8, 91:16(15), 103:25, 118:165, 134:17, 138:4, 141:5(4), 145:3, 146:5. Only five times is the contracted form used: 31:9, 72:4, 85:8, 143:14, 144:3.

The uncontracted negative as the equivalent for οὐκ ἔστιν is preferred in the Harklean New Testament and usually the Syrohexapla. However, in some Syrohexaplaric books, as in the Peshitta, the preference is for the contracted form: III Kingdoms, by a count of eleven (3:18, 5:4[18] *bis*, 6[20], 10:7, 12:16, 18:10, 43, 20[21]:15, 22:7, 33) to one (22:17); IV Kingdoms, all nine occurrences (3:11, 4:2, 6, 14, 5:15, 7:5, 10, 9:10, 19:3); Song of Songs, all four occurrences (4:2, 7, 6:6[5], 8); Daniel, by a count of five (3:33, 38, 40, 96[29], 10:17) to two (2:11, 27).

The contracted form of the negative is typical of Syl of Isaiah (43:11, 13, 44:6, 45:5, 6 *bis*, 14, 18, 21 *bis*, 22, 46:9, 47:8, 10 *bis*, 48:22) and the Crawford Apocalypse (17:8 *bis*, 11, 21:1). The Four Minor Catholic Epistles have no instance of οὐκ with any form of εἰμί, but note the following Philoxenian equivalencies: II Jn. 9, οὐκ ἔχει = ܠܝܬ ܠܗ; III Jn. 4, οὐκ ἔχω = ܠܝܬ ܠܝ; Jude 19, μὴ ἔχοντες = ܠܝܬ ܠܗܘܢ. These are the only places in the Four Minor Catholic Epistles where ἔχω is preceded by a negative.

[60]SyrPs translates μακάριος with the ܛܘܒܬܐ root twenty-three times: 1:1, 31:1, 2, 32:12, 33:9(8), 39:5(4), 40:2(1), 64:5(4), 83:5(4), 6(5), 13(12), 88:16(15), 93:12, 111:1, 118:1, 2, 126:5, 127:1, 2, 136:8, 9, 143:15, 145:5. Only twice is the ܛܘܒܘܗܝ form used (2:12, 105:3). The preference for ܛܘܒܬܐ accords with normal Syrohexaplaric and Harklean usage. Significantly, however, the ܛܘܒܘܗܝ form is preferred to ܛܘܒܬܐ etc. in Syh of Isaiah by a count of three (30:18, 32:20, 56:2) to one (31:9). It is also the Syh equivalent for μακάριος in III Kingdoms (10:8 *bis*) and Daniel (12:12). All three of these books exhibit more than one characteristic of the *Philoxeniana*.

The usual equivalent for μακάριος in the Crawford Apocalypse is the ܛܘܒܘܗܝ form: 14:13, 16:15, 19:9, 22:7, 14. However, ܛܘܒܬܐ does occur once in its opening Harklean section (1:3), while ܛܘܒܐ also appears just once towards the end of the book (20:6). Neither Syl of Isaiah nor the Pococke Epistles have occasion to render μακάριος.

[61]SyrPs translates ἀνομία with ܠܐ ܢܡܘܣܘܬܐ seventy-six times: 5:5(4), 6(5), 6:9(8), 7:15(14), 13:4, 17:5(4), 24(23), 25:10, 30:19(18), 31:1, 5 *bis*, 35:3(2), 4(3), 5(4), 13(12), 36:1, 37:19(18), 38:9(8), 12(11), 40:7(6), 44:8(7), 48:6(5), 49:21, 50:4(2), 5(3), 7(5), 11(9), 51:3(1), 52:2(1), 5(4), 54:4(3), 10(9), 11(10), 56:2(1), 57:3(2), 58:3(2), 4(3), 5(4), 6(5), 63:7(6), 68:28(27) *bis*, 72:19, 73:20, 78:8, 84:3(2), 88:23(22), 33(32), 89:8, 91:8(7), 10(9), 93:4, 16, 20, 23, 100:8, 102:3, 10, 12, 105:43, 106:17 *bis*, 42, 108:14, 118:3, 133, 150, 124:3, 5, 128:3, 129:3, 8, 138:24, 140:4, 9. A similar composite form, ܠܐ ܢܡܘܣܝܬܐ, is used in two additional instances: 37:5(4), 39:13(12). The usual Syrohexaplaric and Harklean equivalent is ܠܐ ܢܡܘܣܘܬܐ. In Syl of Isaiah, the word used is ܥܘܠܐ (43:25, 26, 44:22). The Four Minor Catholic Epistles and the Apocalypse

do not contain ἀνομία.

[62]In SyrPs, εἰρήνη is always translated by ܫܝܢܐ: 4:9(8), 13:3, 27:3, 28:11, 33:15(14), 34:27, 36:11, 37:4(3), 40:10(9), 54:19(18), 71:3, 7, 72:3, 75:3(2), 84:9(8), 11(10), 118:165, 119:7, 121:6, 7, 8, 124:5, 127:6, 147:3(14). This equivalency characterizes the Syrohexapla and the Harklean version as well. In Syl of Isaiah (45:7, 48:18, 66:12; cf. also Is. 53:5 in *Tractatus tres*, p. 163, l. 9), the Pococke Epistles (II Pet. 1:2, 3:14; II Jn. 3; III Jn. 15; Jude 2), and the Crawford Apocalypse (6:4), the equivalent is ܫܠܡܐ. Only in Crawford Apocalypse 1:4, which is part of the initial Harklean section, is ܫܝܢܐ employed.

It will be noted, however, that the previously discussed reading attributed to the Philoxenian version in the Isaiah scholion of the Ambrosian Ms has ܫܝܢܐ in all four places where the underlying Greek text had εἰρήνη. The scholion's preference for the independent possessive pronoun over against the directly attached pronominal suffix, and for the uncontracted negative, ܠܐ ܐܝܬ, as opposed to the contracted form, ܠܝܬ, is likewise Syrohexaplaric/Harklean but non-Philoxenian in character. The existence of such features in the reading does not, however, preclude the possibility that it was drawn from the Philoxenian Isaiah. Instead, their presence may merely indicate that the scholion's author (presumably Paul of Tella), whose apparent purpose in recording the variant reading was to include the longer text of the Philoxenian version, revised the Philoxenian original (see Delekat, "Die syrolukianische Übersetzung," pp. 23-4).

[63]The SyrPs equivalent for θηρίον is always the typical Syrohexaplaric/Harklean term, ܚܝܘܬ ܒܪܐ: 49:10, 67:31(30), 73:19, 78:2, 103:11, 20, 148:10. The sole equivalent in both Syl of Isaiah (43:20, 46:1) and the Crawford Apocalypse (6:8, 11:7, 13:1, 2, 3, 4 *ter*, 11, 12 *bis*, 14 *bis*, 15 *bis*, 17, 18, 14:9, 11, 15:2, 16:2, 10, 13, 17:3, 7, 8 *bis*, 11, 12, 13, 16, 17, 19:19, 20 *bis*, 20:4, 10) is ܚܝܘܬܐ. The Four Minor Catholic Epistles do not contain θηρίον.

[64]The penchant for revising existing Syriac versions of the Bible towards the Greek characterized a good deal of sixth and seventh century Syrian scholarship (see Vööbus, *The Apocalypse in the Harklean Version*, pp. 6-7; S. Brock, "The Resolution of the Philoxenian/Harclean Problem," *New Testament Textual Criticism—Its Significance for Exegesis: Essays in Honour of Bruce M. Metzger*, E. J. Epp and G. D. Fee, eds. [Oxford: Clarendon Press, 1981], pp. 340-1).

For examples of disagreements between SyrPs and the Peshitta, see notes 56 and 57.

[65]In the portions of the Syrohexapla of Isaiah which correspond to Syl, ܗܢܘܢ translates the article of the plural articulated participle on twenty-two occasions (42:24, 25, 44:3, 9 *ter*, 10, 45:20 *bis*, 24, 46:3, 5, 6, 8, 12, 47:13, 48:1 *bis*, 49:17, 66:14 *bis*, 17), whereas both ܗܠܝܢ (28:17, 42:19, 23, 44:7) and ܐܠܝܢ (28:9 *bis*, 45:11, 16) do so four times. The preference for the demonstratives, ܗܢܘܢ and ܗܠܝܢ, is usual in the

Syrohexapla. In Wisdom of Solomon, Sirach, Daniel, and Bel and the Dragon, however, ܐܠܝܢ is favoured. This anomaly may be due to the fact that there were a number of workers involved in the preparation of the Syrohexapla (see the IV Kingdoms colophon of Ms Par. syr. 27, folio 90a, published by Middeldorpf in *Codex Syriaco-Hexaplaris*, p. 66, and by Lagarde in *Bibliothecae Syriacae*, p. 256).

In the Harklean version of the Four Minor Catholic Epistles, the article of the participle is translated by ܗܢܘܢ eight times (II Pet. 1:1, 2:18; II Jn. 7; III Jn. 10; Jude 4, 6, 12, 19), by ܗܠܝܢ five times (II Pet. 2:10, 18; II Jn. 1; Jude 5, 17), but by ܐܠܝܢ not at all. In the Apocalypse, too, these demonstratives are favoured. The pronoun ܗܢܘܢ is employed forty times: 1:3 *bis*, 3:9, 10, 6:9, 11, 7:4, 14, 8:13, 9:14, 15, 17, 11:1, 10, 16, 18, 12:12, 13:12, 14 *bis*, 14:6, 12, 13, 15:2, 16:2 *bis*, 17:8, 18:9, 15, 19, 24, 19:5, 9, 10, 18, 20:12, 21:9 *bis*, 27, 22:14; ܗܠܝܢ is used twenty-five times: 2:2 (which actually has ܠܗܝܢ, evidently a mistake for ܠܗܠܝܢ), 9, 22, 6:10, 8:6, 9, 13, 11:4, 10, 11, 18, 12:17, 13:6, 8, 14:4, 11, 15:6, 17:1, 2, 19:17 (sup. lin.), 20 *bis*, 20:4, 22:18, 19. As in the Harklean Four Minor Catholic Epistles, ܐܠܝܢ is not used to render the article of the plural articulated participle.

[66]In those parts of Syh of Isaiah which correspond to Syl, the ܕܝܠ form is preferred to the attached suffix by a count of 151 to 25. In the Harklean version of the Four Minor Catholic Epistles, the ܕܝܠ form occurs sixty-seven times, and the attached suffix only nine times. The same preference is exhibited in the Harklean Apocalypse. For example, in chapters 1-10, the independent possessive pronoun is favoured by a count of 121 to 18. The ܕܝܠ form is characteristic of both the Syrohexapla and the Harklean New Testament.

The preference for the ܕܝܠ form in Pss. 1-24 of SyrPs must stem from the fact that SyrPs is a revision of the Philoxenian Psalter—a Psalter in which the attached suffix would have been preferred throughout. However, either this revision was never fully carried out (at least with respect to the substitution of ܕܝܠ forms) or it was only partially incorporated into an exemplar from which the extant Mss of SyrPs derive. I have not been able to isolate any other SyrPs characteristic in regard to which such a dramatic switch in usage occurs.

[67]Apart from the three instances of the θέλω = ܒܥܐ equivalency in the Syrohexapla of Isaiah, there are only three scattered occurrences of it in the books of the Syrohexapla contained in the Ambrosian codex, Lagarde's *Bibliothecae Syriacae*, and the Midyat Ms of the Pentateuch (A. Vööbus, *The Pentateuch in the Version of the Syro-Hexapla*, CSCO, Subsidia 45 [Louvain: Secrétariat du CorpusSCO, 1975]): Deut. 21:14; Ecclesiastes 8:3; Mal. 3:1 (SyrPs, it will be remembered, employs ܒܥܐ seven times as a rendering for θέλω). In contrast, θέλω = ܨܒܐ occurs sixty-nine times: Gen. 37:35, 39:8, 48:19; Ex. 2:7, 8:28(32), 10:4, 11:10; Num. 20:21, 22:14; Deut. 1:26, 2:30, 10:10, 23:5, 22, 25:7 *bis*, 29:20(19); Josh. 24:10; Judg. 11:17, 20, 13:23, 19:10, 25, 20:5;

III Kingd. 9:1, 10:9, 13, 21(20):8, 35, 22:50; IV Kingd. 8:19, 13:23, 24:4; Prov. 1:30, 21:1; Song of Songs 2:7, 3:5, 8:4; Wisd. of Sol. 9:13, 11:25, 12:18, 13:6, 14:5; Sir. 6:32, 35, 7:13, 15:15, 16, 23:14, 39:6; Hos. 6:6(7), 11:5; Jer. 5:3 *bis*, 8:5, 9:5(6), 11:10, 27(50):33, 38(31):15, 45(38):21; Ez. 3:7, 18:23, 32, 20:8; Dan. 1:13, 2:3, 4:17(14), 7:19, 8:4. In the Harklean version of the Four Minor Catholic Epistles and the Apocalypse, the equivalent is always ܨܒܐ: II Pet. 3:5; III Jn. 13; Apoc. 2:21, 11:5 *bis*, 6, 22:17.

[68]The τίμιος = ܝܩܝܪ equivalency occurs only three times in the books of the Ambrosian codex apart from the Psalter: Job 28:16; Prov. 8:19; Jer. 15:19. Elsewhere in that codex and in Lagarde's *Bibliothecae Syriacae*, ܡܝܩܪ is the equivalent (some twenty-two times): III Kingd. 6:1a(5:31), 7:46(9), 47(10), 48(11), 10:2, 10, 11; Job 28:10; Prov. 3:15 *bis*, 6:26, 8:11, 12:27, 20:6, 24:4, 31:10; Ecclesiastes 10:1; Wisd. of Sol. 4:8, 12:7; Hos. 11:7 (mg); Lam. 4:2; Is. 60:6 (mg). The word τίμιος is not found in the Pentateuch. In the Harklean version of the Four Minor Catholic Epistles and the Apocalypse, ܡܝܩܪ is always the rendering for τίμιος: II Pet. 1:4; Apoc. 17:4, 18:12 *bis*, 16, 21:11, 19.

[69]The διδαχή = ܡܠܦܢܘܬܐ equivalency is consistent in the Harklean Four Minor Catholic Epistles and Apocalypse: II Jn. 9 *bis*, 10; Apoc. 2:14, 15, 24. The same is true elsewhere in White's Harklean edition (Heb. 13:9 is not extant in White's edition—which breaks off at Heb. 11:27—and unfortunately *The Harklean Version of the Epistle to the Hebrews, Chap. XI,28-XIII,25* published by R. L. Bensly [Cambridge: University Press, 1889] is not available to me): Mt. 7:28, 16:12, 22:33; Mk. 1:22, 27, 4:2, 11:18, 12:38; Lk. 4:32; Jn. 7:16, 17, 18:19; Acts 2:42, 5:28, 13:12, 17:19; Rom. 6:17, 16:17; I Cor. 14:6, 26; II Tim. 4:2; Tit. 1:9; Heb. 6:2.

[70]Ceriani, *Esaiae fragmenta*, pp. 7-8; Wright, *Catalogue*, vol. 1, p. 39.

[71]I have examined the text of these fragments and found it to be an eclectic one. It is based on the Peshitta, but incorporates non-Peshitta readings which are attested in Lucianic, hexaplaric, and other sources.

[72]In the Isaiah fragments, where the Greek has a plural articulated participle, ܗܢܘܢ precedes plural participles thirteen times (28:1, 9, 46:3, 5, 6, 8, 12, 47:13, 48:1 *bis*, 49:17, 19 *bis*), ܗܠܝܢ does so three times (28:17, 45:11, 49:19), and ܐܝܠܝܢ just once (45:16). Furthermore, ܠܝܬ is preferred to ܠܐ ܐܝܬ in places where the Greek has οὐκ ἔστιν by a count of four (45:14, 47:8, 10, 48:22) to two (46:9, 47:10). In SyrPs, ܐܝܠܝܢ and ܠܐ ܐܝܬ are favoured.

[73]Jacob's text has ܩܘܫܬܐ where the Greek has ἀλήθεια (48:1). Where εἰρήνη occurs, Jacob uses both ܫܠܡܐ (48:18; ܫܠܡܐ in 48:22 equals the Peshitta, the MT, Clement of Alexandria, and οἱ γ′ [οἱ λ′ according to Chrysostom]) and ܫܝܢܐ (45:7). In SyrPs, the usual equivalent for ἀλήθεια is ܫܪܪܐ (but never ܩܘܫܬܐ), and the exclusive equivalent for εἰρήνη is ܫܝܢܐ.

[74]The IV Kingdoms colophon of Ms Par. syr. 27 names a certain Thomas, the minister (or deacon, i. e. ܡܫܡܫܢܐ) and syncellus ("cellmate" and domestic chaplain) of the Antiochian patriarch, Athanasius, as the one in charge of the rest of the co-workers. Apparently, Thomas of Harkel and Athanasius had earlier spent time at the renowned Syrian Monophysite center of Graeco-Syro studies, the Monastery of Qennešrê (*A Dictionary of Christian Biography*, s. v. "Thomas (17) Harklensis," by J. Gwynn), so a close association of the sort described in the colophon would not be surprising. The assertion that the Thomas of the colophon must have been someone other than Thomas of Harkel who, as bishop of Mabbūg, would not have been introduced as merely a minister and syncellus is less than convincing (see Ceriani, *Prolegomena in editionem versionis syriacae ex textu LXX*, Monumenta sacra et profana, vol. 1, fasc. 1 [Milan: Typis et impensis Bibliothecae Ambrosianae, 1861], p. V f.; Vööbus, *Hexapla*, pp. 40-2). It is quite conceivable that, during his time of exile from his see, the bishop of Mabbūg could have assumed the duties of syncellus to the patriarch. It is also possible that Thomas was the author of this colophon, and that, as in his New Testament colophons, he modestly avoided the mention of his episcopal title (*A Dictionary of Christian Biography*, s. v. "Thomas (17) Harklensis," by J. Gwynn). The appearance of "bishop of Mabbūg" in the colophon to the Harklean Corpus Paulinum appears not to have been Thomas' doing, but would seem to constitute an insertion by a respectful copyist (see Vööbus, *The Apocalypse*, p. 56, n. 67).

[75]Gwynn, *Remnants*, pt. 1, pp. lxxi, 41-6. However, Gwynn and others have raised the possibility that the Paul mentioned in the Ms colophons reproduced in *Remnants* may have been the Monophysite bishop of Edessa of the same name who fled to Cyprus in the first part of the seventh century to escape the Persian invasion (*Remnants*, pt. 1, p. lxxi, note *; S. Brock, *The Syriac Version of the Pseudo-Nonnos Mythological Scholia* [Cambridge: University Press, 1971], p. 30).

[76]In Isaiah where, if Jenkins is correct, Paul revised Philoxenian Syl ("Quotations from Isaiah," p. 34, n. 22), Paul's revision (Syh) appears to have been more thorough since Syh, with Ms 88, comprises Ziegler's hexaplaric *ol* group (*Isaias*, pp. 36, 41-3).

[77]The fact that there is a noticeable decrease in the number of substantive variant readings in Mss *hj* following Ps. 27 (as a glance at the apparatus accompanying this edition will show) makes it clear that the most distinctive section of these Mss ends with that Psalm. Verse 6 is singled out because it contains the last instance of the characteristic *hj* equivalency, δέησις = ܐܬܟܫܦܘܬܐ (previously 5:3[2], 6:10[9], 16:1, 21:25[24], 27:2). After 27:6, this pair agrees with SyrPs on the equivalency which the latter has in each passage just cited, δέησις = ܒܥܘܬܐ: 30:23(22), 33:16(15), 38:13(12), 39:2(1), 54:2(1), 60:2(1), 65:19, 85:6, 87:3(2), 101:1(inscr.), 18(17), 105:44, 114:1, 118:169, 129:2, 139:7(6), 140:1, 141:3(2), 7(6), 142:1, 144:19. Furthermore, 27:7 is the

first place in which *hj* agree with SyrPs on the ὑπερασπιστής = ܡܣܬܪܢܐ equivalency, as they do ever afterward: 27:8, 30:3(2), 5(4), 32:20, 36:39, 39:18(17), 58:12(11), 70:3, 83:10(9), 113:17(115:9), 18(10), 19(11), 143:2. Prior to 27:7, SyrPs has the same equivalency, but *hj* have ὑπερασπιστής = ܡܣܝܥܢܐ: 17:3(2), 31(30), 26:1.

[78]Characteristic examples of this greater servility to the Greek in SyrPs^a^ are:

17:18(17) καὶ ἐκ τῶν μισούντων με LXX
ܘܡܢ ܗܢܘܢ ܕܣܢܝܢ ܠܝ SyrPs^a^ (*hj*)
ܘܡܢ ܣܢܐܝ Pesh SyrPs (*abce*)

22:1 καὶ οὐδέν με ὑστερήσει LXX
ܘܠܐ ܡܕܡ ܠܝ ܢܚܣܪ SyrPs^a^ (*hj*)
ܘܡܕܡ ܠܐ ܢܚܣܪ ܠܝ Pesh SyrPs (*ace*)

22:2 ἐκεῖ με κατεσκήνωσεν LXX
ܬܡܢ ܠܝ ܐܫܪܝ SyrPs^a^ (*hj*)
ܢܫܪܝܢܝ Pesh
ܬܡܢ ܐܫܪܝܢܝ SyrPs (*acef*)

27:1 τοῖς καταβαίνουσιν LXX
ܠܗܢܘܢ ܕܢܚܬܝܢ SyrPs^a^ (*hj*)
ܥܡ ܢܚܬܝ Pesh
ܠܢܚܬܝ SyrPs (*abcef*)

That SyrPs^a^ is no more hexaplaric than SyrPs has been demonstrated in the concluding summary of chapter three in the present study. It must be admitted that demonstrating the existence of a relationship between SyrPs^a^ and the Philoxenian Psalter (see note 95 for a possible example) is more difficult to do than it is for SyrPs because, as will be shown below, in places where SyrPs shares characteristics with the *Philoxeniana*, SyrPs^a^ normally has Syrohexaplaric/Harklean characteristics. The other possible base text for revision would be the precursor of the Philoxenian Psalter, the Peshitta Psalter. Yet where SyrPs^a^ and SyrPs disagree, SyrPs agrees with the Peshitta more often than SyrPs^a^ does. For example, by my count, in Pss. 2-10(11) SyrPs has ninety-eight readings which agree with, or more closely reflect, the Peshitta, whereas SyrPs^a^ has forty-seven. In Pss. 20(21)-22(23), SyrPs has fifty-two while SyrPs^a^ has thirty-three. Thus, SyrPs^a^ does not give evidence of an extraordinary degree of dependence on the Peshitta. This observation, and the fact that SyrPs^a^ follows the Greek closely, argue for a base text already conformed to a significant extent to the Greek—namely, the Philoxenian.

[79]The typical Syrohexaplaric/Harklean θέλω = ܨܒܐ equivalency in 17:20(19) of SyrPs^a^ (where the SyrPs equivalent is ܒܥܐ) may, however, be due to Peshitta influence, since ܨܒܐ, the usual Peshitta word in passages where the LXX Psalter has θέλω (see note 47 for the Greek/SyrPs references) occurs here in the Peshitta. The Peshitta has ܨܒܐ everywhere except 37(36):23 and 112(111):1 where it

has other readings. There is no equivalent for θέλω in 21:9(8) of SyrPs[a], since the relevant stich has been omitted. In the remaining passages where the SyrPs equivalent is ܨܒܐ, Mss *hj* show agreement (these passages fall outside the bounds of the SyrPs[a] text in *hj*): 33:13(12), 34:27 *bis*, 39:15(14), 77:10. There is agreement too in places where SyrPs translates θέλω with ܪܓܐ (see note 47 for references).

Mss *hj* also follow SyrPs in having the διδαχή = ܡܠܦܢܐ equivalency in Ps. 59:1(inscr.), a passage which is likewise beyond the borders of the SyrPs[a] text in *hj*.

[80]SyrPs[a] translates the article of a participle with ܗܢܘܢ where SyrPs has ܐܝܠܝܢ in 3:8(7), 5:12(11) *bis*, 13:4, 16:7 *bis*, 9, 17:31(30), 21:8(7), 30(29), 23:1, 24:3 *bis*, 10, 14. The article of the second participle in 9:11(10) is rendered by ܗܢܘܢ in *j*, but by ܐܝܠܝܢ in *h* (and SyrPs). The equivalent for the article of the first participle in 9:11(10) is ܐܝܠܝܢ in both *h* and *j* (as well as SyrPs). The same is true for the articles of plural articulated participles in 2:12 and 21:27(26). Only once is ܗܠܝܢ the equivalent of such an article in SyrPs[a] where SyrPs has ܐܝܠܝܢ (8:9[8]). After Ps. 27:6, Mss *hj* normally agree with SyrPs in cases where the latter has ܐܝܠܝܢ as the equivalent for the article of the plural participle. For example, in Pss. 27:7–50:21(19), this occurs without exception (see note 37 for references).

[81]Such is the case in Mss *hj* throughout the Psalter.

[82]18:11(10), 20:4(3). The τίμιος = ܡܝܩܪ equivalency occurs also in 115:6(116:15) of Mss *hj*. This passage, which contains the only other instance of τίμιος in the LXX Psalter, does not fall within the SyrPs[a] section of these Mss.

[83]2:12. Mss *hj* also have the μακάριος = ܛܘܒܬܢܐ equivalency in the only other place where SyrPs renders μακάριος with the ܛܘܒܝܗܘܢ form, 105:3. This passage also falls outside the SyrPs[a] section of *hj*. Otherwise, SyrPs and this pair agree on the μακάριος = ܛܘܒܬܢܐ equivalency (see note 60).

[84]Here are some examples of passages in which SyrPs[a] has distinctive composite terms:

9:26(25) κατακυριεύσει LXX
ܢܗܘܐ ܡܪܐ *hj*
ܢܬܡܪܐ *af*
ܥܠܐ Pesh

9:31(30) ἐν τῷ αὐτὸν κατακυριεῦσαι LXX
ܟܕ ܢܗܘܐ ܡܪܐ *hj*
ܥܠ ܕܢܬܡܪܐ *af*
ܘܒܣܥܪܘܗܝ Pesh

9:39(38) τοῦ μεγαλαυχεῖν LXX
ܠܡܪܒܘ ܪܒܐ *hj*
ܠܡܫܬܒܗܪܘ *acf*

ܠܡܘܡܝܗ Pesh

11:4(3) μεγαλορήμονα LXX
ܡܘܪܒ ܡ̈ܠܠ *hj*
ܡܬܪܘܪܒܢܐ *α*, c. sey. *cf*
ܕܡܡܠܠܢ ܪ̈ܘܪܒܬܐ Pesh

21:22(21) μονοκερώτων LXX
ܕܚܕܩܪ̈ܢܝܢ ܡ̈ܢܐ *j*, primum uerbum s. sey. *h*
ܕܪ̈ܝܡܐ *αef*
ܪܡܬܐ Pesh

See note 61 for the discussion on the ἀνομία = ܠܐ ܢܡܘܣܘܬܐ equivalency, which SyrPs[a] shares with SyrPs.

[85]The θηρίον = ܚܝܘܬܐ ܒܪܐ equivalency, however, does not fall within the SyrPs[a] section of Mss *hj* (see note 63).

[86]See the description of *h* in chapter one for what is actually extant within this section of the Ms. Note also that *h* gives way to h_1 in 146:8.

[87]Ms *k* shares with *hj* both stylistic features (e. g. the highly consistent use of the ܕܠܐ form—*k* is totally consistent where extant) and distinctive readings (the lemma appears first, followed by the *hjk* reading):

e. g. 73:8 ܚܒ̈ܪܝܐ] ܚܒ̈ܪܘܗܝ
77:30 ܡܐܟܘܠܬܐ] ܡܐܟܘܠܬܗܘܢ
79:11(10) ܠܐܣ̈ܝܪܐ] ܠܐܣ̈ܝܪܘܗ
79:14(13) ܘܚܝܘܬܐ ܕܒܪܐ] ܘܡܥܘܣܘܗ

However, *k* also diverges from this pair (and SyrPs) at various junctures:

e. g. 70:7 om. ܡܪܝܐ
70:13 ܠܗ ܚܬܝܬܐ] tr.
73:11 om. ܡܢ
73:11 fin.] + ܠܥܠܡ
77:37 om. ܕܝ
79:15(14) ܘܣܥܘܪ] + ܒܗ

Thus, the eighth century *k* will not have been the exemplar from which twelfth century *h* and thirteenth century *j* were copied.

[88]See note 80. The interrogative ܐܝܠܝܢ renders the article of the Greek plural articulated participle in SyrPs[b] also where *k* is extant (70:10, 13 *bis*).

[89]See note 79.

[90]Two representative examples are:

2:7 ܦܘܩܕܢܗ ܕܡܪܝܐ *abf*] ܦܘܩܕܢܐ ܕܡܪܝܐ *hj*

73:12 ܒܥܠܡܬܗ ܕܐܪܥܐ *acef*] ܒܥܠܡܬܐ ܕܐܪܥܐ *hjk*

[91]See note 82.

[92]Interestingly, Scher ("Diarbékir," p. 332) says *h* contains "la version héracléenne," though unfortunately he does not explain the reasoning behind that deduction (cf. I. Vosté, "Notes sur les manuscrits syriaques de Diarbékir et autres localités d'Orient," *Le Muséon* 50 [1937], p. 348). Vööbus reports that the end of the codex (which is lacking in my copy) contains the statement, "Here ends the Book of the Psalms according to the version of the Septuagint" (*Discoveries*, p. 31).

[93]For example, in Ps. 15:10 and Acts 13:35:

Ps. 15:10 οὐδὲ δώσεις τὸν ὅσιόν σου ἰδεῖν διαφθοράν LXX, item praeter Οὐ pro οὐδέ Acts 13:35
ܐܦܠܐ ܬܬܠ ܠܚܣܝܐ ܕܝܠܟ ܠܡܚܙܐ ܚܒܠܐ *hj*
ܠܐ ܬܬܠ ܐܢܬ ܠܚܣܝܟ ܠܡܚܙܐ ܡܬܚܒܠܢܘܬܐ Hark NT
ܘܠܐ ܬܫܒܘܩ ܠܚܣܝܟ ܠܡܚܙܐ ܚܒܠܐ Pesh OT
ܕܠܐ ܬܫܒܘܩ ܠܚܣܝܟ ܕܢܚܙܐ ܚܒܠܐ Pesh NT

[94]For example, in Ps. 8:5(4) and Heb. 2:6:

Ps. 8:5(4)[a] τί ἐστιν ἄνθρωπος, ὅτι μιμνῄσκῃ αὐτοῦ LXX, item Heb. 2:6
ܡܢܐ ܐܝܬܘܗܝ ܒܪܢܫܐ ܕܡܬܕܟܪ ܐܢܬ ܠܗ *hj*
ܡܢܐ ܐܝܬܘܗܝ ܒܪܢܫܐ ܕܡܬܥܗܕ ܐܢܬ ܠܗ Hark NT
ܡܢܘ ܒܪܢܫܐ ܕܬܬܕܟܪܝܘܗܝ Pesh OT
ܡܢܘ ܒܪܢܫܐ ܕܬܥܗܕܝܘܗܝ Pesh NT

Note particularly that SyrPs[a] (*hj*), like SyrPs (*af*), and the Peshitta Old Testament have the ܕܟܪ root, whereas the Harklean and the Peshitta New Testaments have the ܥܗܕ root. Likewise, I suspect that the Philoxenian Psalter had ܕܟܪ, and that the Philoxenian New Testament had ܥܗܕ. Both roots translate μιμνήσκω in the Philoxenian New Testament books: ܥܗܕ in II Pet. 3:2, and ܕܟܪ in Jude 17 and Apoc. 16:19. Significantly, the Harklean version agrees with the choice of root in each of these three passages.

In the Old Testament, Syl of Isaiah always has ܕܟܪ for μιμνήσκω: 43:25, 26, 44:21, 46:8, 9, 47:7, 48:1. This is also the normal equivalent in Syh of Isaiah: 12:4, 17:10, 26:16, 38:3, 43:25, 26, 44:21, 46:8, 9, 47:7, 48:1, 54:4, 57:11, 63:7, 11, 64:5(4), 7(6), 9(8), 65:17, 66:9. Only in 62:6 does Syh show ܥܗܕ. In the Psalter, ܥܗܕ in 102:18 is the sole exception to the consistent employment of ܕܟܪ as the equivalent in both SyrPs[a] and SyrPs: 8:5(4), 9:13(12), 15:4, 19:4(3), 21:28(27), 24:6, 7 *bis*, 41:5(4), 7(6), 44:18(17), 70:16, 73:2, 18, 22, 76:4(3), 6(5), 12(11) *bis*, 77:35, 39, 42, 78:8, 82:5(4), 86:4, 87:6(5), 88:48(47), 51(50), 97:3, 102:14, 104:5, 8, 42, 105:4, 7, 45, 108:16, 110:5, 113:20(115:12), 118:49, 52, 55, 131:1, 135:23, 136:1, 6, 7, 142:5.

[95]For example, the διαθήκη = ܩܝܡܐ equivalency (24:10, 14). The normal Harklean equivalent is a transliteration, ܕܝܬܝܩܐ (Heb. 12:24 and 13:20 are not extant in White's edition; see note 69): Mt. 26:28; Mk. 14:24; Lk. 1:72, 22:20; Acts 3:25, 7:8; Rom. 9:4, 11:27; I Cor. 11:25;

II Cor. 3:6, 14; Gal. 3:15, 17, 4:24; Eph. 2:12; Heb. 7:22, 8:6, 8, 9 *bis*, 10, 9:4 *bis*, 15 *bis*, 16, 17, 20, 10:16, 29; Apoc. 11:19 (note the plurals in Rom. 9:4 [ܘܕܝܐܬܝܩ̈ܣ], Gal. 4:24 [ܕܝܐܬܝܩ̈ܣ], and Eph. 2:12 [ܕܕܝܐܬܝܩ̈ܣ]). In SyrPs and SyrPs[b], the transliteration is always used, with different spellings (ܕܝܬܝܩܐ, ܕܝܬܝܩܝ, ܕܝܐܬܝܩܝ, ܕܝܐܬܝܩܐ) depending on the Ms: 24:10, 14, 43:18(17), 49:5, 16, 54:21(20), 73:20, 77:10, 37, 82:6(5), 88:4(3), 29(28), 35(34), 40(39), 102:18, 104:8, 10, 105:45, 110:5, 9, 131:12. The Peshitta word in each of these Psalter passages is ܩܝܡܐ. This is also the equivalent in all three places in Syl of Isaiah where διαθήκη is translated (28:15, 49:6, 8), though ܕܝܬܐܝܩܝ is used in Crawford Apoc. 11:19. In Syh of Isaiah, ܕܝܬܝܩܐ is always employed: 24:5, 28:15, 18, 33:8, 42:6, 49:6, 8, 54:10, 55:3, 56:4, 6, 59:21, 61:8. The διαθήκη = ܩܝܡܐ equivalency in SyrPs[a] may, then, be due to Peshitta and/or Philoxenian influence.

96 See note 15.

97 *A Dictionary of Christian Biography*, s. v. "Thomas (17) Harklensis," by J. Gwynn; Vööbus, *Early Versions*, pp. 110–19.

98 *Psalmi cum Odis*, pp. 66–7.

APPENDIX

1 A few hexaplaric readings are also found in the margins of Mss *e*, h_1, and *j*.

2 Ms 86 in the prophetic literature is an example of a text which has such marginal notes (see A. Schenker, *Hexaplarische Psalmenbruchstücke*, Orbis biblicus et orientalis 8 [Freiburg: Universitätsverlag; Göttingen: Vandenhoeck & Ruprecht, 1975], p. 4.). The Pentateuch provides examples of other texts which have them: e. g. Mss of groups *C* and *s* in Genesis, *C*, *n*, and *s* in Deuteronomy (J. W. Wevers, THGG, pp. 67–8, 82 and THGD, p. 19; L. Perkins, "The Place of the Syro-Hexapla in the Textual Tradition of the Septuagint of Deuteronomy" [Ph. D. Thesis, University of Toronto, 1980], p. 431, n. 1). The only Greek witnesses to Origen's recension in Rahlfs' edition of the Psalter are the Hexapla fragments of Mss 1098 and 2005, which include the non-LXX materials in the typical columnar format. However, there are other Psalter Mss, like catena text 264, which contain hexaplaric readings in their margins (Schenker, *Psalmenbruchstücke*, p. 4).

3 See Wevers, THGG, pp. 67–8.

4 Undoubtedly the most common difference between *f* and *a* with respect to the marginal hexaplaric apparatus is that *f* will, in whole or in part, fail to attest a given reading found in *a*. The occurrence of such lacunae is not hard to understand, given the fact that *a* antedates *f* by some three to four centuries. Some readings are bound to have been lost in that interval, particularly since the margins of Mss tend to be the first areas to deteriorate, as is amply illustrated by *f* itself.

[5]As always, the verse numbering is that of Rahlfs' *Psalmi cum Odis*, with SyrPss numbers following in parentheses wherever they are different. Field's "Psalmi" segment is contained in volume 2 of *Origenis Hexaplorum quae supersunt*.

[6]See also Reider, pp. 148, 287.

[7]In this and other lists of the appendix, not necessarily all of Field's entry for a given reading is reproduced.

[8]With regard to the correction in *a*, see Ceriani, "Notae," *Codex Syro-Hexaplaris*, p. 11.

[9]With respect to the correction in *b*, see Ceriani, *ibid.*, p. 14.

[10]See Reider, pp. 5, 296; cf. Schenker, *Psalmenbruchstücke*, pp. 97, 299 regarding Ps. 81:2.

[11]*G. Mercati, ed., Psalterii Hexapli reliquiae...Pars prima: Codex rescriptus Bybliothecae Ambrosianae O. 39 Sup.* (Vatican City: In Bybliotheca Vaticana, 1958), p. 69. Note that iota subscript is actually written on the line in this Ms.

[12]It is possible that the σ′ reading in verse 5 could have led to the ascription of this reading to σ′ in *f*.

[13]With regard to α′ and the צרר (*BDB* root III) = θλίβω equivalency, see Field at Ps. 30:12(11). However, note also the σ′ reading for 7:5(4).

[14]With respect to α′ and the צרר (*BDB* root I) = ἐνδεσμέω equivalency, see Field at Ps. 6:8(7), 7:7(6), 68:20(19).

[15]With regard to σ′ and נגינה/ψαλτήριον/ܟܢܪܐ, see Field at 6:1(inscr.), 53:1(inscr.), 54:1(inscr.).

[16]With regard to σ′ and פעל/πρᾶξις, see Field at 27:4 and 76:13(12).

[17]See Field and Ceriani, "Notae," *Codex Syro-Hexaplaris*, p. 28.

[18]Cf. Field at Ps. 103:22. However, note that in the text of the Syrohexapla of Ez. 29:5, ܠܐ ܬܬܟܢܫ translates περισταλῇς.

[19]With respect to α′ and additional instances of מַשְׂכִּיל/ἐπιστήμων/ܡܣܬܟܠܢܐ, see Field at Ps. 31:1(inscr.), 41:1(inscr.), 44:1(inscr.), 51:1(inscr.), 52:1(inscr.), 141:1(inscr.); cf. Reider, pp. 93–4, 312.

[20]Cf. Field at Ps. 87:1(inscr.).

[21]See Field at Ps. 102:4 and 118:154 for גָּאַל = ἀγχιστεύω in α′. For this equivalency and גֹּאֵל = ἀγχιστεύς, see Reider, pp. 4, 269.

[22]With regard to σ′ and חפר/κατορύσσω/ܚܦܪ, cf. Field at 70:24.

[23]With respect to α′ and עברה/ἀνυπερθεσία/ܠܐ ܡܫܬܘܚܪܢܘܬܐ, see Field at Ps. 7:7(6); cf. Reider, p. 23; cf. Schenker, *Psalmenbruchstücke*, pp. 70–1, 154 regarding Ps. 77:49.

[24] This is the reading of the σ′ column of Ms 1098 (except that 1098 has εἰμί which occurs at the end of a line; Mercati, ed., *Psalterii Hexapli reliquiae*, p. 97). It is demonstrably superior to Field's retroversion, at least with respect to the זכר = μνημονεύω equivalency which is unanimous in the extant readings of the σ′ Psalter: 24:7, 73:22, 87:6(5), 88:48(47), 51(50), 96:12, 102:14, 110:5, 118:49 (see H-R, vol. 2, p. 931 and Supplement, p. *209*). Only in Job 21:6 and 28:18 is the זכר = μιμνήσκομαι equivalency which Field posits in this Psalter passage attested for σ′ (see H-R, vol. 2, p. 929 and Supplement, p. *209*). In the text of SyrPss, the ܕܟܪ root translates both Greek terms. The חלד = ἡμερόβιος equivalency occurs only in this Psalter passage in σ′ (H-R, Supplement, p. *205*). However, Field's suggested retroversions, *πρὸς ἡμέραν/ἐφήμερος*, are never attested.

[25] Whenever SyrPss has occasion to translate χάρις, it does so with ܛܝܒܘܬܐ. This is seen in both the text (44:3[2], 83:12[11]) and the margin (30:8[7] σ′; see Field also at 39:12[11]). However, the preferred equivalent for חסד in α′ is ἔλεος (see Reider, pp. 78, 278), whereas χάρις is not attested as an equivalent for that term in any extant Greek witness to α′.

[26] See Field at Ps. 67:8(7) and 105:14 as well as at Ps. 43:20(19) and 67:5(4).

[27] This equivalency is attested in the SyrPss text at 106:40, although note the *j* variant.

[28] With regard to the גמל = εὐεργετέω equivalency in σ′, see Field at Ps. 141:8(7). For SyrPss and the εὐεργετέω = ܥܒܕ ܛܒܬܐ equivalency, see 12:6, 56:3(2), 114:7.

[29] Note that the נחל = χείμαρρος equivalency is attested for α′σ′θ′ in Field at Ps. 73:15. For χείμαρρος = ܢܚܠܬܐ/ܐܢܚܠܬܐ in the text of SyrPss, see 123:4 and 125:4.

[30] Note that the next marginal hexaplaric reading in SyrPss, which occurs in verse 4, is attributed to α′σ′ by *abf*.

[31] See Field at Ps. 58:7(6), 15(14); cf. Reider, p. 180; cf. Schenker, *Psalmenbruchstücke*, pp. 101-2, 323 regarding Ps. 82:3(2).

[32] See Field, vol. 1, p. iii and vol. 2, p. 84.

[33] See Reider, pp. 125, 282.

[34] See Reider, pp. 87, 281; cf. Schenker, *Psalmenbruchstücke*, pp. 86, 244.

[35] See Reider, p. 172.

[36] S. v. "ܢܘܪ," "ܢܘܪܐ." In *Thesaurus Syriacus*, ܢܝܪܐ = *morsus* is listed (s. v. "ܢܝܪܐ"), but this term would hardly seem to fit the present context.

[37] Note, however, that *fg* omit ܠܥܠܡ in the text.

[38]However, as Field suggests, ܡܢܥܗ looks to be the superior reading.

BIBLIOGRAPHY

Aland, K. et al., eds. *The Greek New Testament*. 3rd ed. (corrected). Stuttgart: United Bible Societies, 1983.

Assemanus, J. S. *Bibliotheca Orientalis Clementino-Vaticana*. 3 vols. Rome: Typis sacrae congregationis de propaganda fide, 1719-28.

Baars, W. *New Syro-Hexaplaric Texts*. Leiden: E. J. Brill, 1968.

Barnes, W. E., ed. *The Peshitta Psalter according to the West Syrian Text*. Cambridge: University Press, 1904.

Baumstark, A. *Geschichte der syrischen Literatur*. Bonn: A. Marcus und E. Webers Verlag, 1922.

Biblia sacra iuxta latinam vulgatam versionem. Vol. 10: *Liber Psalmorum*. Rome: Typis Polyglottis Vaticanis, 1953.

Biblia sacra vulgatae editionis Sixti Quinti Pont. Max. iussu recognita atque edita. Rome: Typographia Apostolica Vaticano, 1592.

Brock, S. "A Fourteenth-Century Polyglot Psalter." *Studies in Philology in Honour of Ronald James Williams*. G. E. Kadish and G. E. Freeman, eds. Toronto: SSEA Publications, 1982, pp. 1-15.

———————. "The Resolution of the Philoxenian/Harclean Problem." *New Testament Textual Criticism—Its Significance for Exegesis: Essays in Honour of Bruce M. Metzger*. E. J. Epp and G. D. Fee, eds. Oxford: Clarendon Press, 1981, pp. 325-43.

———————. *The Syriac Version of the Pseudo-Nonnos Mythological Scholia*. Cambridge: University Press, 1971.

Brown, F., Driver, S. R., and Briggs, C. A., eds. *A Hebrew and English Lexicon of the Old Testament*. Oxford: Clarendon Press, 1907 (Repr. 1974).

Browne, E. G. *A Supplementary Hand-List of the Muḥammadan Manuscripts...Preserved in the Libraries of the University and Colleges of Cambridge*. Cambridge: University Press, 1922.

Ceriani, A. *Esaiae fragmenta syriaca versionis anonymae et recensionis Jacobi Edesseni*. Monumenta sacra et profana. Vol. 5, fasc. 1. Milan: Typis et impensis Bibliothecae Ambrosianae, 1868.

———————. *Prolegomena in editionem versionis syriacae ex textu LXX*. Monumenta sacra et profana. Vol. 1, fasc. 1. Milan: Typis et impensis Bibliothecae Ambrosianae, 1861.

———————, ed. *Codex Syro-Hexaplaris Ambrosianus photolithographice editus*. Monumenta sacra et profana. Vol. 7. Milan: Typis et impensis Bibliothecae Ambrosianae, 1874.

Cighera, P., ed. *Psalmi secundum editionem LXX interpretum...ex codice Syro-Estranghelo Bibliothecae Ambrosianae*. Milan: n. p., 1820.

A Compendious Syriac Dictionary. S. v. "ܢܘܙ," "ܢܘܙܐ," "ܐܘܠܘܓܝܣ."

De Halleux, A. *Ēlī de Qartamīn, Mēmrā sur S. Mār Philoxène de Mabbog*. CSCO, Syr. 101. Louvain: Secrétariat du CorpusSCO, 1963.

———. *Philoxène de Mabbog: sa vie, ses écrits, sa théologie*. Louvain: Imprimerie orientaliste, 1963.

———, ed. *Philoxène de Mabbog: Commentaire du prologue johannique (Ms. Br. Mus. Add. 14,534)*. CSCO, Syr. 165. Louvain: Secrétariat du CorpusSCO, 1977.

Delekat, L. "Die syrolukianische Übersetzung des Buches Jesaja und das Postulat einer alttestamentlichen Vetus Syra." *ZAW* N. F. 28 (1957), pp. 21-54.

A Dictionary of Christian Biography. S. v. "Polycarpus (5)," "Thomas (8) Edessenus," "Thomas (17) Harklensis," by J. Gwynn.

Elliger, K., Rudolph, W., et al., eds. *Biblia Hebraica Stuttgartensia*. Stuttgart: Deutsche Bibelstiftung, 1967/77.

Field, F. *Origenis Hexaplorum quae supersunt*. 2 vols. Oxford: Clarendon Press, 1875.

Fox, D. J. *The "Matthew-Luke Commentary" of Philoxenus*. SBL Dissertation Series 43. Missoula: Scholars Press, 1979.

Guidi, I. "Mosè di Aghel e Simeone Abbate." *Rendiconti della R. Accademia dei Lincei* 4/2 (1886), pp. 397-416, 545-57.

Gwynn, J. *Remnants of the Later Syriac Versions of the Bible*. Pt. 1. London: Williams and Norgate, 1909.

———. *The Apocalypse of St. John in a Syriac Version Hitherto Unknown*. Dublin: Hodges, Figgis, and Co. Ltd., 1897.

Hatch, E. and Redpath, H. A. *A Concordance to the Septuagint and the Other Greek Versions of the Old Testament*. 2 vols. including Supplement. Graz: Akademische Druck- u. Verlags-anstalt, 1975.

Holmes, R. and Parsons, J., eds. *Vetus Testamentum Graecum cum variis lectionibus*. Vol. 3. Oxford: Clarendon Press, 1823.

Institut für neutestamentliche Textforschung und vom Rechenzentrum der Universität Münster. *Computer-Konkordanz zum Novum Testamentum Graece von Nestle-Aland, 26. Auflage und zum Greek New Testament, 3rd Edition*. Berlin/New York: Walter de Gruyter, 1980.

Jellicoe, S. *The Septuagint and Modern Study*. Oxford: Oxford University Press, 1968; Ann Arbor: Eisenbrauns, 1978 (Repr.).

Jenkins, R. G. "Some Quotations from Isaiah in the Philoxenian Version." *Abr-Nahrain* 20 (1981-2), pp. 20-36.

Kasser, R. and Testuz, M., eds. *Papyrus Bodmer XXIV*. Cologny-Geneva: Bibliotheca Bodmeriana, 1967.

Lagarde, P. de. *Bibliothecae Syriacae...quae ad philologiam sacram pertinent*. Göttingen: Prostant in aedibus Dieterichianis Luederi Horstmann, 1892.

———. כתבא דמזמורא מן כתבא דאוצר ארזא. *Praetermissorum libri duo*. Göttingen: Sumptibus editoris in officina academica Dieterichiana, 1879.

Lebon, J. "La version philoxénienne de la Bible." *Revue d'histoire ecclésiastique* 12 (1911; repr. 1967), pp. 413-36.

———. *Le monophysisme sévérien*. Louvain: J. van Linthout, 1909.

Lee, S., ed. *Vetus Testamentum Syriace*. London: The Biblical Society, 1823.

Liddell, H. G. and Scott, R. *A Greek-English Lexicon* (with Supplement). Revised by H. S. Jones. Oxford: Clarendon Press, 1968 (Repr. 1976).

Lisowsky, G. *Konkordanz zum hebräischen Alten Testament*. 2nd ed. Stuttgart: Württembergische Bibelanstalt, 1958.

Mai, A., ed. *Scriptorum veterum nova collectio*. 10 vols. Rome: Apud Burliaeum, 1825-38.

Margolis, M. L. and Marx, A. *A History of the Jewish People*. New York: Atheneum, 1972.

Martin, J. P. P. *Introduction à la critique textuelle du Nouveau Testament*. 5 vols. Paris: Maisonneuve frères et C. Leclerc, 1884-5.

Masius, A. *Josuae imperatoris historia illustrata atque explicata*. Antwerp: n. p., 1574.

———. *Syrorum Peculium*. Antwerp: Ex officina Christophori Plantini, 1572.

McReynolds, P. R. "The Claremont Profile Method and the Grouping of Byzantine New Testament Manuscripts." Ph. D. Dissertation, Claremont Graduate School, 1968.

Mercati, G., ed. *Psalterii Hexapli reliquiae...Pars prima: Codex rescriptus Bybliothecae Ambrosianae O. 39 Sup.* Vatican City: In Bybliotheca Vaticana, 1958.

Metzger, B. M. *The Early Versions of the New Testament*. Oxford: Clarendon Press, 1977.

Middeldorpf, H., ed. *Codex Syriaco-Hexaplaris*. Berlin: Enslin, 1835.

Migne, J.-P., ed. "Epistola...ad Sunniam et Fretelam." *Sancti Eusebii Hieronymi...Opera omnia*. Patrologiae cursus completus...Ser. latina 22. Petit-Montrouge: Ex typis Migne, 1845, cols. 837-67.

Mingana, A. "New Documents on Philoxenus of Hierapolis, and on the Philoxenian Version of the Bible." *The Expositor*. 8th series, vol. 19 (1920), pp. 149-60.

Nöldeke, T. *Kurzgefasste syrische Grammatik*. 2nd ed. Leipzig: Tauchnitz, 1898.

The Oxford Dictionary of the Christian Church. 2nd ed. S. v. "Gregory of Nazianus, St.," "Nicaea, First Council of (325)," "Nicene Creed, The."

Perkins, L. "The Place of the Syro-Hexapla in the Textual Tradition of the Septuagint of Deuteronomy." Ph. D. Thesis, University of Toronto, 1980.

———. "The So-Called 'L' Text of Psalms 72-82." *Bulletin of the International Organization for Septuagint and Cognate Studies* 11 (1978), pp. 44-63.

The Peshitta Institute, ed. *List of Old Testament Peshitta Manuscripts*. Preliminary Issue. Leiden: E. J. Brill, 1961.

———. *The Old Testament in Syriac*. Pt. 2, fasc. 3: *The Book of Psalms*. Leiden: E. J. Brill, 1980.

Pietersma, A. "David in the Greek Psalms." *VT* 30 (1980), pp. 213-26.

———. "The Edited Text of *P. Bodmer XXIV*." *Bulletin of the American Society of Papyrologists* 17 (1980), pp. 67-79.

———. "Proto-Lucian and the Greek Psalter." *VT* 28 (1978), pp. 66-72.

———. *Two Manuscripts of the Greek Psalter*. Analecta Biblica 77. Rome: Biblical Institute Press, 1978.

Pigulewskaya, N. "Греко-сиро-арабская рукописб IX В." Палестинский Сборник I (63) (1954), pp. 59-90.

Pococke, E., ed. *Epistolae Quatuor, Petri secunda, Johannis secunda et tertia, et Judae, fratris Jacobi una*. Lugduni Batavorum: Ex officina Bonaventurae & Abrahami Elzeviri, 1630.

Rahlfs, A. *Septuaginta-Studien* 1-3. Göttingen: Vandenhoeck & Ruprecht, 1965.

———. *Verzeichnis der griechischen Handschriften des Alten Testaments*. Mitteilungen des Septuaginta-Unternehmens 2. Berlin: Weidmannsche Buchhandlung, 1914.

———, ed. *Septuaginta*. Vol. 10: *Psalmi cum Odis*. Göttingen: Vandenhoeck & Ruprecht, 1931.

Reider, J. *An Index to Aquila*. Completed and revised by N. Turner. Supplements to Vetus Testamentum 12. Leiden: E. J. Brill, 1966.

Robinson, T. H. *Paradigms and Exercises in Syriac Grammar*. 4th ed. Revised by L. H. Brockington. Oxford: Clarendon Press, 1962 (Repr. 1978).

Schenker, A. *Hexaplarische Psalmenbruchstücke*. Orbis biblicus et orientalis 8. Freiburg: Universitätsverlag; Göttingen: Vandenhoeck & Ruprecht, 1975.

———. *Psalmen in den Hexapla. Erste kritische und vollständige Ausgabe der hexaplarischen Fragmente auf dem Rande der Handschrift Ottobonianus graecus 398 zu den Ps 24–32*. Studi e Testi 295. Vatican City: Biblioteca Apostolica Vaticana, 1982.

Scher, A. "Notice sur les manuscrits syriaques du Musée Borgia aujourd'hui à la Bibliothèque vaticane." *Journal asiatique*. 10th series, vol. 13 (1909), pp. 249–87.

———. "Notice sur les manuscrits syriaques et arabes conservés à l'archevêché chaldéen de Diarbékir." *Journal asiatique*. 10th series, vol. 10 (1907), pp. 331–62, 385–431.

———. "Notice sur les manuscrits syriaques conservés dans la Bibliothèque du patriarcat chaldéen de Mossoul." *Revue des bibliothèques* 17 (1907), pp. 227–60.

Sprengling, M. and Graham, W. C., eds. *Barhebraeus' Scholia on the Old Testament*. The University of Chicago Oriental Institute Publications 13. Chicago: The University of Chicago Press, 1931.

Swete, H. B. *An Introduction to the Old Testament in Greek*. Revised by R. R. Ottley. Cambridge: University Press, 1914; New York: Ktav Publishing House, 1968 (Repr.).

Thesaurus Syriacus. S. v. "ܐܣܪ."

Vaschalde, A., ed. *Philoxeni Mabbugensis: Tractatus tres de Trinitate et Incarnatione*. CSCO, Syr. 9. Paris: E typographeo reipublicae, 1907.

Vööbus, A. *The Apocalypse in the Harklean Version*. CSCO, Subsidia 56. Louvain: Secrétariat du CorpusSCO, 1978.

———. *Discoveries of Very Important Manuscript Sources for the Syro-Hexapla*. Papers of the Estonian Theological Society in Exile 20. Stockholm: ETSE, 1970.

———. *Early Versions of the New Testament*. Papers of the Estonian Theological Society in Exile 6. Stockholm: ETSE, 1954.

———. *The Hexapla and the Syro-Hexapla*. Papers of the Estonian Theological Society in Exile 22. Stockholm: ETSE, 1971.

———. *History of the School of Nisibis*. CSCO, Subsidia 26. Louvain: Secrétariat du CorpusSCO, 1965.

———. "New Data for the Solution of the Problem concerning the Philoxenian Version." *Spiritus et Veritas*. Festschrift K. Kundzinš. Auseklis, ed. Eutin: Andr. Ozolins Buchdruckerei, 1953, pp. 169-86.

———. *The Pentateuch in the Version of the Syro-Hexapla*. CSCO, Subsidia 45. Louvain: Secrétariat du CorpusSCO, 1975.

Vosté, I. "Notes sur les manuscrits syriaques de Diarbékir et autres localités d'Orient." *Le Muséon* 50 (1937), pp. 345-51.

Watt, J. W., ed. *Philoxenus of Mabbug: Fragments of the Commentary on Matthew and Luke*. CSCO, Syr. 171. Louvain: Secrétariat du CorpusSCO, 1978.

Weitzman, M. P. "The Origin of the Peshitta Psalter." *Interpreting the Hebrew Bible: Essays in Honour of E. I. J. Rosenthal*. J. A. Emerton and S. C. Reif, eds. Cambridge: University Press, 1982, pp. 277-98.

Wevers, J. W. *Text History of the Greek Deuteronomy*. Mitteilungen des Septuaginta-Unternehmens 13. Göttingen: Vandenhoeck & Ruprecht, 1978.

———. *Text History of the Greek Genesis*. Mitteilungen des Septuaginta-Unternehmens 11. Göttingen: Vandenhoeck & Ruprecht, 1974.

White, J., ed. *Actuum Apostolorum et Epistolarum tam Catholicarum quam Paulinarum, versio syriaca Philoxeniana*. 2 vols. Oxford: Clarendon Press, 1799-1803.

———. *Sacrorum Evangeliorum versio syriaca Philoxeniana*. Oxford: Clarendon Press, 1778.

Wisse, F. *The Profile Method for the Classification and Evaluation of Manuscript Evidence as Applied to the Continuous Greek Text of the Gospel of Luke*. Studies and Documents 44. Grand Rapids: Eerdmans, 1982.

Wright, W. *Catalogue of Syriac Manuscripts in the British Museum*. 3 vols. London: British Museum, 1870-2.

Wright, W. and Cook, S. A. *A Catalogue of the Syriac Manuscripts Preserved in the Library of the University of Cambridge*. 2 vols. Cambridge: University Press, 1901.

Ziegler, J., ed. *Septuaginta: Vetus Testamentum Graecum*. Vol. 14: *Isaias*. Göttingen: Vandenhoeck & Ruprecht, 1967.

Zotenberg, H. *Manuscrits orientaux. Catalogues des manuscrits syriaques et sabéens (mandaïtes) de la Bibliothèque nationale*. Paris: Imprimerie nationale, 1874.

Zuntz, G. *The Ancestry of the Harklean New Testament*. The British Academy Supplemental Papers 7. London: Oxford University Press, 1945.

INDEXES

A. PROPOSED CORRECTIONS TO THE PSALTER TEXT OF RAHLFS' *PSALMI CUM ODIS*

B. SCRIPTURE REFERENCES

This index does not include Psalter references in the text and apparatuses of the edition of Psalms included in the present study (pp. 20-177). Versions are specified where necessary.

Genesis

Exodus

Numbers

Deuteronomy

Joshua

Judges

I Kingdoms

III Kingdoms

IV Kingdoms

Psalms

Psalms (Cont.)

Psalms (Cont.)

Psalms (Cont.)

Psalms (Cont.)

Psalms (Cont.)

Psalms (Cont.)

Psalms (Cont.)

Odes

Proverbs

Isaiah (Cont.)

Romans (Cont.)

I Corinthians

II Corinthians

Galatians

Ephesians

II Timothy

Titus

Hebrews

II Peter

II John

III John

Jude

Apocalypse

Apocalypse (Cont.)

C. AUTHORS

ROBERT A. KRAFT (editor)
Septuagintal Lexicography (1975)
Code: 06 04 01
Not Available

ROBERT A KRAFT (editor)
1972 Proceedings: Septuagint and Pseudepigrapha Seminars (1973)
Code: 06 04 02
Not Available

RAYMOND A. MARTIN
Syntactical Evidence of Semitic Studies in Greek Documents (1974)
Code: 06 04 03
Not Available

GEORGE W. E. NICKELSBURG, JR. (editor)
Studies on the *Testament of Moses* (1973)
Code: 06 04 04
Not Available

GEORGE W.E. NICKELSBURG, JR. (editor)
Studies on the *Testament of Joseph* (1975)
Code: 06 04 05
Not Available

GEORGE W.E. NICKELSBURG, JR. (editor)
Studies on the *Testament of Abraham* (1976)
Code: 06 04 06

JAMES H. CHARLESWORTH
Pseudepigrapha and Modern Research (1976)
Code: 06 04 07
Not Available

JAMES H. CHARLESWORTH
Pseudepigrapha and Modern Research with a Supplement (1981)
Code: 06 04 07 S

JOHN W. OLLEY
"Righteousness" in the Septuagint of Isaiah: A Contextual Study (1979)
Code: 06 04 08

MELVIN K. H. PETERS
An Analysis of the Textual Character of the Bohairic of Deuteronomy (1980)
Code: 06 04 09
Not Available

DAVID G. BURKE
The Poetry of Baruch (1982)
Code: 06 04 10

JOSEPH L. TRAFTON
Syriac Version of the Psalms of Solomon (1985)
Code: 06 04 11

JOHN COLLINS, GEORGE NICKELSBURG
Ideal Figures in Ancient Judaism: Profiles and Paradigms (1980)
Code: 06 04 12

ROBERT HANN
The Manuscript History of the Psalms of Solomon (1982)
Code: 06 04 13

J.A.L. LEE
A Lexical Study of the Septuagint Version of the Pentateuch (1983)
Code: 06 04 14

MELVIN K. H. PETERS
A Critical Edition of the Coptic (Bohairic) Pentateuch
Vol. 5: Deuteronomy (1983)
Code: 06 04 15

T. MURAOKA
A Greek-Hebrew/Aramaic Index to I Esdras (1984)
Code: 06 04 16

JOHN RUSSIANO MILES
Retroversion and Text Criticism:
The Predictability of Syntax in An Ancient Translation
from Greek to Ethiopic (1985)
Code: 06 04 17

LESLIE J. MCGREGOR
The Greek Text of Ezekiel (1985)
Code: 06 04 18

MELVIN K.H. PETERS
A Critical Edition of the Coptic (Bohairic) Pentateuch,
Vol. 1: Genesis (1985)
Code: 06 04 19

ROBERT A. KRAFT AND EMANUEL TOV (project directors)
Computer Assisted Tools for Septuagint Studies
Vol 1: Ruth (1986)
Code: 06 04 20

CLAUDE E. COX
Hexaplaric Materials Preserved in the Armenian Version (1986)
Code: 06 04 21

MELVIN K.H. PETERS
A Critical Edition of the Coptic (Bohairic) Pentateuch
Vol. 2: Exodus (1986)
Code: 06 04 22

(Continued on previous page)